Basic News Writing

Basic News Writing

Melvin Mencher
Columbia University

wcb

Wm. C. Brown Company Publishers
Dubuque, Iowa

wcb group

Wm. C. Brown
Chairman of the Board

Mark C. Falb
President and Chief Executive Officer

ωcb **Wm. C. Brown Company Publishers, College Division**

Lawrence E. Cremer
President

Marcia H. Stout
Marketing Manager

James L. Romig
Vice-President,
Product Development

William A. Moss
Production Editorial
Manager

David Wm. Smith
Vice-President, Marketing

Marilyn A. Phelps
Manager of Design

E. F. Jogerst
Vice-President, Cost
Analyst

Mary M. Heller
Visual Research Manager

David A. Corona
Vice-President,
Production and Design

Book Team

Judith A. Clayton
Senior Developmental Editor

Kevin J. Pruessner
Designer

Lynne M. Meyers
Production Editor

Faye M. Schilling
Visual Research Editor

Since this page cannot legibly accommodate all the copyright notices, pages 455–58 constitute an extension of the copyright page.

2-04354-03

Contents

Preface

This is a how-to book. It was written to help the newcomer to journalism learn how to put words on paper that accurately and clearly describe and explain ideas and events.

Basic News Writing is designed to show the beginner how to gather information, how to analyze its importance and then how to put the results of the reporting and thinking into news stories.

The techniques recommended here are those of successful news writers, men and women who have struggled to make words do their bidding. The writers who have contributed to *Basic News Writing* know that writing does not come easily. They understand how hard it is to whip words into submission so that they dance or march somberly across the page. They have learned to write through patience, confidence and effort.

Patience is necessary because words have a tendency to go their own way, resisting our efforts to lock them into sentences and paragraphs. It takes time to learn to write well. Few people are born writers.

Confidence is important because sometimes it seems that the right words will never come, that the story just will not blend smoothly but insists on zig-zagging its way from paragraph to paragraph—no matter how patient the writer is. The newcomer should not give up. All of us possess the creative instinct. We all want to make something of our experiences, to tell others what we have seen and heard. With confidence in ourselves, we can do that.

But it does require hard work. The aspiring artist who seeks to transfer a sunset to canvas does not instinctively dip his brush into the precise colors on the palette. Through study and trial and error the artist learns just how much white to mix with red for the clouds. The performer cannot turn words and musical notes into a sad song of lost love the first time she sees the score. It takes hours, sometimes days, before everything comes together and the performance is worth recording. The journalist is no different. Beginner or experienced news writer, effort and hard work lead to well-written stories.

However, unguided effort is wasted work. The purpose of *Basic News Writing* is to serve as compass and sextant. It provides the directions in which the student should point his or her efforts. The techniques, principles and concepts that are suggested here come from the field, from the everyday experience of journalists on the job. Every concept and principle is illustrated with a practical example provided by the experience of a professional.

For the student considering a career in journalism, these illustrations serve another purpose. By watching the journalist at work, the student is able to see the many faces and facets of journalism: The young woman, just out of journalism school, alone in the AP newsroom, who is called on to handle a rooming house fire that kills more than 20 people. The television network news writer who has minutes to write the story of U.S. Navy planes downing two Libyan jets. The newspaper reporter who climbs the stairs of a nearly deserted tenement to interview a family living without heat or running water.

The philosophy of *Basic News Writing* is best summed up by Samuel Johnson's remark, "The end of writing is to enable the readers better to enjoy life, or better to endure it."

For all its practicality, this textbook recognizes that journalism is more calling than trade. Kin to teaching, cousin to preaching, journalism is much more than the sum of its techniques and the advice of its practitioners. Through its many examples, *Basic News Writing* seeks to demonstrate the moral underpinnings of journalism.

Journalism's hope and inspiration are its young men and women. This book was written for them and especially in memory of two young men who were killed in Vietnam, Ron Gallagher and Peter Bushey. Ron was editor of the *University Daily Kansan* when I was its adviser at the University of Kansas, and Peter was one of my students at Columbia University. They loved journalism and had faith in what it could accomplish. They wrote, they took pictures and they aspired to make the world a better place for us all through journalism. To them, journalism was a noble calling.

M.M.

Acknowledgments

Those who have provided help with this book include the following:

Steve Ames
Pepperdine University

Mervin Block
CBS News

Stewart Bowman
The (Louisville) *Courier-Journal*

Bonnie Britt
The Houston Chronicle

Roy Peter Clark
Modern Media Institute

Joelle Cohen
The News Tribune (Tacoma, Wash.)

William J. Connolly, Jr.
The Virginian-Pilot

Claude Cookman
The Miami Herald

Frances D'Emilio
UPI

Stuart Dim
Newsday

Mary Ann Giordano
The Daily News

Douglas Hand
A freelance writer

Stephen Hartgen
The Anniston (Ala.) *Star*

Berkley Hudson
The Providence Journal-Bulletin

Monica Kaufman
WSB-TV (Atlanta)

Terry Keys
University of Kentucky

Mary Ann Laskewicz
The St. Petersburg Times

Dennis Love
The Anniston (Ala.) Star

Frank McCulloch
The Sacramento Bee

Avice Meehan
The Dalton (Mass.) News-Record

Mitch Mendelson
The Birmingham Post-Herald

Bill Mertens
The Hays (Kan.) *Daily News*

Mark Miller
The Berkshire (Mass.) *Eagle*

Cheyenne J. Oldham
University of Kentucky

Susan J. Porter
Scripps-Howard News

Neal Robbins
UPI

Bob Rose
The Blade (Toledo, Ohio)

Christopher Scanlan
The Providence Journal-Bulletin

Howard L. Seemann
Humboldt State University

Rick Sluder
The News & Observer (Raleigh, N.C.)

Mary Voboril
The Miami Herald

Charles Walk
The Bismarck (N.D.) *Tribune*

Lindy Washburn
AP

Jan Wong
The Gazette (Montreal)

Charles M. Young
Rolling Stone

Part One
Journalists in Action

1

In the Newsroom and on the Beat

The news writer gives readers and viewers an accurate, thorough, impartial and timely account of events. The writer does this by applying his or her skills and knowledge to the job of reporting and writing.

The journalistic process is the same for newspapers, radio, television, newsmagazines: facts are gathered and checked, additional information is obtained through research, the story is written and, finally, the news is produced in written or spoken form.

Looking Ahead

The lights are out in the fashionable stores along Fifth Avenue, and the tall buildings in Rockefeller Center loom over the deserted streets. Moviegoers have made their way home from Radio City Music Hall a block away on Sixth Avenue. It is well past midnight in midtown New York.

Although the lights in one Rockefeller Center office building burn brightly, there is an unusual calm here, too. The reporters, editors and operators in the Associated Press newsroom have left for the night. The office is deserted—except for a young woman sitting at one of the desks.

Lindy Washburn is working the early shift—11:30 p.m. to 8 a.m.—in the New York City bureau of the AP. She was hired as a summer vacation replacement after her graduation from journalism school.

As the newcomer in the bureau, she has been taught the ropes: the need for speed, accuracy and brevity, which wires send out sports, radio, local and national news, and the method for transmitting stories she may have to write when the operators are not on duty.

Washburn is responsible for a large area of the East Coast, and she will be on her own most of the morning. This is her first night alone on the early shift.

As the old hands were leaving, one had stopped on his way out to reassure her. "Looks like a quiet night," he had said.

On the Job. Lindy Washburn of the Associated Press takes notes on a video display terminal (VDT) for a breaking news story.

For a while it was quiet. Washburn handled some routine tasks. But suddenly, at 1:40 a.m., the stillness of the office is broken by the ring of the telephone. The night city editor of the *Daily News* is calling. Washburn can sense the urgency in his voice.

Handling a Big Story—Alone

"We have a tip there's a big fire in New Jersey," the *News* editor says. "Have you got anything?" No, she hasn't, she says. She asks him where the fire is. "Bradley Beach," he replies.

Washburn looks at a map and sees that Bradley Beach is a town on the Atlantic shore and is near Asbury Park, a larger city.

She calls long distance information and asks for the telephone numbers of the Bradley Beach police and fire departments and the numbers of the departments in Asbury Park. First, she calls the Bradley Beach fire department.

"Lady, we're busy," a voice says and hangs up. He sounds frantic.

She telephones the Asbury Park fire department.

"What's happening in Bradley Beach?" she asks. "I can't get anything from the department there."

"That's some fire," the dispatcher answers. "We have departments from all over the state fighting it. It looks like a big one."

"Any deaths?" Washburn asks.

"I think it was 20 last time I checked. Could be more now."

Washburn's heart picks up a few beats. This is obviously a big story. She realizes that on a slow night a fire of this size will be given play around the country. She knows that at this time—nearly 2 a.m.—newspapers in the West are readying their front pages. She will have to hurry to catch them.

She asks the dispatcher for the address of the building, what it is used for, when the first alarm had been received. She wants to know what the building looks like—is it wood, brick, stucco? It's a wooden frame building, called the Brinley Inn. The dispatcher says no, he doesn't know the cause. Too early for that.

As she hangs up, another telephone rings. The call is from a radio reporter for a station in Asbury Park. He had called the AP's Newark bureau with information and a tape-recorded message had told him the bureau was closed for the night but that important stories should be phoned to the New York City bureau.

"Have you heard about the fire?" he asks.

"Yes," says Washburn. "How many deaths are there?" She needs the death toll. It's the key to the story. And she must have it confirmed.

"The hospital spokesman on the scene says 23," the radio reporter replies. She gives him the address the dispatcher had provided, and he confirms that.

He then plays a tape of the conversation he had with a doctor from the medical examiner's office who was at the scene of the fire.

Washburn now has almost all she needs. She will have to put something on the wire at once. Then she will have to alert the AP New Jersey staff to start working on the story.

She has been typing notes from her conversations. She looks them over, rearranges them, writes a lead and decides she is ready to file her story. She types in the proper code for an all-points bulletin.

```
o364
    B N ZYVVYXUIV
BNBX NR07 NR05
BNBX
BC-BRADLEY BEACH FIRE
    BRADLEY BEACH, NEW JERSEY (AP)--A MAJOR
FIRE IN BRADLEY BEACH HAS KILLED 23 PEOPLE,
ACCORDING TO FIRE OFFICIALS.
    THE FIRE AT BRINLEY INN, 200 BRINLEY AVE.,
BEGAN AT 11:20 P.M. AND WAS BROUGHT UNDER
CONTROL AT MIDNIGHT, ACCORDING TO CHIEF
THEODORE A. BIANCHI OF THE BRADLEY BEACH FIRE
DEPARTMENT.
    THE CAUSE OF THE FIRE IS UNDETERMINED, HE
SAID.
    THE BRINLEY INN, A THREE-STORY WOOD FRAME
BUILDING, WAS REPORTEDLY OCCUPIED BY 36 PEOPLE
```

AT THE TIME OF THE BLAZE. MANY ELDERLY PERSONS
AND TEENAGERS WERE AMONG THOSE KILLED, THE
OFFICIALS SAID.

DEAD AND INJURED WERE TAKEN TO THE JERSEY
SHORE MEDICAL CENTER AND THE LONG BRANCH
MEDICAL CENTER.

MORE
AP-NY-07-27 0201EDT

Second Lead

All of this is done in about 20 minutes, and Washburn is pleased by her ability to act quickly in a critical situation. (She later learns that she has beaten the opposition, the UPI, by 35 minutes.) But she is not pleased with her story. There are some flubs.

She sees that she should have abbreviated New Jersey in the dateline, and she realizes that the adjective *major* in the lead is extraneous. She also realizes that she should have used *said* instead of *according to* in the lead.

By the time her story has cleared the wire, Washburn is busy gathering more material. She learns that the Brinley Inn is a four-story rooming house, and she has obtained more details about the injured, where the dead had been trapped and the time the fire broke out.

She begins to write a new lead. Her first story had cleared at 2:01 a.m. Her second piece clears at 3:26 a.m.

o365
    B N ZYVVYXWYF
AM-BEACH FIRE, 2ND LD-WRITETHRU,400
EDS: UPDATES, CORRECTS BUILDING
TO FOUR-STORY STRUCTURE, ADDS COLOR
    BRADLEY BEACH, N.J. (AP)--AT LEAST 23
PERSONS WERE KILLED SATURDAY IN A FIRE AT A
ROOMING HOUSE IN THIS SEASIDE RESORT, HOSPITAL
OFFICIALS SAID.
    TWO OTHERS SUFFERED SMOKE INHALATION AND
WERE ADMITTED TO THE JERSEY SHORE MEDICAL
CENTER, SAID HOSPITAL ADMINISTRATOR ERNEST
KOVATS. AN ADDITIONAL 13 PEOPLE WERE EXAMINED
AT THE HOSPITAL, KOVATS SAID.
    AS MANY AS 36 PEOPLE MAY HAVE BEEN INSIDE
THE BRINLEY INN WHEN THE FIRE BROKE OUT AT
11:02 P.M. AND WAS BROUGHT UNDER CONTROL ABOUT
MIDNIGHT, AUTHORITIES SAID.
    WITNESSES SAID MOST OF THE VICTIMS APPEARED
TO BE ELDERLY AND APPEARED TO BE TRAPPED ON THE
TOP FLOORS OF THE FOUR-STORY WOOD-FRAME
BUILDING.
    THE CAUSE OF THE FIRE WAS NOT DETERMINED,
BUT THERE WERE SOME REPORTS OF AN EXPLOSION,
SAID FIRE CHIEF THEODORE A. BIANCHI.

```
    AT LEAST 35 AMBULANCES FROM BRADLEY BEACH
AND SEVERAL MONMOUTH COUNTY COMMUNITIES LINED
UP NEAR THE BUILDING, WAITING TO TRANSPORT THE
BODIES, ACCORDING TO WITNESSES.
    FIREMEN REMOVED THE VICTIMS FROM A THIRD
FLOOR EXIT DOOR ON THE REAR OF THE BUILDING TO
A ROOF WHERE THEY LOWERED THE VICTIMS TO THE
WAITING AMBULANCES.
    TWO DOCTORS, ONE WHO IDENTIFIED HIMSELF AS
A DOCTOR FROM THE MONMOUTH COUNTY MEDICAL
EXAMINER'S OFFICE, WERE ON THE SCENE TO BRIEFLY
EXAMINE THE BODIES BEFORE THEY WERE TRANSPORTED
TO JERSEY SHORE MEDICAL CENTER.
    KOVATS SAID SEVERAL BODIES WERE TRANSPORTED
DIRECTLY TO THE COUNTY MORGUE AT FREEHOLD AREA
HOSPITAL.
    FIREMEN SAID THE BUILDING WAS ENGULFED WHEN
THEY ARRIVED AT THE SCENE, MAKING ENTRY
IMPOSSIBLE.
    THE BUILDING WAS BADLY CHARRED ON THE SOUTH
AND EAST SIDES OF THE FIRST FLOOR OF THE
BUILDING. FIREMEN SAID THE FIRE APPEARED TO
HAVE STARTED ON THE EAST SIDE OF THE BUILDING
ON THE PORCH.
    LOCAL FIRE OFFICIALS, MONMOUTH COUNTY FIRE
MARSHAL FRED LEGGETT, THE STATE POLICE ARSON
SQUAD AND MONMOUTH COUNTY PROSECUTOR ALEXANDER
LEHRER WERE ON THE SCENE CONDUCTING AN INITIAL
INVESTIGATION.
    THE BRINLEY INN WAS THE SCENE OF ANOTHER
FIRE IN SEPTEMBER 1979, ACCORDING TO THE ASBURY
PARK PRESS.

AP-NY-07-27 0326EDT
```

In the UPI's Hong Kong Bureau

A third of the world to the west, in Hong Kong, a young reporter for the UPI is going over stories he plans to put in his files.

"Robbins," the deputy news editor calls. He tells Neal Robbins to find a boat and track down a flotilla of Chinese junks that is approaching Hong Kong.

Chinese sneak into the British colony all the time, Robbins knows. But this is different. This is an influx by sea. It could be a big story in the United States as well as in Asia. Chinese have been leaving the mainland in small groups for political reasons. But this sounded like a large movement.

Robbins is joined by a photographer and they take off.

Soon they are cruising the Hong Kong harbor on the *Xinhua,* a 30-foot boat, looking for a cove that the Chinese are supposedly heading for. As they head out to sea, police boats pass them, spotter planes fly overhead and a helicopter slowly circles above the water.

Seeking Refuge. Part of a flotilla of Chinese junks that found a haven near Hong Kong. This was the first sight that greeted Neal Robbins of the UPI Hong Kong bureau on his assignment to find out why the Chinese had fled China.

They spot the cove. There before them are about 50 traditional Chinese sailing junks. "Their rust-color bat-wing sails make the flotilla seem a well-combed field of wheat," Robbins notes. The boats are anchored, and Robbins directs the captain toward the middle of the flotilla.

The photographer, a Hong Kong Chinese, calls out to some people in a Cantonese dialect. The boat people stare back. Robbins tries his Mandarin, which he learned in college. More stares.

The Unexpected

Finally, they locate a man who speaks Mandarin. The Chinese boat people come from an area in South China, he says. There are 70 of them on the small wooden boat, all members of three families.

No, he replies in answer to a question from Robbins. They are not fleeing China for political reasons. They have come, he says, because the authorities warned them of a massive earthquake that is to strike their area soon. (China was hit by a devastating earthquake in 1976 that killed more than 800,000 people.)

Finding the people friendly, Robbins moves from boat to boat, asking questions. He boards some of the boats. The people are from a fishing area, he is told, and they have been informed that the earthquake was due in about a week. He is also told that gangsters had invaded their area and had stolen valuables and commandeered some fishing boats.

A Final Check

In an hour, Robbins is ready to return to the bureau to write. On the way out of the cove, he stops to interview officials on the police boats. The police had intercepted the junks and herded them into the cove, a police superintendent tells him. The police had counted 55 boats and were told that a hundred more are on the way.

Packed. Crowded in a single junk with all they own, 70 people watch as Robbins and a photographer approach.

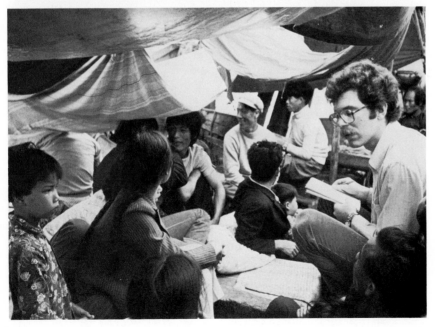

Getting the Story. Robbins asks the Chinese why they fled their homes for Hong Kong. They tell him they were warned a massive earthquake was due soon.

They estimate there are 2,000 people on the boats. Robbins also asks what the superintendent knows about the earthquake, the gangsters and whether the people will be fed and cared for. Finally, he wants to know whether the government will let them stay if they ask to remain.

He obtains the superintendent's exact title and the spelling of his name.

On the way back to the bureau, Robbins reads his notes to get the story straight. Figuring out the lead is not too hard, he thinks.

Clearly, he says to himself, the point is that the boats have arrived and why they are here. The hard part is the wording, trying to make the lead attractive. On a story like this one, good writing is important.

He has arranged his notes, thought of a lead, and there is still time before they land. He starts to write his story in longhand on the boat.

In the bureau, as Robbins seats himself, the editor says, "Keep it short." Back in the States, the President has been shot, and there are ominous stirrings in Poland.

As Robbins types, his editor looks over his shoulder. He asks Robbins about the gangsters.

"That's what they told me," Robbins replies. He says that the account the people gave was a bit confused.

"Bury it," the editor advises him, meaning that it should be put deep in the story.

Robbins agrees that the fear of the earthquake is the central fact.

Here is the beginning of Robbins' story as it went out on UPI's wires from Hong Kong:

```
ZCZC XHA197 NXI
00 HUP NRS
R I
     FLOTILLA 3-31
     BY NEAL ROBBINS
     HONG KONG, MARCH 31 (UPI)--A FLOTILLA OF
CHINESE JUNKS CARRYING SOME 2,000 PEOPLE
ARRIVED IN HONG KONG TUESDAY FEARING AN
IMPENDING EARTHQUAKE IN SOUTHERN CHINA,
OFFICIALS SAID.
     POLICE SUPERINTENDENT BILL RENAHAN TOLD UPI
THAT A WAVE OF 55 OF THE RICKETY WOODEN BOATS
WITH 2,000 MEN, WOMEN AND CHILDREN CAME FROM
HAIFENG AND LUFENG COUNTIES IN GUANGDONG
PROVINCE JUST NORTH OF HONG KONG. THE MAKESHIFT
FLOTILLA LEFT HOME SUNDAY, HE SAID.
     ANOTHER 200 TO 400 VESSELS POWERED BY BAT-
WINGED SAILS ARE STILL OUT AT SEA CARRYING AS
MANY AS 10,000 RESIDENTS OF CHINA, RENAHAN
ESTIMATED.
     BUT HONG KONG GOVERNMENT SOURCES SAID ONLY
78 BOATS HAD BEEN SIGHTED AND 48 OF THEM
CONTAINING 1,800 PEOPLE ARRIVED TUESDAY.
```

```
    RENAHAN SAID THE FLOTILLA WAS THE LARGEST
OF ITS KIND TO HIT THE BRITISH COLONY, WHICH
HAS BEEN FLOODED WITH HUNDREDS OF THOUSANDS OF
ILLEGAL CHINESE IMMIGRANTS SINCE 1978.
    POLICE LAUNCHES CORRALLED THE 20-40 FOOT
(7-13 METER) BOATS IN JOSS HOUSE BAY, A SMALL
COVE SURROUNDED BY UNINHABITED, GRASSY HILLS
JUST IN SIGHT OF THE TOWERING SKYSCRAPERS OF
HONG KONG, BUT OUTSIDE THE MAIN HARBOR.

    MORE
SC1755
CCCCQQE
NNNN
```

Hong Kong authorities were told by Chinese officials that the earth-quake warning was a false alarm. The authorities turned back all the boats, some by force. Nine days later, an earthquake did strike the South China area from which the people had fled. Authorities described it as "moderate" but refused to divulge whether there had been any casualties.

The CBS Evening News

In New York City, it is 5:30 p.m. according to the wall clock in the small lobby of the CBS Broadcast Center at 524 West 57th St. Left through the lobby, down a long, narrow corridor, around a corner, a door with a small glass window opens into a large newsroom-studio. People move quickly in and out the door.

Inside, it is almost an hour before air time for the "CBS Evening News." A large desk sits in the middle of the pale blue studio. At one side, behind large glass panels is the executive producer's room. Dan Rather, the anchor-man for the Evening News, is going over the program with the producer. From time to time, Rather emerges to talk to the writers who are seated next to the central desk in the studio.

They are preparing for the 6:30 program that is shown live to viewers in some cities in the East and Midwest. Half an hour later, the video tape is broadcast for New York City and other places, and later the tape will be shown to viewers on the West Coast.

The Writers

The writers have been at work since 10 in the morning. Their first task is to read several newspapers—*The New York Times, Washington Post, Wall Street Journal* and *Daily News.* Then they scan the wires for the news. Each writer has a different area of responsibility: one handles national news; an-other, foreign; a third, features, disasters and obituaries.

The writers look over the major stories in the newspapers and on the wires, and they are on the lookout for the news items that make for interesting feature stories and takeouts. They are conscious of the visual possibilities of each story. A "tell" story or "reader" in which the anchorman reads from a script is not as interesting to viewers as a story that is accompanied by videotape.

Tell stories are written tightly because time is precious. But stories with good visuals will run five or six times as long.

A writer may collect several thousand words for a story and reduce it to 100 words for the anchorperson to read as a tell story. A story that involves a correspondent in the field may require a discussion with that correspondent. The writer will want to know what Robert Pierpoint or Lesley Stahl in Washington will be stressing in order to write an appropriate lead-in, one that captures the essence of the story without duplicating what the reporter is going to say.

By midafternoon, the writers have a good idea of the day's news, and at 3:30 the executive producer and the editor discuss the news items for the program. The editor needs to know how much time will be needed for each item for Rather and whether it will be a tell story or be told by a reporter on videotape.

Minutes to Go

5:58 Rather leaves the executive producer's office and sits in the chair that he will use for the broadcast. He is holding a sheaf of papers, the items he will read for the Evening News. He manages to bite down on his cigar and move his lips as he reads the script. He is in his early fifties, trim and vigorous. He wears a white shirt and a conservative tie. His hair, flecked with gray, is carefully combed back but rearranges itself as he moves around.

6:02 Rather turns to one of his writers and asks about an item that has been inserted in the newscast, a legal suit involving Richard Nixon.

"You think we should explain this, Charley?" Rather asks Charles West, a tall, middle-aged writer. "If we do, we'll need 10 or 15 more seconds." West, a former AP reporter who has been with the Evening News for 15 years, agrees to add some material.

6:04 Lineup No. 22, a tell story, displeases Rather. He discusses some of the wording with a writer. The item runs for 20 seconds and is 50 words long. They agree on a new wording.

6:05 "Ten is out," someone shouts, and item 10 is scratched to make room for the additional material in the Nixon story.

6:08 The makeup woman enters the studio. The camera crew begins to position itself around the room, and the two people running the prompter machines go over the script. The machines project large type directly in front of Rather so that although he appears to the viewer to be looking directly into the camera he is reading from the script projected in front of him. A system of lenses projects the script over the lens of the camera focused on Rather.

6:10 Rather looks up from editing the lead-all, the first item in the newscast. "Very nice lead, Charley, very nice," he tells West. Rather resumes reading.

6:11 A woman dashes out of the executive producer's office. "We have an emergency," she says. "We need something from the archives." Film is necessary for a news item. It may not be used, but the producer wants to have it available.

6:14 Rather detects an ambiguous statement in one of the stories. The item has just been inserted in the program, and Rather wants to change some of the wording to clarify the story.

6:15 A sudden calm descends on the studio.

In the control room, there is no peace. Seven people are jammed together at a console, each one talking. In the middle front row is the director. He will cue the cameras as they focus on the anchorman and give other cues as the visuals, remotes and videotapes pop on and off the screen.

The goal of the control room staff is to have a tight program, to move neatly from Rather to the Washington correspondent without dead air, without cutting Rather off too soon; to synchronize the visuals that are the backdrop for Rather as he describes a spot in the Pacific (a map appears), a planet (a picture of Saturn looms over his left shoulder), a labor union (its emblem is shown).

6:23 Grim faced, Rather sits in front of a small mirror and is made up. He applies the lip rouge himself.

6:24 Rather shouts, "Sandy, you've got to pump that audio way up." Silence again.

6:25 "Five minutes," the stage manager calls out.

6:29 Rather settles into his chair, again reading the script. This time his lips are immobile.

"Thirty seconds." The deep voice booms in the studio and over a loudspeaker in the control room where the hubbub suddenly ceases. Countdowns are being prepared by the people at the various panels to cue the announcer, Rather, the video tape recorder, correspondents and the visuals. "Ten seconds."

Rather opens the program with a lead-in (introduction) to the big story of the day:

> President Reagan today signed into law his tax and spending cut bills. He called it the beginning of-- quote--"a turnaround of almost half a century, marking the end of a course we have been on of excessive growth, excessive bureaucracy and excessive taxation." End of quote. In other words, a sharp turn from a course begun by the Franklin Roosevelt New Deal. Lesley Stahl reports from the Reagan ranch in California.

> LESLEY STAHL: What made this different from the usual Rose Garden signing ceremonies? Just about everything-- casual ranch clothes, milling ranch dogs, grazing horses and the awkward signing of the budget and tax cut bills with 24 different pens. A thick mountain fog....

Editing a Weekly Newspaper

North of New York, in the small town of Dalton, Mass., Avice Meehan is the managing editor of the weekly newspaper, *The Dalton News-Record*. The newspaper serves eight communities in the area. Meehan had been working for a daily newspaper after graduating from journalism school. When the editorship of the weekly opened up, Meehan grabbed it. She liked the idea of becoming involved with a small town and its people. In her work on the daily, her coverage was limited by her beat.

For the weekly, she does everything. She covers politics, local government and Lions Club luncheons; she writes obituaries and local items. She also designs the front page and takes an occasional picture.

She is busy with the page layout but takes a minute to talk about her work.

"The hours are long, the pay is not terrific, and I generally work six or seven days a week," she says. "But I wouldn't exchange this experience for anything."

Air Time. In the control room, the chatter ceases, all is silent and the countdown begins 10 seconds before the CBS Evening News goes on the air.

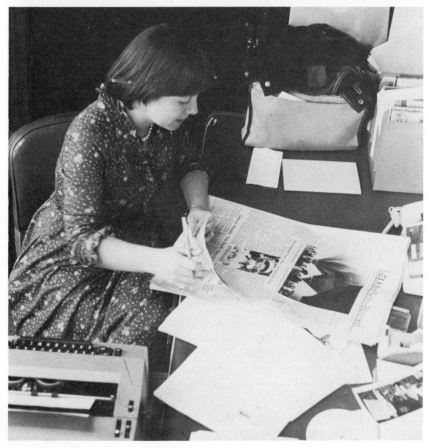

Weekly Editor. Avice Meehan of *The Dalton News-Record* checks a newspaper just off the press. In her job she does it all—writes stories, does the makeup and even takes photos now and then.

Meehan is putting an obituary in the number one spot, upper right-hand, of page one. "You couldn't do this on a daily, unless the president died." Her obituary is of a local volunteer fireman who is well known in town. She wrote it.

"We mainly concentrate on the little things," she says. "Our readers like items about the Boy Scouts and such. We manage some hard-hitting stories, like our series on the state takeover of a local nursing home.

"You can learn on a weekly, and you can experiment. You don't have to be as conventional as you do on a daily newspapers.

"People here take great stock in their children. I cover the schools and children's programs."

She needs some work done on a story, and she dashes over to a machine that feeds the small computer her paper uses in its production process.

"Everything in the paper is local," she says. She points to a story she has just written about the visit by officials of the Vietnam Era Vet Center.

"I was able to bring a national issue—the threat of loss of funds for the Center in a budget cut—to my readers," she says. Here's how she began her story:

DALTON—For many Vietnam veterans the war has not ended.

"We are the flashbacks. We are the nightmares. We want people to get a little frightened. We want the public to cry, too, but no one is crying," said Frank Penacho.

"People commonly think time heals all wounds, but it only decreases the intensity of the wounds. Time is not enough. A lot of guys in World War II are still suffering," said Robert Gillis.

Mr. Penacho and Mr. Gillis are on the staff of the only Vietnam Era Vet Center in Massachusetts. The Vet Center, located in Brockton, took to the road last week at the invitation of the American Legion for a two-day visit here.

The Vet Center opened in 1979, following passage of the Veterans Health Care Amendments Act to provide readjustment counseling to Vietnam-era veterans, a group often neglected by the Veterans Administration.

The program, with a budget of about $13 million, is threatened with elimination by the Reagan administration, although support for it has been growing. If funding continues, centers similar to the one in Brockton may open in Springfield and Albany, N.Y. The Brockton agency has a budget of $140,000. . . .

A Job Tryout

In a luncheonette in Gloucester, Mass., a young man is eating a sandwich. His name is Nicholas Trowbridge and he is recalling for a friend his first few days on the local daily, *The Gloucester Times*. He had just graduated from college where he had majored in philosophy. But he thought he had some knowledge of journalism because he had worked on his college weekly.

"I had a three-day tryout for the job," he recalls. "The editor had told me it would be two days, and by the third day the one suit I had needed cleaning.

"The first day had been a disaster. I was told to condense five stories to capsule length. After two hours at the typewriter, I had five two-page stories.

"The boss looked at them and said, 'When I said brief I meant two grafs, not two pages.'

"So when the third day came and the paper's veteran reporter suggested I do a sidebar to go along with his story on a mayoral election debate at the local Legion Hall, I knew this was it.

"My assignment was to talk to people in the bar downstairs and ask them why they weren't upstairs listening to the debate. The reporter introduced me to the bartender and went upstairs.

The Wise Guys

"I talked to a few of the regulars at the bar and had the beginnings of a story. Then I ran into the wise guys.

"They were playing pool in one of the rooms off the bar, and after I identified myself, one turned to me and said, 'You're new, aren't you?'

"When I told him I hadn't even been hired yet, that I was on trial, he said, 'Well if you want the job, the big story's in the bar. Jack's his name and he set a record last week,'

"The record, they told me with complete sincerity and honesty, was for not going to the toilet. It was going to be published in the *Guinness Book of World Records,* they said."

" 'Come on, you're kidding me,' I laughed.

"They assured me it was no lie. Jack had survived on water, vitamins and beer during the long wait.

"I went into the bar and asked if Jack was in.

" 'Why do you want Jack?' one woman asked as she cradled Seven-and-Seven between her forearms.

" 'I hear he set a record, he's the one who didn't go . . . uh, forget it,' I stammered. 'Why aren't you upstairs, listening to the politicians at the debate?'

" 'One's an idiot and one's retarded,' she answered." "No, that's not it, they're both retarded.'

"I put the quote high in my story and the editor ran it on page one. The next day he told me I had the job and said I could thank the woman in the bar for it. A few days later the paper received an angry letter on my story from one of the two mayoral aspirants who claimed the story was derogatory to those with mental handicaps.

"But it's lucky my story wasn't about a mythical Jack who avoided the call of nature for a record number of days. Had it been, I'd probably still be wandering through the south in search of a job, hitching with truckers through an endless succession of roadside truck stops and hopeless interviews."

Lost in the Crowd

A few weeks later, a wiser and tougher reporter—he thought—he was assigned to journey to Boston with a busload of parishioners who were going to see the Pope during his U.S. tour. He met the people at 7 a.m. in front of a local church and a short time later in Boston they split into four groups to walk to Boston Common where the Pope was to celebrate Mass.

"I decided to stick with the largest group for the day, listen to their comments, watch their reaction to the Pope.

"On the way to the park, I ducked out for a cup of coffee. When I got out of the coffee shop, the group was gone.

"I raced to the Common. They were lost in a sea of people. After a two-hour search, I realized I was wasting my time.

"I went to a pay phone and called the boss, collect.

" 'I've lost them,' I said.

" 'Lost who, Nick?'

" 'The parishioners from St. Ann's. I went into this place to get some coffee, and when I came out they were gone, vanished,' I told him, thinking that his advice would be to continue south to look for another job.

" 'Nick lost the parishioners and he's looking for them on Boston Common,' I could hear him telling the staff.

"I could hear laughter in the newsroom.

" 'Don't worry,' he told me. 'Just get some good quotes on the bus on the way back.'

" 'And don't miss the bus.'

" 'No problem,' I told him. 'I've got it under control.' "

Inside a Newsroom

If we could look in on one of the 1,750 daily newspapers a few hours before press time, we might see a picture of this kind: Telephones ringing with reporters calling in to speak to the city editor about stories they are working on. Teletype machines clacking off reams of AP and UPI copy. Copy editors reading news stories on their video terminal screens, removing the word *felt* and inserting the word *said,* writing a headline for a page one story about a fatal accident.

The news editor is chatting with the managing editor about a weather story out of Florida, and reporters are writing stories on their quiet terminals, looking up now and then at the screen to see whether the lead is just right.

A police siren pierces the evening's stillness outside, and soon the wail of an ambulance is heard. No one pays attention.

A Fatal Accident

The phone on the city editor's desk rings and he picks it up. It is a call from the police reporter at the police station. "Bad accident at an intersection with the bypass," he says. "You want me to get out there or cover from here? They think two people have been killed."

The city editor tells the reporter to sit tight, that with the rain-slick roads and the fog there may be other accidents. The editor doesn't want the reporter to lose touch with police headquarters for awhile.

"Try to get a fix on it," the editor says. "If it's as bad as you say, I think you'd better get out there. I'm sending a photographer anyway."

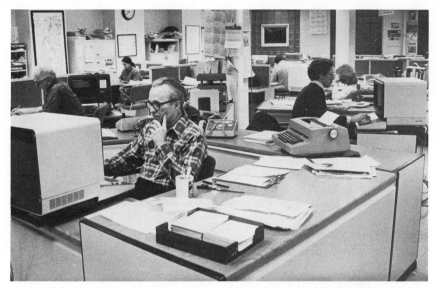

News Center. All local news funnels through the city editor. Here, in the newsroom of *The Berkshire Eagle* in Pittsfield, Mass., city editor Bill Bell looks over local stories for the day on the screen of his video display terminal. On the left, county editor Frank McCarthy writes a headline. Day news editor Charles Bonenti, on the right, edits a reporter's copy on a terminal. In the background, reporters are at work.

For the next half-hour, the police beat reporter monitors the police radio. At the same time, he goes through the notes he has taken from police reports upstairs in the lieutenant's office. He spots a burglary at the First Baptist Church. He recalls that he has notes somewhere in his pad about the theft of religious scrolls from a synagogue on Maple Avenue. He decides he will put the two thefts into one story. He makes a mental note to call the lieutenant to ask whether the same people could have been involved in both burglaries.

Three blocks away in city hall, another reporter is walking into the city council chambers. He greets the city clerk.

At City Hall

"Should be a good meeting tonight, Alice," he says. She nods in agreement.

"The appeal on the zoning decision on Hale's will bring them out," he says. "I'm glad you gave me the background on that one."

He turns to chat with the manager of Hale's Department Store who has entered the room, along with his lawyer. The reporter wants more background on Hale's plans to build a large store in a residential area outside the downtown area.

In the newsroom, a young reporter is bent over several sheets of paper. They are the carbon copies of obituary notices from the advertising department. One of the notices is about the death of a retired school principal. She had taught in local schools for 30 years and was a principal for 13 years. She probably has many former students in town, the reporter thinks. She decides to obtain more information about the woman.

A telephone call interrupts her thoughts. The caller is the president of the United Way. He has the results of the fund drive just completed.

"We worked all day getting the field reports together, and I'm glad to say we've set a record," he says. The reporter asks how much was raised, what accounted for the record donations. Did any particular organization or event raise an unusually large amount of money? The questions continue.

In a corner of the newsroom, the news editor is looking over some wire service stories.

"Hurricane expected to hit Florida," he tells the managing editor. "People boarding up. Worst in a decade, they think."

The managing editor tells him to put the AP and UPI stories together. They might put it on page one, he says. Lots of people in town have friends and relatives who have moved to Florida.

Approaching Deadline

The news for tomorrow's newspaper is being gathered in diverse ways. Some reporters are covering events. Others are taking information from sources over the telephone. News that originates outside the community is coming in on the Associated Press and United Press International news wires.

Not all the information and news being gathered will be used. The police reporter has had reports of two more accidents, and he knows that he will have little time to write up the minor burglaries, break-ins and arrests from his notes. He may do the church and synagogue thefts in a single story, but he knows that he will have to spend the few hours before deadline on the accidents, rounding them up into a single story, probably for page one.

The reporter handling the obituaries has learned that a fund drive is being planned to raise money for a memorial scholarship in honor of the retired school principal who has just died. The scholarship will be called the Rose Harriet Allen Memorial Scholarship, and some of the city's leading citizens—her former students—are serving on the committee to raise money.

The reporter intends to interview these people, not only about their plans to raise money but about their recollections of their school days in Allen's classroom.

The reporter looks at a batch of notes she has taken on several other obituaries. She shrugs. She will have little time for them, and she will have no time for the calls she had planned to make for some of the other obituaries. She realizes that this will displease some readers. Obituaries are one of the newspaper's best-read sections, she knows. If she can, she will spend time on the other obituaries once she has finished the Allen story. She will have to work at twice the usual pace, which, she smiles to herself, is twice as fast as she thought she'd work when she was studying journalism in college.

The wire editor has handed the city editor an AP story from Phoenix about the crash of a small plane. One of the three victims had owned a chain of shoe stores in town until his retirement three years ago. The city editor calls a reporter to his desk.

"Here, rewrite this. Bill Frazier died in a plane crash in Phoenix."

The reporter understands that he will have to localize the wire story, which means putting information about Frazier into the lead. He heads for the newspaper library to dig up background—the number of stores Frazier owned, his civic activities, place of birth, and other details he will need for the combination news story and obituary.

We move from this composite picture of reporters at work on a medium-sized newspaper to the newsroom of a larger daily newspaper, *The Providence Journal.*

Twenty-Eight Years in Confinement

Berkley Hudson is talking about a story he has just finished handling for his newspaper. The story—actually two stories, Hudson says—began one day in the newsroom. "This man had sneaked off the grounds of a state mental hospital, managed to get a bus and walked into the newspaper to tell his story." Hudson arranged to meet him later at the hospital parking lot.

The man had spent five years in the state penitentiary and 23 in a state mental hospital. Most people confined to such places believe they should be freed, but Hudson felt this story was different.

Hudson let the man talk, and the longer he spoke the more Hudson felt that there had been an injustice. Reporters often act on their hunches or intuition, which is actually a highly developed insight gained by experience.

Hudson decided to look into Chester Jefferds' story.

From looking at hospital records and interviewing social workers and administrators at the hospital, Hudson concluded that neither justice nor compassion would be served by keeping Jefferds locked away.

"He doesn't belong here," a social worker told Hudson. That quote was underlined in Hudson's notes. It would have to go high up in the story. He remembered a point his journalism instructor had driven home relentlessly: Good quotes up high.

As angry as Hudson felt about the situation, he knew that the best way to tell the story would be to let it tell itself. The indignation would have to come from the reader. Hudson would lay out all the facts and let the reader reach the conclusion that Jefferds should be freed. The reporting took two weeks.

"When I had all the information I thought I needed, I decided to start writing," Hudson says. He went into the office at 10 a.m. and looked over his notes carefully. As often happens, he discovered he needed additional details, and that took a few hours.

"At 2 o'clock I had organized my notes and was ready to write." With a few breaks, he wrote until about midnight. He spent another hour with the Sunday editor, going over the story, making some changes in the copy. Here is how the story begins:

He survived inside; now he'd like to be free

By BERKLEY HUDSON
Journal-Bulletin Staff Writer

CRANSTON — Chester G. Jefferds Jr. has survived 28 years in confinement. His face has deep, bold wrinkles. His hazel eyes are murky.

He spent five years in the state prison, then 23 more in the state mental hospital. He has seen other prisoners kill themselves — and sometimes each other. His was a world of beatings and rape, strait jackets and electroshock therapy, nurse's needles and attendants' pills.

Chester Jefferds learned how a man labeled crazy stays sane in a mental institution. You keep quiet. You try to forget why you're there. You don't listen to the moans and screams around you.

"You go through the alphabet, saying the letters over and over," he says. "You go through the fraction tables. 7 into 100. 8 into 100."

He has one tooth left. The rest he lost in fights. He has a raspy voice.

"There's only one way to go in this place," he·says. "You keep your mouth shut."

Those who know him call him Jeff. He is 68. It has been 28 years since he was sentenced to life imprisonment for shooting his wife to death. Now he would like his freedom.

★ ★ ★

"HE DOESN'T belong here," says David J. Arone, a social worker at the state General Hospital. "There's plenty of evidence Chester has been able to take care of himself."

Since 1973, psychiatrists, social workers and nurses have been saying what Arone says: Jefferds is not sick, mentally or physically.

The problem, Arone says, is that Jefferds is unique among the 1,400 patients at the medical center. Like others there, he is elderly and has been in a mental hospital for many years, yet he is no longer ill. What makes him different is that he is under a life sentence for murder.

"He's still here because if he weren't here, he'd be at the prison," says Frederick Young, chief of social services at the General Hospital. Jefferds, Young says, doesn't belong in prison either. Mental-health laws require the release of anyone who is not ill, but hospital officials believe that if he were released from the hospital, he would be required to go back to prison.

"Had he been at the prison all this time as a lifer, he'd probably be free now," Young says. "Most of the ques-

Free. Six weeks after Hudson's story appeared, Chester Jefferds was released from the state hospital where he had been confined long past the time he should have been freed.

Six weeks after Hudson's story appeared, Jefferds was on his way to freedom. The state parole board had decided to allow Jefferds to leave the hospital for a halfway house. After three months there, he would be a free man. Hudson went out to the hospital to watch Jefferds pack. He wrote a story about Jefferds' release that began:

Chester Jefferds stood next to his suitcase. It had a rope for a handle. Inside, among his few possessions, was a card from a friend. It read, "Good luck in your new venture."

At 11:15 a.m. on Friday, Jefferds left behind him 28 years of confinement in a world of barred windows, locked wards and moans in the nights. He had spent five years in the Adult Correctional Institution, 22 more at the Institute of Mental Health and one more at the state General Hospital.

A board on March 3 had unanimously approved his request for parole of his life sentence for the murder of his wife, who was shot to death in July, 1952.

For the last eight years, psychiatrists, social workers and nurses have said he is not sick, mentally or physically. Still, he remained confined.

During the last four years, the Parole Board reviewed his case on 10 occasions. Once, in August, 1977, the board approved his removal from the locked wards for the criminally insane, but it required him to continue living at the mental institution.

The story of Chester G. Jefferds Jr., 68, was reported in the *Sunday Journal* on Feb. 8, four days after the Parole Board had considered his case once again and "continued the matter." The board wanted hospital officials to provide "concrete alternatives" on how the man could be released.

Hospital and corrections officials devised a plan to satisfy the board. As a condition of parole, Jefferds must spend at least three months in a halfway house, adjusting to his new life of freedom. . . .

The Journalistic Process

We have been talking with and watching a few of the 47,500 reporters and editors who gather, write and produce the news that is read in the 1,750 daily newspapers and 7,000 weeklies and is heard and watched on 10,000 of the country's radio and television stations.

Veterans and newcomers, young and old, they are engaged in a process that is the same, whether for a weekly in Massachusetts read by a few thousand people or for a television newscast watched by millions across the country.

From our observations, we can see that the journalistic process consists of four distinct parts:

Information gathering—Making observations, interviewing, conducting research

Planning—Checking and verifying information, plotting the story

Writing—Putting the story together in a form that is interesting, clear and succinct

Production—Fitting the news into the newspaper or newscast

In the following chapters, we will concentrate on the writing process, how reporters put their notes into an accurate and clear account of the events we need to know about and those we enjoy hearing about. But we will not lose sight of the other parts in the process—they all bear on the writing, as we shall see.

The job of people who report and write the news is to tell those who weren't at the event what happened. The duty of the reporter is to give an accurate, complete, impartial and timely account of what has happened or what is likely to happen.

To do this requires skill and knowledge. The few words used in each of the stories on the "CBS Evening News" must be carefully chosen to reveal the essentials of the event. The writers must, as we have seen, condense thousands of words into less than a couple of hundred.

Writing the news requires clear thinking under pressure. Lindy Washburn was able, on her first day alone on the job, to handle a national story. She knew what questions to ask her sources, those the reader or listener would want answered. (Chapter 15 discusses the particular information required for two dozen types of stories.)

Washburn was unable to cover the fire in New Jersey personally and had to rely on sources. She used the best she could locate. Neal Robbins was able to go to the event for firsthand reporting, which almost always leads to a more interesting story since the written account will contain the observations that make a story ring true. He, too, sought out the official version of the event.

Fact gathering, which we will examine in detail in chapter 4, includes direct observation, use of sources by telephone and the use of references, documents and records. The police reporter who consulted the records in the lieutenant's office at the police station was making use of official records for his story about the break-ins at the church and the synagogue.

Before we go into any more detail about reporting and writing, let's take a closer look at the journalist. Who are these people who gather and write the news? What traits do they have in common and what skills are they expected to have when they begin their careers? We will talk to several reporters and editors for the answers to these questions.

2

Focus on the Journalist

The journalist is curious and seeks to share the discoveries uncovered by his or her curiosity.

In getting and telling the news, the journalist is committed to fair play, accuracy and honesty. The journalist sticks to the facts and, despite the pressures of deadlines, writes as complete a story as possible.

The journalist is interested in people but is aware of the danger of becoming too close to the individuals in his or her stories and embracing their ideas or causes. A slight distance from people and their concerns makes for objective journalism.

As he was reading a new biography of the American playwright Eugene O'Neill, the Boston University sophomore was struck by one of the scenes in the book. O'Neill is dying and he instructs his wife to burn the unfinished manuscripts of his plays in the fireplace of their Boston hotel room.

The student, Nick Gage, knew that the hotel had become a student dormitory. He was curious. What did the room look like now? He decided to walk across the campus to find out.

"To my surprise," he recalled later, "there was no evidence of a fireplace in the room. Out of curiosity, I looked up the blueprints of the building dating from its construction. Sure enough, there was no fireplace."

Gage, who was a reporter for his college newspaper, wrote a piece about his discovery. The authors of the biography heard about Gage's article and called him. Then they called O'Neill's widow who said that on second thought she might have burned the manuscripts in the basement. The authors corrected the book in its next edition.

Intrigued by the episode, Gage said he had become "bitten by the investigative bug"—so much so that 10 years later he was interviewed for a job with *The New York Times* as an investigative reporter. The man who interviewed and hired Gage was Arthur Gelb, metropolitan editor of the *Times* and the coauthor, with his wife, of the O'Neill biography Gage had been reading years before.

Traits of the Journalist
Curiosity

You might say that Gage's curiosity made him a natural for journalism. An inquisitive nature is fundamental to the journalist. Helen Thomas, who has covered the White House for United Press International for many years, also showed her curiosity early.

"I was an inquisitive child and was constantly reprimanded for prying into the personal lives of visitors who stopped at our home," she recalls. She also enjoyed writing.

"I've never wanted to do anything but write," Thomas says. As a youngster, she worked for her school newspaper. At Wayne State University, she majored in English and continued to write.

The desire to know and the urge to tell others what he or she has found out mark the journalist. Many choose journalism as a career because they want to have a part in the excitement of events—covering the state basketball play-offs, following the campaigns of political candidates, interviewing people who are making news in medicine, agriculture, business and music.

The journalist is there when a new spacecraft is launched from Cape Canaveral and is present when the Dodgers stage a comeback to beat the Yankees in the World Series. The journalist asks the mayor why drunk driving laws are not being strictly enforced and questions the president about his policy in the Middle East.

Journalism puts the journalist on the cutting edge of life, where journalists are happiest.

Journalists have a need to know—to be the first to know and the first to tell everyone.

Commitment

Some of those who become journalists do so because they have a strong urge to set things right. They want to tell people the real story, to correct errors and misconceptions. Some want to change things. A. M. Rosenthal, managing editor of *The New York Times,* says that most reporters are reformers. These reporters root for the underdog. They have a deep sense of compassion. Unlike most people who are frustrated by their inability to do something about injustice, the journalist can. In this sense, journalism is a profession—like law or medicine—because it seeks to render public service.

Listen to Mary Ann Giordano of the *Daily News* talk about the stories she wrote for her newspaper about a decent family caught in the coils of poverty and helplessness:

"It was cold in the eighth-floor office of the *Daily News* Brooklyn bureau. It was Sunday and the landlord doesn't usually give heat on the weekends. It was a bitter cold day—all the more painful because it was late in the winter and the freezing temperatures had been unexpected.

"As we tried to warm ourselves, my editor in Brooklyn, Bill Federici, suggested we do a story about a family without heat. Problem one was how to find one—not a very great problem since in Brooklyn that day there were untold numbers of people living without heat and hot water through the cold spell. But the easiest way, I figured, to get an address was to call the city's Heat Hotline.

"The hotline, I knew, is a city service to process complaints and press landlords into providing that essential service. In the event of an extended emergency, the city can send repairmen to fix boilers and then bill the landlord. But on that cold weekend, the calls were averaging 380 an hour, a supervisor told me.

"One of those callers was Marie Walker. She, her two daughters and their four children had been living all winter without heat and hot water in their abandoned building at 587 Gates Ave. in the Bedford-Stuyvesant section of Brooklyn.

"I called the Walker family to see if they would be interested in talking to us about their heat problem. Though surprised, they agreed and with photographer Ed Molinari I headed out there. It was midday and my deadline was about 3 p.m.

"Bedford-Stuyvesant was virtually deserted in the freeze. The stairway up to the Walker home was dark and creaky. But when I reached the Walker apartment, there was a startling warmth in the back kitchen where Marie Walker sat, water bubbling steadily around her and the stove door propped open.

"The Walkers were lively, cheerful, friendly people. Despite their hardships, they were able to joke about it. The children were well behaved, the apartment spotlessly clean. It only took a brief observation to see that the Walkers were just poor people caught in a bad situation.

"Through interviews with the family members and a quick check through some of their records, I was able to piece together an account of just how such nice people wound up living in an abandoned building with no heat, no hot water, no toilets, no locks on the doors—with rats and junkies as neighbors and fear an ever-present companion."

Giordano spent about two hours with the Walker family. They all sat bundled up in their coats in the front room, where a few rays of sunlight warmed the floor at their feet. She was able to develop a feel for the people and their plight.

"I could now understand how they had fallen into this situation. And I had come to like the Walkers very much."

Giordano next had to think about a story. Here, a characteristic trait of journalists—the ability to organize facts—came into play.

"Heading back to the office, I tried to organize my thoughts," she recalled. "I knew that describing the cold in the apartment was important, and showing how the Walkers coped with it was an essential ingredient of the story.

"I also knew that people would want to know why the Walkers were living that way, and I had to explain that, too.

"I had about 45 minutes to write the story when I returned to the office. The *News* ran the story as I wrote it, word for word."

Here is how Giordano's story began:

It is warm and bright in Marie Walker's kitchen. Four flames glow on the aging stove as a pot of water boils steadily. The door of the oven is open, and she sits in front of it, her sock-covered feet propped on the door as the gas heat warms her toes.

It is the only hot spot in the apartment, the only place in the entire building where warm breath does not send puffs of vapor into the air.

A thermometer in a front room, where the sun shines through a window, registers 52 degrees. That is warm, the Walker family says. Saturday it reached a high of 39 degrees inside.

It is so cold, the pipes burst in the four-story apartment building at 58 Gates Ave. in Bedford-Stuyvesant and the six members of the Walker family must take turns drawing water from a hydrant on the street.

Giordano's complete story appears in Appendix C.

City officials responded to the Walkers' plight and promised to find public housing for them. Knowing how slowly the city wheels can turn, Giordano kept checking, and three weeks later wrote a second story that began:

The plumbing is still broken, the heat is still out, the junkies and rats still roam freely through the lower floors, and the Walker family of Bedford-Stuyvesant is still looking for decent housing.

Three weeks after an article ap-

peared in the *Daily News* detailing the plight of the seven members of the Walker family, they are still trekking through the maze of housing regulations—cruel realities that confront New Yorkers searching for livable housing.

The rest of the story is in Appendix C.

The second article brought action. "Within a short time, the Walkers were in better housing," Giordano said. "They faced last winter without fear of the cold and live today as safely as anyone does in New York."

To the journalist, this sense of accomplishment, the opportunity to be of service, is the greatest of all journalism's rewards.

Journalists are committed to fair play and equal treatment for all. For some, George Orwell, the British writer who sought to set things right-side-up in a topsy-turvy world, is the perfect journalist. Orwell's journalism was on the side of decency, and this intense belief made his writing vivid and forceful. He knew he had to be read to reach people, and his writing was clear and simple, though he often wrote about complex issues.

Orwell, who wrote *Animal Farm* and *1984*—political novels that described the fraud and horror of totalitarian governments—stressed independent thinking. He believed the journalist must never accept unquestioningly a line formulated by a party or an authority. The journalist must work things out for himself or herself.

Journalists are faithful to the facts, whatever the consequences. When he was **Integrity** covering the Nixon administration for CBS television, Dan Rather was under enormous pressure to let up on his dogged coverage of the president.

He said later that the White House had a "journalistic goon squad" that pressured reporters who did not accept at face value the pronouncements from the president's office.

"The idea is to crowd you, to harass you when they can with phone calls complaining about pieces, complaining to other people during the broadcast," he said.

Although some CBS affiliates demanded Rather's resignation after he had a run-in with Nixon and viewer mail was heavily against him, CBS kept him on the job and Rather continued to demand of the president the answers to questions he felt the public would want answered.

"If a truck runs over me tomorrow," he said once, "what I really would love to have someone tell my kids is that their father wouldn't buckle—not under Lyndon Johnson, not under Richard Nixon."

Honesty for the journalist also extends to the use of the language. News stories **Accuracy** should be accurate, no more exciting—through manipulation of words—than the event itself.

We live in a world of exaggeration and lies. A movie reviewer writes that a new motion picture is "spectacular." We pay $4.50 and find it no better than last month's so-so movie. A president says he knows nothing about a break-in, and a vice president swears he never received payoffs in office. Lies. The television comedies we watch have laughter fed into the sound track by machine. The producers do not trust us to find the humor. They manufacture laughter when there is nothing funny. Advertisers laud their products, and we find the two-man rubber raft seats only two five-year-olds comfortably, and the four-man raft is really made for two. The braking mechanism on the expensive new car is faulty and the model has to be recalled.

The journalist is responsible for the truth, which means scratching beneath the surface to find the real story and then choosing appropriate words to describe it.

The journalist matches language to the event. If the meeting of the city council was routine, the news writer does not try to dramatize it with hyperactive prose.

In interviews with editors and reporters and in observations of them at work, **Dependability** dependability continually surfaced as an essential characteristic of the journalist. Dependability encompasses a number of desirable traits:

Sent out on a story, the journalist works at it until it is fit for broadcast or print. Like other professionals engaged in serving the public, the journalist can be depended on to do his or her best.

The journalist shows initiative in digging up story ideas and is relentless and enterprising in pursuing a story. A few months after his graduation from Notre Dame, Phil Cackley was hired by *The Albuquerque Tribune* and given the University of New Mexico beat.

President Shot.
Photographer Ron Edmonds of the Associated Press took these photographs at the moment President Reagan was shot. Reagan waves, looks around and is shoved into the presidential limousine by secret service agents.

"When I got the beat, I didn't expect any major stories to result from it," Cackley said. "My first story was about a student who hatched a duck from an orphan egg."

But Cackley was a digger. Within a few months, he had unearthed one of the biggest sports stories in the country, an academic scandal involving the university's athletic program. Cackley's investigation revealed that grades were faked on the transcripts of certain athletes.

The journalist does not guess or assume. Whether it is the spelling of a word, the address of someone in a story, or the charge that will be filed against a person arrested in connection with a slaying, the journalist checks. The public depends on the journalist to be thorough and accurate. The strength of a story comes from the journalist's observations and verifications.

Readiness

President Reagan had just finished speaking in the Washington Hilton Hotel and was waving to a friendly crowd before entering his limousine.

Suddenly, six shots rang out in rapid order. Bodies were sent sprawling. The president was shoved into his car, and the car sped off. Three people were down. A crowd engulfed the husky young man who had fired the shots.

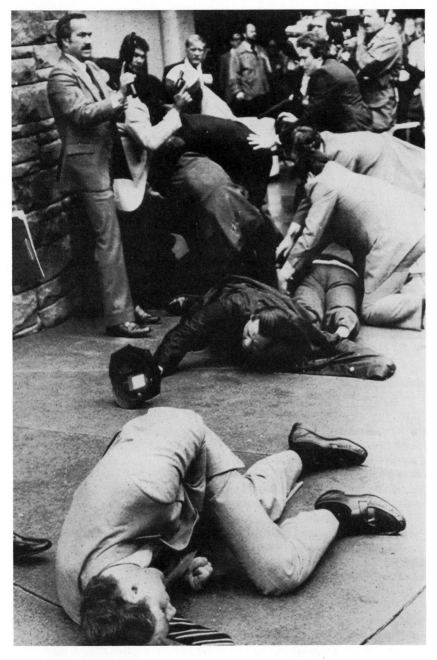

Down by Gunman. Also caught in the fusillade that struck Reagan, three men lie in the street outside a Washington hotel. Edmonds reacted quickly under pressure to snap these photographs. Edmonds' photos won the 1982 Pulitzer Prize for spot news photography.

Though the situation had exploded quickly, moving from the routine to the sensational in seconds, photographers and reporters recorded the scene. Ron Edmonds, an AP photographer, took a picture of Reagan at the precise moment the first shot was fired. Holding his finger on the motor-driven shutter release, Edmonds shot a sequence of pictures in the brief moments immediately following the attack on the president.

Press association reporters raced to telephones and dictated stories that were used around the world. Radio and television stations interrupted their programming with the news, some of it incorrect at first. To those at the scene, the president had seemed unhurt, and this is what the first bulletins reported. They were corrected as more information became available. By being able to respond quickly to the unexpected and to write under pressure, the journalist is able to report news that is informative, timely and accurate.

Deadlines The competent journalist understands the necessity of meeting deadlines. For the press association reporter, there is a deadline every minute. As Lindy Washburn was writing her fire story, she was aware that some newspapers were readying their front pages for the press. At any hour of the day or night, there is a deadline being met by some newspaper or broadcast station.

The ability to write clear, complete and accurate stories despite the pressure of deadlines is the result of self-discipline.

Although many editors push their staff members, the journalist must provide his or her own drive. No one on any newspaper or broadcast station stands over a reporter and coaxes, begs or commands. The writer is personally responsible for writing the story. In this sense, the journalist shares with other creative workers the drive to produce and the pride in the finished product.

Discipline

The ability to work steadily at a task until it meets the highest level of a person's capabilities is a trait common to all who work creatively—writers, musicians, painters, designers, builders, dancers, actors, teachers. Ernest Hemingway labored over his sentences and paragraphs until he was satisfied. He would rewrite a paragraph time after time until it did his bidding.

For all their seeming spontaneity, musicians practice until they have their pieces sounding just right. A world-renowned pianist says he has never missed a day's practice of at least six hours in the 40 years he has been playing. Most singing groups are willing to work day and night to perfect their songs to the last detail.

John McPhee, a *New Yorker* writer who describes himself as a "working journalist," walks into his office at 8:30 in the morning and leaves at 8:30 in the evening. He takes a 90-minute break each day for squash, tennis or racquetball.

McPhee, considered one of the finest journalists in the country, disciplines himself to write.

"People want to be writers without writing," he says. Impossible. After he graduated from college he tried to write television plays. He was learning and so the task was arduous. The temptation to leave the typewriter was so great that he even resorted to tying himself to a chair with his bathrobe sash.

Dan Rather enjoys hunting and fishing, but he has little time for recreation. "I work about 110 hours a week," he says. "It will eat you up, but if it doesn't you have a difficult time being good at it. I think you have to care that much."

Advice from the Consummate Comic

W. C. Fields, one of the greatest film comedians ever, seemed to be a natural comic. Actually, he labored at his craft.

"Show me a comic who isn't a perfectionist and I'll show you a starving man," he said. "You have to sweat and toil and practice indefinitely. A comic should suffer as much over a single line as a man with a hernia would in picking up a heavy barbell."

In his autobiography, Anthony Trollope, the English novelist, describes how he trained himself to write every day, although he held a full-time job for many years. Once, on his way to Egypt to help to set up postal service between the Middle East and England, he became violently seasick. Between bouts of nausea, he managed to write over a thousand words a day.

Openness

The journalist is always willing to learn and ready to experiment. Frances D'Emilio works for the Associated Press in San Francisco. Upon graduation from journalism school, she sought out wire service work to gain experience in being fast, accurate and succinct. She has learned that on the job, and she has welcomed the opportunity to learn from a variety of assignments.

She has covered a kidnapping trial and sumo wrestling. She has written weather and football stories. Every day, she says, she learns something new, either in the craft or in the subject matter of what she covers.

Creative people are always anxious to enlarge their knowledge and skills. Writers read other writers for interviewing techniques, for stylistic innovations, for new ways of expressing ideas. When Tom Wolfe, Gay Talese and other journalists developed the New Journalism, their ideas were picked up by news writers all over the country.

Models for Journalists

Scratch the surface of every journalist and you will find a model or mentor for that journalist. It could be Hemingway or Tom Wolfe, McPhee or a teacher or a musician—people who work hard at their trade, craft or profession and are admired and respected for their work.

Dizzy Gillespie, the jazz trumpet player, is a model for journalists in his openness to new ideas. He is never satisfied with what he has accomplished. He has adapted Afro-Cuban rhythms and the patterns of Rumanian gypsy music to his playing. Gillespie, Charlie Parker and Thelonious Monk turned jazz upside down in the 1940s by experimenting with new forms, just as the New Journalists were to do 20 years later.

Man with a Horn. Dizzy Gillespie, one of the greatest jazz trumpet players, is a model for journalists in his openness to new forms and his dedication to his work.

The journalist tries to say as much as possible in as few words as possible. He or she tries to make every word count. Gillespie, a master at improvisation, has worked steadily at eliminating the unnecessary. What seems to be impulsive, spontaneous brilliance is the result of thought and hard work.

"It's taken me all my life to learn what not to play," says Gillespie.

This sounds like the conclusion of a city editor in New York, Joseph G. Herzberg, who says that journalistic writing consists of knowing what to leave out and condensing the rest. Thomas Jefferson wrote "The most valuable of all talents is that of never using two words when one will do."

All Kinds. The journalist goes into the classroom for news, chats with those who work in the offices and the fields. The journalist hears the cries of the poor and befriends black and white, young and old. In this way, the journalist is able to give readers and viewers a true cross section of the community.

In their openness to new ideas, journalists become involved with people of all kinds. This is not accidental. Journalists seek out a wide range of individuals because they are committed to involvement in the affairs of all people.

Involvement

The news is where people are. News is found in factories and service stations, supermarkets and laundromats, unemployment offices and executive suites, schoolrooms and homes. By seeking out people with varied backgrounds, journalists can hear the heartbeat of their communities.

The Anniston Star regularly sends its reporters out to search for stories and pictures of the people who live in rural Alabama as well as in the city.

Young and old, black and white, these people not only inform the readers of the mood and the feelings of the area; they also educate reporters. Typically, reporters are young and middle class. Their friends are like them. A journalism of the young middle class would be a narrow journalism, a thin slice of the social and economic life of the community.

When Christopher Scanlan and Mark Patinkin of the *Journal-Bulletin* in Providence wanted to know about the black communities in Rhode Island, they set out on a series of interviews that took them into the offices of black lawyers and the homes of welfare mothers. They spoke to business people and hookers. They went to housing projects—monuments of despair to some of the tenants, models of hope to others. Here is one of their interviews:

Voices: Johnny Mitchell on the Projects

"Providence hardly knows these people exist," said Johnny Mitchell. "This project is in crisis, but nobody cares. Nobody hears what we're saying. People in here are in a crisis. A serious social crisis. They just get by. They go to sleep tonight and wake up tomorrow and don't think about the future."

Mitchell is speaking of the 734 people, mostly black, who share his home, the Roger Williams Housing Project in South Providence, perhaps the worst low-income development in the state.

He looked at the black children playing in a patch of dust and rubble and saw the teenagers darting on the glass-specked basketball court and the mothers sitting on the doorstep. For blacks here, he said, nothing has changed.

Blacks make up about 10 percent of Providence's population, but they fill well over 70 percent of the apartments in the city's six low-income family housing projects.

In Roger Williams, which is 98 percent black, all but 10 of the project's 213 families are young women who live alone with children, most on welfare.

"There's excellent hope for those kids, they're all beautiful kids," said Mitchell, "but a lot of them are going mad. No fathers, no real men. Is anybody going to get down and help? Right now, they think they're pimps. The language is unbelievable, too—little kids cussin like men."

The people of the projects, especially of Roger Williams, are not a mirror of the state's black community. They are the extreme, the underclass. In Rhode Island, they form a big underclass.

There are about 931,000 people in Rhode Island. About 27,600, one out of every 34, is black. There are more than 50,000 Rhode Islanders on welfare. More than 8,000, about one out of every six, is black. In other words, close to a third of all blacks in the state are on welfare.

Black poverty is not limited to the inner city. In South Kingston, one out of every five welfare recipients is black. In Newport, one out of every four is black.

Welfare speaks of poverty but it does not tell the whole story. Income figures tell more. The latest U.S. Census figures show that one of every three black families in Rhode Island lives below the poverty level. They account for 11.8 percent of the state's 17,000 poor families, four times the black percentage of state population.

Poverty means other things, such as health problems. In 1976, the infant death rate for whites in Rhode Island was 13.1 deaths per 1,000 births. For non-whites, the rate was 23 deaths for every 1,000 babies born.

Poverty. It also means a higher percentage of blacks are criminals and more are victims of crime.

Scanlan and Patinkin also sought out those who had made garden spots out of the inner city ghetto areas.

Voices: Arthur Strother on success

"They say people who come from projects are ruthless, can't live right," said Arthur Strother, "but look at this. If people are given a chance, they can do it, they can turn it around."

Arthur and his wife Geraldine stand on the groomed lawn outside their new home at 270 Willard Ave. It is a slice of the suburbs in the midst of the slums.

Their piece of South Providence is called Comstock Gardens, an inner-city experiment born of federal dollars. It is a neighborhood of bright new homes owned by families who spent years in projects and tenements.

"I want people to say there are black people who want nice things and they don't have to escape to Cranston or Warwick," said Mrs. Strother. "They can have it right here."

Strother sees change and hope in the neat lawns and mint-condition homes. He and 40 others, many from low-income projects, own houses here. The model neighborhood sits off Prairie Avenue, in the core of the inner city.

"These houses are part of us now, part of South Providence," said Strother, who is 32. "The neighborhood's like a baby again. It's being reborn."

The Strothers are a sign of black success. There are others. . . .

Scanlan said that the assignment was a vast educational project for him. He learned something new every day, he said.

Despite their involvement in the affairs of other people, journalists must be able to distance themselves from the people and the events they are observing. This distance allows for better understanding and objectivity.

Garry Trudeau, the creator of the comic strip "Doonesbury," says that he is able to develop ideas for his work by being an outsider rather than by fraternizing with important people. Like the journalist, Trudeau says he wants his strip to represent the outsider looking at the activities of people.

The journalist must be close enough—physically and emotionally—to his or her subject to understand what is being observed. At the same time, the journalist must maintain a certain distance to keep things in perspective.

Consider two sportswriters in the dressing room of the losing basketball team.

One is interviewing the center who has had a bad game. "Too bad," the writer says, but he presses home his questions. Why did he seem to tire in the last 10 minutes? Are the stories about missing practice true? Why had he failed to execute a key play in the last minute?

Another reporter then interviews the center. He is sympathetic. "Too bad about the game," he says. The center gives him an excuse. The writer nods in sympathy. He lets the player talk but does not press any questions. As he gets up, he pats the player on the shoulder.

Objectivity

Which reporter better serves his readers?

Complete detachment is sometimes impossible. When six-year-old Adam Walsh disappeared from the Sears department store in Hollywood, Fla., reporter Charlie Brennan of the *Sun-Tattler* decided to stay with the story, and his newspaper agreed. A child had disappeared five years before. Her body was discovered in a canal five days later.

Brennan's first story alerted the community:

Reve Walsh usually leaves her son in the toy department at Sears while doing her shopping at the Hollywood Mall. He's always there waiting for her.

But Monday was different. Adam Walsh, six, wasn't there waiting. The Hollywood child hasn't been seen since 12:30 p.m. Monday.

"Everybody's working this one," says police spokesman Fred Barbetta. "Everybody wants this kid to show up."

Adam is the only child of John and Reve Walsh of 1801 McKinely St.

"He's very sheltered," Walsh says. "We never let him out of our sight. He even went on business trips with me."

Hollywood police, the Broward Sheriff's helicopter search team and 47 members of Citizens Crime Watch teamed up Monday night to search for the child throughout Hollywood. Their efforts so far have proven fruitless. . . .

The complete story is in Appendix C.

Every day for two weeks Brennan's stories appeared on page one. In his stories, the 26-year-old reporter described the concern of the entire community and its attempts to find the child. Brennan kept in close touch with the parents, and each day he felt their grief and desperation increase.

Brennan accompanied the parents to New York for their appearance on a television show that discussed the disappearance of children throughout the country.

Three hours after the program, the telephone rang in the couple's hotel room. John Walsh took the call. It was from Hollywood. The search was over.

The remains of a child had been found floating in a canal, and the head was that of Adam Walsh.

Brennan was with Walsh when the news came.

"Oh Christ, Oh Christ, who could do this to my little boy?" the father cried. "Who could cut his head off?"

Brennan mourned with Walsh.

"It was absolutely the worst thing I've ever been associated with," Brennan said. "The parents will never be the same. I don't know if I'll ever be the same."

Of his involvement with the family and its tragedy, Brennan said, "Getting deeply involved was the only way to cover the story. To remain detached would have been inhuman."

The sportswriter who pressed his questions and the reporters for the Providence newspaper who interviewed blacks in Rhode Island did not turn from reality, whether it was the failure of an athlete to give an all-out effort or the poverty, crime and hopelessness of housing project life.

Journalists are loyal to the facts. This dedication sometimes makes them seem heartless. The truth is that the most are just the opposite. They believe that the relentless exposure of truths—no matter how unpleasant—will lead people to change the situation for the better. Journalists, at bottom, are compassionate people. This feeling is what drove Mary Ann Giordano to speak up for the people in the tenement who were without heat or water in the winter. It led Berkley Hudson to help Chester Jefferds in his quest for freedom from a state mental hospital.

The brotherhood of all people is felt by creative workers, journalist and painter, musician and novelist.

Commitment to Democratic Values During a tour in Turkey, Gillespie was to perform at a lawn party. He saw a group of street kids outside peering at the party.

"Dizzy refused to play until they were let in," a friend says. Gillespie told his hosts, "I came here to play for all people."

The journalist, too, performs for all people. The journalist is motivated by the democratic ideal that given the truth people can govern themselves intelligently and will be able to live in harmony. The journalist seeks the truth whatever the obstacles, and he or she presents it in language accessible to all.

When people are denied the opportunities inherent in a democratic system, the journalist is quick to point this out. Some of the greatest stories in the history of American journalism have concerned abuses of people's constitutional rights, such as withholding the vote to blacks, the inequitable administration of justice—one system for the rich, another for the poor—and the persistent denial of equal opportunities to people because of their race, sex, religion or national origin.

The list of traits and qualities characteristic of the journalist may appear overwhelming. Surely, no human being can embody all of these traits. True enough, and the first person to realize this is the journalist.

No reporter ever believes he or she has gathered enough information for the story, dug deeply enough, talked to the right people, ferreted out the real story. Few news writers are content with what they have written.

The Struggle for Perfection Wayne Worcester of the *Journal-Bulletin* in Providence says, "The compulsion is always there to improve, improve, to do better.

"After a while it gets to you. But that's all right. You just keep things in perspective. Waylon Jennings sings a song called, 'I've Always Been Crazy, but It's Kept Me from Going Insane.' "

Reporters must be able to laugh at themselves. They know they have a serious job to do, but they don't let the hassles and the struggles get to them. One of the reasons they are able to cope with deadlines, irascible editors, angry readers and listeners and their own admitted inadequacies is that they like what they do. For them journalism is fun.

The Pleasures of Journalism

At one time, Lynn O'Shaughnessy thought about becoming a lawyer. But after a few months of covering federal court for the *Memphis Press-Scimitar,* she was no longer interested in studying the law as a student.

"Legal writing is too stilted for my taste," she says. "Reporting on the courts is interesting. Lawyers sometimes spend a year or two preparing a case, and I get to cover it right when the excitement happens. Also, I don't cover the everyday cases, just the big ones."

Lew Moores of the *Cincinnati Post* also likes the excitement of journalism. "There's more going on in cities, more things to look into, more successes and failures. I am intensely curious about everything and everyone," he says.

His curiosity led him to seek out some of the victims of city crime, the elderly who are preyed on by muggers.

Here is how Moores' story began:

George Prather sat in a booth at the Mecca Lounge, a bottle of Hudepohl and a glass before him alongside a portable radio tuned to the Reds game. He was joined by George McKindrick and Pete Kindle.

All three men live in apartments above the Bay Horse Saloon, located next door to the Mecca, at 625 Main St., downtown. Last Friday evening, after a Reds game broadcast, Prather walked Kindle, who is 72 years old, home. Home is 25 feet away, a side entrance on Gano Alley.

Prather had his keys out. Six youths sprang from the shadows. Prather saw them first. "Here they come," he said to Kindle, then removed his eyeglasses so they wouldn't splinter in his eyes.

Wednesday, Prather sat in the Mecca with his two friends, and pointed over his shoulder, "The bartender next door's been mugged," he said, then pointed to the end of the bar. "Herb there's been mugged, too."

There are purple commas around the sockets of Prather's eyes, and his upper lip is split and healing. Kindle, who was mugged twice last week, has a large purple welt on the right side of his face—it's becoming the aged's badge of downtown residency.

The Mecca Lounge and Bay Horse Saloon are watering spots for the old downtowners, the men and women who survive on social security checks and live above storefronts. Usually without transportation, they remain close to home, close to friends, close to the bars that appreciate their patronage. Sometimes they drink and become easy prey, sometimes they don't and become prey anyway.

And unless the police find the victims unconscious or wandering around with their wounds, the transgressions often go unreported. . . .

This story begins slowly, just a few friends sitting in a bar listening to a ball game. Swiftly it builds to a climax, then we are back in the bar, chatting with the men. Moores lets the story unfold. He does not overwrite with adjectives and adverbs. He **shows** the reader the situation, painting word pictures.

Many journalists like the action on their beats and the satisfation they have when they can put it into words. Paul Maryniak was an avid reader of mysteries, and when the criminal courts beat opened up on the *Pittsburgh Press,* he told the executive editor he wanted the job. "I'll gladly depart with one of my limbs to get the job," he recalls saying. Nothing that drastic was necessary.

One of the stories he handled—a number of killings linked to the city's massage parlor racket—took nearly six months of research. Because it disclosed a lot about the city's underworld, some law enforcement agents warned him to be careful when it was published.

"A fictional version of this story would be rejected by most publishing houses as being too implausible," Maryniak says.

Satisfaction . . .

Most journalists are happy with their work. Although they gripe about low pay, not many list this as a major problem of the job. In a study of reporters on Iowa daily newspapers, these sentiments emerged as the joys of the job:

We're beholden to nobody. This place has integrity.

I'm involved in what's going on in the community.

The camaraderie of the news staff.

Independence for creative writing.

Being where the action is.

Good discipline, effective on-the-job training.

Opportunity to express opinions on the editorial page.

The freedom of adventure a small newspaper affords.

The responsibility given to me and to each reporter by management.

. . . and Frustration

Charles M. Young is a worrier. He sweats and strains over his stories, never really happy about them. But his stories for *Rolling Stone* about rock groups like Kiss and the Eagles and entertainers like Carly Simon seem to flow like maple syrup over a short stack.

Despite his pain, Young likes to write. It is his affliction and his joy. His smooth writing and his love of words are evident in his stories, especially in his piece "Carly Simon, Life, Liberty and the Pursuit of Roast Beef Hash" that begins:

Most rock writers, it has been observed, would rather be the people they write about; that is, trade in their typewriters to scream nonsense at 20,000 rioting lude freaks while Keith Richard powerchords their brains into Cool Whip. Not me. I don't want to be Mick Jagger. Nor do I want to be Carly Simon and have millions of college students think dirty thoughts about my album covers. I don't even want to be James Taylor, who is married to Carly Simon.

I would trade it all to be Benjamin Taylor. Here is someone with a good deal in life; all Benjamin Taylor has to do is cry and Carly Simon sticks her breast in his mouth. The other 4 billion of us on earth could cry for the rest of our lives and Carly Simon would not stick her breast in our mouths.

Greater injustices have marred human history, I suppose, but I can't think of them right now, because Carly Simon has just placed her breast in Benjamin Taylor's mouth. He is having a good time. I am breaking into a cold sweat, wondering if it is obvious from ten feet away that my eyes are dropping from Carly Simon's face to her uplifted blouse every three seconds.

"This is beginning to look obscene," says Carly Simon in the living room of her huge ten-room Central Park West apartment. Benjamin, a cuter-than-hell miniature of James Taylor, is gymnastically curled around his dinner, which he is clutching with both hands and both feet, as well as his mouth.

The Extraordinary and the Routine

Some people are attracted to journalism because of the glamour of covering the big stories. Richard Dudman, who worked his way up to Washington bureau chief for the *St. Louis Post-Dispatch* from the Oroville (Calif.) *Mercury Register,* has had his share of big stories. He has covered revolutions and wars. In Vietnam, he was shot at by a terrorist at close range. The shots missed Dudman but killed a companion.

For 40 days, Dudman was a prisoner of communist guerillas in Cambodia. He had no idea for most of the 40 days whether he would survive the day.

But he warns anyone thinking of a career in journalism to pass it by if the only attraction is excitement. The daily pursuit of news, which often involves painstaking reporting of the mundane, must interest the young man or woman planning a career, he says. The once-in-a-lifetime stories occur just that often—once in a lifetime.

"You know you have a routine to follow every day," says Pete Lee, for many years editor of the *El Paso Herald-Post*. "But you also know that something totally unexpected will happen. You may talk to a bum one day and the president the next."

The excitement at new discovery and the willingness to adapt to routine are prerequisites for the journalist's job.

Earl Ubell, head of NBC's local television news division, says he looks for people "who are eager to work." In short, the name of the game in journalism is work.

But for all the work involved, there is opportunity and reward. The reward is excellence at the job. McPhee's long hours at the typewriter have led to a superb writing style and recognition as one of the country's foremost nonfiction writers.

The Tough Stories

For every upbeat, enjoyable story written, the journalist encounters another that is offensive, embarrassing, gloomy, or heartbreaking.

Sarah Booth Conroy of *The Washington Post* remembers a particularly sad story she covered as a reporter in Tennessee for *The Knoxville News-Sentinel*. She was sent out to interview a young mother who had been stricken with polio just before Christmas. The woman had been placed in an iron lung to aid her breathing. Conroy's city editor wanted a story and pictures of her three small children wishing their mother a Merry Christmas.

"I was getting along fine," Conroy recalls, "until the children, all below table height, one by one mounted steps to kiss her face, all that was left outside the iron lung."

The city editor is king of his domain, the city staff, and Conroy recalls being told by her editor in the early 1950s, when she was starting out as a reporter, to interview the young wife of Vice President Alben Barkley, who was in his 70s. The Barkleys were visiting Knoxville a few months after their wedding.

"Find out if she's pregnant," the city editor instructed Conroy.

"I went with fear and trembling," Conroy says. "But I was more afraid of Mr. Levitt (the city editor) than Mrs. Barkley.

"She looked appalled by my question," Conroy says. Mrs. Barkley asked her, "Why do you ask?"

"Because my city editor told me to," she replied.

"Go back and tell him," Mrs. Barkley said softly, "I think he must be a horrid man to send a nice little girl like you to ask a question like that."

Death in the Afternoon

In Liberia to do stories about the work of missionaries from the Southwestern Baptist Theological Seminary, the reporter-photographer team for the *Fort Worth Star-Telegram* was suddenly thrust into history's cauldron.

Liberia had erupted with savage violence. A young soldier, Master Sergeant Samuel K. Doe, had led his troops in a military coup. Under Doe's command, soldiers had assassinated the president and then set about eliminating the country's leaders.

The executions were to be carried out on a hot afternoon on a Liberian beach, and the press was invited.

Larry C. Price, the photographer, and Paul Rowan, the reporter, made their way to the beach where thick, sturdy posts 10 feet high were being placed in the white sand. As the posts were being adjusted, Price broke away from

Witness to History. Photographer Larry C. Price of *The Fort Worth Star-Telegram* stood so close to the soldiers in the firing squad on a Liberian beach that an ejected shell casing struck his cheek. "The central thing in photojournalism is that you have to get it when it happens," he said. "There are no second chances. If you miss the shot, it's gone forever." Price won the 1981 Pulitzer Prize for these photographs.

the knot of newsmen gathered 100 yards from the beach. Alone, he walked toward the posts anchored in the sand. As he walked, he snapped pictures. The heavily armed soldiers watched him but did nothing.

Rowan edged closer and took notes. The number of posts grew, Rowan noted on his pad, from four to five, from five to seven, seven to nine. In the middle of the work stood the 27-year-old photographer, snapping pictures.

The men were then brought out.

"They tied nine men, old-looking men, paunchy, gray-haired men, to the posts," Rowan wrote.

Then the shots rang out, and the bodies began to crumple into the sand. Price was so close an ejected shell casing struck his cheek.

He continued to take pictures.

© 1980 Larry C. Price/*Fort Worth Star-Telegram.*

© 1980 Larry C. Price/*Fort Worth Star-Telegram.*

Price's photographs of the deaths of the old rulers won the 1981 Pulitzer Prize for spot news photography. The pictures are horrifying, a grim record of men calculating the death of fellow men, and the moment of death.

Price and Rowan were appalled by what they saw. But their job was to record for their readers, and for history, the momentous event.

"I'm certainly not coldhearted," Price said later. "Taking pictures of tragedy does affect me."

Journalists are witnesses to life's tragedies—sudden death in the afternoon, a youngster mangled beneath the wreckage of his motorcycle, a young mother immobilized by crippling disease and confined to an iron lung.

But the journalist functions. Journalism has been called history in a hurry. Though they laugh off such descriptions, journalists know theirs is an important and serious business that demands self-control and self-discipline.

Women, Minorities and Money

There are 47,500 reporters, copy editors, photographers, artists and news executives on daily newspapers. Of these, about one-third are women and 2,300 are members of minority groups.

Women are heavily represented on the smaller newspapers. The number of women on the larger newspapers is significantly smaller. Fewer than 10 of every hundred editors and news executives are women. The same is true of radio and television stations. The situation is gradually improving, partly as the result of lawsuits brought by women journalists who charged they were discriminated against in promotions and salaries. *The New York Times* and *Washington Post,* for example, agreed in out-of-court settlements to hire more women for managerial positions.

The number of minority journalists is small but has also been increasing. From the mid-1970's to the beginning of the 1980's, minority employment increased by 35 percent. In the 1960's, the number of minority journalists in newspaper editorial jobs was estimated at 1 in a hundred. A 1981 study of 732 dailies found they made up 5.3 percent of the total.

About two-thirds of all journalists are college graduates. Almost all of the newly hired reporters are college graduates, and four of every five new reporters are journalism school graduates or majored in journalism. Most new journalists who did not study journalism in college worked on their high school or college newspapers.

Among the older hands in the newsroom, few graduated from college. Traditionally, many journalists came from working class homes. Dan Rather was born in Wharton, Tex. His father was a pipeliner with oil pipeline construction companies, and his mother was a waitress. He went to Sam Houston State College.

Warren Phillips, who worked his way up the ladder from reporter at *The Wall Street Journal* to chairman of the vast Dow Jones operation, attended Queens College, a New York City public college, which charged no tuition to its students, the sons and daughters of shopkeepers and factory workers.

Most newspapers and many radio and television stations are owned by companies that have several media properties. Of the 1,750 daily newspapers, 65 percent are owned by chains, the name given newspaper groups that own more than one newspaper.

The chains reach 46 million readers every day, which is 75 percent of the circulation of all daily newspapers. The chains with the largest readership are Knight-Ridder, whose 34 newspapers are read by 3.8 million readers, and the Gannett Company, which has 3.7 million readers of its 85 daily and 27 weekly newspapers.

The chains are aggressive buyers of newspapers, and some press critics contend that should the trend of group ownership continue, absentee ownership will mean less sensitivity to local affairs and greater concern with profits.

Newspaper and broadcast station salaries vary according to the size of the paper or station. Usually, the larger the paper, the higher the salary. Reporters on the large metropolitan daily newspapers with contracts with the American Newspaper Guild receive upwards of $500 and $600 a week. The pay is similar at broadcast stations in the major markets.

But beginners cannot expect to land jobs immediately on large papers or stations. Usually, they find niches in small and medium-sized cities. Entry-level salaries in these communities usually range between $150 and $200 a week, sometimes more if the applicant has had some worthwhile experience. A student who has been a stringer or correspondent for a newspaper while in school or who has worked summers or part-time and has the clippings to prove his or her experience will command a higher salary.

Newspapers with Guild contracts usually pay higher salaries than non-Guild newspapers. However, since few small newspapers are organized, the Guild represents fewer than half of the 47,500 news workers.

Editors and managers of large newspapers and stations are paid around $50,000 a year. Salaries for the top people in smaller communities may be half that figure.

Big bucks Salaries for the top people on camera in television are astronomical in comparison. When Walter Cronkite was about to retire in 1980 as the anchorman for The CBS Evening News, the country's most-watched television newscast, Dan Rather was one of those being considered for the job. ABC News reportedly offered Rather $8 million for a five-year contract in an effort to woo him away from CBS. He stayed and succeeded Cronkite. CBS reportedly pays Rather $2 million a year. On a local level, a sports announcer on a New York City television station is paid more than $400,000 a year.

Executives of the large newspaper organizations are also well paid, by newspaper standards, earning $250,000 to $500,000 a year.

3

The Making of the News Story

News gives us information to help us understand the world around us. Gen-erally, newspapers and broadcast stations stress news that has impact on our lives—news of government, world affairs, business activities. People are also interested in learning about unusual events and the activities of well-known people.

The news value of an event can be judged by its impact on people, its unusual nature or the prominence of the people involved. Four additional fac-tors also influence the newsworthiness of an event: conflict, proximity, time-liness and currency.

How the news writer applies these news values determines what people will read in their newspapers and see on television newscasts. In applying these values, the news writer considers the audience's interests and needs.

The county courthouse reporter had two piles of paper in front of her. One, much larger than the other, consisted of court documents that she had looked through for news and had rejected. The other pile included material she had set aside to take notes from for news stories.

She had gone through the day's records at a rapid pace, but the drawer in which the damage suits, pleadings and other documents were filed con-tained still more papers. At one sheaf of papers, she hesitated, then studied the pages closely. She tossed the document on her newsworthy pile. A com-panion, a young reporter learning the beat, asked her why she had decided to take a second look at the document.

"It seems to be important," she answered. "On this beat, you have to make decisions quickly or you'll be snowed under and never have time to write.

"I have two guides I use to separate material. Either the material is important or it's so unusual that I know the reader will want to read about it.

"This one is important because it is a request by a big developer to have the court force the county to issue a building permit for a shopping mall north of town."

She picked up two pages stapled together from her pile of possible news stories.

"Here's one that isn't important at all. But it will make a good little story. It's wild."

The papers described a suit for damages of several thousand dollars by a woman who accused a department store Santa Claus of slapping her six-year-old son.

"Whoever heard of someone suing Santa Claus?" she said. "This is the kind of story readers enjoy."

What Is News?

That evening, the novice reporter thought about what the courthouse reporter had told him. He had recently graduated from college and was being given a tryout by the newspaper. He realized that all his training in how to write would not amount to much unless he could distinguish between what was newsworthy and what wasn't.

He wrote down two definitions:

1. News is material that the public must have because it's important.
2. News is material that is entertaining, that is fun to read.

He recalled reading something that illustrated his first definition of news. He located the clipping with his notes from one of his college journalism courses. The article described the situation in the early 1970s when New York City was on the edge of bankruptcy. The city had outspent its revenues and was running out of money to pay salaries and to buy goods to keep the city going.

An emergency group, the Municipal Assistance Corp., was set up to steer the city through the troubled waters. The group managed to do the job, and several years later the head of the MAC said that the city's newspapers deserved much of the credit for helping to prevent financial chaos.

"I'm absolutely convinced New York City would have gone bankrupt if *The New York Times* and the *Daily News* hadn't been there every day explaining the economic issues to people," the clipping quoted Felix G. Rohatyn, the head of MAC, as saying.

"The press informed the public so that it could support the measures essential to the rescue operation."

The clipping seemed to verify a definition of news that the reporter had been given in one of his classes:

News is information that helps people solve their problems intelligently.

But what about the second category of news, entertainment? Well, as his grandfather used to say, man does not live by bread alone—he has to have an occasional delicacy.

Impact. On Nov. 4, 1979, the U.S. embassy in Tehran was stormed and members of the staff were taken hostage. The story was covered extensively by the press, and ABC News initiated a news program, "The Iran Crisis," that millions watched each evening.

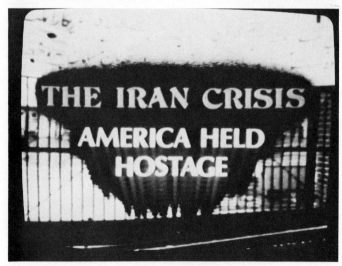

The courthouse reporter's guidelines are helpful in figuring out what makes news. Another way to determine what makes news is to examine newspapers and the transcripts of newscasts. If we were to do this, we would find that news falls into three general categories.

Most news stories are about events that (1) have an **impact** on many people, (2) describe **unusual** or exceptional situations or events, or (3) are about well-known or **prominent** people. The length of a news story is usually determined by the number of people affected by the event and/or the number of people interested in the event.

Three Basic Determinants of News

Unusual. Events that make us stop and stare or shake our heads in wonder are newsworthy.

Impact

By impact, we mean importance or significance. One way to judge impact is to figure out what the results or consequences of the event being reported might be. If many people will be affected, then the reporter knows that the event is important enough for a news story.

Unusual

One of the oldest definitions of news says that when a dog bites a man, it isn't news, but when a man bites a dog, it is news. The interruption in the expected, the different make news. If something makes a reporter stop and stare, wonder, exclaim, then the reporter knows that what he or she is looking at is newsworthy.

The Unusual—The Barefoot Water Skier

The accidental death of one person of no prominence is hardly worth the attention of the AP's main news wire. But because of its unusual, almost freakish nature, this story was given 200 words on the AP wire:

```
     LONG BEACH, CALIF. AP--A 23-YEAR-OLD MAN,
WATER SKIING BAREFOOT AT 109 MPH IN AN ATTEMPT
FOR A WORLD RECORD, LOST HIS BALANCE AND TURNED
SIX TO EIGHT CARTWHEELS BEFORE SINKING INTO THE
WATER WITH FATAL INJURIES, AUTHORITIES SAID.
     ROY MCSHEA, 23, OF HUNTINGTON BEACH DIED OF
EXTENSIVE INJURIES AT 4:55 P.M. SUNDAY AT THE
LONG BEACH COMMUNITY HOSPITAL.
     HE WAS GOING AT A SPEED WHICH MADE IMPACT
WITH THE WATER SIMILAR TO "HITTING CEMENT,"
SAID LIFEGUARD JOHN PATTY.
     LONG BEACH FIRE DEPARMTENT DISPATCHER JOHN
LANDSTROM SAID MCSHEA WAS NOT BREATHING WHEN HE
WAS RESCUED.
     "THERE WERE NO LACERATIONS ON THE OUTSIDE
OF THE BODY, BUT IT BREAKS BLOOD VESSELS AND
ARTERIES," LANDSTROM SAID.
     MCSHEA WAS GOING THROUGH THE QUARTER-MILE
COURSE AT LONG BEACH MARINE STADIUM'S SPEED
SKIING CHAMPIONSHIPS WHEN THE ACCIDENT OCCURRED
AT ABOUT 4 P.M. MCSHEA WAS TIMED AT 109 MPH,
PATTY SAID.
     IN BAREFOOT WATER SKIING, A COMPETITOR
TAKES OFF HIS SKI AS THE BOAT ACCELERATES AND
THEN SKIMS ALONG THE WATER IN HIS BAREFEET,
WHILE THE BOAT STEERS HIM THROUGH A COURSE
WHERE HE IS TIMED, PATTY SAID.
     THE LIFEGUARD SAID THE BEACH WAS JAMMED
WITH SPECTATORS OF THE COMPETITION, WHICH WAS
SPONSORED BY THE INTERNATIONAL SPEED SKIING AND
BAREFOOT ASSOCIATION.

     1050EDT
```

Prominence

People who are well known or who have positions of authority are said to be prominent. These are the newsmakers of our community and country. They may be politicians or car dealers, priests or labor leaders, entertainers or cabinet members. If you recognize the name and think your readers will, chances are that the person is prominent. What prominent people do, even if unimportant, is often newsworthy. Names make news.

Prominence is an important determinant that can be added to the courthouse reporter's list. She talked about the impact an event might have and its exceptional or unusual nature. But if she had been asked, there's no doubt she would have added prominence because in one of her stories the previous week she had written about the failure of the owner of the city's largest industry to pay his personal property taxes. The courthouse records list hundreds of people who are in arrears in their tax payments, but few become the subject of news stories. The reporter had singled this one out for only one reason—the prominence of the businessman.

For several years, many newspapers and news magazines carried stories about the spats of the rock singer Mick Jagger and his wife, Bianca. When they were finally divorced, it was news in a number of publications. The personal life of the Jaggers is hardly significant in the scheme of things, and arguments and divorces are hardly unusual actions these days.

But people like to read about those in the spotlight, whatever they might do. If the president has a cold, the governor spends a week in Wyoming fishing, a television talk show host has an argument in a night club—all this becomes news. We are inquisitive people, and we enjoy reading about the personal lives of the famous.

The Diet Doctor   One of the best-selling books in the last 10 years promised to keep readers trim and healthy if they followed the author's advice. Since obesity is said to be the nation's number one disease, diet books have been popular for some time. But nothing paralleled the popularity of *The Complete Scarsdale Medical Diet,* which sold millions of copies. The author was a doctor, Herman Tarnower, a vigorous bachelor in his late 60s.

Tarnower lived in Purchase, N.Y., and had been involved for 14 years with the head of an exclusive girl's school, Jean Harris. But gradually, Tarnower's ardor cooled and his affections fixed on his office assistant, who was a dozen years younger than the 56-year-old Harris.

During one of her visits to Tarnower's home, Harris discovered the other woman's nightgown and several other personal items in a bedroom closet. Harris was furious, and the two quarreled. She took out a gun and shot Tarnower five times. He died an hour later. Harris was arrested and charged with murder.

The shooting and the trial were carried on the front pages of newspapers in New York City and elsewhere. Even the conservative *New York Times* devoted considerable space to the lurid event. A reporter was assigned to the story, and he wrote a story every day.

At the trial, Harris said she was trying to take her own life in despair but accidentally shot the 69-year-old doctor-author. The prosecutor said she killed Tarnower in a jealous rage over his affair with another woman. Harris was convicted and sentenced to a minimum of 15 years in prison.

Two books were written on the triangle, each by a well-known and respected author. A television movie based on the murder was made. Why so much attention? Jealous wives, husbands and lovers shoot, stab and maim

Conflict. The struggle between athletic teams is an obvious example of conflict. Conflict exists at all levels of life—from the student torn between studying for an exam or going to a dance to the father of four trying to wrest a wage increase from a tight-fisted boss.

their loved ones every day in big cities. They rarely rate more than a one- or two-line mention in the newspapers' police reports. These crimes receive little attention because the people involved are among the cities' anonymous millions. Tarnower's murder was newsworthy because of his prominence.

Another news determinant was involved as well—conflict. There was conflict between Tarnower and the woman he was discarding, and there was conflict between the discarded woman, Harris, and the younger woman who was taking her place. Harris resolved these tensions by the ultimate act of conflict—murder.

Conflict is one of four additional news determinants that we need to examine. Before we do so, it is important to point out that these factors alone do not make an event newsworthy. Impact, the unusual and prominence are the three basic news determinants. The presence of one or more of the four additional determinants will heighten the news value of an event. The four are: **conflict, proximity, timeliness and currency.**

Four Additional Determinants of News

Conflict underlies our lives. There are internal conflicts we are all familiar with. The student must master a list of Spanish verbs for a test the following day, but his friends are leaving for a movie. Conflict. The car owner notices that his car is slow to start. The battery is running down. A new battery will be about $50. He has the money, but he had planned to use it for a special set of tools he saw advertised. Conflict.

Conflict

Almost every meeting of the city council, state legislature or congress involves conflicts between advocates of different points of view. The U.S. Constitution purposely sets governmental powers in conflict so that no one branch of government may prevail over the others.

Men and women are always struggling with something or someone—employers and employees; fathers and sons; husbands and wives; clerks and customers; teenagers with their consciences; adults with their responsibilities. Probably because we are so familiar with strife we overlook its drama except for the most obvious battles and violence. Overt conflict is newsworthy.

Less evident conflicts are the struggles of individuals against adversity—the woman trying to hold a family together on $100 a week, the historian with a view of Thomas Jefferson that conflicts with the established perception, the handicapped youngster trying to play baseball. Some of the best stories a reporter can dig up are the attempts by groups, organizations or individuals to counter prevailing attitudes. When women first banded together to protest what they called a sexist society, few reporters paid attention. In fact, the women were ridiculed as "bra burners."

The few reporters who recognized the movement became acquainted at the outset with what expanded to become a massive and effective drive for sexual equality.

Proximity

"Anything that is close to my readers or listeners is more important than something remote." This is how one reporter defines proximity. When sociology students at the local college stage mock marriages for a class project, that's news in a local newspaper. It's of no interest to newspaper readers in a neighboring state, unless one of the couples decides to elope there.

Proximity usually means something physically or geographically close. The fatal accident that the police reporter was covering in the first chapter was at an intersection near town. The accident would be of no interest to a newspaper or station 100 miles away.

Proximity can also refer to matters that are close in another way. People feel attached to those like themselves and to those with whom they share common interests. Catholics want to read about the activities of their church, and Jews are interested in events in Israel. Stockholders want to know what the board of General Motors has decided about the annual dividend. When a plane crashes in Cyprus, people in the United States wonder whether any Americans were aboard. They have an attachment to fellow citizens, even though the event was thousands of miles away. In carrying the event, newspapers and broadcast stations will tell readers and listeners whether any Americans were aboard. The fewer the number of Americans, the less important the story will be in the United States, regardless of the total number killed.

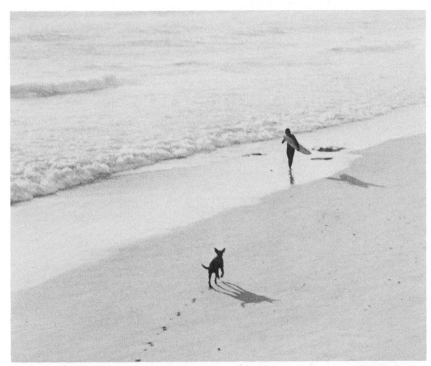

Proximity. We feel close to people and events with which we are familiar. The first warm day that brings out the surfers is big news to young people on the West Coast, and the day that the bluefish start running close to shore is news for surf fishermen.

Prominence and Proximity—Willie Nelson and Distant Death

The United Press International ran these two stories on its major news wire on the same day.

```
    LOUISVILLE, KY. (UPI)--COUNTRY MUSIC
SINGER WILLIE NELSON CANCELED HIS SCHEDULED
APPEARANCE SATURDAY NIGHT AT THE KENTUCKY STATE
FAIR'S CLOSING CONCERT BECAUSE HE IS
HOSPITALIZED WITH A LUNG AILMENT.
    JULIE SHAW, MANAGER OF THE 10-DAY FAIR,
SAID SUNDAY THAT NELSON--THE TOP DRAWING CARD
AT LAST YEAR'S FAIR-HAD BEEN HOSPITALIZED IN
ANOTHER STATE FOR A SERIOUS RESPIRATORY
AILMENT.
    MRS. SHAW SAID SHE HOPED TO ANNOUNCE TODAY
A REPLACEMENT FOR NELSON.

    10:21 AED
```

The story above is not important, but Nelson's **prominence** led the UPI to give it this much space.

The following story is certainly more important than the illness of a country music singer, but its impact is diminished due to lack of **proximity** to readers in the United States.

```
    NEW DELHI, INDIA (UPI)--A BUS FELL INTO A
CANAL TODAY IN THE NORTHERN STATE OF KASHMIR
KILLING 22 PEOPLE, THE PRESS TRUST OF INDIA
REPORTED.
    THE ACCIDENT OCCURRED NEAR PAHALGAON, ABOUT
400 MILES NORTHWEST OF NEW DELHI.
```

Timeliness

For some reason, we always want to know the latest, what's happening now. We march to the minute hand on the clock. Our all-news radio stations, our newspapers and our television stations rattle out a drumfire of news for us. We awake to the morning news, and we eat lunch to news and music. Driving to and from school or work, the news is with us in our cars. At home, we read the evening newspaper and turn to the network and local newscasts on television for news of the election returns or the high school football game.

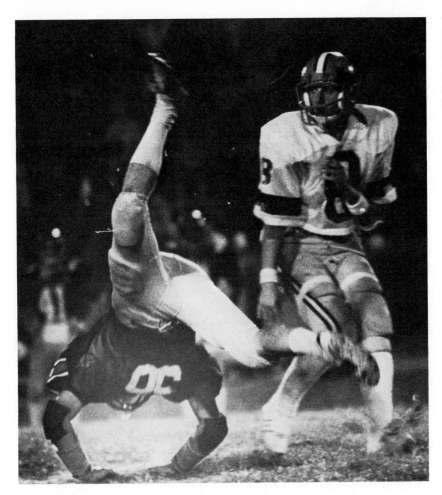

Timeliness. Readers and listeners want to know the latest from the White House and from the high school football field. The more recent the news, the greater its news value.

News has a short lifespan in this barrage. Reporters recognize that what occurs today has greater impact than an event that occurred a week ago, even if that event was not reported at the time. This is why newspaper leads usually include the word *today*. News writers want to impress their readers with the timeliness of the story.

People will read about past events if they are highly significant or extraordinary. Some stories are always timely. Berkley Hudson's story (in chap. 1) of a man held years too long in confinement attracted readers. Investigative reporters are always digging into the past to unearth stories.

Important stories will always attract readers. So will a story about a situation that has been around a long time but never written about in detail. This takes us to the last of our news determinants.

Since the end of World War II, public schools have been educating large numbers of young people who in previous years would not have finished high school or attended college. At the same time, some educators and parents were not too sure about the quality of that education.

This concern has erupted in every decade since the 1940s. In the 1980s, the worry has led to the "back to basics" movement, the substitution of required courses for electives in college and an emphasis on reading and mathematics in the grade schools. These are hardly new ideas. Yet the movement is newsworthy because of the concern expressed over the declining test scores of high school students.

What people talk about makes news. Although school vandalism is an old story, it became news in the 1970s when taxpayers became conscious of the enormous cost of repairing desks and windows and painting over graffiti. In some school districts, vandalism costs more than school supplies.

Reporters who are good listeners and who frequent the places people gather are likely to discover news that fits into this category. A reporter for a California newspaper who was taking a break from a political convention sat in the hotel lobby and overheard delegates chatting. They were not talking about any of the items on the agenda nor were they exchanging political gossip. What concerned them was the rising property tax.

The reporter put the discussion in the back of his mind and the following week when he had time he looked into it. He was able to gather information from a number of cities and wrote a series that predicted what later became known as the taxpayers' revolt in California.

We have now sketched out the seven determinants of news: impact, the unusual, prominence, conflict, proximity, timeliness and currency. As we have pointed out, the first three are the most important. The other four extend or diminish the news value of an event by their presence or absence.

The Guide: Importance

The single most important guide to whether something is worth a news story is its importance. Another way of looking at news values is to put the event to this test: Does it meet the "primary purpose" of journalism? This purpose is described by the American Society of Newspaper Editors in "A Statement of Principles" this way:

> The primary purpose of gathering and distributing news and opinion is to serve the general welfare by informing the people and enabling them to make judgments on the issues of the time.

Obviously, not everything in the newspaper or on newscasts is about a major issue. Newspapers, radio and television stations and newsmagazines try to reach a large audience of different needs and tastes. Still, if a study were to be made of the newspapers, stations and magazines we consider the best, we would find most of their articles to be about important issues.

A bit of advice at this point: Learning to differentiate the important from the inconsequential, the unusual from the ordinary, and the prominent from the little known comes with experience. Reporters learn from reading newspapers, listening to newscasts and seeing how the professionals handle news. Every reporter sooner or later develops what is called news sense. Without it, a journalist cannot function.

We can apply the seven news determinants to the work of the reporters we observed in chapter 1. **Putting the Determinants to Work**

The police reporter decided to devote most of his time to the fatal accident. He knew this would have greater **impact** on his readers than the petty thefts, lost dogs and brush fires that he had picked up at the police station. Obviously, **timeliness** and **proximity** were also involved as determinants.

The city hall reporter chose to write about the zoning appeal by the department store because of the **prominence** of the store and the **impact** of the proposal on the community. The original request had been important enough for a news story, but the appeal had the added ingredient of **conflict** to make it even more newsworthy. Readers were interested in the vehement opposition of people living in the residential area near the proposed building site.

The editor's decision to use the Phoenix plane crash involved the element of **prominence.** Although the event was far away, the victim was so well known the story had to be carried. Another distant event made the newspaper that day, the Florida hurricane. Even though the storm was more than a thousand miles away and storms in this season are not unusual in Florida, the story described this as a "killer storm." This makes the storm **exceptional,** unlike the usual storms that batter the state this time of year.

Lindy Washburn knew she had a big story when she learned that more than 20 people had been killed in a New Jersey fire. Disasters make news. Had one or two people been killed, the story would not have been carried on the Associated Press wires. But 23 deaths has considerable **impact.**

In Hong Kong, Neal Robbins was interested in the flight of hundreds of Chinese from the mainland because he knew such a large exodus was **unusual.** Usually, the Chinese came individually or in twos or threes. Their arrival in colorful junks made the story even more unusual.

The lead story on the "CBS Evening News" was a major tax story, which obviously had great **impact** on the public. Although most of the stories on the newscast were significant to large numbers of people, the program also included a feature on a midwestern family with three brilliant children who were being taught at home by their parents—an **exceptional** family educating their children in an **unusual** way.

We are now ready to use these news determinants, or news values, to help write news stories.

Finding the Focus

The first step the news writer takes before writing a news story is to determine its focus or main point. **What's this event about?** the writer asks himself or herself. At least nine times out of ten, the answer to the reporter's question is that the story is about either:

1. A person who has said or done something important or interesting or a person who has had something important or interesting happen to him or her.
2. An event of importance or interest to many people.

If we look carefully at the first paragraphs of news stories in today's newspaper we can verify this. The beginning of the news story, or **lead,** usually summarizes the main theme of the story. Look at a batch of news stories. Almost all of them will begin with a lead that answers one of these two questions:

1. **Who** said or did what? What was it that happened **to the person?**
2. **What** happened?

This takes us to the heart of news writing. When a reporter sits down to write, there are almost always two choices:

1. If a person is central to the event, the writer answers the question: **What did the person say or do; what happened to the person?**
2. When the event, occurrence or happening is important or unusual, the writer answers the question: **What happened of significance or was exceptional or unusual?**

Look back at the three sets of numbered items. They are parallel. All the items numbered 1 are related, as are items numbered 2. They are presented in detail because they are the starting point for news writing.

You might ask at this point what happened to the news determinants. Look closely at all the items and you will see that they embody the three key determinants—impact or significance, the unusual, exceptional or interesting and prominence.

Focusing on the Person

When the event involves an individual saying or doing something, or when the individual has something happen to him or her, the writer first must decide whether the person is prominent. Will readers and listeners recognize the name?

Is the singer Mick Jagger or Ralph Martin? If it is Jagger, most people will recognize the name, and "Jagger" will go into the lead. If it is Martin, few will know that name, and some kind of **identifying label** will have to be used: "A 26-year-old rock singer," for example.

Focus on Person. When the news event involves a well-known person, the news story centers on that person's statements or actions. The lead will contain the name of the person. The story answers the questions: Who said it, who did it?

Here are some leads using the **name** of the person involved in the news event:

Who? (name) **said what?**

SANTA BARBARA, Calif. (UPI)—*President Reagan said* Thursday he *has offered to hold a summit meeting with Leonid Brezhnev* once the administration has decided on its proposals for "legitimate arms reduction."

Who? (name) **did what**

MALDEN, Mass. (AP)—*Malden Police Commissioner William A. Davidson* yesterday *ordered two police officers fired* after they arrested him for drunk driving.

Who? (name) **said what?**

SPRINGFIELD—*Chancellor William E. Barnes told* entering freshmen today *the way to academic success is through* "unstinting effort."

If the person central to the event is not well known to the news writer's audience, a label must be used that allows the reader or listener to quickly visualize the person. Sometimes, the label is **age** and **address** or **home town:**

Who? (label) **had something happen to him**

A 39-year-old Kansas City, Kansas, man was charged Monday in Wyandotte County District Court *with the fatal shooting* early Saturday *of a patron* at a tavern in that city.

—*Kansas City Times*

The label can also be the **occupation** of the person:

Who? (label) **had something happen to him?**

A Kentucky State Police detective was *shot to death* yesterday afternoon while searching for marijuana in a field in rural Edmonson County.

—*Lexington (Ky.) Herald*

A person's **title** may be used as the identifying label. This is frequently done on radio and television news:

Who? (label) **did what?**

A federal judge in Brooklyn today *imposed prison terms* on four former congressmen and two other codefendants convicted in the FBI's Abscam sting operation.

—CBS Evening News

When the person's **connection to the event** identifies him or her, that relationship can be used as the identifying label:

Who? (label) **had something happen to him?**

HOUSTON (UPI)—*A Rolling Stones fan was stabbed to death* during the British rock group's near-sellout show at the Astrodome, police said Thursday.

When **the event** is the most important aspect of the story, the writer uses the lead to describe what occurred in the briefest way possible:

What happened?

> WASHINGTON—*Congress* yesterday *appropriated $3.5 million to fulfill the government's part of the out-of-court settlement of the Narragansett Indian land claim.*
> —The Providence Evening Bulletin

What happened?

> THROOP, Pa. (AP)—*Eight teenage party-goers were crushed to death* when their car swerved into a guard rail, plunged some 190 feet through the air and crashed on its roof, officials said Friday.

What happened?

> CHICAGO (AP)—*DePaul University's student newspaper was shut down* Friday after printing a story about a rape on campus, in defiance of orders from the director of student publications, the editor said.

Look back over these 10 leads for a minute. Use the courthouse reporter's two guidelines to determine what kind of events the leads describe: important or unusual.

Direct and Delayed Leads

Clearly, each of the 10 is important or significant. This is why the leads are written in a straightforward, direct manner. But suppose the event you are writing about has no great importance or significance. Suppose it is more bizarre than significant, as Diana Jones of the *Herald-Dispatch* in Huntington, W. Va., considered an event she covered. Her story begins this way:

The students knew something was up.

At Milton High School, they watched sheriff's deputies and two corrections officers leading German shepherds into the school at about 8:30 yesterday morning.

At Huntington High, two girls leaning out a window called to another girl. "They're keeping everyone inside. They won't let anybody out."

"Are you serious?" the girl outside called back.

But it wasn't until the drug-sniffing dogs and law enforcement officers had left the school that the students and teachers were told what was happening and why: Sheriff Bob Bailey was leading a series of surprise drug investigations at area high schools, using the specially trained dogs to try to detect drugs in the students' lockers. . . .

Focus on Event. When the news event concerns something that has happened, the event or occurrence is emphasized. Horse race, or flood, or fire, the story answers the question: What happened?

The same kind of indirect, leisurely beginning was used by the courthouse reporter when she wrote the story about the woman who sued a department store whose Santa Claus had, she said, slapped her son. Her story began this way:

Santa Claus is a child's best friend.

The kindly old gent pats little boys on the head and little girls on the cheek.

But two weeks ago, says Mrs. Carolyn Elliott, a Zale's Department store Santa whacked her six-year-old son, Dennis.

The dog-sniffing story and the Santa Claus suit story begin informally. The writing is relaxed. Most important, they do not get to the main theme of the event immediately.

When the event is important or significant, the story gets to the main point at once. The lead is **direct.** When the story is about an unusual, odd or strange event, the story does not need to describe what happened or what was said at once. The lead, or main point, can be **delayed** a bit.

This leads us to these guidelines:

Direct leads are used on important news stories.
Delayed leads are used on feature stories.

A Delayed Lead News writers have to decide how important an event is before writing. When David Stacks was sent to cover an arm-wrestling tournament, he had a good idea that his story for *The Anniston Star* probably would not be the most important in the newspaper the next day. He was fairly sure that he would be writing a feature story, which would mean he would be writing a delayed lead. And that is just what he did:

Sweat beaded on Bruce Jernigan's forehead. His biceps swelled as blood rushed through his strong chest and into his right arm. His face grimaced with exertion.

Bruce's opponent, Claude Bradford, smiled in seeming defiance as the two boys' fists—locked in an arm-wrestler's grip, teetered slowly back and forth over the tabletop.

Then, with a burst of energy, 14-year-old Claude overcame his opponent's balanced show of strength. Both boys fell from near exhaustion as the referee declared the match concluded.

Theirs was a test of strength, endurance and will. In the end, Claude managed to wear down his friend and adversary Bruce, 14, in the Anniston Park and Recreation Department's first arm-wrestling tournament Saturday morning at Carver Community Center on West 14th Street.

"It's all in the way you move," Claude said afterwards.

Arm-wrestling is an ancient contest of power in which two opponents grasp each other's hands with their elbows resting on a flat surface. The one who forces the other's arm down to the surface wins.

Ancient people of the world regarded arm-wrestling as a non-violent test of strength where one adversary could defeat the other.

The contest Saturday was staged for a different reason, said Zebedee Murphy, the city recreation leader who coordinated the event and acted as referee.

"We're trying to get them (the boys) interested in something new," he said. Murphy said he used to arm-wrestle with other kids on the block when he was growing up, but this was the first time the city had ever sponsored such a tournament.

"We'll probably do it again next year," Murphy said.

About 20 boys from the Carver area of Anniston participated in the contest Saturday. Officials divided them into three age groups and pitted contestants against each other arbitrarily, Murphy said.

The winner in the 12-and-under age group was Larry Johnson, 12, of H-4 14th Street, a seventh-grader at Cobb Junior High School. Claude Bradford at H-1 14th Street, a seventh-grade student at Carver Junior High School, walked off with the peanut for the 13–15 age group. Tony Graham, 16 of F-2 14th St., can show his prize to classmates at Anniston High School where he is a senior.

The three winners were awarded first-place ribbons, Murphy said: Second- and third-prize winners also received ribbons for their achievements. The boys who were eliminated in early rounds were given certificates of participation.

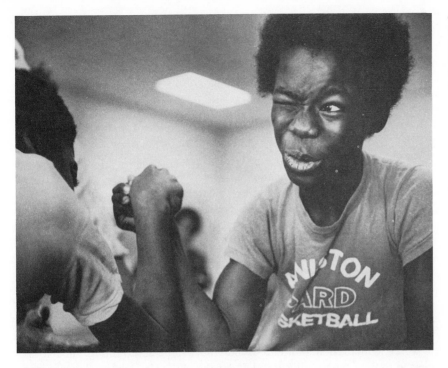

For a minute, suppose that Stacks had decided on a direct lead. It might have been written this way:

```
Claude Bradford, 14, won the first arm-wrestling
tournament held by the Anniston Park and Recreation
Department on Saturday.
    Bradford defeated....
```

"Big deal," a reader might say and pass on to real news. But with the delayed lead Stacks put on his story, the reader settles back and says, "Let's have some fun with this story." The reader knows at once that he or she will be reading a feature story.

Feature Story

The courthouse reporter who came across the document involving Santa Claus knew at once that she would write a short feature story. Her problem was how to write an entertaining lead. Before she sat down to write the story, she had a few ideas. The best one, she thought, was that although Santa Claus is considered a kindly old man, here he was accused of a cruel act. She decided to put this idea of contrasts into her lead:

```
Santa Claus, that paragon of kindness, is being sued
for cruelty to a child.
```

As with most first efforts, this wasn't exactly right. The idea was sound, she still felt, but not the way she had put it. Writers should use simple language, but here she was using the word "paragon," which not many people would understand. Although the lead was short, she preferred to have as little punctuation as possible in it. She tried again:

```
Kindly Santa Claus is being sued for being cruel to a
youngster.
```

She was more satisfied with this. But perhaps she should localize it, put the local department store's name in the lead. No, readers would know it was a local story because there would be no dateline.

The lead was still too flat, too close to a straight news lead. She knew that the lead is the most important part of the story, that it either attracts the reader at once or turns the reader away. "Hook him at once, or he's gone," an editor had once told her. This lead wouldn't even tempt the reader, she decided.

The tone was wrong. The beginning of a feature should be relaxed. It should beckon the reader and say to him or her: slow down a minute—I've got something funny I want to tell you.

Suddenly she realized there was a more serious problem than her choice of words, punctuation and tone. In her effort to be entertaining, she had neglected to be scrupulously careful about the facts. Her lead mistakenly identified the party the suit was brought against, the defendant.

It was not Santa Claus, as both drafts of her lead had stated. It was the department store. Some feature writers, she knew, are known for shading the facts in the interest of a well-written story. She did not want to give herself that kind of reputation. She had heard about their guideline: "Never let the facts get in the way of a good story."

She knew that she did not have too much space, so she could not spin out the tale for more than five or six paragraphs. After her leisurely beginning, she would have to get to the facts—name and address of mother, description of the incident, damages sought. She wrote:

Santa Claus is a child's best friend.

The kindly old gent pats little boys on the head and little girls on the cheek.

But two weeks ago, says Mrs. Carolyn Elliott, a Zale's Department Store Santa whacked her six-year-old son, Dennis.

Mrs. Elliott, of 49 East End Ave., wants $10,000 for her "humiliation and embarrassment" and her son's "nervous reaction." She filed suit against the store in the Grant County District Court yesterday.

The department store had no comment.

Next, let's look at the straight news story. In chapter 1, we watched a reporter **Straight News Story** begin to write the obituary of Rose Harriet Allen, former school teacher and principal. The event contains two news determinants, prominence and impact. Allen was well known, and her death and the fund drive will have an impact on the readers.

This means the story will be written in a straightforward manner, as most obituaries are, that it will be given a direct lead.

Just what the lead will say is not as obvious. We have two answers worthy of the lead when we ask the two questions that will give us the story focus:

1. What was it that happened to the person?
    Rose Harriet Allen died.
2. What happened?
    A scholarship fund is being set up.

Which should be the lead? One or the other, or both? Let's listen in on the writer's thinking:

"Everyone in town knows Allen, so I'll start with that and immediately go to the fund drive. The lead will include both elements."

> Rose Harriet Allen, 71, of 33 Fulton Ave., who taught school here for 30 years and was a school principal for 13 years before her retirement, died yesterday in the Community Hospital. A fund drive will be....

"No, that won't do. The first paragraph will be a blockbuster, much too long. Maybe the better lead is the fund drive since that has lasting significance. Obviously, with that as a beginning Allen's name will be worked into the story since the drive is in her memory."

> A college scholarship fund is being set up in memory of Rose Harriet Allen, 71, who died yesterday after a career of 43 years in the local public schools.

"That's better. It's shorter and it combines the two elements."

She continues to write, and in the middle of the fourth paragraph she suddenly stops and slowly reads what she has written.

"This is becoming a story about a fund drive, not the death of a well-known teacher who probably has thousands of friends in town. The impact, the real significance, is not the fund drive but her death. Allen's death will affect many of our readers.

"The lead should concentrate on Allen's death and the fund drive should go lower in the story."

> Rose Hariett Allen, whose teaching and administrative career spanned 43 years in local public schools, died here yesterday at the age of 71.
> Allen died in the Community Hospital where she had been since suffering a heart attack last week in her home at 33 Fulton Ave.
> For 30 years, Allen taught in several of the city's elementary schools. For the next 13 years of her educational career, she was the principal of the Lincoln School. She retired six years ago.
> She is remembered as a friendly, outgoing teacher. As a principal, she delighted in taking a class for a teacher who was ill.
> "She was strict," recalled Albert Green, a local lawyer. "If you didn't do your homework, she wanted to see your parents in school the next day."
> Green and some of Allen's other former students said they are planning to establish a college scholarship fund in her memory.
> "Miss Allen came from a poor farm family." Green said. "She used to tell us how hard it was for her to stay in school at State Teachers College, how she worked for a family for her room and board and did chores six hours a day, went to class, and studied."....

This version satisfied her. She was able to balance both important elements of the story, Allen's death and the fund drive. She had good quotes that told something of Allen's personality as a teacher. The personal details about Allen helped the reader to visualize the kind of person she was.

Selection and Judgment

Walter Lippmann, a newspaper columnist and author of many books, said that "in our world the facts are infinitely many." He added, "We have to select some facts rather than others, and in doing that we are using not only our legs but our selective judgment of what is interesting or important or both."

Both in the reporting and the writing, the journalist has to exercise judgment. The news story is a keyhole view of the event. It does not pretend to tell all. However, it should give the "interesting or important" aspects of the event. It will, if the journalist has the ability to select the essentials of the event and the judgment to weigh their relative merits.

Selection and judgment come into play in reporting as well as in writing. No news story, no matter how well written, can be any better than the facts that go into it. In chapter 4 we'll look at reporting, which is another word for fact or information gathering. But before we do, a cautionary remark.

In chapter 1, we saw how the police reporter and the obituary writer decided to emphasize one story (the fatal accident and the death of Rose Harriet Allen) and to ignore or quickly pass over others. When Neal Robbins returned to the bureau he thought he had a big story. But because of more important news on the wires (the assassination attempt on the president and stirrings in Poland), the story had to be cut down to a length shorter than anticipated.

News Values Are Not Absolute

The news story that is worth 500 words on a slow news day may be shortened to 250 words on a busy news day. A story newsworthy on a day the newspaper is fat with advertising, thus allowing considerable space for news, might not be printed on a Saturday, when the paper is thin and news must be carefully chosen for the little available space.

Because readers, listeners and viewers are accustomed to a wide variety of news in their newspapers and newscasts, no story can run too long, no matter what its importance may be. Room must be made for features, business news, local news, obituaries, personal items, weather, sports and so on.

The nature of the audience influences news selection. An announcement from the Vatican will be given space in *The Bridgeport Post* because of the large Catholic readership in the industrial community. But it may not be carried in *The Advocate* in nearby Stamford, which has a diverse, white collar readership.

The Audience

News from Washington about crop support payments is of little or no importance to New York readers but has considerable impact in the Midwest. Although a story about a meeting of the board of Eastman Kodak will not be carried in many newspapers, *The Wall Street Journal* will run it for its readers, whose average net worth exceeds $400,000 and who invest in stocks and bonds.

The New York Post is loaded with gossip about television and movie stars and has large headlines about sex crimes. *The New York Times* emphasizes international news, carries little local news on page one and has a reporter who writes about wine.

The *Post* ran a story about an incident at a performance by Abba, one of the biggest-selling groups in pop music history but ignored a meeting in Chicago of governors of the midwestern states, to which The *Times* devoted almost a column. The *Post* is high on entertainment; the *Times* emphasizes information. The *Post* tries to reach workers on their way home on the subway. Hence, the eye-catching, lurid headlines and the short, breezy stories. The *Times,* read over a leisurely breakfast or by the commuter, is interested in the affluent, college-educated reader who skis in the Swiss Alps, keeps up with the fashions, reads a book a week and spends more than a $100 on dinner and the theater twice a month.

The journalist who goes to work for the *Post,* the *Times,* or any newspaper or broadcast station quickly learns to tailor news decisions to fit the interests of the audience. A story that would be played up with explicit language in the *Post* might not be used in Huntington, W. Va., and if it were, the four-letter words and the sexual references would probably be eliminated.

Figure 3.1 Readers Determine News. In this agricultural area of Minnesota, a wind and hail storm is big news because of the damage to crops, out buildings and homes. *The Free Press* in Mankato devoted its entire front page to news of the storm.

THE FREE PRESS

Vol. 95   No. 73   28 pages   2 sections plus supplements
June 24, 1981 Mankato-North Mankato, Minn. 56001 25¢

Wednesday

A wet ending to a wild afternoon

While traffic creeps along flooded Carney Avenue in West Mankato Tuesday afternoon, Tom Browne, 934 Charles Ave., plants one foot and his hoe along a boulevard for security and fishes for a debris-clogged storm sewer grate. Portions of several city streets were closed temporarily.

John Cross photo

Mother Nature does it again

By Staff Writers
A storm 40 miles wide, carrying hail and high winds, ravaged trees and crops and created openings for water damage in Blue Earth County Tuesday.

The brunt of the storm, with gusts of nearly 80 miles per hour, apparently passed directly over Mankato-North Mankato, causing flooding of streets and basements. At least half of

See related articles, photos on Pages 4 and 15

the Greater Mankato area was left without electrical power. West Mankato, where numerous large trees were uprooted, appeared hardest hit. The storm also struck the Lake Crystal and St. Clair areas.

TOTAL DAMAGE in the county, including the destruction of about 50 buildings, was estimated at $3.5 million by Blue Earth County Sheriff LeRoy Wiebold.

"As far as I'm concerned, Blue Earth County is a disaster area," he said.

Two Mankato area people were admitted to Immanuel-St. Joseph's Hospital, one with a back injury and one with an injury to the left eye, as a result of the Tuesday afternoon storm.

A hospital spokeswoman said seven residents were treated in the hospital emergency room for minor cuts and bruises following the storm, and released.

No tornadoes were spotted, although some people witnessed funnel clouds over Mankato.

MANY PEOPLE in Mankato watched the storm's approach. Ample warning was given, with stress sounding long before the first drops fell. As the storm neared from the northwest, a wide band of white appeared, announcing the arrival

See STORM
(Please turn to Page 8)

Strong winds, hail strip crops from fields

• Redwood Falls

Minnesota River

New Ulm

Mankato

Why us? Meteorologist says to blame the terrain

The Minnesota River Valley's rough terrain magnified Tuesday's storm by about 30 percent, National Weather Service meteorologist John Graf said today.

Actually, Graf said, several storm systems struck southwestern Minnesota Tuesday, but the storm along the 100-mile long river valley from Montevideo to Mankato was particularly severe because of the valley's rolling terrain.

"Changes in the height and contour of the valley magnify a storm," Graf said. "The initial inflection point of the storm began in the upper sections of the valley, and 'lifting mechanisms' in the atmosphere were magnified by the rough terrain."

The Minnesota River Valley is an "ideal storm producer," Graf said, particularly when a storm flows in a northwest-southeast direction as it did Tuesday.

"The valley makes a storm generate more energy than it would normally, and once a storm gets under way, it perpetuates itself," Graf said.

The meteorologist said a storm system "pulsates; it elongates and contracts, like a living mechanism, something you might see in the sea."

Graf also said that Tuesday's storm was unusually long-lived, with severe weather lasting up to 40 minutes at some points along the storm path.

By MICHAEL FLAHERTY
Free Press Staff Writer

In some parts of Blue Earth County, it looks as though farmers never planted a crop. The fields, which only Tuesday nurtured promising young plants, lay black — completely stripped of foliage.

The storm that struck Tuesday will be billed as one of the worst disasters ever to strike Blue Earth County farmers.

Large hail whipped by high winds slashed fields and pasted young soybean and corn plants to the ground throughout the county. Observers estimate between 70 and 85 percent of the county's crops have been damaged, but the number of acres destroyed will not be known until farmers have had time to see how much of their corn crop recovers.

MOST OF the county's soybeans are gone. Soybeans even bruised by hailstones usually have to be replanted. And Tuesday's hail smashed most of Blue Earth County's crop. Agronomists say farmers still have about a week to plant a new crop of soybeans.

Corn plants are usually more

A helping hand

Need help with storm cleanup?

Hundreds of people in The Free Press circulation area need assistance to restore their homes and yards. Many students, 12 years and older, need summer jobs.

In an effort to help everybody, The Free Press is offering any student a free seven-day want ad between June 26 and July 1.

Details in the classified section.

resilient. In order to be killed, corn plants have to be severely damaged below the plant's growing point, which Tuesday was 3 to 6 inches from the ground.

But even parts of the corn crop have been wiped out. Elevator operators throughout the county say that many of their customers have given up hope that the shredded corn crop will recover.

Some farmers are going to try to replant the corn using an early maturing variety of seed, but many feel it is too late —

that corn planted now would only have a ghost of a chance of producing a crop.

"But we'll just have to wait and see how much of the corn was hurt," said Byron Kunkel, county extension agent. "Corn will usually come back, and I don't want to get into a guessing game on how much was destroyed until we wait a few days."

Kunkel said the storm was the worst he'd seen in this area.

See CROPS
(Please turn to Page 8)

Bill Alfrow photo

Knee-high by the Fourth of July may be a tall order for some of Blue Earth County's corn crop battered Tuesday by strong winds and hail.

The Inside Story

Mud Hens flying high

Although the major leaguers are striking, baseball still lives in cities like Toledo, Ohio, the top farm club of the Minnesota Twins. And in Toledo, the club makes it fun to come to the ball park. Find out more about the legendary Mud Hens in Sports, Page 21.

Dancing to 90

When anyone approaches the century mark, everyone else wants to know his secret of long life. For Julius Peterson, it's dancing, and that's how he'll celebrate his 90th birthday on Friday. Mr. Peterson tells how he started dancing, in a story on Page 5.

Index

Accent	5,6,7	Markets	17
Business	16	Opinion	12
Comics	20	Outdoors	23
Deaths	19	Public Notices	24
Dear Abby	6	Records	6
Dr. Donohue	20	Sports	21-23
Horoscope	20	World	21-23
In the Nation	2		

Less dramatic

Clear to partly cloudy tonight and Thursday. Lows in the middle to upper 50s and highs in the lower to middle 80s. Wind northwest 5 to 15 mph tonight. Extended outlook: Partly cloudy Friday and Saturday. Chance of thunderstorms Sunday. Highs in the 70s, north and 80s south. Lows mid 40s to mid 50s Friday and in the 50s Saturday and Sunday.

Drought. To some people, this is just a picture of a dead fish washed ashore; but to readers in drought-stricken areas of the Midwest, it is a symbol of caked fields and withered corn stalks. News values depend on the interests of readers and listeners.

Next, let's see what happens to the news story when the reporter has finished writing it.

Moving the Story
Broadcast Copy

Broadcast news stories move from the writer to the news editor or to the person who will be reading the copy. The copy is edited to see that it can be read aloud without trouble. Factual errors are corrected, and the copy is checked for broadcast style. Numerals are written out. The number 20 becomes twenty; 500,000 becomes 500 thousand.

Correspondents in the field write their own copy and read it on the air. Sometimes, they "wing it," meaning they speak without written copy.

In smaller stations with no news staff, announcers take wire copy directly from the AP or UPI teletype machines and read it with little advance checking. This is called "rip and read," and it is the cause of many of the bloopers that are collected on records and sold as entertainment.

Newspaper Copy

The routing of copy for a newspaper is considerably more complicated. After a story has been written, it is turned in to the city desk. If it has been written on a video display terminal, the city desk calls it up for examination on the screen at the city desk.

The city editor or assistant city editor reads through the copy to see that it is satisfactory: the lead contains the main news point and all questions the reader may have are answered. If the story is defective, it is sent back to the news writer for further work. If acceptable, the story moves on to the next stage, the copy desk.

Figure 3.2 How a Story Moves. The copy that a reporter writes goes through several hands before it appears in the newspaper. The city editor or assistant city editor examines it, a news editor reads through it at the news desk and then a copy editor reads it closely and writes a headline for the story.

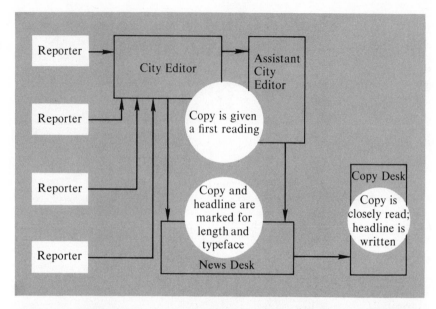

Writing the Head. A copy editor for *The Wall Street Journal* counts letters and spaces to make sure that his headline will fit.

At the copy desk, the story is given a thorough reading. Grammar, punctuation and spelling are checked. The writing is made to conform to the newspaper's style—Street may be abbreviated to St., fourteen changed to 14. (A newspaper stylebook is included in Appendix B.)

If the paper is tight that day, the copy editor trims the story, usually from the bottom. Unnecessary adjectives and adverbs are removed, even when the paper is open—meaning there is plenty of room for news. Redundancies (true facts, circulated around, 7 a.m. in the morning) are corrected. Sentences in the passive voice are changed to the active: "The burglar was seen by one of the children" becomes "One of the children saw the burglar."

A copy editor may spot something the city editor missed. If the problem is minor, the city desk will solve it, but if it is major the story is sent back to

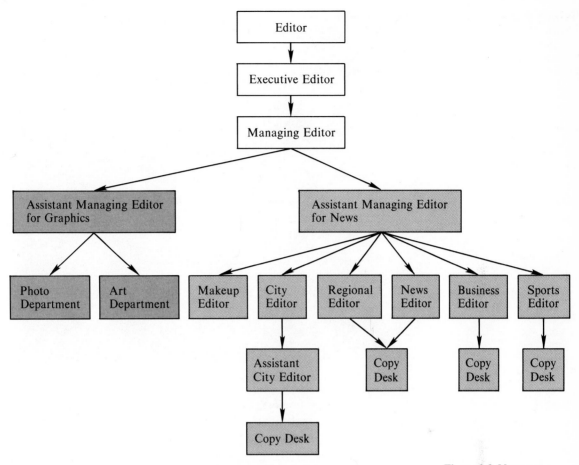

the writer. If the education reporter used too much jargon—the specialized language of educators—the copy editor replaces the technical wording with everyday words and phrases.

When the editing is completed, the copy editor writes a headline for the story. The size of the headline is determined by the city editor if the story is local, by the news editor or managing editor if it is national or international.

Nonlocal stories are usually taken from the wire service machines, AP, UPI or others. If the newspaper subscribes to more than one wire service and the news editor wants to combine the dispatches of two or more of them into a single story, he or she may ask the managing editor to assign the job to a news writer.

On large newspapers, such as the one diagrammed in figure 3.3, a regional editor goes over news from correspondents in nearby communities, the business editor handles news from the business staff and from the wires that the news editor or wire editor has turned over to the business desk and the sports editor handles sports copy.

Each of these specialized departments has a copy desk of its own. On smaller newspapers, all copy is channeled to a single copy desk.

Figure 3.3 Newsroom Organization. Newspaper newsrooms are organized along these lines of authority; the editor at the top and various departmental editors and their copy desks under the editor. This diagram shows the organization of a large newspaper. Smaller newspapers may have just one copy desk—called a universal desk—that handles all copy but sports and social news.

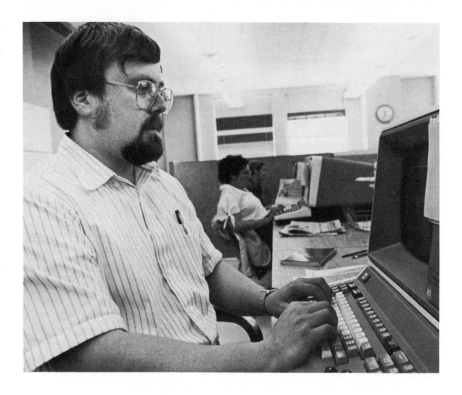

Headline Writing on VDT. Charles Edgren of the *El Paso Herald-Post* uses the video display terminal to write a headline.

As the news day develops, the makeup editor decides how to lay out the newspaper—where to put the stories. Material for the inside pages is laid out first: columns, editorials, comic strips and secondary stories.

On large newspapers, the decision about where to put, or **play,** stories is made at a story, or news, conference. There, the editors of the various sections present the best of their stories to the managing editor. The city editor discusses last night's city council meeting, the national news editor mentions a story from Washington about the federal budget. On some newspapers, a foreign editor is also present.

The managing editor decides what stories will go on page one and which will be given top play. The number one story is usually spotted on the upper-right-hand side of the page.

On smaller newspapers, the decisions on play are less formal. The managing editor and the city editor chat with each other during the day and then instruct the makeup editor about their decisions.

In both cases, the photo editor, or assistant managing editor for graphics, informs the managing editor or another editor about the local and wire photos that are available to accompany the major stories.

Once the decisions have been made about play, it is up to the makeup editor to produce a pleasing display of the news for page one and for other section pages—those pages that begin different sections of the newspaper.

Increasingly, newspapers are being edited and made up on video screens. Just as the video terminal has replaced the typewriter, the video screen is replacing the copy editor's pencil and the layout sheets, called **dummies,** of the makeup staff.

Once the newsroom work is completed, the stories laid out are on plates, which are usually made up by photocomposition and then sent to the pressroom.

In this chapter, we have discussed the way news stories are written. We have presumed that the facts of the stories have already been gathered. Before we go into more detail about news writing, it is a good idea to look at the business of fact gathering. Chapters 4 and 5 will discuss what it is that reporters look for in order to make their stories interesting, complete and relevant to the needs of readers and listeners. We will see how reporting and writing are part of one overall process. This is an important point that can never be repeated often enough: News writers write reporting.

Reporting

Part Two
Reporting

4

Finding Information and Gathering Facts

News is developed from the journalist's observation of events, from interviews with the people involved and by research through records, files and reference material. To adequately report an event, the journalist must know how things work—how city government functions, how the school system operates, how the local court system works. This knowledge is part of the general background the journalist applies to his or her reporting and writing. To obtain this knowledge, the journalist seeks a wide range of experiences, reads widely and knows how to use a variety of reference materials.

Looking Ahead

The news story stands on facts, and the facts that carry the most weight are those that the reporter gathers by direct observation.

A Firsthand Look

Penny Lernoux, who covers Latin America for a number of newspapers and magazines, was doing a story on tin miners in Bolivia who work under difficult conditions high in the Andes. Lernoux was determined to see for herself how the miners worked, although she had heard that the miners threw dynamite at visitors and were especially suspicious of women, whom they believed brought them bad luck.

She disguised herself as a man and went along with an engineer who had volunteered to show her the inside of a mine.

She was deep inside the Siglo Veinte mine, she recalled, "when a miner approached, a smile on his face and a stick of dynamite in his hand."

"Don't panic," the engineer shouted. "Just run."

Fortunately, there was a sharp bend in the corridor, which they scrambled around just as the dynamite exploded. Lernoux survived, and she had her story.

In Philadelphia, newspapers carried stories of crime, delays, fires and accidents in the city's subways. One story reported the case of a well-known Philadelphia lawyer who was brutally beaten, raped and left for dead in the darkened track area. She was discovered 18 hours after the attack.

Terror Underground

Mike Mallowe of *Philadelphia* magazine decided to look into the subway system. He interviewed crime victims, patrolled with the police, worked with the subway motormen and rode the subway for months as a commuter. His piece, "Tunnel of Terror," included his findings:

. . . . a trunk line to hell . . . 40 miles of dark, deadly terror . . . 40 miles of drunks collapsed in their own vomit; of howling teenage punks pissing in public; of hulking panhandlers, not asking, but demanding money; it's 40 miles of old people too terrified to look around them; of women alone, too scared to speak. . . .

Only direct observation could fuel the tension and terror in these lines.

A Fish Story

On a skyway over Tampa Bay, a couple of fishermen are trying their luck. Jeff Klinkenberg, an outdoors reporter for *The St. Petersburg Times,* and another reporter are "catching nothing," as Klinkenberg puts it, when a fisherman walks by with what seems to be about 60 pounds of equipment.

He looks at Klinkenberg and his companion and laughs. "You'll never catch anything with that," he says to them, pointing to their equipment.

Then he begins talking about a shark he is determined to catch, name of "Old Hitler." Klinkenberg manages to get in a few questions before the fisherman goes his way. The reporters resume fishing, but Klinkenberg is distracted. He is thinking, this guy is worth a story.

Two weeks later, Klinkenberg called the shark fisherman and made arrangements to meet him on the skyway.

"I went back out there with him. We went to the bridge about 6 p.m. and stayed until 2 a.m., fooling around with sharks and ladyfish," Klinkenberg says.

Klinkenberg returned to the newspaper and typed up three pages of single-spaced notes for his story. Then he wrote. Here is how the story began:

Ron Swint moaned in the dark about the shark called Old Hitler, the largest shark in Tampa Bay, as traffic roared by on the Skyway Bridge. Somebody in a car shouted and Swint automatically winced. He has been hit by beer cans thrown from passing cars. A huge truck rumbled by so fast the bridge shook. Diesel fumes hung in the air.

The first shark to come along was not Old Hitler, but it was a big one, a shark Swint later estimated at 500 pounds, a shark that swallowed a three-pound live ladyfish bait and swam toward the lights of Tampa. The shark almost killed Swint.

The complete story is in Appendix C.

Again, we see that the reporter who has observed the event is able to make the story come alive for readers. The reader is swept up by the details the reporter is able to put into the story.

It is not always possible to witness the event. A bank is robbed, a truck slams into a car, a flash flood rips out a bridge. These happen so quickly, only sheer luck would have the reporter there at the moment the news breaks. In these situations, the reporter turns to sources for information—eyewitnesses and authorities.

When Bonnie Van Gilder was assigned to do a story about New York City street gangs for her journalism class, she hoped to observe a gang on the prowl. She was unable to do so, and so she had to settle for other sources.

The Crazy Bishops

For her story, Van Gilder could have used the police alone for information. She did interview police officers. She also examined police documents, along with news clippings, for background—the third source of information for news stories. But she wanted more direct contact with a gang. She managed to locate a Times Square gang, the Crazy Bishops, and she was able to interview some members.

Here is her story:

NEW YORK—"China," a female member of a Times Square teen gang called the Crazy Bishops, narrowed her black eyes and declared, "If you want to be a Bishop, you got to mug people and beat them up and take whatever you can."

Like most of the other Crazy Bishops, China, 15, comes from a broken home, is a runaway and has an extensive arrest record. Police have identified 60 Bishops, but suspect as many as 200 Hispanic boys and girls, ranging in age from 14 to 19, are associated with the gang.

Detective John McNamee knew where to find China. When the 42nd Street policemen change shifts at 7:30 a.m., the Bishops come out of a nearby park where they sleep. They go to a local coffee shop or sit on the stoops of pornography and peep show businesses that line 42nd Street.

At night they work the streets and vast network of area subway tunnels. The gang has rampaged through the theater district, looting stores, mugging tourists and harassing transients.

"When you're a Bishop, you don't have no pity for people," China said, "You got to hustle to survive."

Area merchants complain about the gang. But, police say they can arrest the Bishops only for disorderly conduct unless they are caught committing a more serious crime.

Louis Corbo, head of the Youth Gang Information Unit of the New York City Police, said, "We think this gang grew out of the film 'The Warriors.' It may just be coincidence, but there was never a gang around Times Square before."

Corbo said the Crazy Bishops are unlike any other youth gang he has investigated. Usually gangs are made up of neighborhood kids, living within the same 10-block residential area. But the Crazy Bishops operate in a commercial district and recruit members from gangs in the Bronx, Brooklyn or New Jersey. Also they recruit runaways at the New York Port Authority and outside "Under 21"—a church-operated organization that houses and feeds runaways.

To become a member of the Crazy Bishops, a boy must hand over $50 from robberies and allow a high-ranking gang officer to cut a one-inch gash in his arm. The initiation is different for the girls. To become a full-fledged Queen Bishop, a girl must sleep with several gang members.

"You got to prove you're hard," one gang member said, "They put you to the test when the godfather—the top man—cuts you."

The gang has an elaborate hierarchy. "Dice," 19, is the "pres," or top man, because he is older and shrewd. "Sinbad" is the war chancellor in charge of rip-offs and fights, and is said to be one of the most violent gang members. The group also has a vice president and an intelligence officer, who keeps track of treaties with rival gangs and arrest records for the Crazy Bishops.

"They aren't angels," said McNamee. "They usually don't carry guns. But they have makeshift weapons—sticks, belts with sharpened buckles or homemade blackjacks."

China admitted the gang carries chains and knives, but "stashes them" when the "heat is on." She said female gang members usually carry the weapons because they can't be searched by police officers.

"We do most of our stuff at night," China said. "We put a knife to a white boy's side and tell him to walk. When you get him to the park, you slice him up or beat the— out of him."

The Crazy Bishops are what the police call a horizontal gang because there are other divisions in other boroughs. Members of the Times Square Bishops—the third division—wear a rabbit's foot around their necks or a bandana around their legs for identification. There are no rumbles between Bishop divisions, but sometimes there are turf wars with rival gangs.

"When gang members 'fly their colors' (wear jackets with the gang's name emblazoned on the back), that usually means a turf war," Corbo said.

Recently the Crazy Homicides—a Coney Island deaf-mute gang—flew their colors in Bishop territory. About 60 Bishops and Homicides fought with chains in 42nd Street subway tunnels. The police, however, were tipped off in advance. They stopped the fighting and arrested nine Bishops.

Talk to Participants

Van Gilder's vivid story stands out because she went beyond official sources to those directly involved in the event, the gang members themselves.

The reporter covering a flood will try to reach those on the scene, someone who saw the water's surge carry off the bridge. If not, the reporter will settle for quotes from someone who can attest to the storm's fury.

The reporter covering a fatal accident will try to talk to a passenger or the driver, if the accident is worth a detailed story. If not, the reporter will try to reconstruct the event from the investigating officers' written report.

A bank robbery story will be given the detail and color necessary through interviews with bank employees and customers who were in the bank at the time. The teller who was held up will be interviewed in detail.

We have sketched out the three basic sources of information for news stories:

1. Direct observation.
2. Human sources. People who have witnessed the event; authorities and experts who know about the subject, and people who are involved in the event.
3. Reports, documents, reference material. This includes minutes of meetings; tape recordings; court, police and legislative records; budgets; tax records.

Three Basic Sources of Information

Know It All. Biking and ballet . . . Shakespeare and surfing . . . politics and pottery. . . . The journalist is expected to know something about everything. The journalist may be sent out to cover a political rally one day and to interview a famous ballerina the next. Wide-ranging reading and a variety of experience help the journalist to build the knowledge and information necessary to write accurate and informative stories.

Most stories combine all three types of sources. Lernoux used her observations from her trip into the bowels of the Bolivian mine. She collected detailed material about the production of these mines, the salaries of miners, the profits of the mining companies from records and documents. Finally, she gathered information from interviews with engineers, mining officials and others connected with the mines.

Mallowe rode the subways, talked to passengers, motormen, transit officials and read all the newspaper clips he could dig up about the subway system.

We should add a fourth ingredient here. It is not precisely a means of gathering news, but it is essential to the content of the news story. This is the background knowledge of the reporter, the information he or she has about the subject.

Background Is Essential

As an outdoors reporter, Klinkenberg knew about fishing. He was able to add to his story of the shark fisherman from his wide knowledge. He was also able to ask questions more intelligently, to understand some of the points Swint was making about the difficulties in landing a 500-pound shark from a bridge far over the water.

When a reporter is sent out on an unfamiliar story, he or she has to take a quick course in the nature of the event. The reporter sent to interview a country music singer will do some quick reading if all the reporter knows is rock or jazz. When the singer says he is true to the tradition of Jimmie Rodgers and that other singers are cashing in on the bland commercial sound introduced by the Nashville record producers, the reporter should know what the singer is talking about.

Reporters are expected to have a broad general knowledge as well as a lot of specific information. "A reporter has to know something about everything," says an editor of *The Charlotte Observer.* That's a tall order, but reporters do have to know a lot because, as the editor says, readers expect "a well-rounded story." By this, the editor means that readers expect to be told everything that is relevant to the event, even material that comes out of the reporter's own background knowledge.

Examine the Facts

During the border war between Iraq and Iran that began in 1980, a correspondent for the British news service Reuters was expelled by Iraqi authorities. In his account of the event, John Kifner of *The New York Times* wrote that an "official said it was because he had written 'lies about Iraq' in a story saying there was a shortage of gasoline in Basra and that the price of food was going up. The story was true."

Notice that last sentence. It is Kifner's own knowledge that is the basis of the information. Without it, the reader would not know that the Reuters correspondent had been expelled for telling the truth.

During a mayoral compaign, a reporter followed a candidate as he moved through the city to a tumultous welcome. Stated in this straightforward fashion, the story would indicate the candidate had a good chance to win. But the reporter, Deirdre Carmody of *The New York Times,* knew that crowds sometimes turn out for reasons other than to show their support for a candidate. ". . . crowd reaction is often hard to interpret in terms of potential votes," she wrote. "Some wild shows of enthusiasm often turn out to be for the benefit of television cameras instead of the candidate."

Then, to buttress the point that the size of street crowds can be misleading, she interviewed people in the crowd. She wrote in her story that several people who battled through the crowd to get the candidate's autograph "have admitted to newsmen later that they were not going to vote for him."

Rewriting Publicity and Press Releases

Press releases and publicity handouts, additional sources of news, flood the newsroom. Some basic reporting steps are taken before they are rewritten for the newspaper or station.

One of the first discoveries new journalists make is their sudden popularity. They are sought out and courted. Most of these new-found friends, it turns out, have something they want to see in print or hear on the 7 o'clock news. The friends call and write, and the organized ones among them have material sent by press agents and public relations firms.

Some of this material does make good news stories. These sources account for as much as half the news in some newspapers. They supply information about the fresh air fund drive that is soliciting money to send needy youngsters to summer camp, and they tell the press when the governor will be in town to speak.

The proud mother calls in to tell the social news or lifestyle reporter about her daughter's marriage, and the bank's information officer announces the hiring of an executive assistant to the president. The local college sends out a press release about an award given to a professor of chemistry.

Whatever the source, however perfect the material may seem, the reporter always checks before writing a news story. Nothing is accepted at face value. The first check is with the newspaper files. The governor might be making his first visit locally since elected; the press release did not mention that. The professor of chemistry may have recently been denied tenure; the college press office neglected to mention that. And the proud mother may have forgotten to tell the newspaper her daughter is a former Miss California in the Miss America contest.

The short item in the *Boston Herald American* read:

Avoiding Errors

The Civic Symphony Orchestra of Boston, Max Hobart, conductor, will present the Beethoven Piano Concerto No. 4 with Stephanie Brown, soloist, in Jordan Hall, tomorrow night at 8:30. There'll also be an exhibition of pictures by Moussorgsky.

To many readers of the newspaper, the item was hilarious. Those who knew classical music realized that the reporter did not. Moussorgsky is a Russian composer who wrote a piece called "Pictures at an Exhibition." It was to be played along with the piano concerto.

To an editor of *The New York Times*, the mistakes he had been seeing in the newspaper were far from funny. "Inexcusable," he wrote in a staff memo that also pointed out:

```
    National Organization of Women. (It's not "of" but
"for.")
    Proctor & Gamble. (It is Procter.)
    Roosevelt Hotel at 45th Street and Park Avenue.
     (The hotel is at 45th Street and Madison Avenue.)
    The state's four largest cities--New York, Rochester,
Syracuse and Buffalo. (Yonkers replaced Syracuse years
ago.)
```

A news writer whose wide range of knowledge included all kinds of music would not have made the error committed by the writer for the *Boston Herald American*. No one is expected to know every detail of every subject. But editors do expect their writers and copy editors to consult the appropriate references. The errors in the *Herald American* and the *Times* were unnecessary because a quick check of reference works would have caught them.

A good dictionary usually includes a list of biographical names, and Moussorgsky's is among them. News clippings would have shown the *Times* news writers their mistakes before their copy saw print. The facts, said the *Times* editor, were "readily available."

Before we examine in detail the reference works with which every journalist should be familiar, let's see what reporters are expected to know.

A Reporter's Range of Knowledge
Know the Beat

A reporter should know **how things work on his or her beat.** The police reporter knows the chain of command in the police department, why police officers sometimes throw the book at offenders and how juveniles are used by drug pushers to avoid felony arrests. The courthouse reporter knows the wheelers and dealers among the courthouse lawyers, the process from arraignment to trial, what plea bargaining is and why damage suits are settled out of court so often.

The Education Beat Let's look at what an education reporter needs to know in order to cover his or her beat properly. The reporter must know how a school system is organized and how it is financed, how the board sets the property tax. The reporter understands the politics of setting the property tax. Property owners want good schools for their children, but they resist increasing taxes. The educators usually want smaller classes, more visual aids, larger athletic programs, a school band, a bigger library. All of this costs money, which is raised through taxes.

The board is usually caught in the middle. It is responsive to property owners since many board members are property owners themselves and often represent interests in the community with a concern for lower taxes. At the same time the board is also responsive to the educators.

In addition to knowing the system, the reporter keeps up with current affairs through visits to the classroom and by constant reading. The education reporter knows that public education is being attacked for failing to educate large numbers of youngsters. Through reading several magazine articles about educational problems, the reporter has established several guidelines for judging schools. She has them listed in a notebook so that on visits to schools her observations can be judged according to these guidelines.

Strong principal

Disciplined atmosphere

High expectations for students

Homework

Individual attention to students

Emphasis on basic skills

Systematic evaluation of pupil and teacher performance

In the Classroom. The education reporter keeps up with events by frequent visits to classrooms and by reading about current topics in education. The beat reporter understands the need for background knowledge that will keep him or her in touch with the latest developments.

Knowledge of the beat, says an editor at the Long Island, N.Y., newspaper *Newsday,* helps the reporter ask questions. It is the answers to these questions that make it possible to write a complete story. The education reporter on visits to schools will base questions on the guidelines.

"Too many reporters don't ask enough questions," says *Newsday* editor Stuart Dim. "Reporters have to be like vacuum cleaners. They must suck up everything in sight—facts, colorful material, quotes, scenery." But to be able to ask questions that get to the real story, reporters must know the beat, he says.

City Boy on the Farm Beat Editors want a reporter who can go out on a beat and take hold quickly. They do not have time to wait until the reporter learns at his or her pace. A veteran reporter recalls the problem he had the first time he went out on a beat. A city boy, he was assigned by his newspaper in the southwest to cover agriculture. His first days on the job coincided with the county fair. The editor told him to do a story on the agricultural exhibits and judging.

The reporter took careful notes of his editor's instructions and drove out to the fairgrounds. He located the exhibit area and looked at his instructions. He deciphered his handwriting carefully, but the best he could make out of one key word was "barrows." He had no idea what that meant. Must be wheelbarrows, he thought, some new kind of mechanical device for the farm.

His search for wheelbarrows got him nowhere. He asked a farm equipment salesman what kind of machinery a "barrow" is.

"Must mean harrows," the salesman replied. So the reporter took copious notes about harrows, but he had no idea how he would work that into the story since the salesman said that there hadn't been any new developments with the cultivator in a few years.

The reporter drifted over to the barns to get the results of the livestock judging. An official handed him several slips of paper with the results. At the top of the first slip was a single word, *Barrows*.

The reporter tossed away all the notes he had taken about harrows and made a beeline for the youngster whose barrows had taken the blue ribbon. (A barrow, for city folks, is a castrated hog.)

Know the Community

The reporter should also know **how things work in the community.** The reporter should know about:

The political process—how the mayor and city council are elected; who appoints the police chief; whether the mayor or the council is the source of power; how the judicial system works.

The social setting—who the influential people in town are; how people get along with each other; the racial, religious and ethnic makeup of the community.

The economics of the city—how people make a living; the major employers; who the power brokers are; the relationship of business and politics.

Know the People

Experience is an invaluable teacher for the beginning reporter who wants to know the community. To achieve meaningful experience, the young journalist has to pull himself or herself out of the social setting and the age group in which he or she feels comfortable.

Journalism requires a knowledge of all people. To write about the elderly, it's not enough to consult some clippings and to read the latest report from the Commission on Aging. The best stories come from direct observation, as we have seen, and this means that the reporter must be able to talk to older people, watch them as they scrutinize the costs of chicken wings and baloney, walk with them as they carefully steer their way through dangerous streets.

To write about the problems of the poor and of minorities, the journalist must be able to talk to people of all races and classes without condescension or fear.

By being open with all kinds of people, journalists find people open up to them. When Christopher Scanlan and Mark Patinkin did their series on the blacks of Rhode Island, their willingness to listen was obvious to their sources, who felt at ease talking to them. This kind of reporter-source relationship leads to good stories, insights into the dreams and despairs of people. Here is one of the Scanlan-Patinkin interviews from *The Providence Journal-Bulletin* that helped the community understand some of its neighbors:

Voices: Willy Bradford on luck

"There are people who say the white man is screwing you." said Willy Bradford. "The thing is, you gotta go out there and drive. You can't keep saying they're doing me wrong. You gotta go out there and do it."

Bradford, 24, stands on the sidewalk in front of his apartment on Sayles Street in Woonsocket. He speaks of escape from his childhood ghetto.

"There's no doubt about it," he says. "If I'd stayed in Chester, Pa., I'd be dead or a junkie. I never would have had the drive I have now."

He didn't stay. Eleven years ago, when he was 13, his family left the Chester ghetto and came north to Rhode Island.

Here, they settled in Woonsocket. Here, in 1973, he graduated from high school and joined the National Guard. And here, hungry to succeed, he went hunting for a job. For weeks he hunted, for months. The hunt went nowhere.

"What was I doing?" he said. "I wasn't doing nothing. I was begging for a job."

It was that way for two years. Nothing came through, not a steady job, not a good one.

As he talked, two of his brothers were out of work and a third had just begun a temporary job as a federally-financed janitor.

Bradford was bitter, but did not give up, knocked on more doors than he can remember. In 1976, he showed up at a construction site in Woonsocket and said he wanted to go to work, wanted to learn, wanted to do anything. He was hired as an apprentice.

From his jeans pocket he pulls a small green book, a union book, the one he got when he joined the apprentice program two years ago. He speaks of what it means.

"It means security. That's the main thing. It means knowing you're going to have a job."

But last August, Willy Bradford was the only black in Local 5 of the Bricklayers Union. Some of his own brothers don't have jobs and the ones that do don't get $7.70 an hour.

"I got lucky," he said, grinning. "I know it."

Still, it is not enough. Again he speaks of escape, from Constitution Hill, the black section of Woonsocket. There's too much partying here, he said, too many people out of work, too much hustling.

Now, he wants to move to a nicer neighborhood, a nicer apartment.

Willy Bradford wants the good life.

Fun and Games. Young journalists must be able to move out of the familiar world of their age group and into that of their elders.

Adjusting to the World of the Reporter Moving from the people one knows best and is most comfortable with to those usually seen from a distance is difficult for the young journalist. The young have been segregated in our society. They live in a culture with interests and a language of its own, unlike the young of 50 years ago who were sent off to work at an early age to help support the family, usually married young and had families of their own to support in their early 20s.

Today's youngsters need to stay in school to prepare for more complicated work than their parents and grandparents performed. They move from home to classroom to hangouts, and their talk is of cars, sports and the opposite sex. Almost all their friends are the same age and have the same interests. Standards are set by these friends. Many of the young do work, but usually at part-time jobs.

Sociologists say that young men and women are cut off from adult society. Yet it is in adult society that the journalist must move, through city hall, the county courthouse, executive suites and into homes for the aged, hospitals and factories.

The adjustment is not difficult for most young journalists. When a person's living depends on wearing a tie and a suit to the job instead of an open-necked shirt and jeans, the informal wear is put into the closet for weekends. Young reporters soon learn to understand the dramatic story possibilities of a couple that depends on social security payments to keep themselves in food, pay the rent and have something left for a movie once a month. The outcome of a Saturday afternoon basketball game seems insignificant in comparison.

Press Law and History

Journalists also need to know press law, the history of the press and the special needs of their newspapers and stations. An understanding of the laws of libel and privacy helps reporters avoid troublesome legal suits and encourages them to be venturesome. (The law of the press is examined in Part 3.)

Understanding the history of the press opens the past to the journalist. Knowledge of those who helped to make the press a bastion of democracy gives the journalist courage when attacked, stamina when the routine approaches drudgery and inspiration when journalism is belittled. All these have been endured and overcome, the past tells us. Journalism has emerged as indispensable to a free society.

When Dan Rather was covering President Nixon for CBS television, the White House chief of staff accused him of inaccurate and biased reporting and tried to have him removed from the beat. His tough coverage of the president antagonized Nixon and his aides. Rather's home in Washington was broken into. The only material taken was his files. Many people were convinced the theft was engineered by the same "White House plumbers" who broke into Democratic headquarters in Watergate and eventually proved the undoing of the Nixon administration.

Rather did not buckle. He knew what a journalist is supposed to do, and he persevered in his job.

Rather was described by one television critic as "the only person whom the network news system of journalism has produced since Edward R. Murrow who can conceivably supply the conscience missing from television news."

Murrow's name is prominent in any broadcast journalist's hall of fame. As a radio and television reporter, he took broadcast journalism from the routine reporting of official activities to the task of digging behind the pronouncements. His tradition remains powerful in broadcast journalism.

The Perpetual Student

The reporter never stops learning. He or she is always replenishing the storehouse of knowledge so essential to the journalist.

"A good reporter is a student all his or her life," says Joseph Galloway Jr., a veteran foreign correspondent for the UPI. "Each new assignment demands a crash course in the theory and practice of yet another profession or system.

"From station house to courthouse, you have to find out what the official sitting in the chair knows, and you cannot recognize the truth from a position of blind ignorance."

Trying to accumulate knowledge of all kinds may seem to spread a person so thin he or she cannot learn much about a single subject, the subject that is the basis of the reporter's beat. It doesn't work that way. Information has a way of spreading, like ink on cloth. As the journalist finds out, often to his or her amazement, knowledge comes together.

There is also a practical side to the matter. The journalist never knows when he or she will be called on to handle a story far off the beat. Most news staffs are shorthanded. The police reporter often has to cover an arraignment in court, and the courthouse reporter may double as an education reporter now and then. This is the rule on small newspapers. On radio and television, only the networks have beat reporters assigned to a specialty. Most broadcast reporters cover fires, arrests, political speeches and city council meetings.

Current Events

The journalist also keeps up to date by knowing what is happening in the community, state, nation and the world.

Technology has brought the far corners of the world closer together. The people of the world now live in one neighborhood, and the journalist who knows what goes on next door is better able to serve those in his or her home. Reporters keep up by moving among all kinds of people and seeking out a diversity of experience. But experience is not enough. Journalists read—they read everything from novels, which are great teachers of writing, to geography and history, which help the reporter to understand the relationship of people, place and time.

"To be a good reporter, you must read," says Galloway, who worked his way up from a small daily in Texas to serve as UPI's bureau manager in Moscow after combat correspondence in Vietnam.

"If in this electronic era you are not accustomed to it, then you must train yourself to gulp down the printed word with the same thirst of someone who has covered the last 15 miles of Death Valley on his belly.

"Read for your life.

"Read every newspaper that comes under your eye for style, for content, for ideas, for pleasure. And the books, my God, the books. The world of modern publishing has a 500-year headstart on you and is pulling further ahead every year.

"Never mind your transcript or your resume. Let me see your bookshelves at home and your library card."

Newspapers and Magazines Reporters keep current by reading newspapers and magazines. They read their own newspaper every day, watch the network news regularly and try to scan the regional newspapers and national newspapers, such as *The Christian Science Monitor, The Wall Street Journal* and *The New York Times*. The *Journal* has some of the best writing in U.S. newspapers today.

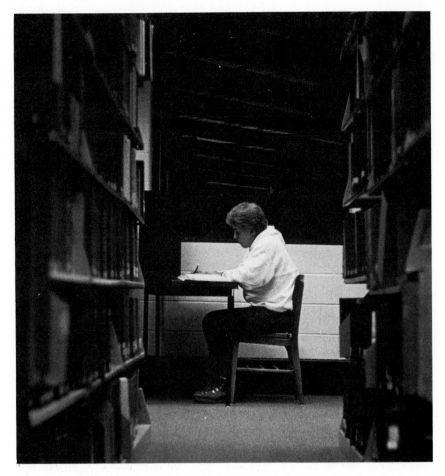

Food for the Mind.
Journalists are readers.
They devour the daily
newspaper, and they read a
weekly newsmagazine
without fail. They also read
plays and history, short
stories and politics. These
are the minerals and
vitamins of the mind.
Without constant reading,
the journalist is
intellectually malnourished.

The New York Times Sunday edition has a number of special sections
that can provide information and ideas for local reporters. Its book section
reviews the best new books, some of which journalists should consider reading.

Ideas and information also valuable to journalists can be found in magazines. A reporter for a New Mexico newspaper wrote a prize-winning series
of articles about drunk driving after reading an article in *The New Republic*
about the cost of alcoholism in this country. Another reporter obtained a major
local story after reading a magazine article about mining the ocean floor. His
reporting revealed that a large local mining industry would be affected if international agreements are worked out to permit large-scale underwater mining.

Keeping up also involves learning what the tangled events of the nation
and the world mean. This requires the journalist to seek out interpretative
columns in newspapers and in magazines of opinion. Among the magazines
that are read by journalists are *The Nation, The New Yorker, National Review, The New Republic, Commentary, Harper's* and *Atlantic Magazine.*

| Favorite Authors | Books are helpful in two ways. Nonfiction books can aid the reporter in the accumulation of background information. Fiction has been an inspiration to many news writers, teaching style and the use of dialogue and description. |

Favorite Authors

Books are helpful in two ways. Nonfiction books can aid the reporter in the accumulation of background information. Fiction has been an inspiration to many news writers, teaching style and the use of dialogue and description.

Some journalists find Ernest Hemingway a good model for their writing. As a young man, Hemingway was a reporter in Kansas City and the journalistic style can be seen in his fiction. The prose in his novels and short stories is cut to the bone. Hemingway was an avid reader. "Thank God for books," he wrote a friend. He most admired Mark Twain. Hemingway wrote:

"All modern American literature comes from one book by Mark Twain called Huckleberry Finn. . . . It's the best book we've had. All American writing comes from that. There was nothing before. There has been nothing as good since."

All writers have favorite authors. John McPhee of *The New Yorker* says he always reads Shakespeare with awe. There is nothing Shakespeare cannot do, he says. Dickens is a favorite of others who admire his feeling for the poor and defenseless, his powerful writing and his amazing output. Words tumbled from his pen.

A modern essayist many journalists respect is E. B. White, for years a writer for *The New Yorker.* Other American writers that journalists respect and learn from are: Eugene O'Neill, the playwright; John Steinbeck, William Faulkner and F. Scott Fitzgerald, novelists; and John O'Hara, short story writer and novelist. Among the current generation of writers, journalists have learned from Gay Talese, Tom Wolfe, Hunter S. Thompson and the fiction writers John Updike, Norman Mailer, J. D. Salinger and Saul Bellow.

Some news writers have learned how to pace their stories from the mysteries of Raymond Chandler and Dashiell Hammett.

Reference Works

Journalists may go through their lives without reading Hemingway, Mark Twain, *The Wall Street Journal* or *Harper's,* but they will be helpless without a mastery of basic references.

These references begin with the telephone directory and the dictionary. In cities where there is a city directory, this should be added to the list of essentials. The telephone directory is the authoritative reference for the spelling of names and for addresses and telephone numbers.

A number of good dictionaries are available, and some reporters carry a pocket size dictionary to take with them when they go on assignment out of town or have to send copy from outside the office. The dictionary is the authoritative source for correct spelling.

Editors may excuse a buried lead or a story that is disorganized. Even the best writers have their bad days. Editors accept this. But they snarl at misspellings. There is no excuse for an incorrectly spelled word. Worse, editors consider the reporter who consistently misspells to be lazy, too indolent to check the dictionary. The reporter who hasn't the energy to turn the pages of a dictionary doesn't belong on the news staff, editors have told poor spellers.

The city directory (fig. 4.1) is invaluable in checking information about individuals and businesses.

ALPHABETICAL DIRECTORY
WHITE PAGES

(h) HOUSEHOLDER   (r) RESIDENT OR ROOMER

Figure 4.1 City Directory. This basic reference can provide the news writer with a wide variety of information. Here is a sample page from a city directory published by R. L. Polk & Co.

correct full name ——— Landon Edw G & Charlotte D; servmn B F Goodrich h1215 Oak Dr

occupation and employer ——— Landon Fred M & Mary E; supvr Reliance Elec h60 Norman Av

complete street address including apartment number ——— Landon Kenneth A & Carol L; clk First Natl Bk h1400 E Main St Apt 14

student 18 years of age or older ——— Landon Kenneth A Jr studt r1400 E Main St Apt 14

Landon Virginia E r1641 W 4th St

Lane See Also Layne

cross reference of surnames ——— Lane Allen M & Joan M (Allen's Bakery) h1234 Grand Blvd

Lane Avenue Restaurant (Ernest G Long) 216 Lane Av

out-of-town resident employed in area ——— Lane James M & Betty B; brkmn Penn Central r Rt 1 Jefferson O

armed force member and branch of service ——— Lane Marvin L USA r1234 Grand Blvd

Lane Robt B & Margt E; retd h1402 N High St

Lane Walter M r1234 Grand Blvd

Layne See Also Lane

Layne Agnes E Mrs v-pres Layne Co h2325 Eureka Rd

wife's name and initial ——— Layne Albert M & Minnie B; slsmn Hoover Co h19 Bellows Av

corporation showing officers and nature of business ——— Layne Co Inc Thos E Layne Pres Mrs Agnes E Layne V-Pres Edw T Layne Sec-Treas bldg contrs 100 N High St

Layne Edw T & Diane E; sec-treas Layne Co h140 Oakwood Dr

Layne Ralph P & Gladys M; formn Layne Co h1687 Maple Dr

Layne Thos E & Agnes E; pres Layne Co h2325 Eureka Rd

suburban designation ——— Leach See Also Leech

retiree ——— Leach Wm E USMC r1209 Ravenscroft Rd (EF)

Lee Alf M & Celia J; retd h2106 Oakwood Dr

business partnership showing partners in parenthesis ——— Lee Bros (Louis J And Harry M Lee) plmbs 151 Abbott St

Lee Harry M & Karen L (Lee Bros) h2023 Stone Rd

husband and wife employed ——— Lee Louis J & Martha B (Lee Bros) h1616 Fulton

Lee Martha B Mrs ofc sec Lee Bros h1616 Fulton

Lee Minnie M Mrs h87 Eastview Dr

"r" resident or roomer ——— Lee Muriel E r810 LaForge St

"h" householders ——— Lee Sterling T & Nadine S; mtcemn Eastview Apts h202 Wilson St Apt 1

Lee Thos W & Effie M (Tom's Men's Wear) r Rt 23

owner of business showing name of business in parenthesis ———
bold type denotes paid listing ——— **LEE'S PHARMACY (Lee A Shaw) Prescriptions Carefully Compounded, Complete Line Of Toiletries And Cosmetics, Fountain Service, Greeting Cards, 1705 N High St (21505) Tel**

business firm showing name of owner in parenthesis ——— Leech See Also Leach

Leech Doris E tchr North High Sch h1323 W McLean St

Leech Joseph B & Lucy V; slsmn Metropolitan Dept Store h824 Wilson St

Leech Joseph B Jr studt r824 Wilson St

unmarried and unemployed resident ——— Leech Marcia M clk Community Hosp r1323 W McLean St

more than one adult in household ——— Lewis Anne M Mrs clk County Hwy Dept h914 Wilson Av

Lewis Ernest W studt r914 Wilson Av

Lewis Harold G & Anne M; mgr Cooper Paint Store h914 Wilson Av

Lewis Robt B lab County Hwy Dept r1410 Union Hwy Rt 2

church showing name of pastor ——— Lewistown Methodist Church Rev John R Allen Pastor 515 Maple Valley Rd

Know How to Use
City directory
Bartlett's Familiar Quotations
Reader's Guide to Periodical Literature
New York Times Index
Who's Who in America
Dictionary of American Biography
Current Biography

Every reporter should own the following:

Dictionary
World almanac
Grammar book
Atlas and road maps

The reporter also should have a copy of the newspaper or station style-book, a guide to consistent usage in spelling, punctuation and grammar. (A stylebook is included in Appendix B. Use it.)

Stories often require more detailed checking than newspaper clips contain. The reporter who wrote the series on drunk driving wanted to check what other work had been done on the subject.

First, he looked at *The New York Times Index,* a guide to all stories that have appeared in the *Times.* The index contains a brief description of the story and the date, which is used to consult the microfilms of the daily and Sunday editions of the newspaper. Many newspapers subscribe to the index and have the microfilms. This reporter's newspaper did not, so he used the material at the public library.

He also wanted to know whether any magazines had carried articles about the subject. He consulted the *Reader's Guide to Periodical Literature.* It contains summaries of articles from all the major magazines. Knowing the date the article appeared, the reporter can usually obtain the original article from the library. If it is not available, magazine publishers will send copies of their magazines for a small fee.

Avoiding Bloopers Some of the most embarrassing boners have been produced by writers who thought they were quoting a famous author correctly. For a front page picture about the return of spring weather to Chicago, a newspaper ran some lines of poetry. It attributed the lines to Shakespeare. They were actually from a poem by Elizabeth Barrett Browning. The writer would have been saved ever-lasting humiliation had he or she consulted *Bartlett's Familiar Quotations.*

For background on living Americans, *Who's Who in America* or *Current Biography* are indispensable. The *Dictionary of American Biography* contains biographical sketches of people of prominence who have died.

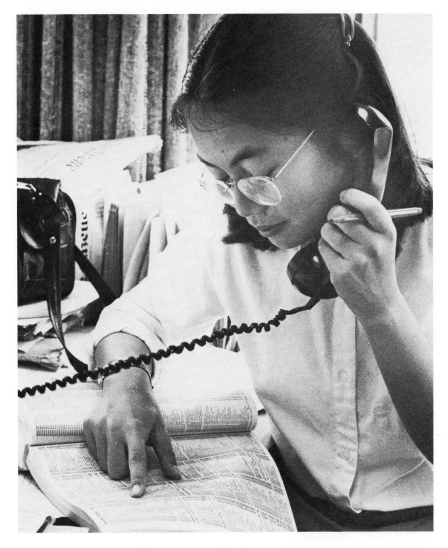

Check and Double-check. As she calls a source, Jan Wong of *The Gazette* verifies the spelling of his name. Though new to her job, Wong quickly made a reputation for herself as a careful, accurate reporter.

Sometimes an assignment is so complicated or so unfamiliar to a reporter that he or she hardly knows where to begin. The clips on the subject prove to be too sketchy, and the references presume some knowledge of the subject. The reporter needs a crash course in the topic, but the assignment is due and there is no time for in-depth research.

This is what happened to Jan Wong on her second day as the marine news reporter for *The Gazette* in Montreal. She had been told to do the piece quickly because she would have another assignment the next day. She was literally at sea.

Wong did what reporters do in such circumstances. She turned to people who know what is going on, authoritative sources.

"I must have called 20 people," she says. "I called everyone I could find in the marine directory. People were very helpful, but I felt I was drowning."

When All Else Fails

The people she called were patient. Gradually, she learned enough from the sources to make sense of the clippings and to take advantage of other resource material in the newspaper library.

"I learned an awful lot in that one day about sources, phone books, the library and clippings," she says.

"I worked at the story until I was sure I had it right, and when I submitted it to the editor, he looked it over and approved it with minor changes."

"The very next day, I had to write a story about the acquisition of Canada's largest shipyard by Canada's largest petroleum company. That was just as hard as the previous day's story. I had no idea what was involved.

"But again, a million calls and reading the clips saved me. The story made the front page of the business section."

Wong has become more confident since her initial learning period, which all new reporters go through. She is a bit embarrassed by the questions she had to ask in her first days on the job though.

"I'm sure my sources thought I was asking dumb questions," she says.

For a reporter gathering information and background for a story, there are no dumb questions, and sources who have an interest in seeing that the stories about themselves and their concerns are reported accurately know this. They do, however, expect the reporter to learn the beat after a while.

Wong has done just that, and her stories are given major play in her newspaper.

Purposeful Writing

Journalism is writing with a purpose. The news writer tells the reader, listener or viewer something definite, something specific.

In the stories that have been reprinted in this text, every one was written with a specific news point in mind:

A fire killed 23 people.

Chester Jefferds should be released.

Many Chinese are fleeing a possible earthquake.

President Reagan signed a tax bill.

Obviously, each news writer had a particular news point in mind as he or she wrote the story. How did the writer get the idea? Did it suddenly occur to the writer in a burst of inspiration?

The answer may be surprising. It is the key to good news writing. We will watch some reporters at work to find the answer.

5

How Reporters Work

Looking Ahead

Reporters develop an idea or framework for their stories before they do the reporting. This initial idea guides their observations and determines the questions they ask their sources.

If a reporter's observations or the statements of sources point in a different direction, the reporter adopts a new idea for the story. Reporters follow the facts.

When the idea or framework is supported by facts, it becomes the lead of the story and the supporting facts become the body of the story.

Give Direction to Your Reporting

Fred Zimmerman knew that he had a good story for his college newspaper. A teacher at nearby Emporia State College had been summarily fired. The teacher was young, bearded and had unconventional political and social ideas.

"I raced all over Emporia, interviewed everybody I could think of," Zimmerman recalls. "I filled two notebooks."

"Then I sat down at a typewriter—where I found I didn't have the foggiest notion of what I wanted my story to look like."

Early in his newspaper career, Zimmerman learned about the reporting process that underlies news writing. He discovered that reporters begin to visualize their stories as soon as they are given an assignment, even before they begin their reporting. They are able to develop ideas for their stories from the nature of their assignments and from general knowledge. By the time a reporter sits down to write, he or she usually has a lead and most of the important themes for the story firmly in mind.

After his experience at the University of Kansas, Zimmerman went on to an extensive reporting career with *The Wall Street Journal,* which included covering the White House.

As a reporter, Zimmerman always had an idea or two in mind when he went out on a story. His ideas were developed from his familiarity with the beat and with the Washington political scene. A check of the clips and other background material refined his ideas.

These initial ideas would give Zimmerman a framework from which to make his observations and to ask questions of his sources. If his observations or the answers to his questions indicated he was on the wrong track, he would ditch his original idea for one that better suited his findings.

The reporter who is assigned to interview a local banker about the steep rise in interest rates may banter with the banker about the weather for a few minutes. But the reporter knows exactly what he is there to find out: How has this increase affected local home building? Can people afford to build when they have to borrow at record-high interest rates?

The reporter who has been told to find out the reaction of university officials to a bare-bones budget just adopted by the state legislature knows what the focus of his story will be: What cuts will have to be made by the university? Will courses or programs have to be eliminated?

The reporting process is much like any other investigative process, whether it is conducted by a detective, a nuclear physicist or an astronomer. First, the investigator develops a theory. The investigator's observations will then either support the theory or not. If it is not supported by the facts, the investigator develops a new theory.

In his classic, *The Hound of the Baskervilles,* Arthur Conan Doyle described Sherlock Holmes sitting in seclusion in his Baker Street residence after learning of the murder of Sir Charles Baskerville. Holmes "weighed every particle of evidence, constructed alternative theories, balanced one against the other, and made up his mind as to which points were essential and which immaterial." Holmes needed a starting point for his inquiry, long before he visited the scene of the murder.

Unlike the master detective, the reporter cannot spend hours in seclusion mulling over particles of evidence. The reporter usually has only minutes to prepare. Remarkable as it may seem, reporters develop the ability to generate useful ideas under pressure.

The Sheriff Was a Criminal

Linda Kramer had done a number of spot news stories for the AP about Sheriff Richard Hongisto, who had an unusual approach to law enforcement. Now, she wanted to do a profile of the man who had once gone to jail on a contempt of court charge and was now in charge of the county jail in San Francisco.

Kramer said she first took time to "read years of clips on his doings and to interview people about him." She began to develop an idea for her story that crystallized when she spent a day walking around the county jail with him.

"His rapport with inmates and his pride in jail improvements showed the man in his element," she says. On her tour of the jail, she picked up quotes from the inmates and she made observations that buttressed the idea she had developed for her story of a new-style sheriff who was friendly with inmates and nontraditional in his approach to his work.

When she was ready to write, she knew how she wanted to begin her piece. She chose an illustration from her tour of the county jail that revealed his easygoing relationship with the men behind bars:

SAN FRANCISCO (AP)—At a desk, he checks the .38-caliber revolver he wears in a holster at the waist of his dapper, pin-striped suit and enters the county prison for an inspection tour.

"Hey, sheriff," an inmate sings out, "we hear you was in jail."

"Yeah," sheriff Richard Hongisto replies, "you mind being seen with a criminal?"

Laughing, he saunters past. The inmate looks after him, admiringly. "He's different than most sheriffs," he says. "Sometimes I doubt if he's a sheriff at all."

Others have been similarly bemused since Hongisto, a former city cop, took office in 1971 and began shaking up traditional notions of how sheriffs should act.

Establishing the Framework

Look again at how Berkley Hudson handled his story. When Chester Jefferds told Hudson about his lengthy confinement, Hudson developed an idea for the article: Jefferds was held without reason.

Hudson's early reporting was directed at seeing whether this theme was accurate. His reporting substantiated his original idea and it became the backbone of his piece.

When Bob Rose of *The Blade* of Toledo, Ohio, was told to interview the former president of the American Cancer Society, he had a framework in mind. He would ask about the major kinds of cancer and their causes. When he arrived at the hotel at which the doctor was staying, he picked up a copy of the day's events at the hotel desk.

On the schedule was a room number for the R. J. Reynolds Tobacco Co. The company had rented a suite to instruct workers involved in a local advertising campaign. Rose quickly changed his plans. He decided to focus on lung cancer and cigarettes. Here is the story that emerged from his interviews:

2 Men Worlds Apart On Smoking

Both In Toledo
To Promote Cause

By BOB ROSE
Blade Staff Writer

Two men who have a deep interest in whether Americans smoke cigarettes were in downtown Toledo Tuesday morning.

They were a floor apart in the Commodore Perry Motor Inn, but they were a world apart in what they said.

One was the immediate past president of the American Cancer Society. The other was a representative of the R.J. Reynolds Tobacco Co.

In an interview on the second floor, Dr. Lasalle Leffall, Jr. talked about what a killer lung cancer is.

In a talk to 14 temporary workers one floor above Dr. Leffall, the R.J. Reynolds man talked about handing out free samples of his firm's products.

Dr. Leffall, who until last week was president of the American Cancer Society, was eager to talk, to warn people about the more than 100 types of cancer.

The Reynolds man was not so eager. "The media is an entity that we do not deal with," he told his group in the smoke-filled room.

Dr. Leffall told about what he does when he meets a smoker. "If someone asks me if I mind if they smoke, I say, 'Yes, I do.' In doing that, I emphasize

— Blade Photo
DR. LASALLE LEFFALL
Eager to warn of cancer

that they are doing something dangerous to my health and dangerous to their health."

The Reynolds man recommended a different routine in handing out cigarettes:

"Are you a smoker or a nonsmoker? Regular or menthol? Full flavor or lights? Longs or regular length?"

Dr. Leffall would not like the euphemism, "full flavor." He'd say "High tar and nicotine."

And he would recommend neither high nor low tar. "The American Cancer Society believes that there is no safe cigarette, but that if you must smoke, the lower tar cigarettes cause fewer changes in your system that lead to lung cancer."

Dr. Leffall said he hopes smokers will kick the habit at least on Thursday, the date of the society's annual "great American smokeout."

Not willing to fight such an effort, the R.J. Reynolds man told his people to take the day off.

Dr. Leffall, who is chairman of the surgery department at Howard University's college of medicine in Washington, D.C., said the biggest opposition to the anti-smoking drive is the person who continues to smoke in spite of all the evidence that it can be deadly.

"We're not winning the battle," he said. "We're making progress, but we're not winning the battle."

The R.J. Reynolds man, who declined to give his name, said he has no quarrel with the American Cancer Society.

"They have their job to do," he said. "And we have our job to do."

Rose sums up the process: "You know what you want to write and how you want to write it while you are doing the reporting." But whenever there is a hitch, be prepared to change plans.

The County Fair

When the Hamilton County Fair opened in Carthage, Ann Marie Laskiewicz of *The Cincinnati Post* had an idea for a story about the company that furnished the amusement rides. She had heard that the firm had been sued by people who claimed they were injured on the rides.

"I wanted to do a piece on how unsafe amusement rides are," she said. Then she started her reporting. She called a state agency that regulates portable amusement rides.

"I found out this company was one of the most safety conscious in the state and that they had never been cited for an infraction of the state's safety regulations." Her whole approach changed.

"The evidence suggested another view. Instead of the original story, I wrote a story that detailed the difficulties for owners in keeping rides safe and the regulations that make Ohio one of the strictest states in the eyes of owners of portable amusement rides."

Super Loop. A ride at the Hamilton County Fair suspends riders upside down 70 feet above the ground and reaches speeds of 48 miles an hour.

Here is a portion of Laskiewicz' story:

There's no room to cut corners in ride safety

By Ann 'Marie Laskiewicz
Post Staff Reporter

The Super-Loops amusement ride, 62,000 pounds of thrill machinery, started up with a sound that was a cross between a whoosh and a groan.

Run by an engine as powerful as 15 automobiles and guided by 4000 rubber wheels, the ride's green train and its passengers Thursday were soon hurling in a circle that gave them a bird's eye view of the Hamilton County Fairgrounds in Carthage.

Within seconds, they were skimming along at 48 mph. Seconds later, the ride performed well and came to an abrupt standstill, suspending the riders upside down 70 feet in the air.

The Super-Loops is one of 24 rides at the county fair that closes Sunday night.

MOST FAIRGOERS have no idea what it takes to move each week from fair to fair, keeping a ride like the Super-Loops or the bumper cars or the ferris wheel operating safely, said Geary Bates. Bates is partner in the Bates Brothers Amusement Co. of Wintersville, which is at the Hamilton County fair for the first time.

Bates is one of 50 companies in Ohio that operate portable amusement rides. With equipment worth $2 million, a payroll of $7000 a week and sizable bills for fuel and parts, Bates expects a profit of $10,000 at this fair. He is sharing the grounds with Dennis Kopcheck, an amusement rides owner from Little Washington, Pa.

Keeping their rides thrilling but safe is expensive. Nevertheless, the companies must spend money for safety because the Ohio Department of Agriculture enforces some rather strict safety regulations.

IN OHIO, portable amusement ride companies must pass a yearly inspection to renew their licenses. The state's fair inspectors turn up at the 704 fairs and carnivals in Ohio, where they spend from 30 minutes to an hour inspecting each ride nearly every time the operator sets up at a new carnival or fair. The department's 26 inspectors have the authority to shut down a ride if it isn't safe.

State laws also require the companies to have liability insurance. The Bates firm has insurance that would pay more than $1 million for each accident on the company's rides, Geary Bates said.

Ohio and Michigan have relatively stringent safety regulations for portable amusement rides, but 42 other states leave safety completely in the hands of owners.

Safety in the business is especially on the mind of state officials' this summer after an incident that occurred last month.

AT A CHURCH carnival July 6 in East Cleveland, two children were hurt when an arm and cables of a helicopter ride broke. Investigators blamed a 3-inch crack that had been invisible to safety inspectors. There was insufficient evidence to charge owner Carl Bayer with any recklessness, federal inspectors said. Two other rides owned by Bayer collided and killed one person in 1978 in Cleveland.

That was the last fatality on a portable ride in the state. But about 20 people each year suffer broken bones, concussions or other serious injuries on portable rides in Ohio.

The state does keep tabs on ride owners, said Fred Brown, chief of the state's fairs and

| Back in Hong Kong | When Neal Robbins was told that a large group of Chinese had arrived near Hong Kong by boat, his immediate reaction was that they, like thousands before them, had fled China for political reasons. This was his tentative theme. When he arrived at the cove and found someone he could interview in Mandarin, his first question was an attempt to corroborate his idea: |

"Did you leave China for political reasons?"

The answer was no, not for politics but from fear of an impending earthquake.

Because Robbins' original theme was not substantiated, he discarded it and worked on the theme that the source had given him. He revised the questions he intended to ask and asked the questions he needed to round out his story. His major questions were directed at gathering information about the departure of the Chinese because of their fear of an earthquake. He knew that this would be the lead.

By now, an important point should be clear. After it is substantiated, the idea or framework becomes the lead of the story, and the supporting evidence—the observations, quotes and research—makes up the body of the story. This is the reason we are spending so much time on this concept. An understanding of the process of news reporting makes writing the news story easier. All the professionals know this.

Remember: The idea or framework is always tentative or experimental. It is used to get the reporting moving. It is never used in the story unless the facts obtained in the reporting support the idea. The framework is only as strong as the beams and joints supplied by the reporting.

| Working on Spot News Stories | Breaking news stories might seem an exception to this approach. After all, the reporter never knows what to expect on such a story. The fact is that most spot news stories do fit a pattern, and if the reporter knows the pattern, it is much easier to report and write the story. You could call this pattern the necessities or essentials of the story. |

Look back at Lindy Washburn covering a fire for the AP. As soon as she heard that the fire in Bradley Beach was a big one, ideas came to mind and a framework developed. Her first question to the fire department dispatcher in Asbury Park was, "Any deaths?"

Washburn knew that a fire story usually centers on the number of dead and injured. There are other necessities or essentials of a fire story, and if we look at Washburn's questions we can see what these essentials are. She asked the dispatcher for the address of the building, what it was being used for, when the first alarm had been received. She wanted to know the cause of the fire and, what the building looked like. The answers to these questions would shape her story, Washburn knew.

The obituary writer also had a series of questions to ask because she also knew that the answers would be essential to her story: The name and identification of the deceased. Past accomplishments. Survivors. Funeral plans.

These essentials can be established for various types of stories. Part 4 lists the basic ingredients or necessities for more than 20 types of stories.

No one can predict what turns and twists a news event will take. When the obituary writer learned that a memorial scholarship fund would be set up for Rose Harriett Allen, that was an unexpected element and it became an important part of her story. The standard questions she asked did start her on the way, and the answers provided considerable material for her story.

At a city council meeting with six items on the agenda, the reporter checks off those he or she thinks will be the most important. Our friend the city hall reporter in the first chapter was prepared for the zoning board appeal by the department store and had looked at the clips and taken notes. Since he knew that this would be an important item, he interviewed people before the meeting began for background.

Be Prepared for Surprises

The reporter was also prepared for surprises. He was alert to the possible introduction of some unexpected item, some sudden development that would make the department store material secondary. To handle situations such as these—the spontaneous eruption of a news item—the reporter falls back on general knowledge and all-around competence.

The reporters and photographers accompanying President Reagan as he left the Hilton Hotel one afternoon were thrust suddenly into a totally unpredictable situation. In fact, one of the wire service photographers later said that he had the wrong lens on his camera for the kind of situation he unexpectedly faced.

The reporters, though surprised, did have a framework for such an event. Just as Lindy Washburn knew that for a fire story she had to include in her story certain essentials—number of dead and injured, location of fire and so on—the White House correspondents with President Reagan knew that the story of an assassination attempt had to be structured around one central fact: Was the president struck by any of the shots?

In fact, in their haste to answer that question, they were at first misled into presuming he was unhurt. Although three others were hit and sent sprawling into the street, the president continued into his car. The reporters jumped to the conclusion the shots had missed him. The truth was quickly put on the news wires when they learned that the president had been taken to a hospital emergency ward.

As soon as he was told that he would have to cover an announcement by the president of the local college about the school's athletic program, the reporter began to plan. He checked the newspaper library for clippings about the college, and he learned that the school had been trying to improve its intercollegiate athletic program. It had recently hired a basketball coach from a Big Ten team. Another clipping described the activities of a booster club that was trying to raise money for the football team.

Trouble on the Playing Field

The reporter covered the college as a beat, but he was not too well acquainted with the athletic program since the sports department handled that aspect of the campus. He knew he had to amass a lot of information in a short time, so he made a few telephone calls to people on the campus he considered good sources.

A psychology professor who had once served on the college athletic board told him that there had been talk among the players of special favors and even of under-the-table payments. Perhaps the president was going to comment on these rumors. The reporter called the college public relations office and asked the head of the office, an old friend, about his theory. He hit his friend with the key question at once.

"Tom, is the president going to talk about the rumors of payoffs to players today?"

Tom was too old a hand to become flustered, and he laughed.

"I won't confirm that," he replied. A pause. "But I won't deny it either."

This last comment indicated to the reporter that he was on the right track. When he arrived at the news conference, he was not surprised to see the college athletic director and two coaches with the president. Nor was he surprised to hear the president deny the allegations about under-the-table payments to athletes. He had expected that.

No wonder that when the reporter returned to the office, he was able to write quickly and to have a comprehensive story ready for the early edition in an hour. He had been prepared with background information, and he had a concept of what the event might be—the denial of wrongdoing.

It seems simple. It is not. One of the most difficult tasks for the reporter who covered the press conference was selecting what to use from the lengthy conference. The president had spoken, and so had the college athletic director and two coaches. The reporters asked questions. Thousands of words and at least a dozen ideas had swirled through the room, but the reporter was told to hold his story to about 350 to 400 words. The reporter used his judgment to select material that was relevant to his story.

Selective Judgment

Walter Lippmann, one of the great figures in American journalism, once observed that there are too many facts for the reporter to gather and that even if a reporter could gather them all, nobody would want to read all that. The nature of journalism, he said, is selective judgment.

News stories are capsuled reality. They can hold just so much—one, two, perhaps three major themes. The job of the journalist is to select the theme or themes that best describe and summarize the event. Since events are often disorganized and time is always short, the reporter seeks to get a jump, to have a headstart on fact gathering by developing an idea of the story as quickly as possible after receiving the assignment.

Then the task is to make the observations, ask the questions and do the background research that provides the details that make up the supporting or buttressing material that is placed in the body of the story.

The word *framework* has been used to describe the ideas reporters have when they begin their reporting. It is appropriate because these preconceptions are the possible scaffolding from which news writers hang the story's details. It is the details that make all stories unique. Every fire story is unlike every other fire story, and no two basketball games are alike. The details make them different. Only solid reporting will dig up the details that make stories unique.

Details Make the Difference

The following story came into the office of *Newsday* from one of its bureaus:

Keep Digging

```
     PLAINVIEW--A 12-YEAR-OLD NEWSBOY DIED
WEDNESDAY AFTER HE WAS STRUCK BY A CAR WHILE
DELIVERING PAPERS BY BICYCLE, POLICE REPORTED.
     PHILLIP GOLDSTEIN, OF 6 RAMSEY RD., LEFT
HIS HOME AT 5:48 AM AND RODE HIS BIKE TO OLD
COUNTRY ROAD, WHERE POLICE SAID HE CROSSED THE
PATH OF A CAR DRIVEN BY JOSEPH HAVRANCK, 53, OF
7 TIMON CT., HUNTINGTON. HAVRANCK, WHO WAS
UNHURT AND WAS NOT CHARGED IN THE INCIDENT,
TOLD POLICE HIS CAR SKIDDED ON WET PAVEMENT
WHEN HE ATTEMPTED TO STOP.
     THE GOLDSTEIN BOY WAS TAKEN TO CENTRAL
GENERAL HOSPITAL, IN PLAINVIEW, AND WAS LATER
TRANSFERRED TO NASSAU COUNTY MEDICAL CENTER,
EAST MEADOW, FOR SURGERY. HE WAS PRONOUNCED
DEAD AT 2:40 PM.
```

An editor at the newspaper sensed there was more to the story, and he asked a reporter to dig further. Here is the new story written by Jeff Sommer:

PLAINVIEW—By 9 AM Tuesday, doctors at Nassau County Medical Center told Gerald and Barbara Goldstein there was little chance that their 12½-year-old-son, Philip, injured in an auto accident, would live.

The Goldsteins thought of Philip's bar mitzvah—his ceremonial coming of age as a Jew—which was scheduled for tomorrow. And they thought of a close friend of Philip's who was to attend the bar mitzvah. The friend was confined to a Manhattan hospital, where he recently received a kidney transplant from his father.

"We decided immediately to donate his [Philip's] kidneys for transplants," Gerald Goldstein said yesterday, sitting in the sunlit yard of the family's Plainview home. "Philip was a very sensitive, compassionate boy. He was very concerned about his friend. We're sure he would've wanted it this way."

The seventh-grader, who hoped one day to attend Harvard Medical School and become a doctor, died Wednesday. And yesterday at Stony Brook University Hospital two young Suffolk residents who Philip never knew received his kidneys. Philip's parents say their son lives on, symbolically.

"I hope some day my wife and I will be able to break bread with these people," Goldstein, a Manhattan lawyer, said. "We have been told that they share our grief and we hope to be able to share their joy in this gift from our son."

The kidney recipients—Kathy Kuhl, 22, of 16 Reynolds St., Huntington Station, and Robert Tagliaferro, 23, of 15 Longacre Court, Port Jefferson—were in stable condition last night at the hospital, resting after their operations performed by a team of 30 medical personnel, headed by Dr. Felix Rapaport.

The recipients, who had been undergoing dialysis treatments because their own kidneys had failed, were chosen from among 60 people for whom the hospital is seeking kidneys, according to Winnie Mack, the hospital's transplant coordinator.

The tissues of Philip and of the recipients are so well matched that the chance the operations will be successful is more than 75 percent—"as good as a parent-to-child transplant," Rapaport said at 4 PM yesterday, nearly 16 hours after the operations began.

Eva Kuhl, Kathy's mother, said last night she hoped the transplant would allow her daughter "to be independent . . . She's been through hell . . . If it doesn't take, she won't be any further back than when she started." Kathy has been a diabetic since age 12. She is legally blind but she "is a fighter," Mrs. Kuhl said.

The Goldsteins said they are not bitter about the accident, which occurred on Old Country Road while Philip was delivering newspapers on his bicycle. No charges were brought in the accident. "He was such a good, bright boy," Goldstein said. "But now all we can do is hope something good comes of it."

Rabbi Louis Stein had expected to see Philip bar mitzvahed tomorrow at Temple Beth Elohim in Old Bethpage. Instead, the rabbi was to officiate at the boy's funeral at 10:30 this morning at Gutterman's Funeral Home, Westbury. Burial was to be private.

"He was sure a fine, all-around boy," Stein said last night. "He was active in our congregation, in his school band, in the local soccer league. He had friends throughout the community . . . His parents have made a very thoughtful gesture—by extending life for others while their child has lost his own."

Good Reporting = Good Writing

Why is the second account so much better than the first? Only one reason—better reporting. This is an important lesson that journalists learn and relearn. It is what editors mean when they tell their reporters: You don't write writing; you write reporting.

No matter how proficient a news writer may become at manipulating words, there is just so much even the most gifted news writer can do unless he or she has the material to work with.

Listen to the latest songs; watch the television talk shows; recall the last movie you saw. When the material is ordinary and run-of-the-mill, not even the most gifted performer can make it come alive. Not every piece REO Speedwagon records becomes a gold record, and Linda Ronstadt cannot turn a so-so tune into a hit. Some of Bette Midler's performances are flat. All of Johnny Carson's nimble wit cannot bring a dull guest to life. Even Burt Reynolds and Jane Fonda have appeared in some lemons they and their fans prefer to forget.

But given good material, the singer, rock group, talk show host, talented actor or actress can make you sit up and exclaim, "That's something." So can the news writer who makes perceptive observations and uses interesting quotes and relevant background.

On the Beat

The heart of news gathering for the newspaper is the beat. Reporters are placed at strategic locations where news usually develops, and these locations are designated as beats—the police station, the county courthouse, city hall, the federal courthouse. The reporters assigned to these locations are called beat reporters.

Some reporters have topical rather than geographical beats. While the police and the city hall reporters are confined most of their time to one location (a geographical beat), the education reporter moves over a wide territory and examines a variety of topics to cover this beat (a topical beat). The education reporter visits schools, looks in on community colleges, attends sessions of the various school boards and even goes to the state capital to cover legislative sessions that deal with educational matters.

Other topical beats include medicine, science, labor, agriculture, politics and the performing arts. Sports is usually considered a topical beat since the sports reporter usually handles a variety of sports events.

Because radio and television stations have fewer reporters, almost all stations make general assignment reporters of their staffers. Only the networks and the largest stations have beat reporters.

Know the Subject Matter

Beat reporters are expected to have a thorough knowledge of the subject matter of their beats. This enables them to work quickly and accurately, whatever the deadline pressure. Their knowledge of how things work on their beats also enables reporters to do **enterprise** stories. These are the stories that are dug up by the reporter on his or her initiative. The coverage of a crime is a spot news story; the enterprising reporter delves into statistics to find that most crimes are committed between 9 p.m. and 2 a.m. by males in their teens.

Persistence and good sources are essential. Persistence is necessary because news often has to be pried from reluctant sources, and good sources are essential because all news is not laid out in the open like a flea market for the reporter to shop around and to pick out what he or she wants.

Persistence Pays Off

Authorities have a way of shrugging off reporters, and those who accept the turndowns often miss good stories. When Jan Wong of *The Gazette* heard that Mariners House, a place for seamen to stay, had been secretly sold, she wanted to do a story. There were two sides to the story, but she was able to obtain only the official version.

She needed to know the whole story to explain why the sale was made in such secrecy that even some members of the board of directors had no idea what was happening. Not even those who were living there had been told, not until the sale had been completed.

Covering the Beat. Beat reporters do most of the reporting on newspapers. The police reporter handles motor vehicle accidents, usually from the police station. For a serious accident, the city editor may send the police reporter to the scene. The cultural affairs reporter covers news of entertainment and may review performances. The education reporter covers school board meetings, visits classrooms and walks school corridors. Sports reporters are usually called on to cover a variety of sports—basketball and baseball, track and football, soccer and swimming.

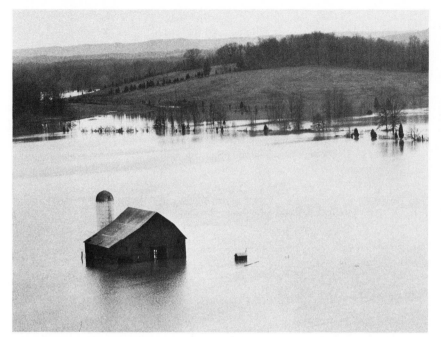

"I got yelled at and thrown out of the building when I tried to interview the manager," Wong says. "I was getting discouraged until that point, but that got me mad, and I regained my enthusiasm for the story.

"Every time someone tries to cover up something to keep it from me, I am even more determined to find it out, and I do."

"If you keep poking long enough, you'll find somebody willing to talk."

On another story, Wong had heard that there had been legal action in a dispute at a major Canadian port. But, she said, "nobody would talk to me about it." She wanted to see the legal documents for her story, but her sources were adamant. After many phone calls and as her deadline drew near, a lawyer finally called.

"He agreed to meet me in a bar and to hand over the court papers and explain the whole situation to me. With that, the whole story fell into place. The lesson: Never give up."

Develop Good Sources

Good sources are indispensable to a reporter covering a beat. A reporter cannot be everywhere on the beat. In the courthouse, where hundreds of transactions occur daily, the reporter who has good sources will be called by a lawyer who is about to file a request for an injunction. Or the court clerk will leave a call for the reporter to check with her about the injunction.

In city hall, when a developer files a plan for a large housing project with the planning office, a secretary may spot the reporter in the hall and beckon him into the office to show him the plans.

Five Keys to Covering the News Beat

Know how things work. Know the laws that guide those in charge, the regulations and rules and the processes that underlie the daily activities of the agency, department or unit.

Cultivate sources. Good sources are not always those in charge. Secretaries, elevator operators, clerks, deputies, telephone operators can provide valuable information.

Keep abreast. Know what is happening in the field you are covering by reading good newspapers and specialized journals.

Be persistent. Dig beneath the handout and the press release. Do not take "no comment" for an answer from public officials.

Anticipate developments. Follow developments on the beat closely so that you have a sense of what logically must follow the present situation.

A school principal will call the education reporter to invite the reporter to spend some time looking over a new reading program he intends to use in the fourth grade.

Sources are essential on every beat. When Dan Rather covered the White House for CBS News he said he survived the highly competitive race for news by relying on his personal sources.

"They didn't pass me notes in invisible ink, but I made it my business to know them—secretaries, chauffeurs, elevator operators and waiters," Rather says. "They see a lot of papers and overhear conversations."

"I take them to dinner and keep them in cigars or whatever turns them on."

Courtesy, a cheerful word or two and personal interest in people is often enough to make friends of potential sources. People on the fringes like to be thought to be close to those in power and to feel they are a part of important activities. They do this by feeding information to journalists.

Sources are also essential in background stories. Every reporter has friends who can be counted on to explain complexities of certain stories. When Marcia Chambers covered the criminal courts for *The New York Times,* she knew a few judges who could explain to her the fine points of the law, and when she moved on to cover education she developed sources on the school board who helped her penetrate the bureaucratic jungle she often encountered.

Chambers knew that although her readers were well informed, they needed guidance, and she often wrote background stories explaining why plea bargaining is essential to the judicial system and how administrative hiring policies caused severe strains within the educational system. For these and some of her spot news stories, she had the help of knowledgeable sources.

Beat reporters face two dangers in dealing with sources: writing for them and getting too close to them. Sometimes, a reporter will become too technical in writing on a specific topic. The sources will understand, but the average reader will be lost. Since reporters are in frequent contact with their sources and can only visualize their readers and listeners, the tendency often is to write for the sources.

A more insidious danger is becoming too close to sources, so close that the reporter may be soft on his or her friends. A reporter may not want to risk losing a good source by writing a tough story. A certain distance must always be maintained between the reporter and a source. Distance lends perspective.

Investigative Reporting

Once a reporter has shown that he or she understands the way organizations, agencies and branches of government work in the community, the reporter may be given the go-ahead to do investigative reporting.

Investigative reporters seek to uncover material that people want to hide. Some of the cover-ups are illegal, and some are legal but abusive. By abusive, we mean that the practices in some way hurt people or deny them their rights. *The Philadelphia Inquirer* was awarded a Pulitzer Prize in 1978 for uncovering abuses of power by the Philadelphia police department.

In recent years, investigative reporters have turned their attention to the affairs of private industry and organizations. In 1981, *The Charlotte Observer* won a Pulitzer Prize for meritorious public service for a series on the effects of unsafe and unsanitary conditions in southern textile mills. The series was titled "Brown Lung—a Case of Deadly Neglect." The previous year, the Gannett News Service won the prize for exposing the phony charitable activities of a Catholic order, the Pauline Fathers.

Investigative reporting is based on digging, the scrutiny of records, documents and files. To do this, these reporters have to know their way through the mazes of officialdom. They also rely on sources for tips and inside information. Good sources enabled two young reporters, Bob Woodward and Carl Bernstein, to explode the cover-up of Watergate for *The Washington Post*. These sources provided the reporters with enough information for them to reveal the fact that the so-called Watergate burglary was part of a plan by the Nixon administration to win reelection.

Although some reporters are assigned investigative reporting as a special beat, all reporters are expected to dig out information on their beats. The reporter who is content to accept handouts and press releases and who relies on the assertions of authorities without checking them fails to inform readers and listeners of the full dimension of his or her beat. Such a reporter can never hope to do investigative reporting.

Editors not only want reporters who can dig out the truth beneath a layer of public relations releases, they want reporters who can do interpretative reporting and writing.

Interpretative Stories

The reporter who knows his or her beat, who has good sources and who can put current events in context is often asked to write interpretative pieces. These articles, sometimes in the form of columns, sometimes called news analyses, give the **causes** and **consequences** of events.

For instance, a writer might try to show how a city ordinance came into existence—the groups that pushed for it, the organizations that opposed it and lost and the reasons for their positions. The writer will also describe the effect of the new ordinance.

The term **interpretative reporting** means that the writer seeks to find the meaning of the event. This is not editorial writing. Editorial writers tell readers or listeners that something is good or bad. That is, they make judgments. The interpretative news writer puts the event in its context.

By putting an event in context, we mean that the interpretative writer's job is to place the news event in the stream of cause and effect. An event that is isolated for a news story is plucked from a larger cycle or stream of related events. The interpretative story puts the news event into this cycle or stream.

A city council decision to allow a developer to build homes on a small tract near the city limits may affect traffic, school population and utility services in the area. The action can be shown to be the consequence of population pressure, people in the inner city wanting to move out of decaying homes into newer houses. The reporter will show this to be an increasingly common occurrence in the area and throughout the United States—the loss of farm land to urban sprawl.

Aids and Impediments to Reporting

In our discussion of reporting we have stressed the logical, thoughtful approach to reporting. We have talked about reporters adopting tentative ideas, then going out on the story to find supporting material. If the material is not there, the reporter adopts another idea. This approach is useful for reporters because it helps them operate despite the huge array of facts they must contend with in a limited time.

All of this makes the reporter seem cool and detached, dispassionately jotting down data from his or her observations, a scientist tracking electrons. Most journalists don't work that way. Like everyone else, they have feelings, attitudes and personal values. No one is exempt from these emotions, prejudices and biases. Some are positive and can reinforce good journalism.

Moral Indignation

The persistent underlying sentiment of many investigative reporters is a sense of moral indignation. They want to make the world a better place to live, and they cannot abide the misuse and abuse of wealth and power that makes life painful and arduous for so many.

This sense of indignation leads reporters to see things differently. Not content with official statements, versions or excuses, reporters blessed—or afflicted—with moral indignation get things done. Look at what radio station WIND in Chicago did.

Accidents in big cities are frequent, so frequent they are not given much attention by the media. But this accident bothered the staff of the radio station. It involved a woman and her two children.

Their car had stalled on the Dan Ryan Expressway. The three waited almost two hours as thousands of cars passed, including several police cars. No one offered to help.

Finally, the mother and her 12-year-old son went to seek assistance. They left the other son, a paraplegic, behind in the car. But they never found help. As the older son watched from the car, his mother and brother were struck by an oncoming car and killed.

The deaths angered a staff member of WIND. The stories and editorials the station carried revealed the need for a communications system on the 125 miles of expressways around Chicago. During the campaign, people called in with horror stories of their own. One man said his son had been driving on the Eisenhower Expressway when his windshield was shot out by a passing motorist.

"The car swerved, banged into the median and threw the boy out of the car," the station quoted the father as saying. "He lay by the side of the damaged car for nearly an hour before help came."

The campaign by WIND won the Sigma Delta Chi Award for public service by a radio station in 1980.

Although emotional involvement can lead to good stories, some feelings and attitudes can distort observations and can blind the reporter to some kinds of stories.

As we have seen, news reporting and writing is the art of selection. Reporters choose what they want to observe, and then they select from those observations the elements they want to put into their stories. The reporter who believes that the poor bring about their own misery would not have recognized the story that Mary Ann Giordano did when she wrote about the plight of a family living in a tenement without heat or water.

The reporter who grew up in a home with liberal political views may be convinced that Republicans are well-to-do people whose philosophy is built on keeping taxes low so they can have more. The reporter may see all Republican candidates in this mold.

The reporter who was convinced as a college freshman that conservative values are the only valid political concepts may conclude that liberals—especially the kind found in the big cities—believe in a tax-and-spend theory of government that will bankrupt the nation.

If these reporters were assigned to cover politics, their stereotyped beliefs would produce slanted stories.

Unquestionably, many reporters do have strong political views, but they hold them in check. They realize that the complexities of life cannot be reduced to the simplistic absolutes of our young liberal and conservative. The good reporter understands that there are few black-and-white situations.

Personal Biases

The problem for some reporters is that they are often unaware of their biases, of the distorted pictures they carry around with them. We all grew up with images of those things and people we like and dislike, of ideas we find compatible and those we consider repulsive. Our parents, our church or synagogue, our friends, our schools, our favorite television programs—all these and more influence us to see the world in certain ways. Journalists have these pictures, too, and sometimes they can distort a journalist's perceptions.

Journalistc Bigotry

The National Press Club in Washington, whose members are some of the country's leading reporters, for 90 years refused to allow women reporters to join. It also closed its doors to blacks.

In 1943, I. F. Stone, a well-known journalist and a member of the press club, took a source, William H. Hastie, to lunch at the club. Hastie was one of the most prestigious judges on the federal bench.

When they arrived, there were few diners, but the waiters stood by without serving them. Judge Hastie sat for more than an hour without so much as a glass of water.

Although Stone knew that few dining places in Washington were open to blacks, he felt that the press club would not practice the then-pervasive segregation of blacks.

Failing to obtain service, they left and Stone decided to appeal to the board of the press club to change its racial policies. The board refused. Stone tried to obtain the signatures of 25 club members for a petition to change the club's bylaws. He could obtain only nine.

In anger, Stone resigned.

Ten years later, friends suggested that Stone let bygones be bygones and they urged him to reapply for membership. By then, the club had changed its policy, welcoming black members. But his colleagues would not forgive Stone. They turned him down.

In 1981, all was righted. At age 73, Stone was guest of honor in the press club building. He accepted a membership card, but he would not let his friends forget.

"This town was full of such cowards," Stone recalled. Their actions, he said, "are the crises of the future. There's a lesson to be drawn from them."

Useless Baggage

To the aspiring journalist, the lesson could be that no one, not even those whose credo calls for an open mind, compassion and a commitment to democratic values, is exempt from the prejudices of time and place.

To act on this lesson is difficult. First, it requires jettisoning the customs, beliefs and ideas that may go back to childhood: A parent's prejudice against Jews and Italians, a teacher's indifference to the slow learner, friends' hostility to blacks and Puerto Ricans, a church's intolerance of freethinkers.

One of the most difficult tasks young journalists face in freeing themselves from the weight of the past is establishing a proper attitude toward authority. The youngster is taught to respect and abide by authority—parents, teachers, experts. As children, we grew up doing what others told us to do.

Then there was the period of rebellion. If father is so smart, how come he can't meet his bills? If the politicians are so wise, why did they get us involved in the disaster in Vietnam? As for teachers, every high school and college student has a favorite tale that proves teachers are hopeless cases. As someone said, "Those who can, do. Those who can't, teach."

There is a middle road. The journalist must be skeptical of authority. An assertion is not necessarily true simply because someone in power or an expert said so. The journalist's task is to check statements, claims and declarations, no matter how authoritative the source.

Skepticism is not cynicism. It makes no sense to turn away from someone in authority merely because the person is an expert. An open mind, a broad outlook, association with all kinds of people and the realization that while people have much in common they are still individuals are all necessary to counter the pictures in our heads that can distort reality.

As we've said, journalism begins with the reporter looking at an event with an open mind, taking notes and then checking what he or she has seen or been told. We are now ready for the next step, the arrangement of this material into an accurate and interesting written account.

Part Three
Writing

6

Planning the Story

Planning precedes writing. The news writer decides before writing whether the story will be a straight news article or a feature, how long it will be, the kind of lead that will be used and the structure of the story.

Looking Ahead

The lead for the news story and the feature story contains the most important aspect of the event, and the body includes supporting facts. These supporting or buttressing facts are quotes, anecdotes, incidents and significant details. The lead is usually placed in the first paragraph of the straight news story. For the feature story a delayed lead usually is used. The lead can be placed in any of the first four paragraphs of the story.

The basic sentence structure for all news stories is S-V-O: the subject, followed closely by the verb and then the object of the verb.

The city editor of a California newspaper who was known for his nasty temper and quick judgments would stride through the newsroom like the captain of a man-of-war. Although he did not whip the poor devils under his command, he had steely eye and a rasping voice that made his victims squirm.

George was the last, or one of the last, of the old-fashioned city editors who believed that might made right.

One day during a midafternoon stroll after the final edition had been put to bed, he spotted a new reporter sitting at his desk and staring at the ceiling. The reporter had a piece of blank copy paper in his typewriter.

"What do you think you're doing," George snarled at the reporter.

"Thinking, George," the reporter answered.

"You're paid to write, not think," the city editor shot back.

"George, you can't write if you can't think," said the reporter, and he resumed his communion with the newsroom ceiling.

For the first time in the memory of the oldest reporter on the staff, George had no reply. His mouth opened, shut, and he walked back to his desk without a word. He sat down and stared out a window. George had come across something so true, so profound—for him—that he ceased his newsroom wanderings thereafter.

First Steps

The reporter knew what he was talking about. Clear thinking underlies clear news writing. The reporter must have a plan before he or she starts to write. To begin with, the reporter has to decide:

> Is this a feature or a straight news story?
>
> If a feature, what anecdote or illustration will best begin the story?
>
> If a straight news story, what is the major fact I have to put into the lead, and what are the secondary or less important facts?
>
> How entertaining or important is the event? How long should the story be?
>
> How do I structure the story? In other words, what goes where?

Some stories require considerable planning, while others seem to write themselves. With experience, the planning period becomes shorter. But for the beginner, it takes time to plan every story.

Feature or News Story?

A story takes its form from its purpose. If the purpose is to tell people quickly about an important event, then the reporter writes a spot news story. If the purpose is to entertain, the reporter writes a feature story. Each type of story has a different kind of lead and structure.

The news story wastes no time in getting to the point. The main element—the most important item—is in the lead. The feature story may begin leisurely and get to the point of the story after three or four paragraphs.

Let's imagine that you have been told about a fire that damaged a student hangout, the Pork Parlor, located near the campus. You are to write a story for class. You gather information from the fire department and the owner. Here is the story you write:

> A favorite student dining spot, the Pork Parlor, at 150 College Lane, was damaged today by a fire that started in the kitchen.
>
> The fire destroyed the kitchen and caused some damage in the dining area. Fire department officials said fat in a frying pan caught fire at around 6:30 a.m.
>
> The fire was under control in about 15 minutes, an official said. No one was hurt.
>
> Damage was estimated at $25,000. The owner, Steve Poulton, said insurance covered the loss. He said he plans to reopen in three weeks.

This is a straightforward news story. But suppose you also heard that one of the part-time employees, a college student, lost something valuable in the fire. A fire department official says he recalls her looking through some charred equipment in the kitchen. He thinks he heard her ask about a manuscript she had left there. You call Poulton and learn her name, Karen Yount.

You manage to reach her and she says that she had just finished a term paper for her English class and had put it with her books in a cabinet in a corner of the kitchen when she went to work. The paper was to be the basis of her grade in the course. She is an English major and needs the course credit to graduate. But now. . . . Her voice trails off.

Now what do you do? Do you still write a straight news story and add Karen's loss to the piece with this paragraph at the end:

> But Karen Yount, a college senior, has no insurance for her loss. Her term paper for an English class was destroyed by the fire. She had put it in the kitchen when she went to work this morning at the Pork Parlor.

That's not a bad ending to the story. But would it have made a better beginning? Should Karen's misfortune have been put into the lead of a straight news story? No, that would have been overplaying her loss, which obviously has less impact on the community than the damage to the restaurant.

On the other hand, the fire was not that serious. No one was hurt and $25,000 in damage is not large. Actually, as fires go it is an ordinary, routine fire. What makes it different from other fires is Yount's loss.

All this reasoning could lead you to conclude that the fire might make a better news-feature story than a straight news account. You call Yount and obtain more information, and you write:

> For three months, Karen Yount spent most of her evenings in the library and over a typewriter.
> A college senior, she was writing a term paper on the woman novelist George Eliot. It was to be the basis of her grade in the class and, she hoped, strong enough to impress the admissions committee at the University of Michigan, where she hopes to do graduate work.
> But her paper, and perhaps her grade and her hopes, went up in flames this morning.
> A fire in the kitchen of the Pork Parlor at 150 College Lane, where Yount works, destroyed the kitchen. Yount had put her term paper and books in a corner of the kitchen.
> The fire broke out at....

Most editors would prefer this account, a feature version of the story, to the straight news account.

Deciding whether the story should be a news or feature story is an exercise in judgment. The question for the reporter to decide is whether the event is significant or unusual. This takes us back to news determinants we discussed in chapter 3. In the case of the Pork Parlor fire, there was little impact on large numbers of people, and Yount's story was unusual. So on balance, the event is given a feature treatment. Had someone been hurt or killed in the fire or had it destroyed the restaurant, the story would be too serious to make into a feature.

Washing Up. A student organization has collected $450 for a Toys for Tots fund drive in a one-day car-washing operation on campus.

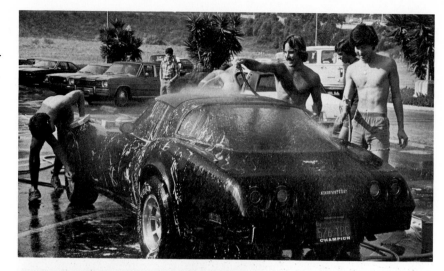

Rock Star. Rod Stewart is interviewed after a concert and discusses how his style has changed with the years.

Feature or Straight News Story?

Burnout. Two people were injured and their hiking gear and personal belongings were destroyed in this fire on the freeway.

Coming Event. Gordon Lightfoot's press agent gives you a photograph and information about the performer's local appearance next month.

Storm. A hurricane last night along the coast has caused $5 million in damage to homes and businesses.

Length

Before a story can be written, the writer has to know how long it will be. Just as a tailor cuts a suit or a coat to measure, so a news writer writes to measurements. On large newspapers, the city editor instructs the reporter on length after hearing the reporter's summary of the story. On smaller newspapers, the reporter must use his or her judgment.

Length is determined by importance and reader interest. An important story merits more space than a less important story. Obviously. But sometimes a story that interests readers and that is of little importance is given plenty of space.

Jan Wong usually writes a page one news story for the marine news section of *The Gazette* that is directed at commercial and business interests. But her feature story about an old salt who builds miniature ships in bottles was so interesting it was given the full page.

Here is how Wong began her story:

George McKee adjusts his spectacles and carefully eases a miniature clipper ship through the neck of an empty Dewar's whisky bottle.

"It takes a strong gale to push it in," he says with a wink and a trace of his native Irish brogue.

At 79, McKee is a retired seaman with 51 years of sailing under his belt. From "old salts" in the days of steampower when he was a youth on the "Australian run," McKee learned how to fill empty bottles with ships.

"When we got to Australia, we used to sell them for a bottle of beer," he says with a chuckle.

McKee still has the ruddy skin of a sailor—and the deep blue tattoos on his arms to prove it. Although he needs a hearing aid for each ear, his hands are steady. He holds them out for a visitor's scrutiny. "Not bad for an old man," he says proudly.

Nowadays, McKee spends long hours in his immaculate basement workshop, redolent with glue and paint fumes that exacerbate his emphysema.

Standards Vary There are no absolute guidelines for the length of a story. Some newspapers have a policy of keeping everything short in an attempt to have as many different items as possible, much like the half-hour newscast that includes as many as 20 news stories. A reporter on such a newspaper is conscious of brevity and generally will write short, crisp stories.

Most editors agree that brevity is dangerous when made absolute. In 1970, there were 10 million college graduates. In 1980, there were 15 million. In 1990, there will be 25 million. Educated readers will not settle for a skimming of the news.

"I'm damned tired of journalism seminars that say you can tell the second coming of Christ in 700 words," says Eugene L. Roberts, the executive editor of *The Philadelphia Inquirer*. "Our task as editors is to make our newspapers more meaningful and relevant and readable for our readers, and sometimes the best way to do that is short, and sometimes it is long."

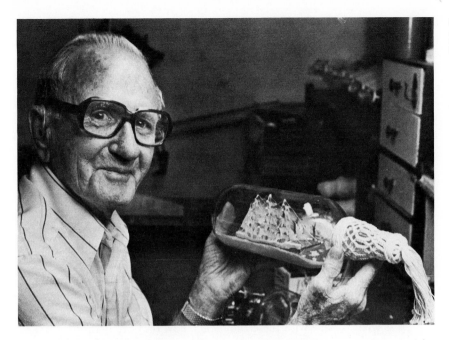

"Sometimes it is simple, and sometimes it is complex. Just like American society. Just like the cities and counties we live in. Just like life itself which, after all, is what we are supposed to be covering."

Roberts says that when the *Inquirer* ran 25,000 words on an accident to a nearby nuclear reactor, the readers were pleased. It ran 10 pages. "And it was probably as well read as anything we've ever printed," Roberts said.

After the reporter determines whether the story will be a feature or a straight news story and estimates the length of the story, the reporter can then plan the lead and the story structure.

Lead and Structure

If the story is to be a feature, the news writer can use a delayed lead, the kind of lead used in the second version of the Pork Parlor fire story. A delayed lead means that the writer holds off, or delays, telling the reader the theme. The theme in the featurized version of the fire—the actual lead to the story—is in the third and the fourth paragraphs of the feature version.

If the story is a straight news piece, as the first version was, then a direct lead is put on the piece. It moves directly to the point of the event in the first paragraph.

We will examine delayed and direct leads in greater detail in chapter 8. These are the only two types of leads you need to know.

The structure of the story also follows its intent or purpose. The feature story can move in a relaxed manner, allowing the reader or listener to savor the situation or the fun the writer is having with the subject.

But the straight news story is highly structured. Beginning with the direct lead, it moves methodically from point to point. If the news story has one major element, the lead contains that element and the body of the story is devoted to explaining, buttressing, elaborating that single element.

If the news story has one major element and some secondary material, the secondary material is put into the body as soon as the reporter has finished elaborating the major element:

Lead: Theme A
Body: More on theme A
Secondary material

We will read more about the structure of the story in chapter 7.

These essentials of the news writer's trade may seem rigid or mechanical. But every trade or profession has forms, outlines and directions that the craftsman or practitioner follows. A carpenter could not lay the floor, the roofer put on the shingles or the electrician lay out the wiring of a new house without strict attention to right angles, slope, voltage and the other essentials that underlie all construction. There are rudiments they all must follow.

It is what is done with these rudiments, how they are used, that makes an A-frame house so different from a ranch bungalow, the paintings of Vermeer differ from those of Rembrandt, and the music of the Stones unlike that of the Beatles.

Sometimes, a new form comes along that becomes the basis of a new line of creative expression. Bach, Beethoven and Wagner revolutionized classical music in their time, as did the Impressionists and Picasso in painting. Jazz, be-bop, rhythm and blues and rock were new forms of popular music. The delayed lead was this type of innovation for journalism.

The delayed lead was born of the need to tell unusual stories in an interesting manner. Because the direct lead was formal, it took the fun out of story telling. The delayed lead had to do battle against one of the oldest writing forms in journalism, the inverted pyramid.

Inverted Pyramid

For generations, beginners in journalism were told to structure all news stories in the form of an inverted pyramid. This meant that all the important material should be placed high up in the story, preferably in the lead, and the less important material inserted as the story moves on. This type of story can be diagrammed as shown in figure 6.1.

Five *W*'s and an *H*

In order to include as much information as possible in the lead, reporters were told to follow the rule of the "Five *W*'s and an *H*." All events—activities, speeches, interviews—could be reduced to this formula:

Who	Where
What	Why
When	How

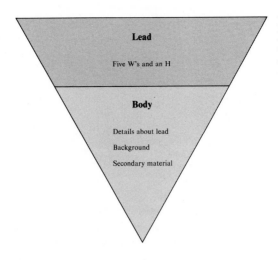

Figure 6.1 The inverted pyramid is an established and proven method, which can be used to organize nearly all news stories.

The formula works well enough, as we can see in these leads:

Gov. Bernard Carberry will be the featured speaker tomorrow at 7:30 p.m. in the Civic Auditorium for a discussion of "Crime and its Solutions" sponsored by several local organizations.

John Whitticomb, 22, of Hampton, a college senior, was seriously injured last night when the motorcycle he was driving struck a tree after he lost control of the vehicle on a section of Highway 28 that had recently been damaged by a washout.

There is so much information in these leads that they can just about stand alone as the entire story. For brief items, such as these, the Five *W*'s and an *H* works well. On longer or more complicated stories, the length of the lead repels rather than attracts readers. Few news writers rely on the Five *W*'s and an *H* anymore as the basis of the lead, but the questions are helpful in directing the new writer to the key elements in a story.

In analyzing a news event, you may want to list on a sheet of copy paper the six questions and then answer them with phrases or sentences taken from your notes. These answers should give you the important aspects of the story.

It's simpler, however, to remember our two basic news writing questions from chapter 3:

Who said or did what?
What happened?

The truth is that the Five *W*'s and an *H* and the inverted pyramid are survivors of a past necessity. When news stories that originated out of town were sent to the home office they were transmitted by telegraph, expensive and sometimes undependable. Reporters crammed as much information as possible into the first part of their stories, and that's often how the stories would appear in print.

In the newsroom, layout was at best a good guess. Stories were frequently too long for the space allocated, and extra type was removed by workers in the back shop. They were instructed to remove paragraphs from the bottom, where the less important material had been put. Hence, the inverted pyramid. Reporters put everything important high in their pieces, or they ran the risk of seeing the climax tossed into the lead pot.

Nowadays, the inverted pyramid survives for straight news stories, but for features it is ignored. Many features have a punch line or climax at the end. Editors make sure that there is ample space for these stories.

Even some news stories ignore the inverted pyramid. Pieces that take a delayed lead—and increasingly newspapers are putting delayed leads on news stories—violate the principle of the inverted pyramid. Occasionally, the writer of a news story will deliberately save the climax for the ending, as story tellers do. The story form is diagrammed in figure 6.2.

Box Structure

The spot news story, which almost always takes a direct lead, includes the lead in the first paragraph:

> A Bath County couple has filed a $200,000 suit in Rowan County Circuit Court against St. Claire Medical Center relating to the hospital's switching of their baby with a Morehead couple's son last year.
>
> —*Morehead* (Ky.) *News*

Summing Up

No news writer will want to play with a delayed lead in this kind of situation.

When the situation lends itself to a more relaxed approach, the lead can be placed anywhere in the first four paragraphs and still conform to our box structure, as Maryjean Wall did in the following story:

> When Helen Alexander shipped her Nijinsky colt to the Fasig-Tipton sales last week, she thought he might bring $300,000.

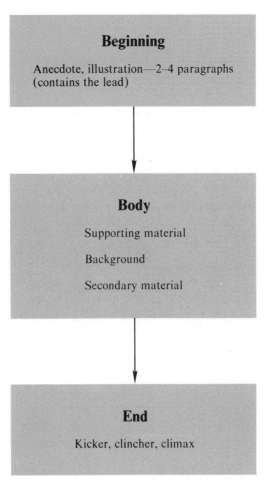

Figure 6.2 The box structure follows the style of storytellers, saving the kicker or climax for the end of the story.

He was a good-looking colt with a pedigree, and capable of selling for that kind of price. But she cautioned herself not to get her hopes too high. "I've always had this feeling," she said, "that thinking too big can put the jinx on a horse."

Lead   But when the colt brought $1.3 million last night in the closing session of the two-day auction, Alexander couldn't believe her good fortune.

"I'm in seventh heaven; I'm in another world," Alexander, the 29-year-old mistress of King Ranch, was saying after the colt shattered all yearling records for the Kentucky division of the sales company.

The British Bloodstock Agency-Ireland, representing English soccer pools magnate Robert Sangster and a Los Angeles lawyer, Daniel Schwartz, outbid a group of Arabs to get the colt.

"He really stood out in our opinion," said British bloodstock agent Tom Cooper, who signed the ticket for the agency. Cooper said the colt, who is out of the Cavan mare Fairness, will be sent to Ireland and put in training under the internationally renowned Vincent O'Brien.

—Lexington Herald-Leader

This news story would interest many people in Kentucky. Yet it has a feature lead. How does the writer know when to put the main theme in the first paragraph—making it a direct lead—and when to put the main idea in the third paragraph as Wall did—making it a delayed lead? Judgment.

The news writer learns that a spot news story of considerable impact or consequence almost always takes a direct news lead. A feature story and a news story of less significance can take a delayed lead.

Facts, Facts, Facts

The news story and feature are only as convincing as the supporting material the reporter includes. One way of describing both news stories and features is to say that each consists of a statement (the lead) and the proof (the body of the story). A summary of the most important fact or facts goes into the lead, and the rest of the story includes the material that supports and buttresses the lead and secondary themes.

A reporter who has decided on the lead and is ready to write will flip through his or her note pad and circle or check all the facts that pertain to the lead element. These additional facts provide the main stem of the story. If the reporter sticks to this plan, it will prevent the story from becoming disorganized or from losing focus.

This advice is important. Think about it. Ninety percent of the problems news writers have with their copy consist of either putting the wrong lead on stories or disorganization. By disorganization, we mean that the story does not move logically from fact to fact.

In looking through their notes for buttressing and supporting facts, news writers are on the prowl for two kinds of material—quotes and anecdotes or illustrations. They add zest to the story.

One of the best buttressing facts is the quote. It not only supports the lead with a statement by the main character or another involved in the event, but it puts the human element into the story.

Quotes help us to visualize the people involved. They add drama and excitement to a story. Look at this quotation from a worker recalling a sit-down strike during the period in the 1930s when labor was trying to win recognition for its unions:

> We were nervous and we didn't know we could do it. Those machines had kept going as long as we could remember. When we finally pulled the switch and there was some quiet, I finally remembered something . . . that I was a human being, that I could stop those machines, that I was *better* than those machines anytime.

After Jeff Klinkenberg had written his story about Old Hitler for *The St. Petersburg Times,* Roy Peter Clark of the Modern Media Institute talked to him about the story.

"Is it a general method of yours to organize your story around quotations you've collected?" Clark asked.

Klinkenberg replied: "Yes. One of the things I've done when I've had the time: I'll type them out, and then I'll assign different values to different quotes. My best quotes I'll try to get up high in the story and then proceed in kind of descending order.

"I'll try to save a couple of good ones for the end. I think it's a good way to organize a story."

In an interview with Howell Raines, who went from *The St. Petersburg Times* to the Washington bureau of *The New York Times,* Clark asked about Raines's use of quotations.

Raines answered: "In political profiles, quotes serve two purposes, I think: one, they are the blocks of fact that you deal with. I want to have the actual words spoken by the man so there is no dispute about what he said or meant. I don't paraphrase much. I try to use direct quotes or fragments of quotes rather than my own language. Because you cannot get around the authority of a quote.

"And, two, quotation establishes character. Quotes make a politician assume a personality in a story. One of the best political reporters I know is a good reporter in the sense of gathering information. But he writes without quotes, so his copy is dead."

When Klinkenberg was organizing his story, he did two things after he typed up his notes.

He underlined his "best quotes," he said, and he broke up the story "into anecdotes." In addition to looking for good quotes, then, reporters search their notes and their memories for the anecdotes and illustrations that also support the lead. These, like the quotes, are used to add life to the body of the story.

Show, Don't Tell

The anecdotes and illustrations that the news writer selects for his or her story are used to **show** the reader what the person has done or was thinking. They introduce drama to the story.

The technique is borrowed from writers of fiction who use dramatic incidents and situations to give their readers deeper insights into their characters than mere **telling** allows.

If you look back at the beginning of Klinkenberg's story about the shark fisherman you can see how Klinkenberg **shows** us his fisherman on the bridge. The story begins this way:

> Ron Swint moaned in the dark about the shark called Old Hitler, the largest shark in Tampa Bay, as traffic roared by on the Sky-way Bridge. Somebody in a car shouted and Swint automatically winced. . . .

The reader is thrust on the bridge with Swint, in the dark, in the middle of traffic, hearing Swint moan, seeing the traffic roar past.

Telling this would have led to something like this:

> Ron Swint is after the largest shark in Tampa Bay, Old Hitler, and he fishes from the Skyway Bridge in the dark, as traffic roars by.

That's not the worst lead that can be written, but it pales beside Klinkenberg's. **Showing** lets the reader see, feel, smell and even taste:

> The food at political picnics in Vadonia County starts with chowder, large bowls of it with the clams so thick you can hardly see the broth. Then there are the vegetables—green beans, long and slender; zucchini, sliced lengthwise and chopped and—take your pick—fried or boiled; corn, heaped in bowls, a large gob of butter slowly melting into the kernels; beets, red and succulent, sweet as candy. . . .

Simply **telling** the reader takes away the joy of feeling, tasting, smelling:

> The food at political picnics in Vadonia County is plentiful. There is clam chowder, various vegetables and several kinds of meat to choose from.

Might as well write menus for the fried chicken outfit down the street with a writing touch like that.

The next step in planning the story is deciding on a writing approach.

Writing Style

Write the way you talk. This has become an axiom in the newsroom. It is obviously useful to broadcast news writers, and it has become increasingly important in the writing style of the newspaper news writer.

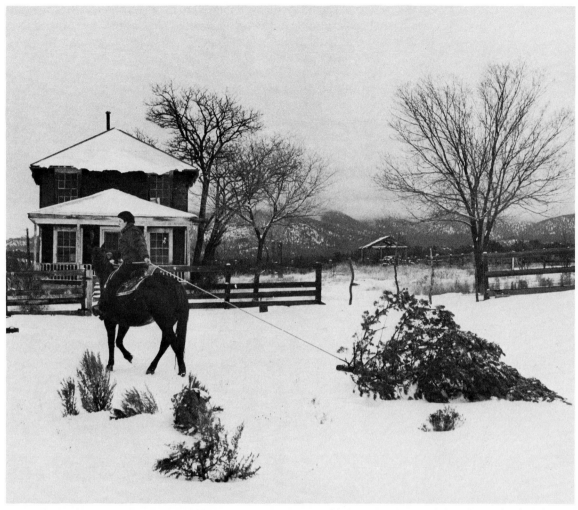

Ranch Christmas. A writer describing Christmas preparations on this New Mexico ranch lets the reader feel the snap in the air, hear the soft thud of the horse's hooves and smell the resiny, new cut sharpness of the fir as the Christmas tree is being brought home to a waiting family.

If you listen carefully to a conversation, a pattern of sentence structure will emerge. Most sentences begin with the name of a person or a thing, a noun:

> **Sam** asked me to help him wash his car.
> The **car** was a mess.
> **I** wasn't going to get roped into that.
> So **I** told him to forget it.
> **He** found someone else.

You can detect something else in these spoken sentences: Often the verb closely follows the name of the person or thing that begins the sentence:

The Wildcats **lost** a close one.
Hooper **blew** it in the last two minutes.
He **called** the wrong play.
I **think** they ought to fire him.
If he **loses** another one, that's curtains for him.
We **need** a new coach.

The third point to notice is that the verb is closely followed by the object when a transitive (action) verb is used.

We have described the basic structure of the sentence pattern most of us use in dialogue: Subject-verb-object.

S-V-O

The S-V-O pattern of some of the sentences in the first group is:

S—Sam	S—I	S—He
V—asked	V—told	V—found
O—me	O—him	O—someone

Look at the second set of sentences, which contain many action verbs. The S-V-O pattern is:

S—Wildcats	S—He	S—he
V—lost	V—called	V—loses
O—one	O—play	O—one
S—Hooper	S—I	S—We
V—blew	V—think	V—need
O—it	O—they	O—coach

Notice the positioning of the subjects and verbs in these spoken sentences. They are snug, the subjects close to the verbs. This kind of positioning makes the sentences clear. By keeping the verbs as close as possible to the subjects, the listener knows who or what is losing, blowing games, calling plays, or thinking. Clarity—which is the goal of good writing—is achieved this way.

The S-V-O sentence arrangement probably should be the way three-fourths of your sentences are written. Because a barrage of S-V-O sentences would be boring, they should be varied with an occasional sentence that has a different structure, such as the use of a clause or phrase to begin a sentence—as this sentence begins.

In planning the story, the news writer must be conscious of these three requirements:

Follow the S-V-O structure.

Use action verbs.

Keep the verb as close to the subject as possible.

Fit the Writing to the Story

In applying these requirements or principles of news writing, the news writer makes them fit the nature of the story. By this, writers mean that certain types of stories take certain writing styles. A presidential assassination attempt is a fast-breaking spot news story. It will take a short-sentence style, almost a rattle of short S-V-O sentences. An obituary of a long-time resident of the community will take a more solemn style, which means somewhat longer sentences.

Before writing, the news writer has to decide what kind of mood he or she wants to evoke in the reader or listener. If the mood is to be one of excitement, then the style and sentence structure follow that goal. If the mood is to be thoughtful, reflective, then the writing will be consistent—the sentences will be longer, the verbs will not be sharp or piercing.

The Active Voice

By staying with the S-V-O structure, the news writer will avoid a problem that seems to plague some writers. This is the use of the passive voice. By passive voice, we mean that the subject of the sentence is being acted upon. By active voice, we mean that the subject is the doer of the action. Here are some examples:

Passive: Your letter was received and read by me.

Active: I received and read your letter.

Passive: The car was seen speeding toward the spectators.

Active: The spectators saw the car speeding toward them.

Look at the passive voice sentences. They lack strength and emphasis. The words sit limply, passively. Active-voice sentences march across the page.

It's easy to avoid the passive voice; simply stay with the S-V-O structure. The problem is solved so long as the news writer thinks of the verb as an action verb. A more difficult habit to break and one that plagues beginners is the tendency to put opinion into stories.

How do these sentences differ?

No Opinions, Please

1. The city council last night gave city workers an undeserved wage increase of 15 percent.
2. The city council last night gave city workers a wage increase of only 15 percent.
3. The city council last night gave city workers a 15 percent wage increase.

If your answer is that sentences 1 and 2 express opinions you are correct. Neither belongs in a news story, unless attributed to a source. The writer cannot make these statements.

The opinion in the first sentence is obvious. The word *undeserved* clearly states that the news writer believes the workers should not have been given such an increase. Opinions of this sort belong in the editorial section of the newspaper.

The second sentence implies that the workers deserve more than the 15 percent increase granted to them: They received an increase of *only* 5 percent. The third sentence is acceptable because it states the fact without opinion.

Opinion is the writer's injection of his or her feelings about the subject. Usually, it is an expression that indicates the writer's approval or disapproval. Sentence 1 implies the writer's disapproval, as does the second sentence. A lead like the following expresses approval, which is common in sports copy when the reporter becomes a fan instead of an unbiased observer.

> The Spartans lost in overtime 58-53 last night to the
> LaGrange Wildcats, but the state champion visitors knew
> that they had met their match in the courageous Spartans.

At first glance, this may not seem to be opinion, and that's the trouble with opinions in copy. Nine times out of 10, the writer is unaware that they are there. Usually, opinions insinuate themselves into the story when the writer gets too close to the subject of the story. No question that the sports writer who wrote this lead was carried away by the home team's valiant effort.

Good advice for writers: Keep cool. This is especially sound advice for sports writers. They have no business rooting for any team. Unlike radio and television sports announcers who are hired by local teams, the sports reporter should be as nonpartisan as the political reporter.

Look at this sentence:

> The city council last night adopted a property tax
> increase of only $2 after rejecting a proposal for a $7
> hike.

Seems OK. It isn't. The word *only* sneaked in when the writer wasn't looking. The writer is saying that the increase was a small amount, "only $2." Small to whom? To the elderly couple living on social security who can barely make it now?

One more point about writing preparations. Since we are talking about little things, it's appropriate to point out here that it is the details, the little things, that give a news story its completeness.

"You have a hole in this story large enough for a truck to get through," the city editor says. The story states that a thief had knocked the night guard unconscious and had taken "several items from the construction site."

A pair of pliers, two lunch kits and a hammer? An air conditioning unit, a generator and three boxes of light fixtures?

No one will know because all the reporter has written is "several items." "Be specific," the editor tells the reporter. "Anticipate and answer all the reader's questions."

In planning the story the news writer makes sure that all holes are plugged, all vague statements made concrete, estimates made specific if possible. When the story lacks specifics and concrete detail, the reader feels cheated:

> The profile of a high school mile runner said he had been approached by a number of eastern colleges after running a fast mile in a state meet. But the story never gave the names of the colleges.

> The reporter wrote that the jury had deliberated "half the night before retiring." But how many hours is that, and what time did the jury retire?

Most of these problems are avoided by seeking details while reporting. When President Reagan was hospitalized following an assassination attempt, Helen Thomas, the White House correspondent for the UPI, dug for details. She even asked what color Jello the president had been served for lunch.

"I was only trying to get the details into my story that would make readers feel as though they were here," she said.

This chapter has made one major point. To write a complete and accurate story, the reporter must be organized in reporting and writing. This means thinking through just what he or she wants to say. Next, we will look at the 10 rudiments of every news story, from accuracy through verification.

7

Rudiments of the News Story

Just as the basketball player must abide by the rules of the game and the downtown businessman must conform to city regulations, so the news writer must adhere to a set of guidelines. These guidelines, also known as rudiments of the news story, are accuracy, attribution of statements, balance, brevity, clarity, human interest, proper identification of those named in the story, focus on the news point, objectivity and verification of information.

By following these guidelines, the news writer will write stories that are accurate, thorough, fair and readable.

For several days, the *Kansas City Times* had published a number of important stories on page one. The editor, Michael J. Davies, was pleased with his newspaper and the work of his staff. This is what first-class journalism is all about, he was thinking one day when he received a telephone call from the owner of a funeral home.

The caller said he wanted to talk about the accuracy of some of the obituaries appearing in the *Times*. He had some complaints to make.

"He wasn't shouting," Davies said. "He seemed resigned."

Davies first reaction was irritation. Didn't this man appreciate the great job the newspaper had been doing? However, Davies agreed to examine the obituaries and get back to the caller.

"I was shocked by what I unearthed," Davies said. "We checked every obit in the *Times* the next day."

"There was an error of some kind—spelling, fact, you name it—in many obits."

Davies took immediate action to guarantee greater accuracy.

"If we can't get obits right, how can we expect readers to believe our page one stories?" he said.

The list of the basic requirements for a news story begins with accuracy—words spelled correctly, the correct middle initial in names and the exact address of people in stories.

Accuracy

In their lectures on libel law, journalism instructors often reach into their bag of stories to find the one about the wrong initial. In one particular case, the courthouse reporter hastily wrote a *T* instead of an *F* when he was taking notes on a divorce action. In checking the telephone book later for the address of the divorcing couple, naturally he looked up the name under the initial *T*.

A couple of days after the story ran, the newspaper received notice from a lawyer for the nondivorcing couple. A libel suit was on the way.

The story brings forth the desired shudders among students, for a minute or two, and then they shrug it off as just another of those scare stories they have been hearing all semester.

Shrug away. These stories happen to be based on fact. Most libel suits begin with a little mistake, a foolish error, a lapse in accuracy. Some could have been avoided with a check of references and sources. Not this kind of error, though. After all, if the reporter has John T. Smith in his notes, why should he think it's wrong? We do verify many details, but everyone, including the reporter himself, presumes reporters can copy material accurately.

Thus, accuracy begins with the reporter's painstaking attention to every detail when gathering facts and information. Initials, spelling of names, correct addresses, exact quotes, the precise number of fire trucks that answered the alarm. Check and double-check.

When there is the slightest doubt, the reporter checks with the source or a reference. If in doubt about the spelling of a word, the reporter uses the dictionary. A misspelled word is a gross inaccuracy. If the reporter is not sure about the source of the idiom, "Out of the frying pan into the fire," *Bartlett's Familiar Quotations* can provide it. The exact number of deaths this year to date at the junction of highway 495 and interstate 95 can be found in the newspaper clips.

Should there be an error, the reporter writes a correction. No reporter likes this, but it is essential. For a long time, newspapers would not admit they made mistakes; they refused to run corrections. Now, almost every newspaper has a permanent place for corrections (first page of the second section in *The New York Times*) or will place them in the section or on the page where the error occurred.

Next time you are too rushed to double-check an initial or name or are too lazy to look up something in a reference work, remember this correction and the embarrassment it caused all concerned:

> Mai Thai Finn is one of the students in the program and was in the center of the photo. We incorrectly listed her as one of the items on the menu.

Mercifully, no mention will be made of the publication that committed this blunder.

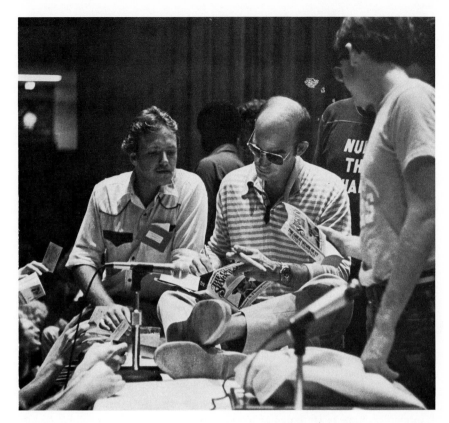

Accuracy. Reporters covering an autograph-signing session by *Rolling Stone* writer Hunter S. Thompson made sure to include his middle initial in their stories. Accuracy requires exactness.

All information and statements, except the most obvious, must be attributed to the source of the material:

Attribution

> The police reported two people were killed when. . . .
>
> Mayor Sam Walker today urged. . . .
>
> Childhood diseases are declining, the agency said. . . .
>
> "College grades are meaningless," Prof. Alvin Goodman told. . . .

However, no attribution is necessary for these assertions:

> July 4th falls on Tuesday.
>
> Lincoln was loved and hated in his day.
>
> The cost of living has steadily increased.

Notice the use of attribution in the following lead:

> Police said today they antici-
> pate major roads out of the city to
> be heavily traveled beginning Fri-
> day at midafternoon. The holiday
> weekend will run from Saturday
> through Monday.

The first statement is attributed. The second is stated as fact because it is obvious.

Actions are attributed to the person or group committing or performing them:

> Mayor George Albritton or-
> dered all city offices closed next
> Monday in memory of the city's
> first mayor, Richard Beatty, who
> died last week at 104 years of age.

> The state Republican Party yes-
> terday took the first steps toward
> holding its November state conven-
> tion. The party. . . .

Generally, when we speak of attribution, we refer to what is called "sourcing" a quote or statement. That is, reponsibility for the material is placed with the source. When there is no attribution, the reporter, newspaper or station is considered the source.

The reporter needs no attribution for events he or she has witnessed. In the unlikely case of reporter being on the scene at a bank robbery, he or she need not attribute to the police what he or she has seen.

Attribution to a source does not guarantee to the reader or viewer the truth of the statement. All it does is place responsibility for the assertion. When reporters doubts the accuracy or truth of a statement, they try to verify it.

In his interview with Jeff Klinkenberg, who wrote about the shark fisherman, Roy Peter Clark wondered about some of the angler's statements.

"I notice at various points in the story you are careful to attribute statements he had made about what he can do with the sharks once he has caught them. Fishermen are notorious BS artists. . . . Do you often encounter problems of credibility in the people you interview?"

Klinkenberg replied, "No, but in this instance, some of the stuff he was telling me was so remarkable I had to protect myself a little bit. Many of the things he told me I double-checked and found to be true. Things I couldn't check I went with an attribution. And there are quite a few in this story."

Attribution. When the reporter sees a volleyball game he or she can describe the event without attributing the action comments to a source. The reporter who is not present when an automobile accident occurs must reconstruct the event from police reports and the comments of any eyewitnesses and attribute the account to these sources.

With the name and the title or occupation of the source given in the story, the reader or listener can place responsibility. After a while, the public learns just how trustworthy the source is. This is important in writing about those in public life. They must be held accountable for their actions and their statements. A reporter who spots a distortion or a lie in a statement may well run it and alongside the inaccuracy give the accurate or truthful account. That way the source is on record, as is the truth.

Attribution should be repeated throughout the story if it is not clear who the source is. Once the source is evident, such as the police, the mayor or the president, it need not be repeated for every assertion. However, the source should not be given only in the lead and then dropped. Repeat the source when necessary to avoid confusion for the reader. Quotes should always be attributed so that the reader knows who is speaking.

Placement within the Story Some news writers say that attribution in the lead sometimes makes it too long or spoils the intended effect. They prefer to cite the source in the second or third paragraph.

Placing the Attribution in the Sentence

In his work as a broadcast news writer, Mervin Block uses this guideline: Attribution precedes assertion.

Placing the source of the information up front is essential for radio and television writing. Newspaper writers also will often begin their leads with the attribution. Write the way you talk is becoming the guide for all news writers.

This works, but only if the material is from an official record or document or is noncontroversial. Notice how Mary Voboril of *The Miami Herald* is able to write a dramatic lead by putting the source (the court) in the second paragraph:

Oswaldo Jordan's version of the American dream turned into a $1.8 million nightmare for the Miami Beach savings and loan where he worked his way from janitor to vice president.

Jordan, a Cuban-born accountant with a degree in mathematics from the University of Havana, was sentenced to four years in federal prison Thursday after pleading guilty to embezzling from the Washington Federal Savings and Loan branch at 1701 Meridan Ave.

No source is necessary in this lead because the event is obviously on record with the police:

Three dead men were found afloat—in two Dade canals and a lake—at midday Sunday by a fisherman, golfers and a scavenger in search of scrap metal.

However, attribution is essential in any lead that contains accusations and charges:

G. Arthur Levy today charged the state liquor authority with "capricious decisions" in denying liquor licenses to two of his clients.

Now and then a reporter will try to make the lead to a story like this more exciting by writing:

The state liquor authority today stands accused of "capricious decisions" in denying two liquor licenses.

This kind of lead is unfair to the reader, who may conclude that the charge has been made in the courts or by some official body. When the source is finally revealed, the reader may feel cheated.

Sometimes, sources seek anonymity. They will offer information only if their identity is not revealed. Newspapers are reluctant to run this kind of material since it absolves the source of responsibility for his or her statements.

Anonymous Sources

When anonymity is promised to a source, the reporter may not use the name under any circumstances. Some editors demand that they be told the source of all such material, and if this is the case, the source must be informed that his or her name will be given to the editor. As a guideline, here is a memo from the UPI to its 200 bureaus around the world on unattributed information:

```
The United Press International discourages the use of
anonymous sources in all its stories. We prefer to list
people by name and title. Where this is not possible, we
seek to give the reader or listener the best possible clue
as to the source's credibility, such as a Defense
Department spokesman, a White House official, a
Democratic party representative, and so forth.
```

When officials request anonymity, the reporter is in a difficult spot. The reporter who is told that without anonymity there will be no statement also knows that some officials like to float trial balloons. That is, an official will make a suggestion without attaching his or her name, watch the public response, and then walk away from the statement if the response is negative. Reporters do not like to be used that way. *The Washington Post* has accepted such material but has published pictures of the source with the source's official title, but not his or her name, under the picture. The message is obvious: We are going to let our readers know your identity. They are entitled to know.

Balance and Fairness

Most of the criticism directed at the press concerns its lack of balance and fairness. Much of the criticism has been deserved. In the past, it was not unusual for newspaper publishers and editors to use their newspapers to attack ideas, groups, individuals and officials. These attacks were made in news columns, which were supposedly free of opinion.

If a newspaper disagreed with or disapproved of an individual or group, the newspaper simply ignored them in its coverage. Not only did the newspapers tend to ignore controversial or minority views, they sometimes even refused to cover major political parties and their candidates.

In his book *The Powers That Be* (New York: Alfred A. Knopf, 1979), David Halberstam describes a visit a *New York Times* reporter made to California in 1934 to cover the campaign for governor. Upton Sinclair, the author of many books and a believer in social and political change, was running against

Frank Merriam, the Republican candidate. The campaign had attracted national attention because of its intensity. Sinclair was considered a wild-eyed socialist by his opponents.

On his arrival in Los Angeles, the New York reporter picked up a copy of *The Los Angeles Times* to look for news about the campaign, especially to learn something about Sinclair, who was a national figure. The only story he could find about Sinclair was one saying that he was un-Christian.

That night, the reporter went to dinner with the chief political correspondent of *The Los Angeles Times*. The reporter asked where Sinclair would be speaking so that he could cover some of his rallies.

As *The New York Times* reporter recalls, he was told, "Forget it. We don't go in for that kind of crap you have back in New York of being obliged to print both sides. We're going to beat this son of a bitch Sinclair any way we can. We're going to kill him." And Halberstam adds: "Which they did."

A quarter of a century later, in 1958, another New York reporter went out to California to cover the turbulent political scene. The same Los Angeles correspondent was directing political coverage. He helped his eastern colleague with background about the Republicans. What about the Democrats? asked his visitor. "Oh, we don't bother with them," was the answer.

Those days of outrageous favoritism in the news are gone, except in some isolated instances. Today, *The Los Angeles Times* is listed among the best newspapers in the country. Although newspapers have recognized their responsibilities, a lack of fairness and balance does creep into stories now and then, usually because of carelessness.

By balance we mean that both sides in a controversy must be given their say. In a political campaign, all candidates should be given enough space and time to present their major points. In debates, each speaker is entitled to reach the reader.

By fairness, we mean that all parties involved in the news are treated without favoritism. If someone makes a charge against another person and the newspaper or station carries a story that includes this allegation, it is obliged to obtain the other side and to put it in the story that contains the charge. Fairness requires that the reporter put the charge and answer as close together as possible.

Let's go back to the lawyer who said his clients had been mistreated by the state liquor authority. The reporter sought the response of the authority and put it high in the story so that it would read this way:

G. Arthur Levy today charged the state liquor authority with "capricious decisions" in denying liquor licenses to two of his clients.

Levy, a local attorney, said the authority had no reason to turn down Fred P. Schmidt and Alice Long, both of whom sought licenses for outlets in shopping centers north of the city.

The executive director of the authority, Theodore Landau, denied that the state agency had acted without reason. He said the applicants had failed to satisfy the authority about their backgrounds. . . .

Balance. The reporter always gives both sides of an argument in a news story. When a charge is made against a person, the accused is sought out and his or her response is put into the story with the charge.

The Tacoma City Council was unhappy with a piece of art a panel of artists had recommended for installation in a municipal building. The jibes of the mayor and council members made good reading:

"This makes me think about my little boy," said an incredulous Mayor Mike Parker after looking at the three-dimensional work. "I've seen this pattern countless times on my kitchen floor, after he's been playing with crayons."

Joelle Cohen, who covered the council meeting for *The News Tribune,* also included the responses of members of the panel, giving them as much space as those who attacked the work.

Fairness means completeness and relevance, giving the reader all the pertinent information so that he or she can see the event in all its dimensions and reach a conclusion.

Fairness also involves the honest use of words. Look at these statements:

Jones admitted he had seen the documents.

Jones said he had seen the documents.

What's the difference? To most readers, the first sentence implies that Jones is under attack for having done something wrong, whereas the second sentence is neutral. There are appropriate occasions when admit, refuse, complain and other words that imply an attitude or a behavior pattern can be used. But these are loaded words. They signal caution. The writer must be fair in his or her use of language.

Brevity

News writing, we have seen, is the art of knowing what to leave out and condensing the rest. Don Murray, a University of New Hampshire professor and newspaper writing coach, says the most effective stories say one dominant thing. In other words, the best stories seem to consist of one major element.

Still, news writers can be counted on to run on and on if they drop their guard. They are born story tellers and tend to be long-winded. Actually, the news writer can include more facts than he or she thinks and still be brief. There are some tricks of the trade.

One way to make a little go a long way is to make one word do the work of three. You already have a method of doing just this—writing sentences with the S-V-O structure.

The S-V-O structure helps to cut sentences to the bone, as Hemingway knew. By choosing a concrete noun, a noun that refers to an actual person, place or thing, the news writer can avoid adjectives. By using action verbs that leap, sing and shout, the news writer can avoid adverbs. Good writers try to make their nouns and verbs work for them. They consider the overuse of adjectives and adverbs as an admission of weak writing.

When George Eliot, the English novelist, was writing the novel *Daniel Deronda,* she wrote this sentence: "She began to sob hysterically." Eliot's manuscript showed that she crossed off the adverb *hysterically*, realizing that the verb *sob* was strong enough to carry the meaning she intended.

Look at these sentences. The weak ones are the wordy sentences. The strong sentences make their points succinctly.

Weak: He was hardly able to walk.
Strong: He staggered. (He stumbled. He faltered.)
Weak: He left the room as quickly as possible.
Strong: He ran out. (He rushed out. He dashed out.)

Action verbs work for the news writer. Action verbs do not need to be propped up by adverbs.

Concrete nouns are words that stand for something we can point to as real: table, desk, chalk, crayon, basket, Ted Kennedy, Prince Charles.

Brevity. You don't need a moving van to pack all your belongings when you leave for summer vacation. Neither does the news writer need 10 paragraphs and 600 words to tell every story he or she writes.

Cool Cal—A Man of Few Words

After Calvin Coolidge returned from a church service, a friend asked the president what the sermon had been about.

"Sin," replied Coolidge.

The friend asked what the clergyman had said. Coolidge replied:

"He said he was against it."

Abstract nouns have no physical reference: patriotism, perception, motherhood, freedom, values, hope. These words mean different things to different people. The news writer should avoid using such words, except in direct quotes. When that happens, the reporter should ask the source how the word is being used.

Another cause of unwanted length is the piling on of irrelevant themes and details. As we have stressed, the average news story has one, two or sometimes three themes. It's up to the reporter to pick the most important. Some reporters want to include everything that happened. The news story will sag out of shape with that overload, bulging like a fullback who has trained on beer.

After the theme(s) has been selected, the reporter must pick the best quotes, anecdotes and illustrations for the supporting detail. A few quotes and a single pertinent illustration are all that are necessary to prove the point.

Relevance

If an event is loaded with interesting and relevant material, the writer can use a device to summarize the secondary material. The additional material is listed at the end of the story:

The city council also:
1. Approved an expenditure of $5,000 for paving Grant Street between Arrow and Baltic Avenues.
2. Appointed Frank C. Barnes of 103 Elm Ave. assistant to the sanitary engineer.
3. Put off until next month consideration of a proposal to adopt an anti-litter ordinance.

The reporter did not believe these items were worth any more than a brief mention. This technique also can be used in an interview:

Nelson ranged widely over the field of music in his remarks:
"Country western will be around as long as people are romantics."
"The mainstream singers give people what they think people want. They're wrong. People want authenticity."
"Travel is no way to make a living, but it's our only way. We are today's minstrels."
"Country music appeals to grandpa and his granddaughter."

Clarity

Ask editors or readers what they want most from the people who write the news and the response will be almost unanimous: clear stories.

Reporters also regard the ability to write stories that are clear and interesting as a highly valuable skill. The reason is simple enough. Life is becoming more complex. Information at the source is often dense and technical. Tax rates. Arms control. Budgets. Foreign assistance. Stadium financing. Trends in crime.

All this and more confronts the reporter and demands to be translated into everyday English.

Clear Thinking

There are several ways the reporter achieves clarity. The common starting point is clear thinking.

"There is only one trick to writing clearly," says a Chicago editor. "The writer must understand the event before writing." If the writer has the information under control, then he or she can put it into understandable language. Reporter Jan Wong often consults references and makes dozens of telephone calls before she writes a story. She needs to have all aspects of the event she is reporting under her control before she writes.

Badly written stories often are the result of muddy thinking.

George Orwell, the author of *1984* and *Animal Farm,* is admired for his ability to express complicated ideas in simple language. His journalism and novels are marked by plain, uncluttered colloquial prose.

Orwell said that the key to clear writing is clear thinking. If the thinking is uncertain and confused, so is the writing. He criticized writers who hide their ignorance of the subject with "purple passages, sentences without meaning, decorative adjectives and humbug generally."

Clear thinking extends to the writing as well as to the subject matter. That is, the reporter has to find the lead that will best summarize the event and arrange all the supporting material in a logical and organized fashion.

When the lead is buried or the piece lacks focus, the reader is confused. News writers visualize themselves as guides leading the reader through the thicket of events. But some inept guides lead their followers in circles or into a swamp of confusion.

Figures are hard to digest. Barry Kramer of *The Wall Street Journal* begins a data story without frightening his readers with statistics:

Guiding the Reader

Health experts have begun an investigation of statistics that show a startling increase in the cancer death rate this year.

They are at a loss so far to explain figures released by the National Center for Health Statistics that show that more than 216,000 Americans died of cancer in the first seven months of this year, or a rate of 176.3 deaths per 100,000 population.

Court documents often are complicated. Look at how Mary Voboril of *The Miami Herald* tries to engage the reader by beginning her piece like a story teller:

Ethiopian Zion Coptic Church members told a teenage cancer victim he would live to be 700 years old if he gave up chemotherapy and embraced their way of life, which includes smoking marijuana, the boy's mother says.

Tony Baron believed them. Then 17, he refused conventional cancer treatment, joined the Coptics, smoked their marijuana—and died less than a year later, says Rosario Baron.

She sued the Coptics and their leader, Brother Louv, in a wrongful death suit Wednesday in Dade Circuit Court. Filed by Miami attorney Ellis Rubin, the suit was in the form of a second amended complaint. Two other complaints have been found faulty by a Dade Circuit judge.

The lead is long. Voboril knew that. So the first sentence of her second paragraph is short, four words. The second sentence of this paragraph is dramatic. The dash and what follows are intended as a slap of cold water on the reader.

The third paragraph describes the details of the suit. Voboril knows she must get back to the spine of her story, the Coptics and young Tony Baron as soon as possible. This narrative, she knows, will fascinate her readers. Her next few paragraphs pick up the drama:

Baron says her son suffered from bone cancer. But the Coptics told him "he did not have cancer and that all he needed to retain good health was ganja [marijuana] and other herbs, tonics and potions, which they furnished," she says.

The Coptics told her son, " 'Like the prophets, he would live to 700 years,' " so long as he followed church teachings and used the herbs they recommended, Baron says. One church teaching says smoking marijuana is a sacrament.

Tony Baron had attended Miami Beach High, earned $100 a week as a pool attendant, gave his mother part of his money and helped around the house, Baron says. All that stopped in May 1978, when he joined the Coptics, she says. Their literature induced him to join, and he was further intrigued by their prescriptions for good health, she says.

Here is another court story that is made clear by the writer's obvious knowledge of the subject and by his ability to translate legal jargon into everyday language. This is how Neil Skene of *The St. Petersburg Times* began a story about a complicated legal question:

Do you know where your curtilage is?

No, it's not in your leg. That's cartilage. Do you know where your curtilage is?

The Supreme Court is trying to find out.

"Curtilage" is lawyer talk for the area immediately surrounding a house. Generally speaking, your house is your castle and your yard is your curtilage. But what if you have a fenced-in, five-acre tract with a house in the middle? Justice Ben Overton asks. Is all of that curtilage? Or is some of it open field?

Skene is trying to make clear to the reader some issues the Florida Supreme Court was trying to resolve. He knows that readers do not understand the specialized language of the law, and he knows that readers cannot digest too many facts too quickly. So he eases the reader into the story. He paces the story at a walk rather than a run, the usual gait of most news stories.

To sum up, clarity in writing begins with the reporter's full understanding of the event. It depends also on the proper lead and the organized structure of the story. By this we mean that the story should march logically from start to finish, with no detours or side trips into irrelevant material. Finally, clarity is enhanced by the writing style: clear S-V-O sentences, short average sentence length, story telling in an informal style when appropriate.

Explain, Explain

A news writer whose stories are invariably clear and interesting says he has only one guideline: "I write as though I'm talking to someone who is intelligent enough to know what I'm getting at if I make it clear enough." To make technical matters understandable, he sometimes inserts explanatory material in his copy:

Explanatory material

Gold was sentenced to three to five years in the state penitentiary for his part in the confidence game.

One of the prosecutors said that with time off for good behavior, Gold would be out of prison in a little more than two years. "We need determinate sentences in this state," Assistant District Attorney Oliver Payne said.

A determinate sentence means that the person sentenced must serve that period and cannot be released by a parole board before that time has been served. Many states have adopted the determinate sentence in response to criticism of lenient sentencing.

The third paragraph is entirely the reporter's. That is, he was the source for this background. Without it, the reader may have no idea what the prosecutor is talking about. With it, a public issue of importance is explained.

Technical and complex subjects can be made clear and interesting with the introduction of the human element, and this is our next news story essential.

Human Interest

The campus correspondent for a newspaper showed the city editor a story he had written for his college newspaper. He wanted to know whether it would interest the editor. The story began this way:

College students face problems ranging from alcohol abuse to loneliness, but the difficulties can be handled with a little friendly assistance, say members of the Campus Ministerial Association.

The organization's members, composed of ministers representing six denominations, do not feel that students here are any different from those at other schools.

"Students are not that different from anyone else," the Rev. . . .

The city editor looked up after reading the story. The piece has possibilities, he told the student. "You've done a lot of work. You quote the director of the Wesley Foundation, the director of the Baptist Student Center, a Catholic priest and an Episcopal vicar.

"They have interesting things to say about students experimenting with drugs, sex and alcohol and then feeling guilty or lost.

"But the story is missing a key element. It's about the problems of students, but there are no students in it. You haven't talked to any students. You don't have any case studies.

"It lacks human interest. It moves all around the subject but never shows us the people directly involved."

He suggested the student reporter return to his sources and ask for some typical cases. The reporter could promise not to use names. Some of the sources might even know students who would allow the reporter to interview them, the editor said. Whatever he did, he would have to include the human element.

Almost every news story involves people, and reporters are being told these days that readers and listeners want to see, hear and read about the way people are affected by events. Reporters are instructed to include people—their reactions, their expectations, their concerns—in their news stories. Since the human element catches the reader's interest, it should be put high in the story. Tell the story in human terms. This is essential.

Beyond the Statistics

We all want to get behind the walls and fences people construct around themselves, and we want to pierce the anonymity of the city. We want to know what went on inside a room down the hall last night when someone screamed. Or whose 10-speed bike was left chained to a post and stripped of every single part but the frame. Or what happened to the family whose home burned down last night. Who took them in? Have they any clothes?

We want to know what people do under stress, what they think about when they have problems. We wonder why the striking postal worker cannot make it on his present salary, what people do when their home is flooded. What, we ask ourselves, does the unemployed teenager want—a job or a handout? The church page has the usual sermons, but nothing about what the seven-year-old child or the old woman in the black shawl are praying for. The newlyweds are honeymooning in the Lake of the Ozarks, but the wedding story says nothing about why they chose this particular place.

Good stories answer our questions. They give us the information we need and want.

After high waters flooded three Kentucky counties, R. G. Dunlop of *The Courier-Journal* talked to some of the people in the area. He began his account with a human interest detail.

SALYERSVILLE, KY.—For the second time in less than three years, Anita Frazier will be shopping for new carpet.

The old rugs in her home on East Maple Street didn't wear out—they were soaked useless by flood waters.

December 1978 was the first time the water had ever crept into the house where Mrs. Frazier has lived since 1920.

Monday morning was the second time.

Residents in Magoffin, Morgan and Bath counties continued to clean up yesterday in the wake of flooding that damaged many roads and bridges and an estimated 300 homes, and that laid waste to countless acres of tobacco, corn and family gardens.

Magoffin Judge-Executive Calloway Montgomery estimated yesterday that 60 percent of the county's gardens and corn and tobacco crops were destroyed.

In Salyersville, Mrs. Frazier's home was fairly typical of the ef-

forts to bounce back from nature's blows.

Volunteers swept puddles outside and washed grimy floors and baseboards.

A box of quilts, salvaged from a flooded pantry, rested on a bed, and furniture was stacked up in the dining room.

Water continued to seep through the tiles on the kitchen floor, almost as fast as Mrs. Frazier mopped it up.

The remains of her carpet and its padding lay in a soggy heap on the front porch. Out back, the propane gas tank that had nearly floated away was strapped to a post.

"This was the quickest and the dirtiest flood I've ever seen," Mrs. Frazier said. "I'm getting tired of replacing this carpet. I hope it's the last time."

So does city Fire Chief Harry Puckett, who watched 4 feet of water creep into the fire station and. . . .

Mop-Up. The flood waters that poured over three Kentucky counties soaked the floor of the Family Federal Savings and Loan in Salyersville. Readers like the human details behind the data and statistics.

When postal workers went on strike, Marcia Chambers, then with *The News Tribune* in Perth Amboy, N.J., dug beneath the union and government statements to look into the life of a striking worker. Here is how her story began:

This March Joe Capik will have worked as a mail carrier in Perth Amboy for 20 years. He takes care of his wife and four children on $110 a week.

Mostly he and his four children, who live at 56 Maplewood Avenue in a Cape Cod bungalow in Keasbey, eat dinners of stews and soups and spaghetti. Things were bad enough last year, he said, that he applied for food stamps. But the county turned him down.

As a mail carrier, he cannot afford much more than stews and spaghetti.

Last week Joe Capik went out on strike for the first time in his life. He joined 49 letter carriers who were on strike for the first time in the 195-year history of the postal system.

"I don't feel right about striking. I really don't," he said outside the deserted post office in Perth Amboy.

"But it's a question of desperation. The situation has been forced upon us," he said.

He was still in uniform, a pleasant, smiling man of 49 whose maroon tie was perfectly knotted. He wore his hat with the number 16, which has been his number for 20 years.

"I feel chagrined," he said, as he smiled to an occasional customer who walked into the post office. "I am disappointed in an employer of this scope who makes it necessary because of inaction and gross unconcern—for us to strike."

Capik was referring to a pay raise of 5.4 percent the postal carriers were supposed to get last October, but which has been held up in congressional committee.

"How come it is so easy for Congress to vote itself raises and their raises never get bottled up in committee?" Capik asked, not really expecting an answer.

Human interest takes the reader to the heart of the event. A strike involves people seeking to change their circumstances. Joe Capik represents that human desire.

Another dimension of a strike was seen by Marilyn Greenwald of the *Citizen-Journal* of Columbus, Ohio, in her story about a strike and its consequences for those touched by its ripples. She singled out a family with school children to show what happened when non-teaching employees struck in Columbus. Here is her story:

Human interest introduction in the first 10 paragraphs

A few weeks before school started this fall, Barbara Eberts had visions of staying home alone during the day and relaxing for the first time in 15 years.

The youngest of her four sons would enter first grade, and she thought she would have time to take some classes at Ohio State University.

Unfortunately, Mrs. Eberts made those plans before the start of a strike by bus drivers and other non-teaching employees of the Columbus schools; since the strike, she has become a full-time chauffeur and transportation planner for her four children, all of whom attend different schools.

"This was going to be free time," she said Thursday afternoon.

Instead, Mrs. Eberts has found she spends most of her time sitting in her Buick Skylark.

She gets up at 6:30 a.m. each day to help sons Howard, 15, Matthew, 6, Joseph, 11, and Michael, 14, get ready for school. About 7:30 a.m. she begins a trek to either Fairwood Elementary School or St. Charles, or sometimes both, depending on her car-pool schedule that day.

About five hours after returning to her home at 5159 Holbrook Drive, Mrs. Eberts begins the journey back to St. Charles, Yorktown Middle School, Fairwood or any combination thereof.

During the day, she refuels and helps arrange schedules among the nine parents who participate in the three car pools of which she is a member.

Parents in her neighborhood are already accustomed to driving large groups of children to school and have even identified "favorite" routes, she said.

When she learned earlier in the week that state officials will reimburse parents about 55 cents a day for driving their children to school, "I laughed," Mrs. Eberts said. "That won't even start your car."

General news—final six paragraphs

Columbus school officials said Thursday that more students continue to enroll in the district despite the strike by members of the Ohio Association of Public School Employees that entered its sixth day.

About 90 percent of the 73,000 expected in class enrolled by Thursday, Superintendent Joseph L. Davis said.

Although 14 bus drivers reported to work, most of the 439 drivers are still on strike, school officials said. Eight bus drivers worked Wednesday.

About 42 percent of the district's 2,600 non-teaching employees were on the job Thursday. About a third worked Sept. 4, the first day of school and the strike.

Assistant Superintendent Frank Maraffa said private trash haulers who serve some schools will not cross the picket lines, causing an accumulation of trash.

School officials are continuing to advise parents to send children to school with packed lunches, although lunchroom operations were running in 58 schools Thursday.

Notice that after she has described the problems Mrs. Eberts faces, Greenwald shifts the focus of the story to the general strike situation. This happens in the 11th paragraph.

Sharp Observations

As the dean listened to students presenting a student council study of dormitory regulations, he drummed his fingers on the desk in front of him. He frequently looked at the clock on the wall above the door, and now and then he stared out the window for half a minute or more.

What do you think that the dean thought of the student presentation? Whatever he might have said about the study, his actions seem to speak eloquently of this impatience and boredom. A story that includes these observations would capture the full dimension, the human dimension, of the event.

We can tell the reader or listener a great deal by including these human interest details. The house whose lawn is littered with beer bottles says as much about the people living there as any direct quotes from the residents themselves.

At the Job Market

Let's say you are sent to cover the annual convention of college and university teachers of English and foreign languages. The convention, which draws thousands of instructors from over the country, is devoted mainly to the exchange of scholarly papers, seminars and discussions. It also attracts hundreds of graduate students who hope to buttonhole the heads of departments for jobs. Thus, the convention is also a job market.

You have written a story about the general meeting that opens the convention and you decide to look into the job market aspect. You learn immediately that it is a tight market for the young men and women seeking employment. You could begin your story this way:

```
    The hundreds of graduate students seeking jobs at the
annual convention of the Modern Language Association are
having poor luck.
    "This is not a good year for them," said Prof. Calder W.
Nolan, head of a committee that makes arrangements for
job interviews.
    "We have about four applicants for every job opening,"
he estimated.
```

There is nothing wrong with this beginning. But many editors would want this redone. Remember the advice of the editor who was shown the story about the problems of college students at the start of this section on human interest? He told the college journalist to go directly to the students themselves instead of quoting people who help them and to make the students the center of the piece. Here, too, the focus is off-center.

The story would be more interesting, and more valid, if it centered on the job-seeking students. You return to the convention and interview a number of students about their experiences. Then you focus on a particular student and begin your story this way:

Patrick Mead and several hundred other graduate students were learning a lesson here today not covered in their postgraduate studies: The academic job market is extremely tight in the humanities.

The reader is at once engaged and wants to know about Mead's problems and the problems of students in general who seek work. You go on:

The annual convention of the Modern Language Association has as its main business the exchange of scholarly material. But for Mead and his fellow students it serves as a job market.

They are not having too much luck. Mead sent scores of resumes to college and universities saying he would be at the convention. He asked for appointments for interviews. He received four positive replies.

But these difficulties have not dampened Mead's enthusiasm. He has spent four years studying 18th Century British literature at Rice University in Houston. He knows how to be patient.

Other students and Prof. Nolan can then be quoted on the general employment situation, and the story can end with some of Mead's experiences at the convention.

The Wall Street Journal pioneered the technique of beginning a news story with the human element. The idea was to make complicated stories easier to understand by showing the effect on people of the situation being reported.

The device works for many types of stories, but discretion has to be used. It cannot always be used on spot news stories. As with so much else in journalism, the journalist gradually learns when to use the human interest lead.

Human interest can also be introduced in a story with the use of personal pronouns and concrete nouns:

Words That Signal Human Interest

1. Johnson put **his** pencil down and closed **his** book.
2. Johnson put the pencil down and closed the book.
3. For a textbook, he thought, it was as lively as one of **Prof. Albrecht's** good lectures.
4. For a textbook, he thought, it was as lively as a good lecture.

Sentences 1 and 3 have human interest: 1 contains a personal pronoun, and 3 has the name of a teacher, a concrete noun. Compare the following sentences and indicate which have human interest:

5. It had a bad odor.
6. It smelled like burned rubber.
7. His back ached.
8. His back felt like the football team had practiced on it.

Sentences 6 and 8 introduce the human senses. Reporters should always try to do this by asking their sources what it smelled like, just how bad it felt, what the noise reminded them of, and so on.

The historian G. M. Young wrote, "The real, central theme of history is not what happened, but what people felt about it when it was happening; in Philip Sidney's phrase, 'the affects, the whisperings, the motions of the people.' " For journalists—historians of the moment—this is good advice.

Identification

Writers identify the people they are writing about so that readers and listeners can visualize, locate and identify these people. The standard identifying material is **name, age, address** and **occupation.** These are often included in general news stories and always in obituaries.

> Vincent Trevino, 74, of 540 Newton Ave., died last night at Harbor General Hospital after suffering a stroke earlier in the day. He was a retired electrician.

Another kind of identification is essential in stories that quote a source as an authority. In this situation, the source must be identified by title or background to give the person the credibility to speak on the subject on which he or she is being quoted:

"Freedom of the press is guaranteed only to those who own one," A. J. Liebling wrote. Liebling, a reporter who turned to magazine and book writing, was a staunch critic of the press. For years he wrote a column called the "Wayward Press" for the *New Yorker* magazine.

Identification is the journalist's way of drawing a quick portrait of the people about whom they write.

Name The best source for the proper spelling of a person's name is the individual. The telephone book and city directory are usually accurate. If a person uses a middle initial, include that in the story. Nicknames are rarely used except in sports stories or features.

Age A person's age should be used only when it bears directly on the story. It is always used in obituaries and in stories about the victims of accidents and fires. It is also used when it helps to make the point of the story:

A 14-year-old girl was released from General Hospital yesterday after a year-long fight against near-fatal burns.

When Ronald Reagan was seeking the Republican nomination for president and later the presidency, his age became an issue.

The older people become in this youth-conscious culture, the more reticent they are about their age. When it is relevant, the reporter is obligated to put it in. This can be done with taste:

She graduated from high school in 1932.

He was 30 when the United States entered World War II, and he immediately volunteered.

Address Where a person lives can tell the reader a great deal. An address in a high-income neighborhood sends one kind of message, an address in a poor neighborhood another. The address also helps the reader to put a person in a setting—large lawns and single residence homes or a low-income city project. The address can indicate a lifestyle.

Occupation Work defines many people. That is, the jobs that people hold often describe their character and personality. Think of the images that you build from the following job titles: hotel maid, film producer, grocer, commercial fisherman, teacher, actor. Obviously, those pictures are general and we cannot push them too far or we will stereotype individuals. But occupation does say something about the person.

These four identifying characteristics give us the broad picture of the person. To fill in the detail, to provide the fine brush-strokes, we need to visualize the individual.

Height, weight, hair color, distinguishing physical characteristics. How a person speaks, his or her posture and mannerisms. All these help us see a person. They are used in profiles and feature stories when the writer is trying to draw a full portrait of the subject.

Race, religion and national origin are sometimes essential to a story but using these characteristics is a touchy matter. Too often a person's race or religion is injected when it has no bearing on the story.

The New York Times Manual of Style and Usage cautions writers:

> Race should be specified only if it is truly pertinent. The same stricture applies to ethnic and religious identifications.

In its in-house publication, *Winners & Sinners,* the *Times* cites a violation of this warning:

> **Race out of place—again.** "All eight men, slashed while they were either asleep or intoxicated, were listed in stable condition yesterday. . . . Four victims were white, three were black and one was a Hispanic man." . . . Our stylebook says we specify the race of a person in the news only if it is truly pertinent . . . the writer must *show* the pertinence.

When the Roman Catholic Church appointed an archbishop in France, news stories pointed out that he was born a Jew. To keep him from death in the Nazi concentration camps, his parents turned him over to a Catholic family, who raised him in the Catholic faith. His parents died in the Holocaust. Obviously, religion was pertinent in this story.

News Point

Every story must have a point, and this point must be made high in the story. Usually, in spot news stories, it is in the lead in the first paragraph. For features, as we indicated in chapter 3, the point may come lower in the story. Few editors will permit the point to be delayed beyond the fourth or fifth paragraph.

The news point is also the main theme of the story. It provides the spine of the story.

The news point is consciously decided upon by the reporter, usually at the scene of the event being covered or while the person is being interviewed. It is done at this time so that the reporter can gather as much supporting and buttressing material as possible for the story. No reporter should sit down to begin to write without knowing what the news point is.

Objectivity

The great strength of American journalism is its objectivity. Unlike the journalism of many countries, objective journalism attempts to present a complete report that is not colored by the opinion of the reporter or the requirements of the prevailing government.

An objective story includes facts that can be shown to correspond to objects, things the reporter can point to. These objects may be physical items: a burned building, a gun, a damaged vehicle. They can also be the documents that record events: the fire and police reports, the tape of a speech, the minutes of a legislative meeting, a bill submitted to congress, a proposed budget. In other words, an objective story contains information that the reporter can prove to exist.

Objectivity also—in the words of James Boylan, who teaches journalism at the University of Massachusetts at Amherst—"has gradually come to be understood not only as an impersonal 'balanced' style of newswriting (which is the commonplace, or newsroom, sense of the word) but also as representing the broader claim of journalism for its position in society—that of an impartial third party, the one that speaks for the general interest."

Boylan says that objectivity's chief philosopher was Walter Lippmann, who "depicted journalism as an institution apart, charged with supplying society with reliable, impartial information."

It's not a coincidence that objectivity in journalism was developed by Americans. The idea that through experience, the amassing of facts, a person may find truth reflects the American style of life. Journalists came naturally to adopt the objective approach of American empiricists and pragmatists.

Objectivity has been criticized because it limits journalists. Facts alone are sometimes insufficient; they must be given meaning through analysis and interpretation. Journalism recognizes this.

If we look back at our discussion of the five W's and an H, we see that two of these elements can involve interpretation—why and how. To tell the reader or listener why or how something happened often takes the writer away from a strictly objective account of events. Properly labelled as such, interpretative stories are used by many newspapers. However, before a reporter is trusted with interpretative reporting, the newcomer must prove he or she can copy the correct middle initial in a lawsuit, add up a column of figures in a budget without a mistake and accurately quote from an interview with the survivor of a fire. Then the reporter will be given wider latitude.

When a reporter checks his or her information against some kind of objective source, we say that the material has been verified. Forty years ago, the password in newspapering was: Go with what you've got. This was recognition of the need for speed. Today, the motto is: Verify what you've got, and then go with it. This is recognition of the need for truth.

Several years ago, AP and UPI received calls informing them that the executive president of the Columbia Broadcast Group had resigned. UPI put the story on its news wire, and 40 minutes later it carried this bulletin:

```
    A KILL IS MANDATORY. MAKE SURE THE STORY IS
NOT PUBLISHED. NO CORRECTED VERSION WILL BE
SENT.
```

AP did not use the information. It had called CBS to verify the call and was told the story was a hoax.

A reporter for a Fort Lauderdale newspaper was walking into a night club when the owner stopped him.

"You just missed Jackie Kennedy," he said. He told the reporter that the secret service men assigned to follow the president's wife had looked over the club and issued orders against any pictures or publicity.

Jackie Kennedy's comings and goings were news during her husband's presidency, and although this story may not seem like much, the doings of attractive, young Jackie were chronicled by an eager press. The Associated Press picked up the story and ran it over its wires.

Two hours later, the AP added an editor's note:

```
    CHECKS THUS FAR FAIL TO CONFIRM THE STORY.
```

The truth, it turned out, was that a woman who resembled the president's wife was in the club. The Fort Lauderdale paper did make a check before going to press and killed the story.

The New York Times has a rule: "Don't trust anybody on anything that is checkable." This rule applies to even the most trustworthy sources. They can make mistakes, such as the press release from an artists' representative who reported a show at a gallery on East 66th Street. The reporter given the release made a routine check in the phone book. The gallery was on East 61st Street.

Don't trust something simply because it is in print. *The New York Times,* probably the most carefully edited newspaper in the country, once carried a story about a trip one of its writers took on the "Superchief Express." No such train. It was the Super Chief. He said he stopped at Raton, Colorado. Raton is in New Mexico. He also described the train as it rolled past Cairo, Illinois, on its way east. The tracks do not go near Cairo.

The story was entertaining all right—but loaded with errors. This leads us to a second rule: "Don't sacrifice accuracy and truth for effect."

Dealing with Hoaxes

For Chicago Bears and Dallas Cowboy football fans, the story Paul Harvey told was a big one: The two teams had traded quarterbacks. Harvey is heard by 5 million people on 774 radio stations over the country. The story had originated with radio station WLS in Chicago, which reported that a vice president for the Bears had called the station with the news.

The caller was an imposter.

Some hoaxsters are ghouls. They delight in calling in death notices for the obituary page. Every veteran reporter can tell at least one story about such an attempt. Most fail because reporters are trained—or learn the hard way—to verify information telephoned in. The simplest tactic is to hang up and phone the number on record for the supposed source—CBS headquarters, the Chicago Bears information office, a hospital, a funeral home, the police, a coroner.

Never ask the source to call back. You, the reporter, make the call.

At 9:45 p.m., the phone rang in the newsroom of WRC-TV, the NBC affiliate in Washington, D.C.

"The mayor has been shot," the caller said. He identified himself as James Taylor, an aide to Mayor Marion Barry. Taylor said Barry was in serious condition with wounds he suffered when he was shot on the front lawn of his home. Barry was in the hospital at Andrews Air Force Base. Two suspects were in custody.

Taylor gave the television station a number to call for confirmation.

Minutes later, the station was on the air with a news bulletin. Soon, three other Washington television stations had the story. At 10:06 p.m. the UPI put the story on its national news wire. CBS and NBC put the news on their 10 p.m. radio newscasts.

One of those watching television at the time of the bulletin was the mayor himself. He was visiting the home of his legal advisor.

After broadcasting the bulletin, the news staff at WRC-TV tried to obtain additional details.

"The cops knew nothing. The hospital knew nothing. All of a sudden, things started to fall apart," an official at the station said. At 11 p.m., a station anchorman confessed to viewers, "We've been had, folks."

The station had gone wrong by using for verification purposes the telephone number that the caller had supplied. What had happened was simple: The imposter had given his own number and verified the hoax when the station called back for confirmation.

The Goal Is Truth

The point of verifying or confirming material is to try to guarantee for the reader or listener its truth. Accuracy is important, but it is not enough.

"The fact without the truth is futile; indeed, the fact without the truth is false." The source is G. K. Chesterton, an English writer who lanced shams and charlatans. This same idea was taken up in the 1950s by Elmer Davis, a radio journalist who was one of the few journalists who sought to determine the truth of the charges of treason and subversion being made by Senator Joe McCarthy of Wisconsin.

While it was a fact that McCarthy said many people prominent in government were members of the Communist Party or sympathizers—and the press reported that McCarthy had said this—Davis asked: Is it true? He asked further: Does the press have an obligation to tell people the truth of the fact?

Attribution does take the responsibility of assertions, charges and declarations from the shoulders of the press. But in serious matters, shouldn't the press try to dig out the truth on its own?

Davis said yes, and the press through the years has come to agree with him. Reporters have made independent verification of charges, statements, accusations, even of convictions in court.

Paul Henderson of *The Seattle Times* took seriously the protestations of innocence of a man convicted of first-degree rape, which in Washington carries a penalty of three years to life. Henderson dug into the story and five days before the man was to be sentenced he uncovered new evidence that set the innocent man free. The freed man said of Henderson: "He saved my life."

Mr. Reagan on Immigration

During his campaign for the presidency, Ronald Reagan was quoted as saying to an audience in Texas that he favored giving visas to illegal Mexican immigrants for as long as they wished to stay in the United States. Reporters carried this in their stories.

Next day, he denied saying that. He had said, he stated, that they should be given temporary visas. Many reporters were content to include Reagan's denial in their stories. Certainly, this was accurate reporting. It was a fact that he denied having said they should be given permanent visas.

A reporter for *The New York Times* who was accompanying the Reagan campaign sought to find the truth. He was convinced he had quoted Reagan accurately the day before. He consulted tape recordings of the speech Reagan had given that day.

In his story of Reagan's denial he also included a sentence stating that the tapes "clearly show that Mr. Reagan said that he was for Mexican workers staying as long as they liked."

Keeping the Public's Trust

Readers and listeners rely on what they read and hear. They trust their newspapers, and radio and television stations to give them accurate, complete and interesting material in news stories.

To meet this trust, news writers are careful with the facts and painstaking with their writing. Writers realize that much of what people know comes from the news stories they read and hear—the information that reporters gather and write.

By adhering to the requirements of the news story, from accuracy through verification, the news writer—and consequently the public—can be confident that the story will be reliable and, when appropriate, entertaining.

8

Writing the Lead

The lead of a news story describes the most important element of the event. It is a brief statement of the fact or facts that make the event newsworthy.

To write a lead, the news writer asks himself or herself these questions:

1. What do I want to say? What is the theme of this story?
2. Will this be a straight news story or a feature story?
3. Should I use a direct or a delayed lead?
4. What facts should I put into the lead?

The first two questions usually are answered at the scene while covering the event. The other two are asked just before writing.

No one can resist reading a book that begins this way: "Mom and pop were just a couple of kids when they got married. He was eighteen, she was sixteen and I was three."

This is how jazz singer Billie Holiday starts her book of recollections. (It also happens to make a good beginning for a textbook chapter.)

People whose job it is to communicate information, ideas and feelings to others know that the beginning is the most important part of the work—whether it be a poem, play, novel, news story, song or symphony. Not only does an interesting beginning grab the attention of the reader, viewer or listener, it also helps the writer or composer to organize his or her material.

Robert Schumann, the composer, advised a fellow composer, Johannes Brahms, to study the "beginning of the Beethoven symphonies . . . to try to make something like them.

"The beginning is the main thing; if only one makes the beginning, then the end comes of itself."

Schumann could be speaking for the city editor here. If the news writer writes a good lead, the story falls into place. With a lead that is on target, the story almost organizes itself. The reason is that the lead points the writer as well as the reader or listener in a specific direction. Once the theme is expressed in the lead, the writer must run with it in the body of the story.

"With me, it's the first sentence that I wait for, and the rest follows," says Sven Birkerts, a young writer of articles and short stories.

Attracting the Reader

Donald M. Murray, a University of New Hampshire professor of writing who coaches news writers for several newspapers, says the writer must engage the reader at once. "Three seconds and the reader decides to read or turn to the next story," he says.

When we see a lead like the following we want to know more about this con artist:

A 73-year-old man was sentenced Tuesday to 10 years in prison for using the mails and telephone lines to cheat 30 people, including a Kansas City widow and a San Francisco physician, out of more than $500,000.

This crisp lead by Mary Voboril of *The Miami Herald* is inviting:

A Dade Circuit Court jury Friday ordered General Motors to pay $1.5 million for a fiery Christmas Eve collision that left a Dade woman fatally burned and her husband badly scarred.

The reader is lured by the name of the company—many people drive GM vehicles—and by the size of the jury's award. This lead does more: It also tells the reader what the story is going to be about. This is the job of the lead— to lure the reader or listener into the story and to give him or her an idea of what's coming up.

Writing the lead is the most difficult job the writer faces in putting a story together. Let's analyze the lead-writing process to see if we can make the task any easier.

Finding the Theme

News stories usually fall into two general categories: Someone has said or done something important or entertaining; or something significant or unusual has occurred. The first step in determining the theme is to decide whether the event focuses on a person or group or on an occurrence: Who or What.

If an individual or group is central to the event, then the story will be based on the statements and actions of the individual or group. If an action, occurrence or idea is central, then the story is directed at one of these.

Looking back to some stories we have discussed in this book, we can see the differences. In chapter 7 we read about Joe Capik, a mail carrier on strike. This story is about an individual. In chapter 1, we saw how Lindy Washburn covered a fire, a story about an event. Jeff Klinkenberg's story was about Ron Swint, a shark fisherman, and Dan Rather's lead story in chapter 1 was about signing a tax bill, an occurrence.

Once we identify the focus of the story—person or occurrence—we can isolate the person's statement or action that best describes what was said or done, or we can isolate the action that best sums up what happened.

There are two practical ways to do this. The first is to jot down a skeleton summary by using the Subject-Verb-Object form:

Who said or did what

S—Joe Capik   S—Ron Swint
V—cannot afford   V—fishes for
O—much   O—Old Hitler

What happened

S—Fire   S—President
V—kills   V—signs
O—23 people   O—tax bill

The other approach to finding the theme uses the "Five Ws and an H." By writing down the answers to these questions, the writer will have the starting points or possible themes for a lead. Applying this technique to Neal Robbins' story from Hong Kong gives us these answers to our six questions:

Who—Hundreds of Chinese
What—arrived in Hong Kong
When—today
Where—in a cove
Why—fear of an earthquake
How—in their junks

It's all there, waiting to be rearranged in a lead. If this procedure works, use it. If the S-V-O skeleton does the job, use that.

Underlying our selection of the theme or themes of the story is one of the definitions of news from chapter 3, the practical definition: The stories that are published in newspapers and are used on newscasts almost always concern events that have **impact,** involve **prominent** people, or are **unusual** or **exceptional.**

A good idea for beginners is to write down the gist or main point of the event. This requires selective judgment. There is no formula for getting to the heart of a story. It takes practice.

News or Feature?

Once you've determined the theme, the second step is to decide whether the story is important or entertaining. If it is serious, a straight news story will be written. If entertaining, it will be a feature story. This decision is important because the lead and the structure differ for each type of story.

Look back at the four stories for which we constructed the S-V-O summaries. The fire and tax bill stories are important—news. Ron Swint may take himself seriously, but the story is entertaining—a feature. What about Joe Capik, though? The postal strike developments are a likely topic for a news story. However, news stories usually have some immediacy. The Capik article has no immediacy, and yet it is not exactly entertaining.

For stories like the Joe Capik piece we have a third category, the news feature. Mary Ann Giordano's story about the poor family without heat or water is considered a news feature. So is the story about the muggers who prey on the poor.

For writing purposes, the news feature comes under the general heading of the feature.

Now that we know the criteria for determining the type of story to be written, we can determine the kind of lead to use.

Direct or Delayed Lead?

Although you may have heard differently, there are only two kinds of leads that reporters use. One is the direct lead, the lead that tells the reader at once what the story will be about. This is used for the straight news story. The major theme is in the first sentence of the first paragraph of the story.

The second type of lead is the delayed lead. That is, the major theme is not placed in the first paragraph but is given later in the story, sometimes at the very end of the piece where it is used as a kicker or climax. The point of using the delayed lead is to give the story drama, excitement, color, an entertaining twist.

Although the delayed lead is used most often for news feature and feature stories, it is sometimes effective for a straight news story. Look at this lead:

> Hiram Thompson was taking a mid-morning bath in his Mattapan apartment yesterday when he heard intruders slamming around downstairs in Willie Hodo's flat.

No question that most readers would be tempted to read on. What happened downstairs? What did Thompson do? But suppose the story began this way:

> `Hiram Thompson, 48, shot and seriously wounded an intruder in his building at 50 Meadowlands Ave. yesterday.`

The reader might go on, but if the reader were in Boston, where this incident occurred, he or she probably would not go further. Robberies are frequent and gunplay almost as common.

Joe Heaney and Bob Keeley of the *Boston Herald American* gave the story the drama it needed by using a delayed lead.

This approach should be taken with caution. Events that have great impact cannot be handled this way. A writer cannot begin the story of an attempted presidential assassination by describing the lunch menu or the chit-chat of the president as he left the hotel, and then get to the shooting in the fourth or fifth paragraph.

This delayed lead approach to news stories is frequently used by news magazines, and for good reason. When readers receive the weekly newsmagazines *Time* or *Newsweek*, they already know that the president was shot, the ambassador was sent packing by the Chinese, the revolution squashed. These magazines employ delayed leads for these stories to give them a fresh slant.

Guideline If the event is important and if it requires the use of today, tomorrow, yesterday, in the lead because of timeliness, the story is most likely a straight news story and should take a direct lead.

As we can see, once we determine whether the story is a news or feature piece, the type of lead selects itself. Here are 10 themes, slightly enlarged from the S-V-O summary. Jot down whether each is a news or feature story and the type of lead each requires. We will see what reporters have done with some of them:

Take 10

1. A jetliner on a flight from Los Angeles to Miami runs out of fuel and must put down in Tampa.
2. Disturbances occur in Worcester, Mass., when it is revealed that the Cockroaches, a rock group giving a concert at a local night spot, are actually the Rolling Stones practicing for their first American tour in three years.
3. A group of women block the approach to a nuclear reactor in Diablo Canyon, Calif.
4. A company makes a wage offer to striking steel workers.
5. More city jobs will be eliminated Friday to balance the budget.
6. An 18-year-old high school student in Wisconsin devises a program to teach youngsters about the dangers of alcohol.
7. A New York City radio station switches music formats and becomes the most-listened-to station in the nation.
8. A new state law sends youngsters into the adult court system.
9. A profile of a figure skating champion.
10. A blind man sails a 35-foot sailboat.

We will refer to this list often in the next section as we examine how reporters have dealt with some of these themes in actual stories. Keep your notes about the type of story and lead handy.

We are now ready for the last and most important step.

Study each picture and the accompanying information. Decide whether the story (1) is about a person or event, (2) should be a straight news story or a feature story, and (3) should be given a direct or delayed lead.

Blaze. A fire does $175,000 damage to an ocean-front apartment building. One person is injured.

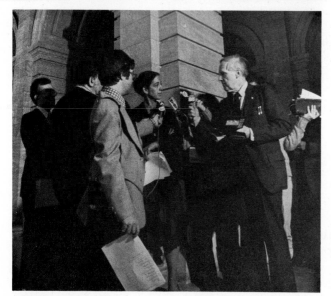

Official. A city official says she will run for mayor. She makes the announcement at a press conference outside city hall.

Shark. A shark-fishing contest began today, and one angler landed this 725-pound, 12½ foot long tiger shark.

Rock. The leader of a local rock group says most young rock musicians are "musically ignorant" and "cannot even read music." He suggests they take music lessons or "forget about trying to make it."

Spring. This is the first day of Spring and the local weather was warm enough for a nap in the sun.

Writing the Lead   The writer doing a straight news story knows he or she must get to the point at once. Major theme (or themes) in mind, the reporter sets to work. Since the lead will revolve about someone saying or doing something, or something happening, the writer begins with the person or the event—Who or What.

If the writer is working from the S-V-O summary, the **Subject** will begin the lead. If the Five W's and an H is being used, **Who** or **What** will start the lead.

The S-V-O of number 1 of our list is:

S—Jet
V—makes
O—emergency landing

The Five W's and an H give us a more complete set of facts to work from:

Who—Jetliner
What—made emergency landing
When—today
Where—in Tampa
Why—ran out of fuel
How—unknown

From either the S-V-O skeleton or the answers to the Five W's and an H, the lead is built. First, the Who or Subject of the sentence is written:

`A DC-10 jetliner on a flight from Los Angeles to Miami`

Notice that we say as much about the jetliner as possible to identify it, to separate this jetliner from the thousands that were flying on this day. We do the same thing when the **Who** or the **Subject** is a person. We don't say a man or a woman. We say a 29-year-old steel worker or Mrs. Mildred Sherman, 69, of 166 Chapel St.

Next, we move to the What or the Verb and the Object:

`made an emergency landing in Tampa today`

Notice that we added the Where and the When here. Place and time are usually placed near the verb or the object.

We could stop here, but the lead would leave people wondering about the cause of the emergency, the Why. So we add:

`when it ran out of fuel.`

Now we have:

> A DC-10 jetliner on a flight from Los Angeles to Miami made an emergency landing in Tampa today when it ran out of fuel.

This is almost a word-for-word duplicate of the wire service leads on the story.

Our presumption in number 1 was that this was a news story that required a direct lead. But what about number 2?

Our first reaction is that this could be serious business—news story, direct lead. For those with good memories or some knowledge of the music scene, it was a disturbance at a Rolling Stones concert in Altamont, Calif., that led to the knifing death of a spectator. But the Cockroaches? There's something funny about that. Maybe a feature would be better. Hold on.

When in doubt, play it straight. That is, if the choice is not obvious, the best way to write the story is with a news approach and a direct lead. This is the safe way. To make light of a serious matter could be offensive.

Number 2 was played straight by most newspapers, though there were no serious injuries. Some damage was done, however, by people cruising through the streets.

Number 3: Straight news story. Direct lead.
Number 4: Straight news story. Direct lead.
Number 5: At first glance, this seems like a straight news story. But is it?

A tipoff to why number 5 is a delayed lead is the word *more*. This means the layoffs are part of a series of layoffs. Words like again, still, continued indicate there is not much new. Thus we lose the news determinant of immediacy.

Bob Rose of *The Blade* in Toledo made the event into a news feature. In his story, he used a delayed lead. The theme does not come until the sixth paragraph:

Delayed lead: Use of incidents to begin the story

> One night this week, some Mabel Street residents went hunting for rats that had moved into their North Toledo neighborhood.
>
> "I called rodent control, and they're closed up," Tom Munger said. "I talked to the mayor's office and the woman who answered the phone said she didn't know what I could do about it. She said I should have voted."

Mr. Munger, who admitted he did not cast a ballot on the payroll-income tax increase issue last month, said he and a neighbor took the problem into their own hands. "I think we got one," he said of the pests.

One night later, L. Michael Duckworth, assistant city manager, got a telephone call at home from someone asking when the city's swimming pools would open.

Transition to theme

City officials know it, but some citizens apparently do not: With 846 layoffs in the last two years, Toledo cannot control rats and it cannot open the pools. It cannot do a lot of things it used to do.

When 262 more city jobs are eliminated Friday, the city will have taken another step toward balancing its budget by bringing the work force down to 2,875. But the list of what it cannot do will grow longer.

"It's hurting," Mayor Doug DeGood said of the city's inability to provide necessary services. "It's hurting."

When times get rough, city officials like to point to silver linings or better times ahead. But with an $11.5 million deficit to erase over the next 18 months, neither Mr. DeGood nor City Manager J. Michael Porter can find much cause for optimism.

Theme: Newspoint

The combination of the 262 layoffs and not filling 67 police and fire division jobs is expected to save $10.2 million for the city's general fund. An additional $377,000 is being chopped off by deferring a 2 percent wage increase for city workers until Jan. 1.

The layoffs will be devastating.

"With no recreation program, biweekly refuse collection, a dwindling police force, and fewer firefighters, some basic services will not be provided at an adequate level," Mr. DeGood said. . . .

The writer has to make two decisions when using a delayed lead. First, he or she must decide just what the lead is. In this case, the S-V-O is: City will eliminate 262 more city jobs Friday. The writer must then find a fitting quote, incident, example that will take the reader right into the lead. Rose chose two examples of the consequences of the layoffs—eliminating the rodent control program and closing down the city's pools.

Rose shows rather than tells the reader what impact the cutbacks will have. Then in the sixth paragraph he explains the cuts the city must make. The next several paragraphs relate the details of the cutbacks. Rose completes the story by recounting the various cutbacks, parks and park buildings closed, golf courses shut down, recreation programs for the handicapped curtailed.

Number 6: This story obviously does not require a today in the lead. It is a news feature, so the AP put a delayed lead on it:

> FOND DU LAC, WIS. (AP)--SOMETIMES THE BEST HELP A JUNIOR HIGH SCHOOL STUDENT CAN RECEIVE COMES NOT FROM A TEACHER OR PARENT BUT FROM A SENIOR HIGH SCHOOL STUDENT.
>
> THAT THEORY, ``KIDS HELPING KIDS,'' IS THE IDEA BEHIND A NEW ALCOHOL AWARENESS PROGRAM DEVELOPED BY A ST. MARY'S SPRINGS HIGH SCHOOL STUDENT FOR ELEMENTARY AND JUNIOR HIGH SCHOOL STUDENTS.
>
> THE PROGRAM WAS DEVELOPED BY JEFF WEINSHROTT, AN 18-YEAR-OLD SPRINGS SENIOR. . . .

The lead idea is: High school student develops program to combat alcoholism. The AP writer realized that the unique or unusual aspect of it was a young student teaching even younger students about the dangers of alcohol. The writer emphasized the unique aspect by using that general idea to begin the story. The lead follows quickly in the second and third paragraphs.

Number 7: What happened here? An FM station switched from mellow music to disco and its ratings jumped. Significant or entertaining? For a magazine devoted to reporting broadcast news, this is significant and a direct lead is in order. Something like this:

> By switching to disco, New York radio station WKTU-FM has become the most-listened-to station in the country.

But for a general audience, the reaction to that lead may well be: So what. For Geoff Walden, a student who wrote this story on assignment for a journalism class, this was an entertaining story, and so he put a delayed lead on the piece. He dramatized the switch this way:

> NEW YORK—Last July 24th, at 5:59 p.m., WKTU-FM "Mellow 92," was playing Neil Young's soft-rock song, "It's Over."
>
> At 6 p.m., WKTU-FM, "The new Disco 92," was playing Donna Summer's "The Last Dance."
>
> For Donna Summer, the song went on to win this year's Oscar for the Best Original Song, for the movie "Thank God It's Friday." For the radio station, the song was the start of an all-disco format that has made WKTU the most-listened-to station in America, with an average of 275,000 people tuning in every quarter hour.

The direct lead tells readers: Here comes something important. Walden's delayed lead tells them: Relax, I'm going to entertain you. But notice that the theme or lead idea is exactly the same for both:

S—Format change
V—makes
O—station most listened-to

Number 8: This falls into the category editors call an update. This type of story brings the reader or listener up to date on something that has happened. An update usually is not a straight news story and does not require a direct lead. How should the story be approached?

Richard Higgins, another journalism student, reasoned that his story should describe youngsters in the adult courts. So he found some young offenders and began his story by portraying them in the new courtroom setting.

> NEW YORK—Rafael Torres and Hector Valdez sat at the brown wooden table, playing with Superman coloring books, combing their hair, waving and occasionally shouting to friends in the room.
>
> It could have been a scene out of the South Bronx junior high school where they are enrolled in the eighth grade. But it was the beginning of an arson and multiple murder trial in the Bronx Criminal Courthouse and the two skinny, squirming boys were not there to learn; they were the defendants.

In the next paragraph Higgins introduces the lead that tells the reader that these youngsters are in court because of a new law and that other youngsters are being tried in the adult courts. He makes a news feature out of his material.

Number 9: For this kind of feature story, Linda Kramer, an AP reporter, says she gathers "piles of material for a story." When she writes, she tries to "weed out the non-essential copy. I want to choose the anecdote that best reflects and highlights what I want to say."

This is a precise description of how the writer must use the anecdote or incident chosen to begin the feature or news feature story. The material must feed directly into the theme or lead.

"In writing about figure-skating champion Linda Fratianne, I led with a description of a lucky charm she pins to her costume during competition. To me, this little touch of superstitiousness illustrated the 17-year-old behind the star," Kramer says. This, then, was her theme—although her magnificent presence on the ice makes her seem almost regal, the real Linda Fratianne is a young girl with a young girl's feelings. Here is Kramer's first paragraph in her delayed lead:

> Tucked in a tiny blue pouch pinned to Linda Fratianne's sequinned skating costume are two four-leaf clovers, a piece of gold foil, and a snip of green yarn.

Just like a little girl, the reader is likely to think.

Number 10: The news writer takes the reader aboard the blind man's sailboat:

> Keeping a grip on the sheet, Albert Adams draws the maximum amount of speed from his 35-foot sailboat.
>
> The yellow-hulled boat responds to Adams' touch and picks up speed. Adams turns to his crew—his wife and two teen-age sons—and asks them to lend a hand.
>
> Adams has been blind since birth. The 33-year-old accountant sails regularly. He can tell from which direction the wind is coming by ear. . . .

Like the beginning of many features, this one **shows** the subject doing something.

Summing Up

Some of these leads, and others in the textbook, might seem beyond you at this stage of your writing development. Don't be concerned. Behind almost every one of the journalists whose work is represented here is an apprenticeship, considerable trial and error. For every good lead that these writers have hammered out, they can tell a sad tale of one they botched.

The trick now is to master the process, to learn the way leads are written. No writer can dash off a lead without going through the four basic steps outlined at the beginning of this chapter.

After these three steps, the lead is ready to be written. Go back to the words you have jotted down as the theme. They may be in the form of the S-V-O skeleton summary, or you may have written a complete sentence. If the lead is a direct lead, make sure that you have the time element (when)—today, yesterday, tomorrow. Make sure that the person, group, or action (who or what) is adequately identified, which means that he, she, or it is named or given an identifying label. Check to be certain that the subject of the action is precise. It is not the council but the city council; not the court but Federal District Court or Grant County Court, and so on.

What to Do and What to Avoid

The journalistic boneyard is littered with the carcasses of young writers gone wrong because they thought clever writing was the beginning and the end of journalism. The largest section of this graveyard is reserved for those who wrote brilliant leads but could not deliver the facts in the body of the story to back up those glorious leads.

Everyone—editors, colleagues, readers and listeners—likes good writing, but the journalist must be honest with his or her words. The words must reflect reality, the actual event. A writer may well tease, cajole, or entice the reader or listener to tarry a while by writing a brilliant lead. But the story must deliver on that promise.

We've all been lured into carnival tents, movie houses, and theaters or to dances, parties, and blind dates only to find that the pitch or come-on was more exciting than the reality. Honesty may not mean much in the entertainment world, or, to be more generous, one person's "best ever" is another's mediocrity. In journalism, honesty is everything. If the writer regularly cheats the reader, the boneyard beckons.

Short and Sweet

Try to make the lead read well. The best test of this is to read it aloud before you hand it in. If it's smooth, fine. If it stutters and stops, ditch it.

If it's too long, cut. There is no last word about the proper length of a lead, but most editors want short leads. That means under 40 words almost everywhere, under 35 most places, under 30 in some.

Reporters like to talk about leads when they get together, the most colorful, the most dramatic, the shortest. H. D. Quigg, a UPI reporter, and Homer Bigart, a veteran of New York City newspapers, once reminisced about the shortest leads they had read. Quigg's favorite went back to 1927, a dispatch in *The New York Times* about Charles Lindbergh's solo flight across the Atlantic Ocean:

PARIS—Lindbergh did it.

Bigart recalled a shorter one he wrote himself. The piece was from West Point, where cadets who were engaged in artillery practice were so far off target that some shells landed in a farmer's field. Bigart knew he had done the *Times* lead one better. His lead had two words. He was not sure whether it was "Oops, missed," or "Cease fire."

To write short leads, the writer needs to keep in mind the guide that the lead should, if at all possible, contain only one basic idea. Here is a UPI lead that can be reworked because it does not conform to the guideline:

```
    WARSAW--FOR THE FIRST TIME IN 36 YEARS,
POLAND'S COMMUNIST LEADERS CELEBRATED A
NATIONAL HOLIDAY MARKING THE 18TH CENTURY
CONSTITUTION THAT PROMPTED A RUSSIAN INVASION,
AND A CHURCH SPEAKER EXPRESSED HOPE THAT
HISTORY WOULD NOT REPEAT ITSELF.
```

Obviously, the writer is trying to put two ideas across. However, two sentences would allow the reader to grasp the ideas with greater ease. A simple solution is to put a period after the word *invasion,* and start a new sentence with "A church speaker. . . ."

Not all long leads are difficult to understand. Good writing, drama, human interest and rhythm can make a long sentence read well. Some operas are boringly long. Mozart's "The Magic Flute" is hours long but no one walks out on it, despite its length. The difference is quality. Bad stuff is boring. A Bruce Springsteen concert can never end for his fans, but the high school rock group makes noises that drive listeners to seek shelter elsewhere.

Look at this lead from the *San Francisco Chronicle* and decide for yourself whether it is too long:

> The tortured young drifter who paralyzed Market Street traffic with random rifle fire during much of the weekend, hanged himself in his jail cell yesterday, confident that the reincarnation he believed awaited him would free him from an existence he found intolerable.

It's long. But it has the ingredients of a tragic novel. Although this writer knew what he was doing, most long leads are the result of thoughtlessness. They go on and on, like the songs of the inept high school rock group, the "Stopped-up Sink."

Imagine what the reporters on the old *Chicago Daily News* had to endure when the newspaper decided that no lead could run over 17 words. One of their star reporters, Edwin A. Lahey, was sent to Connecticut to cover a murder trial shortly after the rule went into effect. One of his leads read this way:

> BRIDGEPORT, CONN.— Witnesses paraded through the chair like customers in a 25-cent barber shop.

Red Smith, the dean of American sports writers, said his favorite lead was by John Lardner about a prize fighter who was murdered in his prime:

> Stanley Ketchel was 24 years old
> when he was fatally shot in the back
> by the common-law husband of the
> lady who was cooking his break-
> fast.

This lead is a gem. It takes less than 30 words to say a lot. Lardner was working on a book about drinking in America at the time of his death. The first sentence in the manuscript was:

> Most of the early settlers of this country had never
> tasted water except for religious or medicinal purposes
> or unless they fell off a bridge.

Humor—Be Careful

Good leads, leads that are remembered, are hard to write, and the hardest of the hard are the humorous leads. Most journalistic humor has a short life, about the time it takes to traverse the distance from the writer's typewriter to the copy desk.

One lead that has endured was written by John Polly of the *Rocky Mountain News*. In the 1930s, Denver was wide open. One night, a disgruntled customer set a house of prostitution afire. Polly wrote this lead:

> There hadn't been so much ex-
> citement at the Silver Dollar since
> the night a patron came in and
> asked for a room.

Howell Raines of *The New York Times* likes to write unusual leads, and he is not above a pun or a play on words. For a story he did about transplanted easterners who immediately buy boots and Stetsons on moving to the West, he began:

> You can tell by his outfit that he
> is a cowboy.

Raines wondered how this went over, and at a journalism writing conference he asked a group of 15 reporters if they got it. Two started humming at once, and one sang the words. The other dozen had no idea what was happening. Raines had borrowed his lead from the old western ballad, "Streets of Laredo."

For another piece, this one about Bruce A. Smathers, a public official in Florida whose father was a United States senator, friend of presidents and a big-time lawyer, Raines wrote this lead:

Will the son also rise?

Raines was asked how he decided on the lead to the Smathers story, which is a takeoff on the title of a novel by Ernest Hemingway, *The Sun Also Rises*. Raines replied:

"This is one of the few times in my career that I used a pun lead. And it seemed so inevitable . . . in talking to Smathers about being his father's son and how he had planned his career . . . the phrase just kept running through my mind.

"I couldn't believe that no one had ever written it because it seemed so obvious. . . . The lead caused a lot of comment, generally favorable, as I recall. I consider that sort of lead a gamble. I was so taken with it, though, that I was prepared for it not to be well thought of. But it was inevitable that I use it."

Some puns and witty leads have become so irresistible that they keep coming back for repeat performances. When a music reviewer hears a school band play off-key all night, his review may begin with this one:

The Fairfield School Band
played Beethoven last night. Beethoven lost.

Of the actress whose emotional range was limited, another critic wrote:

She ran the gamut of emotions
from A to B.

Three great temptations that afflict beginners trying to write good leads are the "question," "quote" and "you" leads.

Forbidden Fruit

The Question Lead:

Looking for something to do today? In Darien, try the
Hindley Happening. In New Canaan, take in the Country
School Clothesline Sale....

The Quote Lead:

"The colleges of this country are in the hands of an
untouchable elite--tenured professors."
This was the charge made last night by....

The You Lead:

> Do you know that the land beneath you rises and falls
> each day by as much as two feet, like the tides of the
> ocean?
>   You don't notice it because, in the words of....

Editors consider question, quote, and you leads the reporter's way of surrendering. They allow the writer to avoid stating a theme.

"This often means that the writer never comes to grips with the story," Lynn Ludlow of *The San Francisco Examiner* says. "As with the question lead, a quote story frequently begins a disorganized narrative in the rambling manner of a memo.

"If a quote is irresistible, keep it short and snappy. Plainly state the theme in the next graph."

Ludlow offers an example of a short and snappy quote lead that worked:

> "Celibacy is like ice skating,"
> said Roman Catholic Bishop Rob-
> ert O'Mooney. "It gets easier with
> practice."

Concrete Nouns, Action Verbs

Good writers know that sentences travel on their nouns and verbs. A noun that refers to a specific thing and a verb that flies, floats, or sizzles makes the sentence move.

Weak writers torture the language with labored similes and not-so-clever phrases. Here's an example from the statehouse bureau of a wire service:

> ALBANY--SEVERAL OF THE TOP NOSES IN GOV.
> HUGH CAREY'S ADMINISTRATION WERE OUT OF JOINT
> TODAY, FOLLOWING CAREY'S CREATION OF A $48,000-
> A-YEAR POSITION FOR A MAN THEY NEVER MET.

Why not say "Carey's associates were muttering" about the appointment. The verb *mutter* has just the ring for this situation.

There is always an exact noun and action verb for the situation the writer is describing. The English language is a writer's language. It has a huge treasure trove of words that convey different shades of meanings: mutter, shout, moan, whisper, croon, sing, coo, sigh. . . .

Down in the coal mines, a canary sings the songs of life. When the canary stops singing, the coal miners get out. They know that if a canary can't live with whatever is in the air, coal miners can't either.

A canary, a kitten, and a puppy died last summer in a mobile home in Dallas. The pets' owner was a little girl who also became sick—with an enlarged liver and toxic hepatitis.

This is how Bonnie Britt of the *Houston Chronicle* began her story about the use of formaldehyde in the woodwork, paneling and walls of mobile homes. The prose flows naturally because of her use of concrete nouns and action verbs.

In Britt's lead we are made aware that something important is happening. Our concern focuses on the little girl's illness. The lead about the governor's appointment makes us notice the writer. Readers and listeners want to know about the subject of the piece. The writer should be invisible.

Summary

Most of the leads we have been discussing in this chapter are single element leads. That is, each story had one basic major theme, and the lead reflected this: jet airliner makes emergency landing, fire kills 23 people, president signs tax bill, student develops alcoholism program.

In chapter 9, we will study stories with two and three major themes. We will also discuss the structure of news and feature stories for events of one, two and more themes.

9

Structuring the Story

The news story is structured according to the number of main elements or themes the writer decides to use in the lead.

The single-element lead is the most common. The body of the news story includes the facts, quotes and incidents that buttress and support the element used in the lead. Less important elements and themes are included in the body of the story after the lead element has been buttressed.

Some stories have two or three important elements. Leads for these stories include all the elements or a summary of the elements. The body of the story takes each element in order and supplies the reader with the supporting material, to buttress each element. After this, the writer includes any secondary material.

The news writer is a builder. From notes and knowledge he or she constructs a logical and complete structure. Like any builder, the news writer works from plans. Just as the builder has one set of plans for an office structure, another for an apartment building and a third for a three-bedroom home, so the news writer has different plans for different types of stories.

First, the writer has to select the main theme or themes and decide whether the event will require a news or feature story. The next decision is how many themes the story will include. The third decision is the type of lead to put on the story. From these decisions, plans are devised that will structure the story.

If one idea, action or occurrence clearly stands out as the most important or unusual aspect of what was said or done, then the writer has a single-theme story. All other points, actions and occurrences are secondary. A single-theme story requires a single-element lead.

When two or three aspects stand out, the writer has a two-element or three-element story. Again, the lead will reflect these elements.

We've seen that the key to deciding whether a story will be a news story or a feature is whether the story is important to a lot of people or is to be used because it is entertaining. A rooming house fire in New Jersey, hundreds of Chinese fleeing their homeland in fear of an earthquake, the sentencing of a swindler to prison and the signing of a new tax bill are straight news stories. There is an immediacy to these events that demands their being told as straight news.

The event that is so unusual that the reporter has an urge to share it with a friend makes a good feature. Santa Claus accused of slapping a child, the college student whose term paper went up in flames and Klinkenberg's tale of the shark fisherman are unusual events, exceptions to the usual run of things.

There is also a hybrid type of story, the news feature. The Pork Parlor fire, Berkley Hudson's story about Chester Jefferds who spent 28 years in confinement, the newsboy whose family donated his kidney for a transplant are news features. That is, they could well be news stories because they describe news events, but they are handled like features because they make better stories told that way.

Once the writer selects the main theme or themes and decides what type of story the event requires, he or she begins to structure the story. The news story usually takes a direct lead and a straightforward approach throughout. That is, the body of the story will amplify the theme or themes in the lead.

The feature or news feature takes a less formal approach. The writer may use a delayed lead and may even put the climax at the end of the story. A feature, then, can have the main point in the first paragraph or in the last. In nearly every case, the straight news story must have the main theme or themes in the first paragraph.

Organizing the Straight News Story

To begin our study of story structure, let's first examine the organization of the straight news story. The starting point is deciding how many major elements or themes the story will include. The story takes its shape from that decision. Stories normally have one, two, or three main themes. A story with more than three is rare.

When we talk about themes or elements we don't mean individual facts. A story may contain many facts but only one, two, or three major themes or elements. You might say that a theme or element of a story is the summary of a set of facts.

The city council votes 4–3 in favor of a street paving program—that becomes the major element for the lead. The arguments for and against the program, the present condition of city streets, the city engineer's statement that twice the proposed amount is needed to fix the streets—all these facts go into the body of the story to support the major element in the lead.

The city council meeting also considered other items that the news writer will include in the story. These additional items are: the hiring of a new director for the city recreation department, a preliminary discussion of a city-county garbage disposal plan and the suggestion that holidays be scheduled so that city employees can have three-day weekends.

These themes are secondary to the street-paving program and are included in the story after the news writer has given ample attention to the street-paving program, which is the major theme.

Single-Element Story. The score in this soccer game is the major element of the sports story and goes into the lead. The names of the players who scored, the key offensive and defensive plays, the changes in the standings and the home team's next game are additional facts that go into the body of the story.

When the writer considers no one element more important than one or two others the two or three elements go into the lead or high up in the story and the facts that support or buttress those elements constitute the body of the story. When these have been written up, the writer goes on to the secondary material.

Donald M. Murray, the news writing coach, says that the lead can be thought of as the promise and the body then makes good on that promise. The lead says to the reader or listener: Hey, look at what I found out. The body says: Let me explain it to you.

No news story should promise so much that the reader or listener will turn away in confusion. This is why the news story must confine itself to only the most important or interesting aspects of the event.

We will now examine the structures of single and multiple element stories.

A plane crash kills three people. A local clothing store is swept by fire. The president flies to Mexico for a conference. A former school principal dies. The Orioles beat the Red Sox.

Single-Element News Story

These are spot news stories, and like most spot news stories, they make for single-element news stories. All single-element news stories take the basic structure shown in figure 9.1.

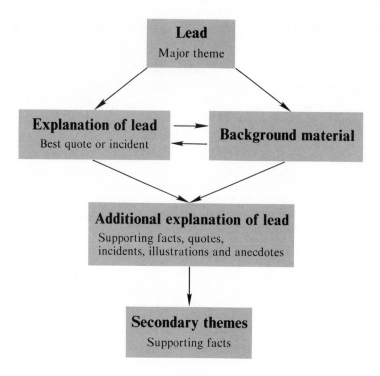

Figure 9.1 Single-element story structure.

Lead
Major theme

Explanation of lead
Best quote or incident

Background material

Additional explanation of lead
Supporting facts, quotes, incidents, illustrations and anecdotes

Secondary themes
Supporting facts

The first paragraph contains the lead. The second paragraph either elaborates on the lead or provides the necessary background. The story continues with supporting and buttressing information about the lead. When the writer has finished with all the relevant material to support the main element of the story, secondary themes are then included in the story.

Forest Fire   The following is an example of a spot news story with a single major theme, a one-element story.

Lead: Fire may spread

A fire in the Daniel Boone National Forest that has destroyed 500 acres of woodland is threatening to spread to private lands.

Explanation of the lead: High winds causing fire to spread

The Kentucky Division of Forestry reported today that high winds have made control of the blaze difficult. The winds are pushing the fire toward timberlands to the northeast, agency officials said.

Background: When started, cause, weather conditions

The fire broke out Thursday. The cause is undetermined. Forest fires are common during periods of dry, warm weather such as the area is now experiencing, an official said.

Additional explanation of the lead	The forestry division has sent 40 firefighters to the area to try to contain the fire. But they have been hampered by the lack of access roads.
More explanation of the lead	No inhabited areas are threatened by the fire, the official said. But there are valuable timberlands to the northeast owned by private growers.
Secondary Theme	The forestry division is trying a new form of forest-fire spray that was developed by the state's engineers. In addition to digging trenches and felling trees in the path of the fire, the firefighters are using a spray that temporarily causes leaves and needles to drop, thus making it more difficult for the fire to spread.

The governor announces that because of financial problems he is ordering an immediate halt in the $25 million construction program on college and university campuses. He also says that he will recommend to the state board of education that all salaries for public school teachers in the state be frozen for next year.

Two-Element News Story

As a reporter on your college newspaper, you want to know whether construction will be halted on your campus. You discover that the order eliminates a $3 million dormitory that was to be built with state funds. This gives you a good single-element story. The freezing of salaries for public school teachers does not directly affect your readers, so it becomes secondary material to be included deep in the body of the story.

Press association reporters and state capital bureau reporters from large daily newspapers realize that both announcements will interest their readers. Because the items are of equal importance, the reporters will construct their stories on a two-element lead.

There are three ways to structure the two-element story:

1. If the two elements conveniently fit into a single sentence, the writer can put them both in the first paragraph. This is the first option.
2. If combining both elements into a single sentence exceeds 35 or 40 words, the writer will have to give each element a sentence of its own. This second option allows the writer to place both sentences in the first paragraph or to make each sentence into a separate paragraph.
3. The third option is the summary lead. This is used when the two elements cannot be squeezed into a sentence (option one) and the writer does not want to write a two-sentence or two-paragraph lead (option two) because it would be too long and cumbersome. A summary lead is just what its name implies: It sums up the two elements by using an introductory statement. Here is an example of a summary lead:

> The Springfield City Council last night took two major steps toward solving the city's budgetary crisis.
>
> The council agreed to hire a consulting firm to study the city administration for possible consolidation of offices.
>
> It also recommended that all city offices and agencies immediately cut spending by 10 percent.

The reporter decided that there was no way to make a one-sentence lead of the two items. He also concluded that to begin the story with a lead that contained a sentence for each of the major elements would be clumsy. He decided that an introductory summary would ease the reader into the story more smoothly and with less confusion.

Money Troubles Let's see what a news writer for a daily in the state capital does with the governor's announcement about financial cutbacks. He takes the options in order. He would prefer a lead that can handle both elements in less than 35 words, the First Option. He writes:

```
Gov. Mark Acosta said today that financial problems
necessitate an immediate halt to a $25 million state
college construction program, and he also said he will
recommend a freeze in salaries for public school
teachers.
```

The lead just makes it by word count, but it has a jammed-up feel to it. He decides to try the second option, two sentences:

```
Gov. Mark Acosta said today financial problems
necessitate an immediate halt to a $25 million state
college construction program. He also said he will
recommend a freeze in salaries for public school
teachers.
```

No. Still jammed-up. What's more, he suddenly sees he has the lead turned around. He should put the wage freeze first since there are obviously more teachers, parents, and children affected by it than those affected by the college construction program.

Even if he does reverse the elements, he still has a bulky lead. As for making each sentence into a paragraph, he does not like two-paragraph leads unless he is forced to use them.

Can he cut down on the number of words? Yes, he can put the reason for the governor's drastic actions in the second paragraph:

```
Gov. Mark Acosta said today he will recommend a freeze
in salaries for public school teachers next year, and he
ordered an immediate halt to a $25 million state college
construction program.
```

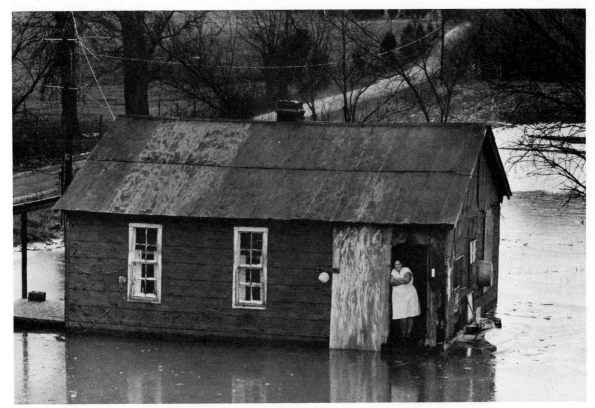

Two-Element Story. A story about a flood that takes several lives and causes considerable property damage has these two elements in the lead. Rescue efforts, loss of power and telephone service, the weather forecast for the rest of the week and closed highways are secondary facts that are placed lower in the story.

```
    The governor said financial problems necessitated his
actions. The governor said that cutbacks in federal aid
for education had not been anticipated when the
construction program was adopted.
```

That's better, he thinks. He has also managed to insert background material into the second paragraph. But the city editor is a short-lead advocate. He likes leads under 25 words, so the reporter now must try a summary lead, the third option. In writing a summary lead, the trick is to find something common to both elements.

The reporter notes that the actions were described by the governor as "drastic" and so he decides to use that as the basis of his lead:

```
    Gov. Mark Acosta said today financial problems have
forced him to take "drastic" action on teacher salaries
and the state college construction program.
```

```
    The governor said he will recommend a freeze on
salaries to the state board of education at its next
meeting. And he ordered an immediate halt to the $25
million construction program.
    The governor said unforeseen federal cutbacks
necessitated his actions....
```

Trouble at the Dump   Here is a two-paragraph lead (the second option) that a reporter wrote about a city countil meeting because he felt the two major elements could not be squeezed into a lead sentence:

```
    The city council last night voted to postpone a
decision on the purchase of acreage north of the city for
a garbage dump after angry residents in the area
disrupted the council meeting.
    In another action, the council voted 4-3 to end
financing of the city's summer educational programs
despite protests from other groups.
```

Too much action for the reader to grasp, the writer thinks. He decides on a summary lead. He has to find a common idea that links the two elements. Obviously, one common idea is that the two actions were taken by the city council. But that's so broad it says next to nothing. Another idea is that the actions are important, but that's too broad also. There is another common idea, the protesting groups. He tries to make something of this:

```
    One group of residents had their way with the city
council last night, but a second group of angry
protestors lost out.
```

Not too bad. Let's accept this and then see what comes next. The writer must immediately turn to the two actions and be specific:

```
    The successful protest was aimed at the council's
consideration of the purchase of acreage north of the
city for a garbage dump. Residents from the area
disrupted the council meeting with their protest.
    The council postponed a decision.
    In the other important action, the council voted 4-3 to
end financing of the city's summer educational programs
despite the protests of various groups.
```

Although the summary lead takes a while to get the reader to the heart of the story, it is preferred by many newspapers and is the way broadcast leads of complex stories are written. It does not overwhelm the reader or listener. The summary lead beckons the reader to come into the story.

So much for the lead. Let's consider the body of the two-element story.

Organize Supporting Material We saw in the single-element story that the body of the story consists of background information and the explanation or elaboration of the lead. Toward the end, additional or secondary material is included. The two-element story follows the same general outline with one major difference.

The important principle to remember in writing multiple-element stories is not to jump around. The writer should not write a paragraph with material that supports lead element A and then jump to a paragraph of supporting material for lead element B, and then back to A, and so forth. The result would be a confused reader or listener.

The guideline is to put the same things with each other. Put all the supporting material about lead element A together before you begin to elaborate on element B. In the city council meeting story, the body includes material about the garbage dump first since that was the first element mentioned in the lead. After the key supporting material about the dump is used in the body, the reporter writes a transition or swing paragraph introducing the summer program, and then the buttressing material for the vote on the summer program is used. Figure 9.2 is a diagram of the two-element story, which outlines the three lead options.

The amount of supporting material that the news writer uses differs from story to story. In some stories, there is a great deal—many quotes, a number of actions and incidents. In some stories, there may be one quote or one action to support each element in the lead. Obviously, the more complicated the event, the more supporting material you will need and the longer the story will be.

Notice in figure 9.2 that your attention is called to a box in the middle of the supporting material: **Transition.**

To jump from lead element A to lead element B would be too abrupt. We need a transition from one element to the other. By this we mean a paragraph, a sentence, even a few words that will swing the reader from one topic to another. Unlike film makers, the writer cannot use a quick cut—now here, next there. Like Tarzan swinging from one tree to the next, the move must be made in a graceful sweep.

The following is a possible transition in the council meeting story from element A (successful protest against the garbage dump) to element B (vote to end the city's summer programs):

> While the garbage-dump protestors were pleased by the council action, the parents hoping to retain the summer programs were disappointed.

A good transition tells readers where they have been and then informs them where they are being taken.

No reporter should be a slave to a diagram. Sometimes, a news writer handling a two-element story will amplify A and B for a paragraph or two before moving into the fairly rigid compartmentalizing of the supporting material for each.

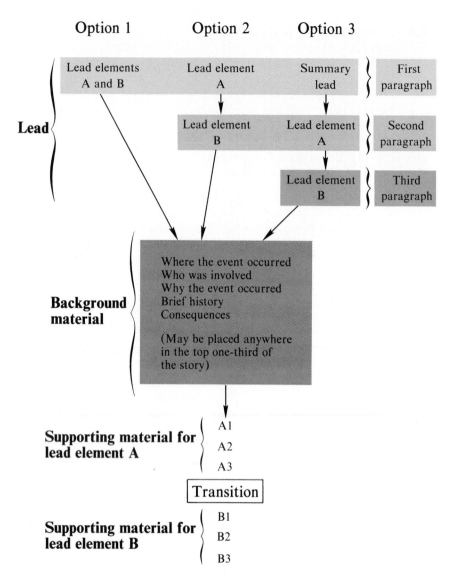

Figure 9.2 Two-element story structure. A and B are the two major elements in the story.

Option 1   Option 2   Option 3

Lead

Lead elements A and B	Lead element A	Summary lead	First paragraph
Lead element B	Lead element A	Second paragraph
Lead element B	Third paragraph

Background material

Where the event occurred
Who was involved
Why the event occurred
Brief history
Consequences

(May be placed anywhere in the top one-third of the story)

Supporting material for lead element A
A1
A2
A3

Transition

Supporting material for lead element B
B1
B2
B3

Additional material { Secondary facts and information

Some news writers will bring up secondary material before they have finished with all the supporting material for the lead elements. They do this when they consider the secondary material to be important but not important enough for the lead.

For beginning news writers, the structures suggested here are good starting points. These structures make for stories that are more easily understood than any other news story structure.

We are now ready to turn to the three-element story. There are no surprises. Our basic approach is the same.

Three-Element Story. The writer covering this speech by gubernatorial candidate Charles Robb decided Robb's three major points were equally important and included all three in the lead.

Here is a three-element lead:

Three-Element
News Story

> JONESVILLE—Residents of Lee County turned out in force yesterday to hear gubernatorial candidate Charles "Chuck" Robb propose more jobs, more efficient use of coal and hope for the small farmer as the young Democrat brought his campaign here.
>
> —*Daily News* (Middlesboro, Ky.)

There were three major elements in Robb's speech: (1) promise of more jobs, (2) more efficient use of coal, and (3) hope for the small farmer. The writer, Cary B. Willis, chose the first option presented in figure 9.3 because the three elements were not complicated.

Still, the lead runs well over 30 words. This is the problem with trying to cram all three elements in the lead. However, this type of lead does immediately tell the reader just what has occurred or what someone has said or done. It also helps the writer with the story structure.

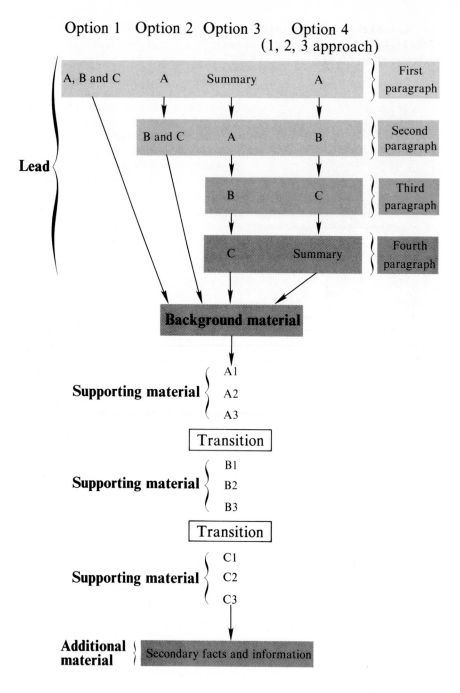

Figure 9.3 Three-element story structure. A, B and C are the major elements in the story.

In the next few paragraphs of the story notice how Willis goes into each of the lead elements, A, B, and C, in order. Then, secondary material and the background are given:

A—jobs

He told a standing-room-only luncheon crowd of close to 200 that he plans to create jobs for 50,000 Virginians if elected to the state's top executive position Nov. 3. He said he had "the most comprehensive plan ever offered by a candidate for governor" to stimulate Virginia's economy.

B—coal

One of the major topics in Robb's brief speech to the audience at the newly-renovated Joyce's Antiques was what he called "Virginia's energy future."

"Coal has to be the cornerstone of Virginia's future," he said in a loud, clear politician's voice. He said the state needs to make better use of its coal reserves, reducing by 20 percent its dependence on outside energy sources within the next 10 years.

"We've got to use more of what we're generating here," he said, stressing the need for a balance between coal that is exported and that which is used locally.

C—farmers

He moved quickly on to agricultural matters, speaking with apparent optimism about this year's tobacco crop in southwest Virginia, as well as mentioning his disappointment with the off year cattle farmers are experiencing.

Secondary matter

He touched on topics common to any good politician's campaign, including education, financial difficulties, roads and care for the elderly.

Background

The 42-year-old Richmond resident, presently serving as lieutenant governor to the outgoing Gov. John Dalton, said Virginia's poor financial condition is one of the most serious challenges the state has faced. . . .

Coping with Crime   A reporter covering an address by the state prison warden to the state legislature decided to emphasize three of the warden's recommendations. In his first lead, the reporter combined the three major elements into a single-sentence lead:

```
State Prison Warden Ralph Newman told state
legislators today that the return of the death penalty, a
new state penitentiary and tougher laws for violent
crimes will halt the spiraling crime rate in the state.
```

The lead has exactly 35 words. Some editors balk at including so many ideas in a single sentence. One idea to a sentence if possible, they tell their writers.

The first option of putting all the elements in a one-sentence lead is infrequently used for the three-element story. The second option—a sentence or paragraph for each element—is sometimes used, usually by making the second paragraph carry two elements in one sentence:

```
State Prison Warden Ralph Newman today called for the
return of the death penalty to help halt the spiraling
crime rate in the state.
He also said that a new state penitentiary and tougher
laws for violent crimes would also help to cut the rate.
```

This is not bad, but many writers prefer the summary lead for any story with more than two major elements. The writer then tried a summary lead:

```
State Prison Warden Ralph Newman today gave state
legislators a plan he said would halt the state's
spiraling crime rate.
```

This is so short the writer decided to add the fact that Newman described it as a three-point plan. Here is the final version:

State Prison Warden Ralph Newman today gave state legislators a three-point plan that he said would halt the state's spiraling crime rate.

Newman recommended the return of the death penalty, the construction of a new state penitentiary and tougher laws for violent crime.

The warden testified at a house-senate committee hearing on crime. Last year's crime rate was up 22 percent over the previous year, with violent crime increasing 27 percent.

Newman said the death penalty would. . . .

After describing the warden's testimony on the death penalty (A), the reporter went to the construction of the prison (B), and then the third set of paragraphs contained buttressing and supporting material for the tougher laws (C).

Teenagers and Dope The city editor has just finished reading a story in the Sunday *New York Times* about youngsters and marijuana. He beckons a reporter and tells her, "Rewrite this. Don't localize it. I want this to be summarized because we are going to have our own series that says about the same thing, and I want to soften up readers who might think we're crying wolf."

The reporter reads through the story and sees that there are three elements: Teenagers can find pot easily, don't feel guilty about using it and have no fear of using it.

The reporter takes three sheets of paper and puts one element at the top of each sheet. Under each element, she lists the supporting data.

On her first sheet, for example, under the heading "Find easily," she writes:

```
Buy from classmates.
Buy from street salesmen.
Even pushers at famous Public Library.
Cocaine and heroin also sold here.
```

She makes the same kind of list on the other two sheets. On a fourth sheet she lists the secondary material, such as the increase in drinking among teenagers.

She is now ready to write. She tries a lead with all three elements:

```
New York teenagers who smoke marijuana can find it
easily, do not feel guilty about using it and have little
fear of being arrested.
    These are the findings of a survey of 1,000 high school
students as reported in "The New York Times" Sunday....
```

Now, all she need do is go to her first sheet and elaborate on the availability of pot. When that is finished, she will write a transition and go to the second sheet about lack of guilt, and so on until she has completed the secondary material.

The 1, 2, 3 Approach Reporters occasionally use a variation of the summary lead for a story with three-elements. Figure 9.3 diagrams the 1, 2, 3 approach, which looks something like this:

```
    The city council took three far-reaching actions at its
meeting last night.
    The council voted to:
    1.Open bids on the controversial community center that
had been stalled in court.
    2.Buy three parcels of land for a new downtown mass
transit center.
    3.Construct a pedestrian overpass over Highway 28
where the Arden Hills Shopping Center will be built.
```

The three items can also be listed right at the outset as Margaret Sullivan does in a story for the *Buffalo News* that begins this way:

• If a woman is really smart and aggressive in business, she's good at hiding the fact that she's smart and aggressive.

• The sexual thing just doesn't go away in business situations.

• Nightmares, depression and stress are the price women pay as they make their way through a male-dominated corporate superstructure.

Those statements—the words of a Buffalo businessman, a local woman accountant and a Stanford University study—just begin to tell the story about women in business, a story that doesn't show up on any company's balance sheet.

Suddenly, without warning, women have become a presence in Buffalo business, and not as glorified secretaries—not by a long shot.

There are a couple of partners in national accounting firms, a bank president and several vice presidents, some owners of mid-sized businesses and a big group of up-and-comers.

So far the sailing hasn't all been smooth, and as women head into the 1980s—a decade that should see them growing in numbers and prominence—they'll face problems most businessmen never even think about.

In the fourth paragraph, Sullivan summarizes her points by saying that the three items are part of the story on women in business. The fifth and sixth paragraphs give background.

Sullivan is then ready to tackle the supporting material to back up her major themes. She needs a transition to swing into the body, and she does it in the seventh paragraph.

Now to the supporting material. To buttress her first theme, she quotes the dean of the School of Management at the State University at Buffalo, Joseph Alutto:

"Business women are often very aggressive and need to be, but it's a trait that people accept better in a man than in a woman."

She also quotes a woman shop owner in Buffalo:

"Women walk a thin line in deciding how forward to be."

To buttress her second theme, sexual relationships in business, she writes:

"The sexual issue does create problems," says Rand Capital Corp. president Donald Ross. "There are lots of liaisons, and they complicate and obscure the real issues."

Romantic involvements are nothing new, these business people note, but they add that it's different now that some women are men's equals on the job.

"No one cared when women were only secretaries and could be replaced like disposable parts," says Susan Jacoby.

"It's always a two-way street, but usually there's a poor, misguided female involved who thinks that's the way to get to the top," observes stockbroker Rosemary Ligotti.

To support her third theme, the price women pay for going into business, she begins with a quick transition and then goes into the subject:

The problems may lie deeper—taking a toll on a woman's emotional well-being.

"Women may not realize the kinds of sacrifices they have to make to forge a successful career," says Miss Ptak.

"They have to realize that it means taking things home, making business calls at night," she continues. "It's not 9-to-5. And it's stressful. They may have to sacrifice their social lives."

Women who try to do it all—manage a family as well as an executive position—are far more likely to become depressed, anxious, and suffer nightmares. They also are four times more likely than men to seek psychological help, according to a Stanford University study of business school graduates.

"These women are very hard on themselves. They feel they constantly have to be proving themselves," says co-author Harvey Weinstein.

The Chronological Approach

Now that we have outlined the basic structure of the straight news story, we will look at a technique that is often used for the dramatic news story.

Ever since humans sat around a fire in a prehistoric cave and listened to the story teller, the tale has been popular. No matter how often it is told, people will listen. Even when they know the outcome, they will hear the speaker out.

This is the reasoning behind the chronological approach to the breaking news story. Essentially, the story is told twice.

The lead tells the reader what happens, and a few paragraphs of buttressing and supporting material amplify the lead. Then there is a transition and the writer turns back to give an account of how the situation occurred— the day the crime was committed, the excitement of two couples as they set out for a wedding party, the first play of the dramatic last two minutes of the game.

Here is how the story of a frightening ride on a school bus began in *The Advocate* in Stamford, Conn.:

Forty junior high school students on school bus 10 were terrified Friday afternoon.

Their normal 15-minute ride home from Cloonan Middle School to the Westover and Long Ridge sections took more than an hour.

The students said they spent the hour watching the bus careen around curves and listening to drivers of oncoming cars honk warnings to slow down.

Some believed they were being kidnapped by their driver, but the school bus company said the man was merely lost.

"All the kids were screaming and some of the kids were crying," said Karen Seren, a seventh-grader, "We screamed to a policeman out the window, but he didn't believe us."

In their fear, eight students jumped out the rear door when the bus stopped at Rippowam High School, and they flagged down a police car for help. All the students eventually were returned home, late but safe.

Allen Graften, assistant superintendent of schools, said he will look into the incident and have some answers by Monday.

In these six paragraphs of this spot news story, Rita Jensen and Kevin Flynn have described the climax and the essentials of the event. The account could stop here. But there is so much local interest in an event of this kind, the writers knew, that they decided to go on. They wrote a transition paragraph and then picked up the chronological account this way:

From accounts of the parents and children who called "The Advocate" and from the manager of ARA bus operations here, the ride of terror and confusion began when. . . .

Notice the word *began*. This tells the reader to sit back while the writer spins out the tale of terror.

Inverted Pyramid—Again If you noticed, these stories do not end with a climax. The climax is at the beginning, in the lead of the one, two, and three-element news stories. The writer gives the major material, then the secondary information. It's the ancient story structure, the inverted pyramid.

This is a perfectly good overall guide to the straight news story. For important events, readers and listeners want to know what happened—now.

However, its use does limit the story-telling abilities of the writer. The chronological approach is one way out, but this approach can be overused.

For a long time writers struggled with the bonds of the inverted pyramid. In fact, they made it the symbol of the limitations of journalistic writing. It became fashionable for gifted writers to scoff at the inverted pyramid.

Writers like Tom Wolfe wanted to tell stories, not live by forms and structures that they saw as chains binding them to a stake labeled "news writing style."

Their protests were valid—to a point. Actually, news writers who had mastered the basic style had for years been able to transcend the inverted pyramid and the traditional structures of the news story—when the occasion permitted it. The last clause bears repeating—when the occasion permitted it.

Long before the New Journalists burst on the scene, A. J. Liebling was writing brilliant, nontraditional stories, as were other journalists. One former newspaperman recalls covering the appearance of Miss America in California with an approach that predated the New Journalists.

Enter: Miss America "I was sent out to a motel where Miss America was to hold a news conference," the former reporter turned journalism teacher recalls. "She had just been crowned and she was making a national tour. That was news in those days, the 1950s, in small and medium size towns."

The two print reporters and a television camera crew and reporter were sent to her suite, and they awaited her arrival in one of the rooms. In a corner was Miss America's mother, ironing a dress. They waited. After a five or 10 minute delay, Miss America entered.

"She was holding a Pepsi, as I recall. Clutching it to her bosom, unopened. On one of the bureaus was a cardboard poster advertising another sponsor of the Miss America pageant," he said. "The whole business seemed arranged, staged."

At that point, he had the idea for his story about Miss America's visit. It would be in the form of a stage play.

He began his story with stage directions:

> *Stage right: Mother ironing blue evening gown. Advertising poster on bureau to left. Opened luggage on low racks. Reporters and camera crew sitting, chatting quietly.*
>
> *Enter from rear of center stage: Miss America. She enters slowly, holding a soda bottle to her breast, unopened. There is a moment of silence. She speaks.*
>
> *Miss America: "Thank you for coming. I have something to say and then I will answer questions. . . .*

The former reporter says that when he handed in his story the city editor laughed, started to hand it back, then decided to run it. "It was a one-day stand. I never wrote another play, but not because the idea was bad. I never had the opportunity. But it fit the occasion."

At that time, such editors were rare. Most stayed with formula writing: Five *W*'s and an *H*, even when the lead ran 50 or 60 words; inverted pyramid structure on most stories. These days, most editors want imagination and color in the writing, and when the event will allow it, they urge their reporters to use the techniques of the feature writer, even on straight news stories. Enter the news feature.

Before we examine the news feature in detail, let's look at the other parent that produced the hybrid we call the news feature—the feature.

Organizing the Feature Story

Everyone knows what a straight news story is. It tells us something we ought to know about a recent occurrence. The feature is journalism's grab bag. It can be about anything under the sun—even the sun itself.

The feature can be as light and fluffy as a cream puff, or as solid and substantial as a rib roast. It can make us cry or laugh. One difference between the straight news story and the feature is that while the news story informs us by involving our reason and logic, the feature informs or entertains us by engaging our feelings.

Another distinctive mark of the feature is its style. The straight news story is just that, a straightforward account of an event. The feature is . . . well, there is no telling what form the feature may take. And this may well be its trade mark. Some are humorous, some somber. And some cannot be catalogued, like this one:

Six-year-old Brian Waters spotted a picket fence down the street from school yesterday and made a detour from his usual way home.

He stared at the iron fence: IIIIIII.

Then he decided to look into the yard through the fence: IIIoIII. But when Brian had seen enough he couldn't pull his head back.

A passerby called the fire department and a fireman approached the fence with a sledgehammer: /

In short order, he had pried apart a couple of the bars: II(o)II. Brian wiped his tears and went on home.

The style of the feature is, as we can see, simple and relaxed. In a feature by Mike Stanton that moved over the Associated Press wires, the story roams around almost as much as its subject—a college student who rode the rails to gather information for a term paper. Despite the rolling, informal style, Stanton gives us enough information by the end of the sixth paragraph so that we have a solid picture of the person and what he did.

Here is the beginning of the story:

AMHERST, MASS. (AP)—Ted Conover's classroom was a rolling boxcar, his first big test a fight with a drunken hobo. He fell off a train, foraged through garbage cans for food and got lice in his hair.

The Amherst College student rode the rails for 3½ months, living the life of a railroad tramp, to research his senior thesis.

He found that it wasn't all bad.

"There's something about jumping on a freight train that just feels right," said Conover, a 23-year-old anthropology major from Denver.

"It's the feeling of the wind in your face and the train pulling you along. I think there's some truth to the saying that every red-blooded American boy should hop a train."

Conover rode the rails for 10,000 miles last fall, criss-crossing the

Writing the Feature

Style: Relaxed, informal. Let the people in the story do things; let them talk. Underwrite. Keep the story moving with quotes and incidents. If possible, use dialogue. That is, have people talking to each other; have them interacting by watching them at work or play. Tom Wolfe, master of the profile, said "realistic dialogue" fascinates readers. Use verbs that make pictures for the reader. When possible, use the present tense to give the reader a sense of continuing action or of being present at the scene.

Lead: Delayed leads are preferred. An anecdote or incident can be used to begin. Stress human interest in the lead by using someone directly involved in the situation being described. Make sure the lead fits into the main theme of the feature.

Body: Avoid overwhelming the reader with detail. A few well-chosen quotes and incidents will tell the story. Selection is the essence of the feature. What is left out is as important as what is put into the piece. A Zen saying makes the point: "To make a vase, you need both clay and the absence of clay." You are not obligated to use everything a source has given you. Remember: One good quote, one telling incident is all the reader needs to put the paper down and say: "That's interesting. I never knew that."

American West to study what author John Steinbeck called "the last free men."

Conover said he didn't want to "suffer in the library" researching his thesis, so he spent a semester observing or interviewing 460 tramps. He estimates there are at least 10,000 hobos living in the United States today.

"They're invisible to most of us," he noted. "But there's a romance about tramps. They've found something valuable that the rest of us have missed."

But Conover also discovered some unpleasant realities about the life of a tramp.

"I went 2½ weeks without a shower once," he said. "My friends thought it sounded romantic to get really dirty. But when I got lice it took away a lot of the romance."

Focus on a Theme

Because the feature has a relaxed, leisurely approach and contains many quotes and several interesting incidents, beginners think all that is necessary to write one is to pile on quotes and anecdotes and then glue them together with a few transitions.

Tom Wolfe says that too many feature writers think "that somehow if you get in enough details, enough random fact—somehow this *trenchant portrait* is going to rise up off the pages."

Yes, he agrees, detail and dialogue are essential, but the good feature writer "piles it all up *very carefully*, building up toward a single point. . . ."

When a news writer sits down to write a feature, some idea of the point of the piece must be clearly in mind. The writer cannot simply toss together detail, fact, quote. That's the potluck dinner approach: Toss a lot of ingredients into the pot and hope someone finds something worth eating. As Wolfe says, the writer must give the reader only those quotes, facts and anecdotes that illustrate and buttress the point the writer intends to make.

In this respect, a feature is no different from any other news story. It must have a main theme, and this must be clear from the beginning, certainly by the fourth or fifth paragraph of the feature.

The main theme is always the spine of the story. Everything else branches from it, and the writer must have it clearly in mind before beginning to write. Most feature writers have a general idea of what they want to say even before they conduct their interviews for their features. At least they have an idea that guides their questions.

If a better theme comes along, they pursue it. The reporter who interviews a rock singer who has just been released from a clinic for alcoholics and drug addicts has a good idea of the questions she needs answered for her feature. So does the sports writer who wants to do a piece about the 38-year-old pitcher who has been named Comeback Player of the Year.

The rock singer may surprise the reporter and say, "I'm through with music. With music, I am going to be back on the habit. Without it, I'll be poor, but alive." The pitcher may be petulant and angry. Instead of being happy about his award, he may take off about his salary, fellow players, and the baseball commissioner. Each reporter will make this unexpected material the main theme of his or her story.

The Ending

Most features have a strong ending. Rather than end on a secondary piece of information, the feature may have what is called a kicker, a punch at the end. It can be a good quote, or a significant anecdote or incident. The ending usually drives home the theme of the feature.

In a story about a woman who visits prisoners in the Dade County Jail to help them with their problems, *Miami Herald* reporter Shula Beyer describes Georgia Jones Ayers as "53, an activist in the black community with a degree of access to the criminal justice system that is unique."

Ayers is shown to be sympathetic to prisoners she believes unjustly accused and imprisoned, but she is no bleeding heart. She does not tolerate crime. To make this point about Ayers, Beyer ends her story with this dramatic incident and quote:

> One of the stories people tell about Georgia Ayers is that she turned over a drug pusher to the police. He was sentenced to eight years. The pusher was her son, Cecil.
> "When my own children do wrong, I don't uphold them. The law is the law. He respects me for what I did. I couldn't afford to see him destroy himself.
> "I would rather see him behind bars than for someone to call me to identify his body in a morgue."

The News Feature

Early one cold Saturday morning, as Bob Rose was at home preparing to go to work at *The* (Toledo) *Blade,* the telephone rang. It was the police reporter. A house a few blocks from Rose's apartment on Parkwood Avenue had caught fire. Could he get over there? Yes, he would.

Rose started out in minutes. He tried to drive but the frost on his car window was unyielding. After a few blocks, he hopped out of the car and ran the rest of the way.

"I arrived in time to see the fireman carry a child out of the house," he said. He spent about an hour at the scene gathering information from fire department officials and from the people who had been driven out of their home.

At the office, he checked the hospital where the injured had been taken, and by early afternoon he had finished his story. But he was not happy with it.

"Somehow it didn't seem right," Rose recalled. He asked the assistant city editor what she thought of the story, and she told him she thought it lacked drama. He worked on it some more and left the office feeling somewhat satisfied.

Soon, he had another call. Ed Whipple, an assistant managing editor, had made a change. "He wanted to bring the reader right into the story. My lead ended up being the third graph, and the scene of the tearful fireman with the dead girl went first," Rose said. The story was put on page one.

In the past, most editors would have wanted Rose's straight news lead. But Whipple wanted a news feature. Here is Rose's story as it appeared in *The Blade*:

Neighbors Aid Firemen

Girl, 4, Dies In Fire; 8 In House Rescued

By BOB ROSE
Blade Staff Writer

It was 7:50 a.m. Saturday when fireman Jack Rynn carried 4-year-old Quanous Russell out of a burning house at 2346 Lawrence Ave.

"She's gone," he said minutes later of the bundle in the blue baby blanket, his eyes welling with tears.

Fighting zero-degree weather and their own emotions, Toledo firemen — aided by alert neighbors — helped save eight other family members in the house.

Timmy Hicks, 2, was rescued by fireman Fred White, who, like Mr. Rynn, struggled through thick smoke and flames to take the child from an upstairs bedroom.

Timmy had stopped breathing, but paramedic Larry LaVigne revived him en route to St. Vincent Hospital, where he was in serious condition Saturday.

Neighbors Help

Before firemen arrived, neighbors had helped others from the home.

Paula Russell, 26, the mother of the dead girl, jumped from a second-floor window into the arms of Bruce Ethridge, who heard her screams from a block away. She was in fair condition at St. Vincent Saturday.

Johnny Hicks, 4, was found on steps in the house by Eron Villanveva, who lives next door. He had summoned firemen after hearing screams and breaking glass.

Others escaped through the front door or were pulled from the roof of the house by firemen who arrived at 7:33 a.m., two minutes after the alarm sounded.

Curtain Was Burning

Kevin Russell, 19, said he was the first to be wakened by the blaze. "Something told me to wake up," he said at a neighbor's house after other family members were taken to the hospital. "When I woke up, my curtain was burning down the side."

An electric space heater in his room had ignited the curtain. He struggled to put the fire out, first by stamping on the curtain and then by running for buckets of water, but the fire was winning.

"It happened so quick, I couldn't even get everybody woke," he said.

His father, Clinton Russell, 72, wearing a tattered coat zipped over his pajama top, shivered as he watched firemen work on the white frame house he has owned since the 1960s. He was the only family member sleeping on the first floor.

"I can't think," he finally said after trying to name other family members who had gone to sleep in the house the night before.

All But 2 Released

They were identified by hospital and fire officials as his daughter, Elizabeth Hicks, 23, who was visiting from Cincinnati with sons Timmy and Johnny. Others were Clinton's wife, Lois, 52, and son, Quincy, 16.

All but Timmy Hicks and Paula Russell were released after treatment.

Toledo Fire Chief William Winkle arrived soon after he was called at home by firemen. "Those guys did a hell of a job," he said of the men who were directed in the freezing weather by acting deputy chief Ron Sturgill.

Chief Sturgill, who estimated damage at $18,000, said the two closest fire hydrants were frozen and water from pumper trucks had to be used while another hydrant was hooked up.

"The first guys there ran into the house without masks (for air) and got to the top of the stairs," Chief Winkle said. "But they couldn't go farther. Guys with masks had to go in to get the kids."

Chief Winkle kicked a snow bank when he talked about the year's first fatal fire. "Damn," he said.

222　　　　　Writing

The news feature takes its content and structure from the feature. In content, it emphasizes human interest and drama. It uses the dramatic quote and the telling incident to point up the major theme. In structure, it may utilize the delayed lead to beckon the reader into the story, and then get to the point of the piece after several paragraphs, or it may put the lead theme in a kicker at the end.

Rose's story puts the reader on the scene at once. We visualize this large man in his dark cold-weather clothing holding tight to a small figure.

The second paragraph stuns the reader with that brief quote. The summary paragraph, which in a straight news account would be part of a first-paragraph lead, comes in the third paragraph. The way the story is told reflects the poignancy of the event more closely than would a straight news story with this direct lead:

> A four-year-old child died and two other family members were hospitalized when their home at 2346 Lawrence Ave. was damaged by a fire this morning.

This straight lead is satisfactory, but the point of this fire is the tragedy of a child's death. A youngster's death is pathetic. Even the fireman was moved. Why not show the reader this and let the reader share the grief. The lead on the published story fits the event.

Many news features use the delayed lead in order to set a mood or establish a scene. The news feature and feature are usually used with single-element stories. The writer will reduce the event, idea or interview to a major theme and emphasize that in the structure. Other information is made secondary in the structure.

Look back to Berkely Hudson's lead on his story about Chester Jefferds. The lead is delayed seven paragraphs, and finally, in the eighth, we are told: Jefferds is not sick; he does not belong in the state institution. The story about the visit of officials from a Vietnam Era Vet Center led Avice Meehan of the Dalton weekly newspaper to put a delayed lead on her story. It began:

> For many Vietnam veterans the war has not ended.

After two paragraphs of quotes, she put the lead in the fourth paragraph: The officials of the center are in Dalton for a visit.

Not many readers will pass by a story that begins as Meehan's does. This is precisely the value of the news feature: It permits the writer a bit more license to entice the reader into the story.

Volunteers to the Dying The news feature is usually built around incidents, examples, anecdotes and quotes that involve people. Human interest is a major factor in the news feature.

Rick Sluder, a reporter for *The News and Observer* in Raleigh, N.C., built his story about a hospice around the people involved. A hospice is an organization that serves the needs of the dying and their families.

The story began with a press release from the recently formed Hospice of Wake County. "My editor felt this was a worthwhile organization and that I should look into it," Sluder said. "Getting the lowdown on how the organization worked was the easy part. Volunteers and officials were eager to meet with me."

Sluder decided that this kind of information was only part of the story. He knew he needed the human element. The story should be about the people the hospice volunteers worked with. He wanted to **show** the hospice at work, not **tell** about it through the words of officials.

"This caused officials to rub their hands for a moment," he said. "Their concern was understandable. Relationships in situations like this are confidential." They did agree to reach some families to ask whether Sluder could talk to them.

"A day or two later, I got the names of the Silvers and the Voelkers. And that's when it became a bit sticky for me. I found myself phoning these people to ask if they would talk to me, a stranger, about the deaths of their loved ones."

Sluder learned what many young reporters find surprising. Despite the tragedies that afflict some people, they are willing to talk to reporters if they believe the reporters are sincere and want to perform a service by writing the story.

Notice how Sluder structures the beginning of his story. This is an example of the delayed lead that is used on news features and features:

Three-year-old Bethany Voelker was sick, and she didn't want any visitors. When Elizabeth Hernandez appeared, she said so.

"Would it be all right if I came to visit you?" Ms. Hernandez asked.

"No," Bethany said. "I'll throw you out."

"I'm going to come anyway."

"Well, I'll throw you out again."

Undaunted, Ms. Hernandez came—and she visited again and again. As days passed, Bethany's uneasiness gave way to tolerance. Friendship followed, and finally, surely, love.

One day the two were together and Bethany was feeling worse than usual. They talked little. As Ms. Hernandez bent to kiss her, Bethany whispered with childhood's sincerity: "I'll be your friend forever."

The bond was sealed. And though Bethany died of leukemia a few weeks ago, it remains strong. Loved ones are not forgotten.

Bethany's parents, Robert and Darlene Voelker of Raleigh, are certain the friendship brightened their daughter's last days of life, just as Ms. Hernandez says she is richer for having known Bethany.

It's a sentiment shared by most of the volunteers with Hospice of Wake County, an organization intended to minister to the needs—physical and emotional—of the dying and their families.

But it's hard to think of Hospice as an organization, with budgets and letterheads and articles of incorporation. Instead, Hospice is people, caring people, who celebrate each second of life by meeting moments of death, accepting death for what it is, refusing to turn away. It is, by any reckoning, in the major leagues of human interaction.

Hospice of Wake County began accepting clients in April. So far it is serving six families; deaths have occurred in five of them.

Its mission is simple, said Dr. William R. Berry, medical director. "We provide medical care for terminally ill patients in the home setting," he said. "We help them and their families any way we can to meet their needs."

In the first nine paragraphs, Sluder shows us how a hospice works, though he never uses that word. It is not until the 10th paragraph that he introduces the hospice, and this and the next three paragraphs provide the lead and background. No question that this is the more effective way to begin the story.

The ending of the news feature and feature must be carefully crafted as well. Unlike the straight news story, which stops when the writer runs out of things to say, the endings of these two kinds of feature stories must leave the reader or listener with a reminder of the point of the piece. Sluder does this with a vivid combination of incidents and quotes about the two families in which deaths occurred, the families of Bethany Voelker and James Silver. Here is the end of his story:

Bethany turned 4 shortly before she died. She got a birthday party her little friends are still talking about. Uncle Paul from TV and Guppy the clown were there. So were many of the Hospice workers, who with some others helped arrange it.

James Silver had a birthday party, too, the Friday before his death on Monday. He had planned it and left instructions it was to be held even if he couldn't attend. "He wanted his friends, the ones who had done so much for him, to have a good time," Mrs. Silver said. The Hospice people were there.

They were there at the two funerals, too. And they're still there, the families said, calling, dropping by, sharing lunch and memories and hopes for the future.

"Sometimes you forget how wonderful people can be," Mrs. Silver said, "but I guess it's like James always said. It isn't how long you're on Earth, it's what you do while you're here."

Cloudy Crystal Ball There is still another way to end the news feature or feature. Put the climax, or kicker, at the end.

A writer for *The Wall Street Journal* decided to have a little fun with a market analyst whose predictions are taken seriously by many people—so seriously that when he told his clients to sell stock, the stock market industrial average fell 23.8 points. The *Journal* sent Alan Bayless to cover a talk by the analyst, and this is how his story began:

> VANCOUVER—Market prophet Joseph Granville made news again Tuesday night, predicting a 16-point selloff of shares in the Dow Jones industrial average on Wednesday . . .

The story then describes some other predictions Granville made, including a Los Angeles earthquake, and then, in the 11th and final paragraph of the story, Bayless writes:

> His prediction for Wednesday was, presumably, a minor matter. Instead of falling the 16 points or so that it was supposed to, the industrial average rose by more than eight points.

So much for the prophet. Notice that Bayless **shows** the reader that Granville failed. By giving Granville's forecast in the lead and then noting the actual market performance at the end, Bayless leaves his readers with the facts to make their own decisions. The kicker has a wallop no reader can miss.

A less experienced writer might have started the story this way:

> Market prophet Joseph Granville flopped miserably in his prediction of a large drop in the stock market Wednesday.

That's telling, not showing. It also gives the story a seriousness that Bayless decided the event did not merit.

Structuring the Feature and News Feature

The feature and news feature are built around the examples, anecdotes and quotations that the writer uses to illustrate the story. The writer is trying to unfold a tale, and the structure depends on whether the writer chooses to get to the point immediately or to hold the reader in suspense. Sometimes the lead will be up high, in the first paragraph or two. This is the first option for the news feature and feature. Often, it comes after an introductory section, as in Sluder's piece about the hospice (second option), or it may be placed at the end, as Bayless did with the market prophet (third option).

These alternatives are diagrammed in figure 9.4.

Option 1	Option 2	Option 3
Lead in the first or second paragraph	Anecdotes, examples, quotes for several paragraphs/must relate to lead	Anecdotes, examples, quotes throughout the story until the end/must build to lead in the kicker
Anecdotes, quotes and examples until the end/ must support lead	Lead	Ending: Lead in the kicker
Ending: Reminder of lead through a summary or an example, anecdote or quote	Additional anecdotes, examples, quotes	
	Ending: Reminder of lead through a summary or an example, anecdote or quote	

Figure 9.4 Alternate story structures for feature and news feature stories.

Look carefully at the material in these columns. Notice that the writer is directed to be selective in using incidents and quotes. Some writers think that they can select any exciting incident, any interesting anecdote or startling quotation and use this as the human interest material at the top of the story. It does not work that way. In fact, the most common error made in writing features is the sloppy selection of anecdotes, illustrations, incidents and quotations for the beginning.

The material selected for the beginning must lead directly to the major theme. Look at how this *Wall Street Journal* story begins:

> It was 1940 when Elmer Novak walked out of his sophomore year in high school and into the coal mines, just as his brothers had before him and his father before them.

Immediately, the reader has a picture of the treadmill life of this family. The reporter follows this beginning with such pieces of information as, "Novak has a mortgage, 10 kids, and black lung." From the present, the reporter looks back: "He quit the mine once, in 1947, after his brother was crushed to death by a coal car, but in a few months he was back, for the money."

The article was part of a series on jobs that are physically draining and mentally numbing. For this piece on coal mining, the incidents and quotes used were selected to make this point.

For his story about opposition to a dam proposed for West Virginia, Douglas Hand focused on a farmer who has battled the project for 40 years. Hand wanted to show that this federal project would wipe out people like Jack Linger, and so he selected the details that make this point. Here is how his magazine article began:

JACK LINGER is seventy years old, but the gold-rimmed spectacles he sometimes wears are his only concession to age. Last spring he was running eighty cattle, forty calves, and forty-one sheep on his farm in West Virginia, with help from his youngest son, Louie. In forty-eight years of farming Jack has developed a habit of being precise. If you ask him how much acreage he owns, he won't answer with a vague generality. He'll concentrate for a few seconds, gnawing on his right index finger, and then tell you, parcel by parcel. There are the 120 acres that he and his wife, Eleanor, bought in 1932, the 50 acres his parents gave him, and the 329 acres he purchased from his parents' estate. He's given away 40 of those acres to the oldest of his two sons. This land is his life, he'll tell you, and he doesn't want you leaving with the impression that he has any more, or any less, than what he does.

Forty years ago Jack took a bus trip to Washington, D.C. He was one of several dozen people who drove ten hours to lodge a protest with their congressman about a U.S. Army Corps of Engineers proposal for a dam on the West Fork River in Lewis County, West Virginia. The dam, in order to provide flood protection for the city of Weston, would flood their farmland. The farmers stayed in Washington less than a day. What effect their protest had is unknown. The dam was not authorized by Congress at that time and the farmland was preserved, but the project just never seemed to go away. On and off for forty years the proposal treaded water, sometimes in a forgotten corner of an appropriations committee hearing room, other times out in the open, threatening actual construction. In the mean-

time, Jack Linger won the Future Farmers of America Established Farmer Award in 1955, the West Virginia Stock Farmer of the Year in 1975, and numerous other state farming awards. But awards can't erase the fact that some people in West Virginia think the best use for his land would be as the bottom of a lake.

"I never thought about giving up until Eleanor died," he says, sitting in his red Ford pickup on a bridge near his property. Eleanor, his wife for more than forty-five years, died unexpectedly in the fall of 1979. "I admit, when she died I considered giving up. I thought maybe this fight just wasn't worth it anymore. But I was feelin' sorry for myself. It's time to move on and live my life. Just last month I bought a mowing machine and a tractor—sixty-eight hundred dollars' worth of machinery. I didn't buy it so I could move away."

He leans out the door of the pickup and spits some tobacco juice. He stares at a sign on the bridge that reads, "If the dam is built the water will be twenty-five feet over this bridge."

"Let me tell you something," he continues. "My daddy and I were fixin' a fence one day. It was some time before we went to Washington, and I got some of that little old two-point barbed wire to fix it with. He looked at me and said, 'Damn it, Jackson, why you usin' that there wire?' And I told him it didn't seem logical to use expensive wire when it was just going to be flooded anyway. And he said, 'Now listen to me. When you do *anything*, you do it *right*. That dam's not built yet.' I always remember that."

"That dam" is the Stonewall Jackson Dam, and Jack Linger has "studied it for forty years and just don't see that it's going to do anybody any good." He's not the only one who's studied it. Many of the approximately 8,000 citizens of Weston have studied it. The Pittsburgh district of the Corps of Engineers has studied it. The West Virginia congressional delegation has studied it. Former governors Hulett Smith and Arch Moore and the present governor, Jay Rockefeller, have studied it. Such study has acted like a growth hormone. The project, when originally proposed in 1937, was for the single purpose of flood control, but it has blossomed into a multipurpose dam with plans for developing the "premier park in West Virginia" around it. When authorized by Congress in 1966, the project was expected to take 9,925 acres of land and cost $34.5 million. The Corps of Engineers now estimates it will take more than 19,500 acres and cost $170 million. Opponents of the project estimate the final cost will be closer to $250 million.

Hand takes his time reaching the facts and figures. In a magazine piece, the writer generally has more space than the newspaper writer. Hand does not waste space. He directs all the details to the point he is trying to make: Men and women who fought the land and earned their living from it would be gone, swept away by the waters of the Stonewall Jackson Dam. Hand's piece, which appeared in the February 1981 *Country Journal,* is titled, "Crossing Swords with Stonewall Jackson—the Farmers Battle the Dam."

Summary

All the diagrams and all the advice and examples presented in this chapter are useless unless the writer has the ability to identify the major theme or themes of the event. No amount of careful structuring can make a story work if the writer picks an unimportant or irrelevant fact as a theme.

Once the theme or themes have been decided, the battle to whip the event into shape is half won.

By listing these themes—mentally or on paper—the writer has them clearly before him or her. If the story is to be a news story, certain options are open. Generally, the theme or themes will be placed in the first paragraph or two. If the story is a feature, other options are open.

With thought and planning, even the novice writer can write stories like those written by professional journalists.

10

Making Words Work

The news writer chooses words that accurately reflect the person or event being described in the news or feature story. **Looking Ahead**

The writer adheres to the rules of grammar and avoids clichés, redundancies and journalese. These words and phrases lead to stories that are flat, tired and uninteresting.

Misspellings, incorrect punctuation, poor grammar and mispronunciation surround us. The sign on the canopy over the pumps at an Exxon service station in Batavia, N.Y., reads:

CLEARENCE   12′   9″

A sign at the entrance to the Publix Supermarket in Homestead, Fla., warns customers:

According to our license, alcoholic beverages may not be drank in this
store or on the parking lot.

A poster in Roosevelt Hospital in New York City invites patients and visitors to a nutrition clinic with this sign:

Want to loose weight?

The AAA Tour Book for Georgia, North Carolina and South Carolina contains an advertisement for the Swamp Fox Motor Inn in Myrtle Beach, S.C., that boasts of a "**seperate** meeting room."

A sign on U.S. 90 invites travelers to visit a "**Tradeing** Post" in Uvalde, Tex.

An article describing the Copper Queen Hotel, built around the turn of the century when Bisbee, Ariz., was the largest copper mining town in the world, says that the town "remains architecturally as it stood in **it's** heyday."

The wrap in the freezer unit of the Safeway market in McKinleyville, Calif., indicates that the packages contain **"sordfish."**

An advertisement for a resort hotel in Pennsylvania suggests to listeners in a radio commercial:

> Why not get out this weekend and lay under a tree?

The people whose job it is to write or to broadcast the news do little better.

The story in *The Miami Herald* about the death of actor William Holden said that after a drinking bout, he fell, gashed his head and "went to **lay** on his bed."

The network sports announcer commented that Notre Dame was completing many passes because the pass defenders "**have overran** the receivers."

The headline in *The San Francisco Examiner* read:

> Climber peaks inside volcano

The Washington Post, New York Times, Boston Globe, Milwaukee Journal and other usually well-edited newspapers have also contributed to the pollution of the written language:

> The *Post* described attempts to keep Northern Virginia's **principle** reservoir from drying up. It mentioned a company that **has became** the first to put a new machine in use.
>
> The *Times* contained this quote: "But I have **alot** of respect for the people. . . . The *Times* describes a character in a movie "struggling to wrap a skimpy towel around his **waste.**"
>
> The *Globe* referred to a man who had been arraigned on a charge of **"negligible homicide."**
>
> The *Journal* ran a story about tourists who "**pour** over English lessons."

The wire services contribute their share to the mess:

> A UPI story from Peking begins—"China's official media **is.** . . ." It describes an attack by nationalists on a United States air base that **"totally destroyed"** eight airplanes.
>
> The AP wrote of the **"first annual** International Congress." From Jackson, Miss., it reported FBI agents "are **pouring** over thousands of pictures. . . ."

The *Surfside News,* a magazine for visitors to the Outer Banks off the coast of North Carolina, reports that a college student "plans to **persue**" his study of geology.

James Reston, the respected columnist for *The New York Times* told his readers of a **"serious crisis"** abroad.

If a carpenter treated his tools the way some journalists treat the language, the carpenter's walls would sag and his floors would slope. He would be on the unemployment line before long.

Granted, language does change. What is considered unacceptable usage one day is acceptable the next. Language grows. Journalists used to be warned to make a distinction between "people" and "persons." People was used for large or uncounted groups of individuals, and persons referred to smaller groups. Now, people is replacing persons for all references to more than one person. But some things never change.

Periods will always be used to end sentences, and the verb will always have to agree with the subject. The spelling of *grammar* will always have *ar* at the end, not *er*, and *sophomore* will undoubtedly always be spelled that way and never *sophmore*.

David Shaw, the media writer for *The Los Angeles Times*, interviewed editors around the country about the problems they were facing.

"Bad grammar. Misspellings. Incorrect punctuations. Poorly constructed sentences. Misused words. Mixed metaphors. Non sequiturs. Clichés. Redundancies. Circumlocutions. Imprecision. Jargon."

This was Shaw's list of deficiencies gathered from his interviews. We will be looking at these errors and those that others have pointed out.

First, an important point needs to be made about why these mistakes occur. Much of the time they are the result of poor thinking, or no thinking at all.

Muddy Thinking = Mistakes

Every person who works with tools knows just what each tool can do. The auto mechanic would not think of using an air pressure gauge to measure the gap of a spark plug. It makes no sense. Writers sometimes fling words around with that kind of abandon. They reach into their word kit and haul out something that looks or sounds as though it can do the job.

```
TWO SOVIET COSMONAUTS SUCCESSFULLY DOCKED
THEIR SOYUZ 35 SPACE CAPSULE. . . .

GOSSIPOL WAS FIRST DISCOVERED IN 1971 AFTER
PEASANTS IN. . . .

ARMED GUNMEN SUNDAY KIDNAPPED THE OWNER AND
EDITOR OF THE WORLD'S LARGEST CIRCULATION. . . .
```

These are from wire service stories. Surely, wire service writers know what they are doing. Let's take a closer look.

The fact that the capsule was docked indicates it was a successful venture. The modifier *successfully* is a wasted word.

The second excerpt has another unnecessary modifying word, *first*. When something is discovered, it is obviously for the first time. It's as though we were to write: Columbus first discovered America in 1492, and then discovered it again a few years later on another voyage.

As for the third sentence, ask your friends if they have ever heard of an *unarmed* gunman.

These three sentences are examples of redundancies, needlessly repetitive words. We'll look into this error in detail later in the chapter.

Another common error is the misused word: *effect* for *affect*, *imply* for *infer*, *disinterested* for *uninterested*. A list of these commonly misused words is included at the end of this chapter.

Misspellings, incorrect punctuation, clichés. Many of these errors can be avoided if writers stop to think about their tools—words.

"Recent reporters have said a number of graduates cannot even read or right," said an editorial in a college newspaper in Kentucky. The editorial writer could not have been thinking when that was written.

"Albert Henry, the disposed former premier of the Cook Islands, has died. . . ." This is from a UPI story. How could the writer confuse disposed with deposed? Obviously, he was not thinking as he wrote.

Word Usage

Writers can sometimes profit from their mistakes and the mistakes of others. Mervin Block, who writes news for network radio and television, watched the wires for the most frequent errors, bloopers and blunders. In a few days he came up with a two-inch pile of redundancies, poor grammar and improper use of words.

What was remarkable about the errors he collected was not that the mistakes were made by professionals but that the same errors occurred time and time again.

Here is some of the material Block contributed:

A pair of small earthquakes about an hour apart. . . .

A trio of bandits held up a. . . .

Some might argue that technically these sentences are acceptable. But not to the journalist, who uses common sense along with the dictionary. To the journalist, shoes come in pairs and trios form singing groups. Be careful when choosing unusual words in place of commonplace words, such as two and three. When writers push too hard they distort language, as in this lead:

A Frankie Valli and the Four Seasons concert—part of Philadelphia's Fourth of July Freedom Festival—ended in tragedy Saturday night when high winds sent 40 spotlights crashing onto a bandstand.

Tragedy is a strong word. Accustomed to accounts of people being trampled at rock concerts, the reader expects the worst. What actually happened: A pianist suffered a broken hand and others had cuts and bruises.

When thieves tunnelled into a bank vault in Massachusetts and made off with the contents of 700 safety deposit boxes, AP described the theft as a robbery. Robbery involves taking by force and is a crime of violence. Burglary is theft of property, which was the case here.

The most frequent misuse of language in Block's collection was the cliché.

If at first you don't succeed, try, try again. Hit the nail on the head. Cool as **Clichés**
a cucumber. Out of the frying pan into the fire. Sadder but wiser. Make hay while the sun shines. Love makes the world go 'round.

At one time these were original and picturesque expressions. But their novelty was their undoing. Writers picked them up and used them, and overused them. They have been ground down to the humdrum and dull, so that today phrases like these are known as clichés. No writer who is proud of his or her writing will resort to using these stale and tired expressions.

George Orwell advised writers to be wary of using any phrase they are accustomed to seeing in print.

Because these sentences and phrases are heard everywhere, all the time, writers have them imprinted on their unconscious, and in the struggle to find an apt expression they pop out. Shove them back in again.

Here is a list of clichés Mervin Block put together from the wires of the press services. Block says these are a small portion of those he gathered in a few days:

```
     CHICAGO--THIS IS THE UNKINDEST CUT OF
ALL. . . .
     KHARTOUM, SUDAN--THE SOVIET MILITARY
INTERVENTION IN AFGHANISTAN AND THE IRANIAN
CRISIS RANG BELLS OF ALARM. . . .
     NEW YORK--THE FIGHT FOR THE NOMINATIONS
SEEMS TO BE ALL OVER SAVE THE SHOUTING.
     NEW YORK--ALEX KARRAS CONTINUES TO BE THE
EXCEPTION THAT PROVES THE RULE. . . .
     FORT WAYNE, IND.--MARTHA COLEMAN . . .
MET WITH FEDERAL AGENTS BEHIND CLOSED
DOORS. . . .
     NEW YORK--ABC AND NBC BELIEVE COMEDY IS
THE WAY TO KEEP LAUGHING ALL THE WAY TO THE
BANK.
     HOLLYWOOD--PAUL LYNDE WILL RETURN TO THE
SAGGING ``HOLLYWOOD SQUARES'' GAME SHOW NEXT
SEASON A SADDER BUT WISER COMEDIAN.
     UNIONDALE, L.I.--THE NEW YORK ISLANDERS
COMPLETE A RAGS-TO-RICHES CLIMB TO. . . .
```

The reader who sees a cliché in print sighs wearily, and the reader who catches a redundancy groans at the writer's incompetence.

Redundancies

In the early part of this chapter we quoted wire service stories that described planes that were "totally destroyed" and a meeting that was the "first annual" Congress. When something is destroyed, that's it. It's gone, a pile of scrap. It cannot be partially destroyed. If a meeting is the first of its kind, it cannot be annual, which means something that has happened yearly. It may be "the first of what its sponsors plan to make an annual. . . ."

David Shaw says that the redundancy "seems to be an occupational hazard for journalists—as witness 'planning ahead' (*Boston Globe*), 'apparent heir apparent' (UPI), and 'ominous portent' (*Los Angeles Times*)." A moment's thought and the absurdity of some of these pairings would be obvious. One way to avoid redundancies and other mistakes is to train yourself to be wary of adjectives and adverbs:

> *totally* destroyed—adverb
> *first* annual—adjective
> *serious* crisis—adjective
> *successfully* docked—adverb

No matter how often writers are told that most adjectives and adverbs are useless, they go on using them. Nouns and verbs do the work in journalistic writing, and all good writing for that matter. Look at this sentence:

```
The workers trudged slowly past the factory in the
rain.
```

The verb *trudged* was picked precisely because it means to walk wearily. It does not need any propping up with the adverb *slowly*.

Some of us learn the hard way. I learned about redundancies when I wrote about a man whose hobby was building "one-wheel unicycles." My city editor pointed out that a unicycle only has one wheel and that what I had written was the equivalent of saying a round circle.

The student who wrote of a professor who "carefully scrutinized" all student papers learned the hard way, too. "Have you ever heard of anyone carelessly scrutinizing papers?" the student was asked in a marginal comment. Puzzled, the student went to the dictionary and looked up the word *scrutinize*. He learned it meant to examine closely, minutely, critically, in detail—all of which certainly implied that the papers were carefully read. His word *carefully* was a waste.

Beware these Redundancies

Here is a list of the most common redundancies seen in newspaper copy. It was compiled by the Minnesota Newspaper Association. You may want to add some of your own.

absolutely necessary	enclosed you will find	reasonable and fair
advance planning	exactly identical	redo again
ask the question	fair and just	refer back
assemble together	fall down	refuse and decline
at a later day	first and foremost	right and proper
attached hereto	friend of mine	rise up
at the present time	gathered together	rules and regulations
canceled out	honest truth	send in
city of Chicago	important essentials	small in size
close proximity	necessary	still remain
consensus of opinion	requirements	temporarily suspended
carbon copy	open up	totally unnecessary
continue on	other alternative	true facts
cooperate together	patently obvious	various and sundry
each and every	plain and simple	
	postpone until later	

Journalese

The dictionary defines journalese as the language style characteristic of newspaper writing. That's the sanitized version. Among journalists, journalese is known as the combination of clichés, hack writing, overwriting, exhausted phrases, and supercharged prose that are the signs of the hopeful beginner or the tired veteran. The AP prepared some guidelines to help writers avoid the pitfalls of journalese (fig. 10.1).

In journalese, costs and the crime rate are always "skyrocketing," and officials who worry about speedy solutions to problems often "raise the red flag."

When a group meets for any period longer than an hour, the meeting is said to last "long hours." The facts raised by in meetings are "cold facts," sometimes "hard facts."

Close elections are always "cliff-hangers," and when someone is elected he or she may "kick off" the term with an inaugural speech. An official who does something unusual is said to have "written a page in the political history books."

Figure 10.1 Take little for granted as you write. Double checking and careful word choice will help you avoid errors like these from AP stories.

 Associated Press
Notes, Nuances and Nits
from the AP News Report

 PROSE & CONS

Number 5   September 28, 1981

Simple Is Better

News copy would be much more readable if writers and editors would keep reminding themselves of one rule: <u>say it simply.</u>

Of course, there is more to good news writing than simplicity. And we realize, too, that one can mock the advice to "say it simply" by composing ridiculous news stories in the "See Jane run" mode.

But simplicity -- clean, tight prose that wastes no words -- is an essential part of readability in newswriting. Reading a newspaper should not be a chore. Readers will go elsewhere.

So, writers and editors must look for those wasted words. Cut them out. They must look for the pompous circumlocutions (like this one). Cut them out.

Unfortunately, examples abound on the wire and in virtually any newspaper. From the wire:

<u>What We Said</u>	<u>What We Meant</u>
announced the names of	identified
use his persuasive powers on behalf of	support
Detroit-area residential real estate holdings	Detroit-area houses
a spate of recent newspaper stories	recent stories
impacted the ground	crashed
a total of seven	seven
for the entire distance of the flight	for the flight
responds specifically to incidents	responds to incidents
a lavish extravaganza	an extravaganza

Louis D. Boccardi, Vice President and Executive Editor

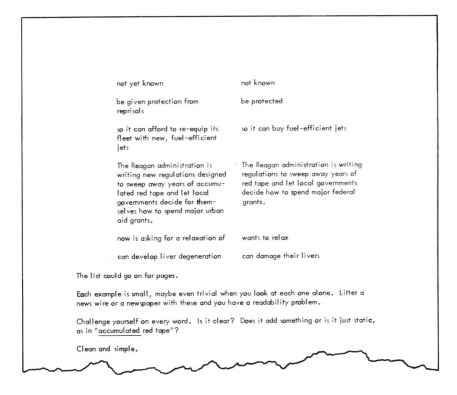

not yet known	not known
be given protection from reprisals	be protected
so it can afford to re-equip its fleet with new, fuel-efficient jets	so it can buy fuel-efficient jets
The Reagan administration is writing new regulations designed to sweep away years of accumulated red tape and let local governments decide for themselves how to spend major urban aid grants.	The Reagan administration is writing regulations to sweep away years of red tape and let local governments decide how to spend major federal grants.
now is asking for a relaxation of	wants to relax
can develop liver degeneration	can damage their livers

The list could go on for pages.

Each example is small, maybe even trivial when you look at each one alone. Litter a news wire or a newspaper with these and you have a readability problem.

Challenge yourself on every word. Is it clear? Does it add something or is it just static, as in "accumulated red tape"?

Clean and simple.

When someone is pleased by something, the person often "hails" the action or statement.

The AP once polled its correspondents to determine the most overworked word or phrase in reporting. They chose the verb *to hail*. Or, as journalese would have it, "to hail took the honors."

Said—
The Scare Word

Another strong entry was the variety of synonyms for the word *said*. For some reason, writers are leery of this four-letter word. They prefer declared, stated, asserted; whispered, shouted, declaimed; repeated, recalled, remembered; inquired, asked; pronounced, related and announced.

The reluctance to use the word *said* has at least two causes. One is a fear of using the same word twice in a news story. If a news writer is doing a piece about Expo '83, it's perfectly all right to use synonyms—exposition, event, exhibition, display, presentation. But *said* catches no one's attention, no matter how often it is used, and substitutes for it usually exaggerate the nature of the statement or mislead the reader.

The other cause is the inherent desire of the writer to strut his or her stuff. Anyone can use the verb *said*. "Look at how many words I can think of to dazzle you," says the writer. In its extreme state, this self-intoxication leads to the refusal to use simple words. A person does not repeat something he or

Watch Out—Trouble Here

Coke This word, like Kleenex, Stetson, Styrofoam and others, is a trademark. Such words are registered by the manufacturer and protectd by law to keep others from using the words. These words must be capitalized.

finalize, prioritize Watch out for invented words, especially those that arise from the unintelligible jargon of government agencies.

irregardless No such word. The word is *regardless*.

minorities Do not use when you mean members of minority groups:
Wrong "When women and minorities are selected to open. . . ."
Right "When women and members of minority groups are selected to open. . . .

The same caution applies to faculty, as in: "Five faculty served with the president." It should be: "Five faculty members served with the president."

miracle Much overused, as in, "Jones miraculously escaped death when. . . ." Leave miracles to the spiritual world.

most unique Delete *most*. Unique means one of a kind. Same for very unique, and quite unique.

presently The word means soon. It does not mean now, although usage may alter the meaning some day.

---

she has heard. He "echoes" it. A project is not completed but "finalized." An event is not set or scheduled to begin but "slated." Future events are "upcoming."

Journalese is contagious. A word or phrase that is unusual is quickly picked up. President Nixon was mocked for using "at this point in time" for *now* and "at that point in time" for *then*. Nevertheless, these cumbersome phrases began to work their way into speech and then into news copy.

"She was credited with the murder of her son." This sentence is from a wire service story. The phrase "credited with" makes the sentence grotesque. Even so, some reporters use it to express causation. A similar phrase is "thanks to," as in this one from a southern newspaper: "Thanks to the recent storm, 600 people were left homeless in the delta area." Soon we may expect to see sports writers writing: "Thanks to Johnson's tackle, Simms suffered three broken ribs and a fractured nose." The political reporter will write: "Thanks to the voters, Mayor C. Cal Evans was overwhelmed yesterday at the polls in his try for reelection."

Some bloopers come about because writers do not visualize the images created by their words. Here is a paragraph from a UPI story:

```
WHITE SOUTH AFRICANS STILL BELIEVE IN
FRONTIER JUSTICE WITH A GUN IN ONE HAND, A
HANGMAN'S NOOSE IN THE OTHER AND A BIBLE--
INTERPRETED TO JUSTIFY WHITE SUPREMACY--
CLUTCHED BETWEEN THEIR TEETH.
```

This is a grim picture indeed, until you visualize the image. Then it becomes ludicrous.

A wire service reporter in Knoxville described Expo '82 as being "centered around energy." Let's see that again. You center **on** something. But to center around something? It's impossible.

It is a good idea to make a mental image of new and unusual combinations of words.

One reporter described the feminist movement as a "slumbering giant newly awakened." Another described a baseball player who broke out of a batting slump as suddenly having "his battery charged."

These words are not only silly but dishonest. They inject the situation with a form of verbal adrenalin. Being honest with language means finding the words that describe the situation accurately and truthfully.

Next, some brief remarks about everyone's favorite subjects—grammar, spelling, and punctuation. If the writer's task is to make the gathered information clear to the reader or listener, then every obstacle in the way of complete understanding must be cleared away. Among the impediments to clear communication are errors in grammar, spelling and punctuation.

Grammar

Grammar seems to have disappeared from the syllabus of the English department. As a consequence, journalism instructors and editors find it necessary to take on the task. Here are some of the basic problems student journalists encounter, according to their instructors.

Agreement

A verb must agree in number with its subject. Writers encounter trouble when they are unsure of the subject or when they can't decide whether the subject is singular or plural.

Uncertainty often arises when there are words between the subject and the verb:

> **Wrong:** John, as well as several others in the class, were unhappy with the instructor.
> **Right:** John, as well as several others in the class, was unhappy with the instructor.
> The subject is *John,* singular.

Wrong: The barrage of traffic noises, telephone calls and similar interruptions make it difficult to study.
Right: The barrage of traffic noises, telephone calls and similar interruptions makes it difficult to study.
The subject is *barrage,* singular.

A collective noun takes a singular verb when the group is considered as a unit and a plural verb when the individuals are thought of separately:

Right: The committee usually votes unanimously.
Right: The family lives around the corner.
Right: The family were gathered around the fire, some reading, some napping.

The pronouns *anybody, anyone, each, either, everyone, everybody, neither, no one, nobody, someone* and *somebody* take the singular verb.
A pronoun must agree in number with its antecedent:

Wrong: The team has added two players to their squad.
Right: The team has added two players to its squad.
Wrong: Everyone does their best.
Right: Everyone does his or her best.
Wrong: Each of the companies reported their profits had declined.
Right: Each of the companies reported its profits had declined.

Dangling Modifier

A word or phrase or clause dangles when it floats in a sentence without clearly referring to some other word. Some dangling modifiers:

Hunting in the winter, the air was cold.
Being an A student, the teacher thought he would succeed.
While in school, my father took sick and died.

These sentences can be corrected by inserting the word the modifier refers to or by rearranging the sentence:

While hunting in the winter, I felt cold.
Jim's teacher thought he would succeed because he was an A student.
While I was in school, my father took sick and died.

Misplaced Words

Related parts of the sentence should not be separated. When they are, the sentence loses clarity.
Adverbs such as *almost, even, hardly, just, merely, scarcely, ever* and *nearly* should be placed immediately before the words they modify:

Vague: He only wanted three keys.
Clear: He wanted only three keys.
Vague: She nearly ate the whole meal.

Clear: She ate nearly the whole meal.

Avoid splitting the subject and verb:

Awkward: She, to make her point, shouted at the bartender.
Better: To make her point, she shouted at the bartender.

Do not separate parts of verb phrases:

Awkward: The governor said he had last year seen the document.
Better: The governor said he had seen the document last year.

Avoid awkward split infinitives:

Awkward: She offered to personally give him the note.
Better: She offered to give him the note personally.

Note: Watch long sentences. Misplaced clauses and phrases can muddy the intended meaning. Read the sentence aloud if you are unsure about the placement of certain words. Generally, the problem can be solved by placing the subject and verb of the main clause together.

The parts of a sentence that express parallel thoughts should be balanced in grammatical form:

Parallel Construction

Unbalanced: The people started to shove and crowding each other.
Balanced: The people started to shove and crowd each other.
Unbalanced: The typewriter can be used for writing and to do finger exercises.
Balanced: The typewriter can be used for writing and for doing finger exercises.

A phrase or a subordinate clause should not be used as a complete sentence:

Sentence Fragments

Fragment: The book was long. And dull.
Correct: The book was long and dull.
Fragment: The score was tied. With only a minute left to play.
Correct: The score was tied with only a minute left to play.
Fragment: He worked all night on the story. And then collapsed in a heap.
Correct: He worked all night on the story and then collapsed in a heap.

Note: Sometimes writers use a sentence fragment for a specific writing purpose, usually for emphasis: When in doubt always use the dictionary. Always.

Tense Sequence	Maintain a logical order of tenses. Keep an eye on the verb in the principal clause as a guide:

Wrong: We wrote him when we had heard of his unhappiness.
Right: We wrote him when we heard of his unhappiness.
Wrong: They enjoyed their lunch after they played all morning.
Right: They enjoyed their lunch after they had played all morning.

Meaning and Punctuation	The story is told of the reporter who was unable to use punctuation properly. His motto was, When in doubt, leave it out. Rather than work on his problem, he left the task up to the copy desk. "I'm the writer," he told one copy editor after the editor had asked him about some punctuation in a story. "You're the copy editor. I write. You supply the commas and periods and that other stuff."

The copy editor was a patient man and waited for his opportunity.

A few weeks after this dialogue, the reporter had a story about a youngster who had been ill for some weeks and had to be fed intravenously. The boy's parents and his grandmother were at the hospital one day, and they fought back their tears as they looked at the child. Benny was pale and had lost much weight. He had not eaten for days.

"Suddenly, Benny looked up," the reporter wrote. "The color seemed to return to his cheeks. He turned to his visitors.

" 'I'm hungry,' he said to them."

And here was the opportunity the copy editor had waited for. He gloated as he left the reporter's final and climactic sentence stand as it was written in the story:

" 'Let's eat Grandma.' "

Appendix B contains a stylebook, which includes a section on the 13 punctuation marks. Refer to it often.

Spelling	The rarest find of all is not the flawless diamond or the white whale but the perfect speller. Everyone has to use the dictionary from time to time. Some use it infrequently, to check unfamiliar words. Others have mental blocks when it comes to spelling certain words and have to refer to the dictionary every time they want to use them. Some examples are *arctic, consensus, embarrass, analyze, separate.*

Good spellers use the dictionary. Poor spellers do not.

Every editor in the land knows that some writers cannot spell well. Editors accept this, but they do not accept excuses for misspelled words. They expect all their reporters to use the dictionary.

The first step in improving spelling is to diagnose the particular spelling problem. One frequent cause of misspellings is mispronunciation. We usually spell as we pronounce, and if we pronounce goverment, sophmore, Febuary, athalete and hinderance, this is how we will spell these words—incorrectly.

One way to conquer a spelling problem is to keep a list of words you often misspell. Poor spellers usually assume they are spelling correctly, which is one reason poor spellers give for not using the dictionary. To start your list, here is a compilation of 50 commonly misspelled words. Look them over. If any surprise you, jot them down.

a lot	environment	occurrence
accommodate	exaggerate	parallel
already	exhilarate	possess
altogether	exorbitant	precede
athlete	February	prejudice
arctic	finally	privilege
calendar	forty	restaurant
career	governor	separate
cemetery	grammar	sophomore
commitment	harass	strictly
competent	hindrance	tragedy
consensus	immediately	truly
dependent	indispensable	undoubtedly
descendant	lightning	vacuum
ecstasy	mathematics	villain
eighth	nickel	weird
embarrass	nuclear	

Don't despair if your list is long, and don't worry if you find you are adding to your list and consulting the dictionary often. That's a lot less embarrassing than finding yourself in the predicament of a writer for a major textbook publisher. The publisher produced a brochure about a book to be mailed to teachers all over the country. It was a handsome and costly effort. One of the sentences read: "There are exercises in spelling, punctuation and grammer." Several thousand brochures had to be burned.

Stylebook

Stylebooks are used by newspapers and broadcast stations to make the use of abbreviations, capitalization and spelling consistent. Is it 145 Meredith St. or Street? Should it be 10 a.m. or 10 A.M.? The federal power commission or Federal Power Commission? The stylebook tells the news writer how to handle each of these.

Newspapers do not use the postal system's abbreviations for states. It is MA for letters, but Mass. for newspapers. The stylebook lists the abbreviations for states.

The stylebook is useful in editing copy, which writers always do before turning in their stories. In addition to checking the content and structure of their story, reporters make changes in spelling, punctuation, grammar, abbreviations and similar technical matters.

When editing their copy, reporters use the copy editing marks that are shown in figure 10.2.

Symbol	Instruction	Original Text with Copy Editing Symbols	Corrected Copy
⬭	Spell out	The (MTA) today decided to increase	Metropolitan Transit Authority
⬭	Use numeral	the bus fare (eighty-five) cents a ride.	85 cents a ride.
⌐	Begin new paragraph	⌐The new fare will go into	The new fare
∧ ／	Insert correction/ lowercase	ₑ̂ffect Thursday at 6 P̸. M̸.	effect/ a.m.
⌐	Run in; no paragraph	More than 100,000 people	6 a.m. More than
＝ ⌣ ∧	Delete word/ insert new word	a day ~~use~~ the city's buses. ^ride	a day ride the
⬭	Abbreviate	The (Metropolitan Transit Authority)	MTA
⌣ ∧	Insert new word	voted 6-2 for the ∧fare. Only new	the new fare
＝	Capital letter	albert Franling and Sue Barker	Albert Franling
∧ ⊙	Insert new word and period/ close up	voted ~~in the negative~~. Barker no⊙	voted no. Barker
∧	Insert comma	said "The state should help	said, "The state
│	Separate	support│our fare. There is	support our fare.
~	Transpose letters	en~~oug~~h in the state treasury	enough in
⊙	Insert period	to lower the fare⊙	the fare."
⬭	Spell out	The (6) in favor agreed that	The six in favor
⌄	Insert apostrophe	the city⌄s funds alone would have	the city's funds
⌣	Close up	to be used⌣.	to be used.

Figure 10.2 Copy editing symbols.

Copy Editing

Here are some examples of how copy editing marks are used. Story A is the news writer's original version. The numbers refer to the errors that the reporter caught before turning the story in to the copy editor.

Story B is the way the story was edited by the reporter. It contains changes the reporter thought were necessary in the original copy. Story C is the way the story appeared.

1.

A man who spend through Brockton with his car hood up

2.

was arrested Sunday morning after losing control of his

3.

car and crashing into the front lawn of a North Brockton

4.

home, Brockton police said today.

5.   *6.*

    Arrested was Josehp Small, 45, of Rockville. He was

charged with drunk driving. His car came to a rest on the

7.   *8.*

law of the home of Peter Ronney, 16 Eastern Avenue. There

was no damage to the Ronney home, police said.

B

1.

A man who spe~~n~~d through Brockton with his car hood up

2. he had lost

was arrested Sunday morning after ~~losing~~ control of his

3. (landed on)

car and ~~crashing into~~ the front lawn of a North Brockton

4.

home, ~~Brockton~~ police said today.

5.   *6.*   *(was arrested and)*

~~Arrested was~~ Josehp Small, 45, of Rockville, ~~He was~~

charged with drunk driving. His car came to rest on the

7. n

law of the home of Peter Ronney, 16 Eastern (Avenue.) There

was no damage to the Ronney home, police said.

Explanation of Editing Marks

1. The word is sped. Black out the *n* and close up the word.
2. I would rather have "lost" than "losing." It goes better with the past tense of the main verb of the sentence.
3. How can you crash into a lawn? Makes no sense. "Landed on" may not make strict sense; after all, he wasn't flying a car. But it's graphic.
4. Don't need Brockton. After all, he was driving in Brockton. No other police could make the arrest. Wasted word.
5. "Arrested was. . . ." is what they call *Time*-ese because *Time* magazine reverses subject and verb. Too cute. Stick with S-V-O. I'll start a new paragraph with the man's name and make one sentence out of two here.

6. Transpose the letters in his first name.
7. That's *lawn.* Insert *n.*
8. Make that *Ave.* The stylebook abbreviates avenue and street in addresses.

C

A man who sped through Brockton with his car hood up was arrested Sunday morning after he lost control of his car and landed on the front lawn of a North Brockton home, police said today.

Joseph Small, 45, of Rockville, was arrested and charged with drunk driving. His car came to rest on the lawn of the home of Peter Ronney, 16 Eastern Ave. There was no damage to the Ronney home, police said.

Stabbing

A

A Brockton man died from stab wounds Monday night after

1.
a dispute with his former girl friend, Barbara Garth, 39,

25 Elm St., had turned violent.

Lee Sam Bensley, 42, died at Bayfront Medical Center
2.   *3.*
Monday evening after the fight, and his former girl

friend was later arrested and booked for investigation
4.   *5.*
into the murder. The incident occurred in Bensley's

apartment at 423 W. 120 St.
     6.
Police said the two had been seeing each other but split

up two months ago when Miss Garth learned he was married.

B

A Brockton man died from stab wounds Monday night after

1.
a dispute with his former girl friend, ~~Barbara Garth, 39,~~

~~25 Elm St.,~~ had turned violent.

Lee Sam Bensley, 42, died at Bayfront Medical Center
2.   *3. The woman, Barbara Garth,*
~~Monday evening after the fight, and~~ his former girl
39, 25 Elm St., was
~~friend was later~~ arrested and booked for investigation

4. death.   5. Bensley was fatally

into the ~~murder.~~ ~~The incident occurred in Bensley's~~

stabbed in his,

apartment at 423 W. 120 St.
      6.
Police said the two had been seeing each other but split

up two months ago when ~~Miss~~ Garth learned he was married.

Explanation of Editing Marks

1. I don't need her name in the lead. No one ever heard of her, and it clutters the lead. I'll save it for the second paragraph.
2. This phrase is a repetition of material in the lead. Tighten up.
3. This is a run-on sentence. Begin a new sentence here and put in her name.
4. Oops. Murder is the finding of a jury after a trial, or a charge. She's only been booked. Call it a "death" and that is safe.
5. Hard to call what seems to be a killing an "incident." I can't say "death" because I've used that. Major surgery necessary.
6. Do I really need this on what may have been a drunken brawl? Might as well let the desk decide. The stylebook says don't use titles on second reference. So *Miss* is deleted.

C

A Brockton man died from stab wounds Monday night after a dispute with his former girl friend had turned violent.

Lee Sam Bensley, 42, died at Bayfront Medical Center. The woman, Barbara Garth, 39, 25 Elm St., was arrested and booked for investigation into the death. Bensley was fatally stabbed in his apartment at 423 W. 120 St.

Police said the two had been seeing each other but split up two months ago when Garth learned he was married.

A   Boots

     1.
For 5 weeks they have been walking, despite the summer

heat, the mosquitoes and their aching, blistered feet.
                              2.   3. 4.
Up over hills. Down sharp rocky hillsides. And along
                              5.   6.
narrow ledges. From 6 a.m. in the morning until 4 or 5 P.M.
     7.   8.
in the evening they walk. The fifteen soldiers have hiked

15 miles a day, even more. They are on the road to . . .

9.
Nowhere!

10.   *11.*
The soldiers have been walking in circles, since the

middle of July they have been walking over a test course.
12.
They are testing a newlydesigned combat boot. By the time
13.
they have completed their rounds the men will have walked
14. 15.   *16.*
nearly 750 miles. "Its wild, wild", said one of the

soliders.

The tests are being conducted on the Aberdeen Proving

Ground in Maryland. The new boot is made of a brown suede.
17.
"No more boot polishing, that's the only thing that makes
18.
this worthwhile," said another.

B

1.
For (5) weeks they have been walking, despite the summer

heat, the mosquitoes and their aching, blistered feet.
2.   *3. 4.*
Up over hills. Down sharp, rocky hillsides. ~~And~~ along
5.   *6.*
narrow ledges. From 6 a.m. ~~in the morning~~ until 4 or 5 P.M.
7.   *8.*
~~in the evening~~ they walk. The (fifteen) soldiers have hiked

15 miles a day, even more. They are on the road to ...
9.
Nowhere X.

10. 11.
The soldiers have been walking in circles, since the

middle of July they have been walking over a test course.
12.
They are testing a newly designed combat boot. By the time
13.
they have completed their rounds, the men will have walked
14. 15.   *16.*
nearly 750 miles. "Its wild, wild", said one of the

soldiers.

The tests are being conducted on the Aberdeen Proving

Ground in Maryland. The new boot is made of brown suede.

"No more boot polishing,⌒that's the only thing that makes

this worthwhile," said another⨯ soldier.

Explanation of Editing Marks

1. Spell out numbers from one through nine. Stylebook rule.
2. Insert a comma between adjectives.
3. *And* does not work. It spoils the parallel structure and rhythm set by the previous two sentences.
4. Capitalize the letter *a*.
5. Redundancy; a.m. means before noon.
6. Lower case P.M.
7. Redundancy; p.m. means after noon.
8. Use the numeral for numbers 10 and above.
9. Delete the exclamation point. Let the reader supply it, the stylebook says.
10. There are two sentences here. Use a period instead of a comma.
11. Capital letter for beginning of sentence.
12. Separate.
13. I want the reader to pause here. There may or may not be a grammatical reason for this, but commas can be used to stop the reader for an instant.
14. New paragraph. The quote introduces a new idea.
15. Troublesome word. Here I need the contraction for it is. Insert apostrophe.
16. Transpose. When ending quotes, the punctuation goes inside the quote mark.
17. Delete the comma, put in a period and close up.
18. Another what? The prior reference to a soldier is too far away.

C

For five weeks they have been walking, despite the summer heat, the mosquitoes and their aching, blistered feet.

Up over hills. Down sharp, rocky hillsides. Along narrow ledges. From 6 a.m. until 4 or 5 p.m. they walk. The 15 soldiers have hiked 15 miles a day, even more. They are on the road to . . .

Nowhere.

The soldiers have been walking in circles. Since the middle of July they have been walking over a test course. They are testing a newly designed combat boot. By the time they have completed their rounds, the men will have walked nearly 750 miles.

"It's wild, wild," said one of the soldiers.

The tests are being conducted on the Aberdeen Proving Ground in Maryland. The new boot is made of brown suede. "No more boot polishing. That's the only thing that makes this worthwhile," said another soldier.

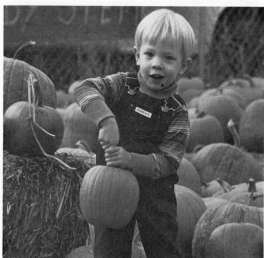

The Right Word. Examine each of these six pictures. Try to find the one word or two that will best describe the action or emotion that each picture projects. If you want to invent a lead, go ahead.

The Right Word

So far we have been concerned with avoiding mistakes. Let's move on to a more pleasant subject, making your writing a pleasure to read.

This involves finding the words that match the situation you are trying to describe. They are out there. The trick is to make your reach long enough to pick them up. The English language has an enormous number of words, so many that the writer can always find the exact word he or she is looking for.

If a child is crying quietly about a neighbor's dog that has been struck by a car, we would not say she is *wailing*. We might say she is *sobbing*. A student who stacks up a heap of library books on his table and then sits there could be said to be *contemplating* the books and his assignment. If his contemplation lasts a long time, we might say he is *avoiding* his assignment.

Avoiding the Wrong Word

accept, except

Sound-alikes that have different meanings.

Accept means to receive.

Except means to exclude.

advice, advise

Advice, a noun, means a recommendation, counsel.

Advise, a verb, means to give advice, counsel or to make a recommendation.

affect, effect

Affect, usually a verb, means to influence or to assume.

The new journalism affected many writers. (influence)

He affected the style of Tom Wolfe. (assumed, took on)

Effect can be used as a verb or a noun. As a verb, it means to bring about.

The council tried to effect a reconciliation with the mayor.

As a noun, effect means result:

The effect of the attempt was failure.

all ready, already

All ready means prepared:

The team was all ready for the big game.

Already means beforehand:

The opposing team was already on the field when they arrived.

all right, alright.

Alright has come to be accepted in some dictionaries. Few newspapers accept it. Use *all right*.

alot, a lot

There is no such word as *alot*. The proper spelling is *a lot*.

allude, elude

Allude means to refer to or to mention indirectly.

Elude means to escape, evade, avoid.

allusion, illusion

An *allusion* is a hint, an indirect reference.

He made an allusion to her vanity.

An *illusion* is an unreal impression, a misconception, an unreal image perception.

He had an illusion he could fly across the sea.

among, between

Among refers to more than two things.

Between refers to two.

Disputes broke out among the men.

Between Sally and Tom there was no agreement.

amount, number

> *Amount* is the quantity of things.
>> The amount of testimony was small.
>
> *Number* refers to individual or separate units in a group.
>> The number of times she testified was too small to make an effect.

and/or

> Use *or*.

as, like

> Use *as* when introducing a clause, as a conjunction:
>> **Right:** The lawyer spoke clearly as good lawyers do.
>> **Wrong:** The lawyer spoke clearly like good lawyers do.
>
> Use *like* to compare phrases and clauses with a noun or pronoun.
>> He played like a professional.

beside, besides

> *Beside* is a preposition that means by the side of, next to.
> *Besides* means in addition to.

bloc, block

> Use *bloc* only when referring to a coalition of people, groups, or nations with a common goal or purpose.

cite, site, sight

> *Cite* means to refer to or to quote.
>> He cited the *World Almanac* for proof.
>
> *Site* is a location.
>> The stadium will go up on the site of the old baseball field.
>
> *Sight* is a view.
>> The sight of the empty room saddened him.

complement, compliment

> *Complement* adds to something to make it complete.
>> The three-cent stamp complemented his collection.
>
> *Compliment* is praise.
>> He complimented her on her gown.

council, counsel

> *Council* is an assembly, usually a legislative body.
> *Counsel* is advice; a lawyer.

disinterested, uninterested

> *Disinterested* means to be impartial, neutral.
>> Journalists are supposed to be disinterested observers.
>
> *Uninterested* means to lack concern for, interest in.
>> He was uninterested in most of the story.

due to, because of

> *Because of* is preferred in journalism.

either, each

Either means one or the other.

Each means one of two or more.

He had to select either the black or white cover.

Wrong: The salt and pepper were on both sides of the plate.

Right: The salt and pepper were on each side of the plate.

emigrate, immigrate

Emigrate means to leave a country. *Immigrate* means to enter a country.

Her family emigrated from Poland in 1939.

Many immigrants experience problems adjusting to the pace of life in this country.

farther, further

Both can be used to describe physical distance. Only *further* is used to mean more, additional.

He said he wanted to hear nothing further about it.

fewer, less

Fewer refers to actual numbers that can be separated in a comparison. *Less* refers to the general number or quantity.

Wrong: There were less boats on the river.

Right: There were fewer boats on the river.

Right: There is less water in the river.

flaunt, flout

Flaunt means to display ostentatiously. *Flout* means to scoff at, to mock, or to show disdain for.

hanged, hung

Hanged refers to human beings; *hung* to objects.

imply, infer

The person speaking *implies,* and the listener *infers.*

He implied the budget was balanced.

On hearing the news, he inferred the worst.

its, it's

Its is the possessive. *It's* is the contraction of it is.

lay, lie

Lay is an action verb that takes a direct object. It means to put or place something. *Lie* is an intransitive verb meaning to recline; it does not take a direct object.

He lay (laid) the newspaper on the table.

The paper lies (is lying) on the table.

The past tense of *lie* is *lay,* which can cause confusion:

I lie on the grass.

Yesterday, I lay on the grass.

leave, let

Leave means to depart from or go away. *Let* means to permit, to allow.

The older woman told him to leave the room.

The judge would not let the contestant participate in the program.

moral, morale

Moral refers to ethics. *Morale* refers to mood or spirits.

The moral life is the good life.

His morale was lifted by the phone call.

over, more than

Some editors are absolutists about the difference: *Over* means higher, above. *More than* is used with figures.

The plane flew over the grandstand.

More than 40 horses were lost in the fire.

persuade, convince

These words are not synonymous. *Persuade* means to induce someone to believe or do something, to plead with or urge. *Convince* means to bring someone to belief or conviction beyond doubt, to satisfy by proof.

Grace has tried to persuade her to change her story.

Finally, she was convinced Grace was right.

principal, principle

Principal means the first or major thing; also, the head of an office. *Principle* means a basic or general truth or guiding rule.

The principal rule for her was silence.

The principal ran the school with an iron hand.

The principles of science are stated in the appendix.

prophecy, prophesy

Prophecy is the noun, meaning a forecast. *Prophesy* is the verb, meaning to predict, foretell, forecast.

His prophecy was for a victory in the big game.

She said she would not prophesy victory or loss.

proven, proved

Both are acceptable, but *proved* is preferred by many editors.

rebut, refute

Rebut means to answer or dispute. *Refute* means to disprove.

Wrong: He refuted her claim she could forecast the weather next week. (He could not prove her wrong until the weather actually occurs.)

Right: He rebutted her claim she could forecast the weather next week. He said that last night he had refuted an earlier prediction of yesterday's weather.

that, which

> They are not interchangeable. *That* restricts or defines.
>
> > The typewriter that is in the corner is broken.
>
> *Which* is nonrestrictive, adds extra but not necessarily essential information.
>
> > The typewriter, which I never liked, is broken.
>
> A simple rule to follow is that when a comma can be inserted, the proper word is *which*.

who, whom

> *whom* is generally the object of an action, and *who* is the subject:
>
> > From whom did you buy the book?
> > She bought it from the woman who lives in her building.

who's, whose

> *Who's* is a contraction of who is. *Whose* is the possessive.
>
> > Who's playing first?
> > Whose glove is this?

Words That
Need Watching

and etc.

> *Etc.* is an abbreviation of the Latin *et* (which means and) and *cetera* (which means others). Never put *and* before *etc.*

annual

> Do not use first with *annual*. Something that occurs for the first time can not be an annual (yearly) event.

anywheres

> *Anywhere* is preferable.

blame . . . on

> Avoid this construction. Make it **blame . . . for.**
>
> > **Awkward:** Don't **blame** it **on** me.
> > **Better:** Don't **blame** me **for** it.

can't hardly

> The word *hardly* has a negative force, which makes *can't hardly* a double negative. The same double negative occurs with *can't scarcely, can't only* and *can't but.*

contact

> *Contact* is often incorrectly used as a verb to mean consult, meet or confer. As a verb, it can mean the touching of physical things.
>
> > His toe **contacted** the football.

could of

> Improper usage. *Could* is sufficient. Also wrong are: *may of, might of, must of, should of, would of.* These are incorrect forms of the contraction of *could have* (*could've*) and so on.

couple of

The *of* is necessary.

Wrong: He passed a couple cars.
Right: A couple of people were present for the signing.

data

The word *data* is plural, as are *media, strata* and *phenomena.*

demolish, destroy

Both words mean to do away with completely. You can't *partially demolish* a building in a fire. It is equally absurd to write *completely destroyed.*

drowned

Don't write that someone *was drowned* unless the person's head was held under water by someone. Just write the person *drowned.*

expect

Expect is not a substitute for suppose.

Wrong: He said he **expected** it was 9 p.m.
Right: He said he **supposed** it was 9 p.m.

funeral service

Redundant. A funeral is a service. Just write *funeral.*

get

Get is a multipurpose verb often used instead of a more precise or exact verb. Use the dictionary to find the appropriate verb.

get around—evade
get over—make clear
get behind—endorse
get—buy, choose, obtain, select

good

Good is often misused in place of *well.*

Wrong: The doctor said she ate **good.**
Right: The doctor said she ate **well.**

in advance of, prior to

Use *before.*

in regards to

Use *in regard to* or *as regards.*

liable

This is not a good substitute for *likely,* unless the event designated is injurious or undesirable.

Wrong: It is **liable** to be sunny and clear.
Right: It is **likely** to be sunny and clear.
Right: It is **liable** to rain.

likewise

Avoid using *likewise* as a transition.
> **Wrong:** He went home. **Likewise,** his sister went.
> **Right:** He went home. So did his sister.

little

Little, like *pretty* and *rather,* is used to qualify another word. It is a wasted word since the qualifier usually adds nothing to the meaning.
> **Unnecessary:** The article was a little long.
> **Unnecessary:** The story was pretty awkward.
> **Unnecessary:** He was rather unhappy.

mad

Mad is not a synonym for *angry. Mad* means insane.

man who

This construction usually adds nothing to the sentence.
> **Weak:** He was a **man who** enjoyed a nap.
> She was a **woman who** was studying dentistry.
> **Better:** He enjoyed a nap.
> She was studying dentistry.

of

Of is an overused preposition. Be selective in your use of the word.
Unnecessary
> inside of the room
> outside of the house
> off of the roof

Acceptable:
> inside of an hour—less than
> outside of fiction—excluding

one

When used in place of **you** it is pretentious. Fats Waller, the pianist, should have buried this usage with his remark: "One never know, do one?"

ought

Ought used in conjunction with *had* is improper English.
> **Wrong:** She hadn't ought to have shouted.
> **Right:** She should not have shouted.
> **Right:** She ought not to have shouted.

over with

With is unnecessary.
> **Wrong:** The game was over with.
> **Right:** The game was over.

presently

Presently means soon, in a little while. It does not mean now.

Wrong: He presently weighs 185 pounds.

Right: He now weighs 185 pounds.

Right: He presently should weigh about 175 pounds.

put in

Put in is colloquial for spend or occupy. Avoid whenever possible.

Wrong: He put in three hours typing the story.

Right: He spent three hours typing the story.

real, really

Generally, avoid these words unless they add to the meaning.

Unnecessary: He was real happy to see her.

Unnecessary: It was a really good talk.

sort of

Like the words *kind of, sort of* is usually used to qualify something in a vague and unclear manner. Avoid such constructions.

Wrong: The story was sort of long.

Wrong: The assignment was kind of difficult.

til or till

Use *until*.

try and

Try and usually serves no purpose.

Wrong: Try and see if you can type.

Right: See if you can type.

unique

Unique means the only one of its kind. It cannot be very unique, somewhat unique, rather unique.

use to

Use to is the incorrect form of *used to*.

Wrong: He use to like sports.

Right: He used to like sports.

very

Very is a much-abused and overused word. Nine times out of 10 it is unnecessary. If you were never to use it, you would lose little.

-wise

Avoid adding this syllable to words to create new words. *Moneywise, healthwise, weightwise, costwise* are not acceptable.

11

Fine Tuning
the Story

News stories are written so people can understand them quickly and without effort. To accomplish this, the news writer uses everyday words in short sentences and paragraphs, structures the story so that it moves logically from beginning to end and includes quotes, incidents and specific details that make the story interesting and convincing.

News writers select a style for each story that reflects the nature of the event. A story about a game decided in the last minute may contain unusually short sentences to give a sense of the quick movement of the game, whereas a story about a teacher retiring after many years will have longer sentences and a relaxed style.

When he was a young reporter struggling to make a name for himself during the rough-and-tumble days of New York tabloid journalism, Jim Bishop was taken aside by a famous columnist and given some advice.

"If you want to write," Mark Hellinger told him, "you are going to have to learn to pound out terse sentences composed of small words."

Bishop took the advice and applied it to all he wrote. He became a successful reporter, then a syndicated columnist and the author of such books as *The Day Lincoln Died, A Day in the Life of President Kennedy* and *The Day Christ Died*. In his stories, columns and books, Bishop wrote short sentences and he used words that are the everyday language of all of us.

The result of Bishop's commitment to short sentences and ordinary words is clarity, one of the most important ingredients of the news story. The news story must be understandable. If it is not, it is nothing.

The good news story has two other ingredients. It is convincing, and it is natural. By this, we mean that the story can be believed and that the style matches the nature of the event. We will examine the ways to achieve these goals in this chapter.

Easy to Understand

Clarity is achieved through language and structure. The language is ordinary language. The words are familiar to everyone. Sentences are short and have the S-V-O pattern.

The story is structured with the reader in mind. From beginning to end, the story moves in a logical progression. A theme is stated in the lead and immediately developed. If there is more than one theme, the themes are developed in the order stated in the lead.

When a delayed lead is used, the incidents and quotes used in the first few paragraphs move directly to the theme. Here is the beginning of an article by Elmer Smith of *The Bulletin* in Philadelphia. Notice how Smith uses a human interest incident to begin the story. The incident is an example of the point that Smith is trying to make, which he spells out in the sixth paragraph: White heroin is returning to the streets.

Human interest example begins story

Kevin Fahy didn't need a newspaper to tell him the United States was losing the battle to keep high-grade white heroin off the city streets.

He could feel it in his veins.

"You get a rush from it. It really puts you on your face," Fahy said.

It was the first encounter Fahy (not his real name) had had with heroin in more than a year. He had confined his daily shoot-up ritual to methamphetamine, because the only heroin on the streets was a weak variety called Mexican brown.

"I ran into an old partner of mine, and he told me he had some white," Fahy said. "I loved it. I went right back to dope."

Lead

Fahy's experience bears out the gloomy forecast of the U.S. Drug Enforcement Administration (DEA), which said part of the impact of the U.S.-Iran standoff and the chaos caused by war in Afghanistan would be the return of white heroin.

The DEA estimated last year that dope factories in Iran and Afghanistan would produce 41 tons of pure heroin worth more than $7 billion. And that white heroin was earmarked for consumption in the United States.

On the other side of the world, but somehow not very far from the hillsides of Southwest Asia, are the treeless streets of Ludlow, a North Philadelphia neighborhood near Girard Avenue and 6th Street. Residents there say heroin is taking over. . . .

The sixth paragraph, which contains the lead, begins with a brief transition or bridge from the opening incident to the lead. The paragraph begins: "Fahy's experience bears out. . . ." The first two words take the reader back to the incident, and the next two move the reader forward to the next idea, the theme.

In another story from *The Bulletin,* William J. Storm uses a two-paragraph delayed lead to move the reader into the story. Notice how many short sentences Storm uses in this excerpt:

Delayed Lead

OLD FORGE, PA.—Until Wednesday night, no one in this Scranton suburb complained much about Joseph Aulisio.

The teen-ager rode a noisy motorcyle up and down the street, one neighbor said. He overturned garbage cans, another claimed—"mostly kid stuff."

Lead

But now Aulisio, 15, is accused of the shotgun slaying of two neighborhood children, Cheryl Ziemba, 8, and her brother Christopher, 4. The neighbors were shocked.

Aulisio, son of a former Old Forge school board member, is being held without bail in Lackawanna County Jail, charged with criminal homicide, kidnaping, hindering an investigation and arrest.

"We never expected anything like this," said Joan Lilli, the mother of a 4½-year-old girl.

"We're all really worried around here," Ms. Lilli said. "We just don't know what's going to happen."

"I was never afraid in my life," said Ceil McGarry, 62, who lives next door to the Ziemba family. "We never had to be afraid in this area, and now I'm numb."

About 500 searchers, including Aulisio and his brother and father, began hunting for Cheryl and Christopher shortly after they were reported missing early Sunday evening. They were last seen in the 18-unit trailer park where Aulisio lives.

Early Monday morning, three bloody sandals and two pieces of rug containing human bone fragments and brain tissue were found at the top of an overgrown, 100-foot-long abandoned strip mine where a neighbor said Aulisio used to ride his motorcycle.

The bodies were discovered shortly after noon Tuesday in a nearby abandoned strip mine pit.

Investigators are checking the possibility that the children were slain in a nearly finished house that Aulisio's father, Robert G. Sr., was building next to the mobile home he shared with Joseph and another son, Robert Jr.

The house is about 500 yards from the children's home on Drakes Lane.

Every sentence is not short. A parade of 10-and 12-word sentences would be tedious. The trick is to set a rhythm balanced with short, concise sentences. (Also, notice the frequent use of quotes.)

Frederick C. Othman, a master reporter for the UPI, was asked to give advice to colleagues about the art of writing. He said: "I shall not repeat any warnings about the need for keeping sentences simple, but I do urge you count words. If you've got a long sentence, make the next one short. Like this.

"The idea is to produce variety, but if your average is more than 25 words per sentence, your reader will desert you. That's been proven scientifically."

Later, we will look at this proof. Now, you can use the work of good writers as proof. Look at the first three sentences in this story from *The Washington Post*:

They came in darkness before the dawn of Dec. 11, 1978. There were six or seven of them, with ski masks over their heads and guns in their hands, and they knew what was supposed to be in the Lufthansa cargo terminal that morning. Millions.

Verbs Provide Action

The sentence lengths are 11, 33, 1. That's 45 words in three sentences, average length 15 words. Just as important, there is rhythm—short, long, very short.

Sentences are given their surge and power by their verbs. Action verbs propel the sentences. They move the subject to the object.

Stanley Walker, a legendary city editor in New York, advised young reporters "to avoid adjectives and to swear by the little verbs that bounce and leap and swim and cut."

Carl Sandburg, the poet, said at age 75, "I'm still studying verbs and the mystery of how they connect nouns. I am more suspicious of adjectives than at any time in all my born days."

Beginners try to reach their readers by injecting their stories with adverbs and adjectives—and failing in the task. Shoving the adjectives "dramatic," "spectacular," "terrifying," "exciting" and others like these into stories is not writing. Nor is the use of adverbs with verbs: "walked quickly," "ran awkwardly," "collided noisily." This is hitting the reader over the head with words.

The good writer does not call attention to his or her writing with these high-school antics. The task of the journalist is to communicate information directly, quickly and clearly. Well-chosen verbs help the writer to do just that. If the reader or listener should stop for a minute and exclaim, "That's a good story," well, so much the better.

Less Is More

As a rewriteman, Robert Peck's job was to take stories whose meaning was cloudy and make them shine clearly. One of the major problems was the long sentence, which was the result, he said, of writers trying to include too much information in the sentence. Peck, acknowledged to have been one of the finest rewritemen ever to work in New York, said he would cut the sentences "to little more than subject, verb, and object."

The result, he said, was a story that gained "grace and speed."

There, in those few words, is the essence of the good story. It is well told, and it moves quickly and gracefully from beginning to end.

Not only would Peck pare down sentences, he also removed extraneous material from the story. Writers gather large amounts of information in their reporting, and they are reluctant to discard any of it, even though some of it may not bear on the major theme or themes.

If the story is about a speaker discussing the need to return to science and mathematics as requirements for college graduation, then his remarks about the beauty of the campus and the bracing spring weather are irrelevant, no matter how clever.

Know Your Audience

Simplicity and clarity are important because of the different kinds of people who read and listen to news. Most journalists are aware that the public is diverse, and they direct their writing at a wide range of readers and listeners.

At one end are those with minimal reading ability. Vice Admiral James D. Watkins said that a study of 23,000 recruits at the San Diego Naval Base showed that 37 percent of them could not read at the 10th grade level. At the Walter Reed Army Hospital in Washington, signs were rewritten to the third-grade level, he said, because many enlisted men found them difficult to understand.

At the other end are college graduates and others who would resent being written down to.

Some journalists have a specific type in mind. Martin Nolan, veteran reporter for the *Boston Globe,* has "a sort of image of the guy who works with his hands but retains a lively interest in what's going on and doesn't need to be given clichés and comfortable slogans in the copy."

Dan Rather of CBS News thinks back to his youth in Texas.

"I know people who work with their back and hands in Texas. A number of them are in my family. And I ask myself, will they understand this story? They're the people I know best . . . good, decent, intelligent people."

Readability

Studies have been made of written material to determine what is easiest and what is most difficult to read. The studies emphasize sentence length. Some also conclude that paragraph length and word length are factors. The UPI gives this table to its reporters:

Average Sentence Length	Readability
8 words or less	Very easy to read
11 words	Easy to read
14 words	Fairly easy to read
17 words	Standard
21 words	Fairly difficult to read
25 words	Difficult to read
29 words or more	Very difficult to read

If the sentences are long, one quick way out of the trouble is to remember the advice of the English author George Orwell, "If it is possible to cut a word out, always cut it out." A good place to start cutting is with adjectives and adverbs. A sentence that repeats a previous idea should be cut. An old rule for journalists is also helpful in cutting down sentence length: One idea to a sentence. Watch for the words *and* and *but*. These words sometimes introduce a second idea. Try putting a period before the *and* or *but*.

Paragraphs should not be too long. In a narrow newspaper column, a long paragraph can discourage a reader. By dividing the number of words in the article by the number of paragraphs, an average paragraph length is obtained. Some editors say they prefer no more than 40 to 50 words to a paragraph. A faster way to check paragraph length is to limit paragraphs to no more than three or four sentences.

Big words, by which we mean words with three or more syllables, are difficult for readers to understand. The fewer big words the better. One long word in 10 at most. Orwell put it simply: "Never use a long word where a short one will do."

Muddy writing can be made clearer with these techniques. But no one can learn to write by using a formula. The formula is a check, a thermometer to measure potential trouble. If you write simply, clearly and directly, if you use quotes and anecdotes and illustrations, and if you write with a firm idea of what you want to say, then your writing will meet these guidelines.

If we were to isolate a single factor that causes trouble to news writers, it is the inability to say something simply. "There are some common defects that we know contribute to bad writing. And, by far, the worst is failure to say it simply," says the AP in a study of readability. The AP says that the heart of all the formulas that have been used to check readability is this: "Say it simply and say it in short, easy-to-understand sentences."

Not only does the reporter have to write each story simply and clearly, he or she must prove the case, must convince the reader that the story is true.

Convincing

A reporter, on assignment in a Central American country that had been ruled by three generations of dictators, beginning with the grandfather of the present ruler, wanted to learn what the people thought of the grandson. The grandfather had been ruthless. One of his favorite methods of torturing opponents was to hang them head down in a well.

The grandson was supposedly enlightened. The reporter went into the countryside to find out what the peasants thought of them. In one of his interviews, he asked an elderly farmer whether there was any difference among the three rulers.

"Un arbol no puede dar tres clases de frutas," the peasant replied, and the reporter wrote this in his story, along with the English translation, "One tree cannot give three kinds of fruits."

Those who read the story understood. Despite the ruler's elaborate and expensive public relations apparatus in the United States, directed at painting him as a democratic president, the reporter's story had the ring of truth. The homespun saying of the peasant carried more weight than the barrage of paid propaganda.

The combination of on-the-scene reporting and good writing carry conviction. By good writing we mean stories that illustrate with examples (show, don't tell), that quote people involved in the event and that contain specific details.

Showing Carries Conviction

When Jeff Klinkenberg interviewed A. J. McClane, a world-famous fisherman, he wanted his readers to draw some conclusions about McClane. He could have said that McClane is world famous. Instead, he **shows** the reader this with the following incident:

Inside ritzy Capriccio's Restaurant where luncheon guests include ITT's board chairman, waiters hover about A. J. McClane like pilotfish around a shark. A waiter lights his cigarette while another pours his drink. The maître d'—and then the owner—stop and ask him if his meal is satisfactory.

We might have taken Klinkenberg's word for it if he had told us McClane was famous. Or we might not. But after reading this incident, we know. We are convinced.

Klinkenberg wants to make a point about the democracy of fishing. On a stream, in a river, at the ocean, all are equal. Klinkenberg uses McClane's voice to provide the incident to make this point. Here is McClane speaking:

> I went fishing once with King Zahir of Afghanistan, but do you know what I remember most about the day? I remember him reaching deep into his wallet and producing a little snapshot of him holding a five-pound trout. Here was this king, and all he wanted was to show me a fish he was proud of. Remarkable! The point is this: Fishing is a universal thing. When people are fishing, it does not matter who they are. They're all the same.

Klinkenberg spent five hours with McClane, read some of his writings and interviewed several people who knew him. The result was a notebook filled with material that showed McClane's abilities as an angler. From these notes, he wrote for nine hours. He revised the story 17 times.

"I would have done better if I didn't have the flu," Klinkenberg said of his effort.

Flu or no, the reader put down Klinkenberg's story with the feeling he or she knew McClane.

Sometimes, the showing can be done quickly. The reader can see a great deal with one shaft of light. When Red Smith, the great sports writer, wanted to tell his readers about the power of the owner of the Los Angeles Dodgers baseball team, he did not say that the owner, Walter O'Malley, was more powerful than Bowie Kuhn, the commissioner of baseball. Smith wrote:

> When O'Malley sends out for coffee, Kuhn asks, "One lump or two?"

Red Smith wrote a column and columnists are given plenty of freedom. However, the point is still valid: Show the reader or listener and conviction follows.

Quotes Convince

Quotes carry conviction. Mervin Block, a former newspaper reporter who writes television and radio news, was assigned to do a magazine piece about the newspaper war between the *Daily News* and *The New York Post*.

He quotes the *Post's* metropolitan editor:

> "What competition?" snaps the Post's metropolitan editor, Steve Dunleavy scornfully. "If it's war, it's a massacre—by the Post. We're gaining two to every one they lose . . . we're so confident we walk around the trenches with our helmets off."

We can visualize the colorful, confident, if not cocky, editor as he talks.

Ten Keys to Good Writing

Begin to write only after you know what you want to say.
Write the way you talk.
Use the S-V-O sentence structure for most sentences.
Use action verbs.
Avoid adjectives and adverbs.
Keep sentences short.
Show, don't tell.
Good quotes up high.
Use words you're familiar with.
Never turn in a story you think you can improve.

Studs Terkel interviewed a telephone solicitor for a Chicago newspaper. The woman, Enid Du Bois, would call people to ask them to subscribe. She worked with about 30 others, mostly women. Four, including Du Bois, were black. She talks to Terkel:

At first I liked the idea of talking to people. But pretty soon, knowing the area I was calling—they couldn't afford to eat, let alone buy a newspaper—my job was getting me down. They'd say, "Lady, I have nine to feed or I would help you." What can you say? One woman I had called early in the morning, she had just gotten out of the hospital. She had to get up and answer the phone.

They would tell me their problems. Some of them couldn't read, honest to God. They weren't educated enough to read a newspaper. Know what I would say? "If you don't read anything but the comic strips . . ." "If you got kids, they have to learn how to read the paper." I'm so ashamed thinking of it.

In the middle-class area, the people were busy and they couldn't talk. But in the poor area, the people really wanted to help the charity I talked about. They said I sounded so nice, they would take it anyway. A lot of them were so happy that someone actually called. They could talk all day long to me. They told me all their problems and I'd listen.

They were so elated to hear someone nice, someone just to listen a few minutes to something that had happened to them. Somehow to show concern about them. I didn't care if there was no order. So I'd listen. I heard a lot of their life stories on the phone. I didn't care if the supervisor clicked in.

Terkel is a master interviewer. Many of his taped interviews have been collected in books. His interviews with working people are included in *Working: People Talk About What They Do All Day and What They Think of While They Do It* (New York: Pantheon Books, 1972).

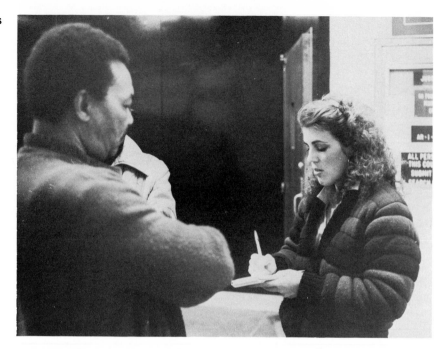

In these quotes, so much is revealed: the compassion of Du Bois, her disgust with her job, the generosity of the poor, the terrible solitude and loneliness of people. All of this in just four paragraphs.

Quotes convince us because we can visualize the people and the circumstances. Quotes are memorable. An international economist recalls being seated in a restaurant next to a family of three, father, mother, and a boy of eight or ten. The waitress brought the menus and waited.

The boy decided. "I want liver and bacon," he said. The mother said she wanted a steak. Father turned to the waitress. "Three steaks," he said. The waitress nodded and replied as she wrote, "Two steaks, one liver and bacon."

The boy turned to his mother. "Mommy," he said, "she thinks I'm real."

No wonder the economist remembered this story. The boy's excited statement sums up the refusal of parents to take their children seriously.

Reporters always listen for the quote and watch for the incident that sums up the situation. Not only will the quote be good reading; it will convince the reader.

Be Specific

Finally, conviction is achieved through specifics. The writer who writes, "There were about a dozen people in the courtroom" is not taken as seriously as the writer who writes, "There were 11 people in the courtroom."

We know that the writer who wrote "11" was there.

If the book stolen from the library was 4 inches by 6 inches, don't say it was a "small book." Say, "The book was 4 inches by 6 inches, small enough to fit into a coat pocket."

Exact Detail. The writer who described a dance performed by the Hartford Ballet as "consisting of several dancers" was not as helpful to the reader, nor as convincing, as he could have been had he written of "six women and three men clad in black."

Readers love details, specific details. Readers can visualize the event if they are told that the suspect was five-foot-four, thin, had blue jogging shoes, a close-cropped haircut and used a small handgun that fitted in the palm of his hand.

The reporter notes sizes, weights, numbers of things, colors, smells. Was it as large as a baseball or a basketball, as heavy as a letter or a book? Did it smell like onions, garlic or newly-cut grass? Was it a deep blue, almost black, or the light blue of a sky after a rainstorm? Did it sound like the snap of a firecracker or the bang of a backfire?

Notice that in these questions, the specifics have been linked to particular things that can be seen, touched, smelled, heard. Writers use images that appeal to the senses to make their specifics spring to life and to give them the exactitude of reality.

Words as well as observations can be abstract. Just as we avoid saying "around a dozen" or "small," we do not use abstractions, such as patriotism, equality, affection, unless they are tied directly to a specific or we are quoting someone.

Abstractions have no agreed-upon meaning. What is obscenity? As a federal judge observed, "One man's lyric is another man's obscenity."

Words must be anchored to real things in nature when we use them. Should the source talk of love, freedom, happiness, fear and anxiety, the reporter is immediately alert. The reporter knows that these words mean all things to all people. Their meanings are elusive. The reporter has to grab the slippery subject and tie it down.

The reporter will ask the source, "Can you give me an example of what you mean by happiness?" As one reporter put it, "I always ask anyone who speaks in generalities for a for-instance."

Natural Style. The writer selects a style for each story that reflects the nature of the event in much the same way as a photographer composes a picture and selects the correct lens opening and filter. Here, photographer Al Cabral highlights the starkness of this abandoned farmhouse by including the weeds, sagging fence and arid land.

Natural Style

Our third component of the well-written story is a natural writing style. By this, we mean that the style of the story fits the subject. Words, sentence patterns, even the length of the paragraphs are chosen to be consistent with the subject matter.

The profile of a young woman who has just won a beauty contest will not be written with the same somber style as the obituary of a well-known local resident. The profile will be breezy, even brash:

Evelyn Marie Welton woke up yesterday morning with a headache.

Last night she went to bed with a head full of dreams.

The 19-year-old Mason City college sophomore was crowned Miss Douglas County at the Civic Auditorium last night. Next month, she goes to the state finals.

"I felt terrible, just terrible all day," Welton said after her victory. "But as soon as I walked into the auditorium, something happened. Like, you know, it snapped."

The lights, the excitement of competition, the possibility of going all the way to the top had its effect.

"I just knew I could do it," she said. . . .

On the other hand the obituary will be somber and reserved:

Albert Funnel, 78, of 45 East Alpine Ave., who served as city clerk for 46 years before retiring, died yesterday after a long illness.

Funnel had been hospitalized a week ago with lung cancer.

The former city worker was known throughout the state for his innovations in the office of city clerk. He instituted a new system of. . . .

Mitch Mendelson had a tragic story to cover, a house fire in which five people died. His style is simple and direct. He lets the facts show the tragedy. The writer gives them no adornment. Here is the beginning of his understated story, which appeared in the *Birmingham Post-Herald:*

A Grim Story

The use of a delayed lead puts reader on the scene.

A coroner stood in the rain yesterday afternoon and poked through the smoldering rubble of what had been a house. She was looking for the bodies of four young children and their great-grandmother.

A helper standing nearby shivered.

One by one, the tiny, charred figures were carefully zipped into black vinyl body bags and carried away.

A chilling quote sums up the tragic event.

As the coroner, Dale Cunningham, was leaving, a passerby asked if there were any bodies left in the ruins. "Five is all," she said. "Five is too many."

The essential facts of the story

> Reginald, 4, Stephanie, 2, Roderick, 2, and Amanda Gardner, 6 months, and Fannie Harvell, 88, were killed by a fire that destroyed their Dolomite home yesterday morning.
>
> The children's mother, Sandra Gardner, 23, was reportedly visiting neighbors when the fire started. Her 19-year-old brother escaped the house. Ms. Gardner was treated for shock at Lloyd Nolan Hospital in Fairfield.
>
> All four of the children were in the same room. One body was found in a corner, another under a bed.
>
> Mrs. Harvell died near the back door.

Mendelson says that he wanted to get behind the tragedy "to find reasons and aggravating circumstances." Once they have been discovered, he says, "the task is to weave the reasons and the message into the dramatic fabric, supporting the themes with facts and vivid descriptions."

In covering the fire, Mendelson learned that there were three possible reasons for the deaths. The burglar bars on the windows may have hampered escape. The community of Dolomite has no fire protection. And, third, the area has no fire hydrants.

Here is the rest of the story. Watch how Mendelson weaves these three possible causes for the tragedy into the account:

Burglar bars

> Preston Countryman, a fire medic from the Hueytown Fire Department, stood in the front yard and picked up one of the steel "burglar bars" that had been on a front window. "Death traps," he said. Every window on the house had burglar bars. "They're good for keeping people out . . . plus keeping people in," he said.

No fire protection

> And Dolomite, an unincorporated area of Jefferson County sandwiched between Hueytown, Pleasant Grove and Midfield, has no fire protection. By the time Hueytown firefighters arrived on the scene about 9:40 a.m., the one-story, wood-frame house at 669 Washington Ave. was, according to firemen, "heavily involved."

No hydrants

Elaboration of possible causes of the deaths

Possible dangers for the future (Mendelson's "message")

Description of the scene

Add a third chilling fact: The area, which is heavily residential with many one-family homes, has no hydrants. Fire companies from Hueytown and Brighton had to shuttle water to the scene.

"The county should furnish protection, but they don't," said Hueytown firefighter Dale Roberts yesterday afternoon as the men cleaned up in the firehouse. "And one thing that hampers firefighting is having to shuttle water. One question that should be asked is, "Why is the Center Point area furnished with fire protection but other unincorporated areas aren't?"

The Hueytown men made it clear they are not required to answer calls outside the city. "We go provided we can get our auxiliary (volunteers) in. We can't send everyone outside of the city," said Roberts.

"It's an awkward situation."

Added volunteer firefighter Luther Brown: "I'm glad that we had enough help that we could go out. It might not happen the next time."

While the two companies had the blaze under control in about 30 minutes, Brown pointed out there was valuable time lost in finding teams to respond. "Five minutes makes a lot of difference," he said.

The rain poured down on the charred ruins yesterday afternoon, and steam rose from the rooms that had been torn apart by the blaze and the men who came on a mission of mercy to fight it. The rain made pools in the front yard where Countryman stood and talked about the burglar bars. It turned to thick mud the yards around the house and the garden in the back.

At the house next door, family, neighbors and friends gathered to console the living and mourn the dead.

Vonnegut on Style—Respect for the Reader

Kurt Vonnegut, the author of *Slaughterhouse Five, Cat's Cradle* and other novels, says that when an author works on his or her writing style it is "a mark of respect" to the reader.

"If you scribble your thoughts any which way," he says, "your readers will surely feel that you care nothing about them. They will mark you down as an egomaniac or a chowderhead—or worse, they will stop reading you."

Vonnegut says that writers must care about the subjects they write about. "It is this genuine caring, and not your games with language, which will be the most compelling and seductive element in your style."

He adds this advice:

Do not ramble.

Keep it simple. He points out that the Bible opens "with a sentence well within the writing skills of a lively fourteen-year-old: 'In the beginning God created the heaven and the earth.' "

Have the guts to cut. Every sentence, he says, has to "illuminate your subject."

Sound like yourself. Write the way you speak.

Say what you mean to say.

Description of the scene (continued)

The rain fell on the twisted pipes that had been a kitchen set and on a scorched refrigerator and on the children's toys in the front yard.

The neighbors stood on their porches and looked out at the dismal scene. A sheriff's officer splashed through the yard and said, "mess," and shook his head.

At the house next door, Shirley Williams, Ms. Gardner's sister, slumped next to a window and looked out at the place where her grandmother and four of her nieces and nephews had died.

Driving home the message

Steve Mahan, another Hueytown fire medic, said at the scene, "Half of our fire department is here and the city is unprotected. But it's hard to say 'No, we can't come.' "

A recent report by the National Fire Data Center said Alabama and other southeastern states have the highest fire death rate in the industrialized world. Birmingham ranks only second to Newark, N.J., in fire death rates among large American cities.

20 Tips for Good Writing

This list was put together by the Gannett newspapers. Most of the tips were supplied by Jim Bishop.

1. Be fair. Presenting all sides of a story is not copping out.
2. Observe good taste.
3. Make the lead provocative, clear and simple.
4. Sentences should be short.
5. Quotes improve a story. Use them.
6. An important story need not be long.
7. Select adjectives carefully. Too many are dangerous.
8. Don't be impressed with an important assignment.
9. Go directly to the source on every story when possible.
10. Leave no reasonable question unanswered. Do not assume readers know the background. And don't be afraid to write a good story you think readers already know.
11. Be polite, but don't be servile.
12. Get details. If your congressman wears high-top shoes, scratches his ears and uses a spittoon, you've created a word picture.
13. Don't be afraid to try something that isn't in the book.
14. Even if you have mastered the language, use short, easy words.
15. Stories are improved by the injection of the time element.
16. After the lead, blend the story from paragraph to paragraph.
17. Don't insult a race, an ethnic group, a minority or other separate entity. Identify when it adds information. The distinction is thin at times.
18. Don't abuse your privileges or the weapons of your industry.
19. Admit errors quickly and fully.
20. Name the source of your story when possible. If it is an exposé from a confidential source, protect that source.

Driving home the message (continued)

> Supplemental heaters, such as space heaters, are considered the biggest cause of fatal fires in the South, the report said.
>
> The cause of yesterday's fire will be investigated by the state fire marshal's office, Roberts said.

As much as Mendelson wants to get his message across, he does not lecture or preach. The message is made by the people he interviews. He lets his sources do the talking.

The story won a writing award from the Scripps-Howard organization, of which the *Birmingham Post-Herald* is a member newspaper. The judges praised Mendelson's "great sensitivity" and for "superbly organizing his facts so that readers when they had finished knew they had read something special."

Resistance to Journalistic Writing

The clear, simple writing in the fire story is typical of good journalistic writing. Despite the clarity of such writing, teachers of high school and college English resist this kind of writing. Worse, they condemn it. Why? Why hasn't journalistic prose won many converts from the cloister of the English classroom?

A study by two professors may provide the answer. In a series of experiments, they found that English teachers are more impressed by wordy, complicated language than by clear and concise writing. Rosemary L. Hake of Chicago State University and Joseph M. Williams of the University of Chicago asked English teachers to rate pairs of student essays that were exactly the same in everything except style.

One of each pair was written in the clear and simple language journalists use. The other essay was devised so that the language was flowery, the sentences complex, the verbs passive.

The two professors discovered that the English teachers consistently preferred the muddy prose to the clear writing. Not only this, but the teachers saw more errors in the clearly written essays than in the complicated essays.

"The teachers tended to find errors of logic and meaning in the verbose papers and mechanical errors in the others—even though the papers were identical in the errors they contained," Dr. Hake said in a newspaper interview.

In other words, the teachers seemed to be impressed by purple prose and turned off by simple writing.

The professors said their findings indicated that many teachers were "encouraging precisely the stylistic values we claim we reject and discouraging precisely the stylistic values we claim we support."

The study, which is described in the September 1981 issue of the journal *College English,* began when the authors became interested in the "obtuse" style of many textbooks on writing. Instead of examining the texts, they decided to look at how teachers actually respond to various writing styles.

The moral of this little excursion into the world of the classroom is this: If you write clearly, people will understand you, but you may have trouble with some of your teachers. If you ever experience this, refer your teacher to the article in *College English.*

Rewriting

Young writers should not be discouraged by the realization that writing requires work. Everyone who writes for a living—reporters, poets, novelists, magazine writers—knows the joy of making ideas come to life on paper. And the agony—especially the pain of rewriting.

"Good writing is rewriting," says Fred Zimmerman, an editor at *The Wall Street Journal.*

"Even on deadline, a good writer will take at least 20 or 30 seconds to glance over a piece of copy, not really editing it, but simply because it is the writer's habit to reflect on what he or she has written before letting go of it," Zimmerman says. The more time the writer has, the more attention he or she will give to the copy.

Clear Writing	Muddy Prose
Simple language	Flowery language
Active verbs	Passive verbs
Straightforward sentences	Complex sentences
Tight writing	Loose writing
Easily understood	Difficult to follow

"Rewrite, rewrite and edit," says Zimmerman.

This has always been the story. The original manuscript of the American classic *Walden* by Henry David Thoreau shows how hard Thoreau worked. He produced seven versions in the six years he worked on the book. Behind the beautiful and clear story of his two years alone by a Concord pond are years of toil.

Caskie Stinnett, an essayist and critic, says that Thoreau "stopped and started, tinkered and rearranged, selected and discarded, chose and reconsidered, and fought with the English language until he forced it to come to terms with him."

Compressing six years into 60 minutes or six, the task for the news writer is the same one Thoreau faced.

Checkpoints for the writer are important as he or she rereads the copy:

1. Is the lead on target or buried? A key to the answer: What is most of the body of the story about? If it is not about the theme selected as the lead, the lead is wrong.
2. If a delayed lead is used, does the quote or incident move directly into the main theme?
3. Is the story organized properly, or does it jump from one topic to another and back? Is secondary information put above primary material in the body?
4. Does the story move? Do the nouns and verbs carry it forward with an internal momentum? Do the facts that are chosen give movement to the piece?

Summary

A copy editor for a newspaper in New York was asked to list some of the most frequent problems he sees in the copy that moves past him.

1. **Not enough self-editing.** Reporters fight so hard to put their words on paper, they have a vested interest in them and are reluctant to change them. No story is perfect on first writing. Don't cherish every word you write. Always ask: Does this word, this sentence, this paragraph move the story forward?

2. **Wrong lead.** The writer has used a secondary theme for the main point of the story. The news writer has to keep asking: What made this event different from all others like it? The answer is the lead.

3. **Poor organization.** This is often the result of not locating the main theme and getting it high in the story. The reader should not be forced to go beyond the first four paragraphs to have a good idea of the thrust of the piece.

4. **Misuse of the delayed lead.** Too many hard news stories are given a soft news approach.

5. **Overwriting.** It's not necessary to use every quote, every observation. In journalism, quantity does not count—the quality of the quote and the observation do.

6. **Dullness.** This can be the result of overwriting. It also stems from poorly selected verbs, long sentences, lack of quotes.

7. **Holes in the story.** Unanswered questions.

First the Formula, then Mastery

The news writer who masters the essentials outlined in these six chapters on writing is on the road to creating a personal writing style.

One of Elvis Presley's song writers said that after five years of writing successful songs for Presley, he realized he was repeating himself. The songs were successful, but they were ground out to a formula, the writer said. There was no reason for Presley to change his style since it had proved to be a huge financial success.

However, the writer felt he was not being challenged, so he decided to move on to new forms of music.

Much of what has been said may seem as much a formula as the ingredients of Presley's hits. Granted. But there is nothing wrong with a formula if it guides the user to successful work. Once the formula is mastered, the writer can move on, like Presley's song writer.

12

Broadcast Writing

Stories written for radio and television are written in conversational style, clearly and simply. The listener or viewer must be able to understand the story at once.

Complicated news stories are simplified by emphasizing only one or two themes. Leads are short and the present tense is used whenever possible. Attribution is always placed first in the sentence so that the listener or viewer knows at once the source of the information.

Monica Kaufman anchors the 6 p.m. and 11 p.m. newscasts on WSB-TV in Atlanta. Her news day begins at 2:30 p.m. and ends at 11:45 that evening. But that's deceptive. She is always working.

"My day starts with reading the morning paper," she says, "and listening to the all-news radio station. If I have time, I tune in the cable news station on television."

By the time she shows up at the station early in the afternoon, Kaufman has a good idea of the day's news.

"My first stop at the station at 2:30 is the assignment desk to see what stories we are covering." These stories will be used on the 6 o'clock newscast.

"My second stop is the producer's desk to see what copy I have to write to fit between stories that reporters have turned in."

Her third stop is the wire machines where the news services click off reams of copy. She tears off the stories that she wants to use.

"Then it's writing time." Kaufman may rewrite the lead-ins that local reporters have written. These are the brief introductions to the reporters' stories. She will change them to conform to her speaking style.

If she is working on a special story of her own, she leaves the station to conduct interviews and to do her research.

"About 5 p.m., we begin to firm up the show. I write a 30-second promo, which is a tease to interest people in the 6 p.m. newscast. I do the promo live at 5:28:11.

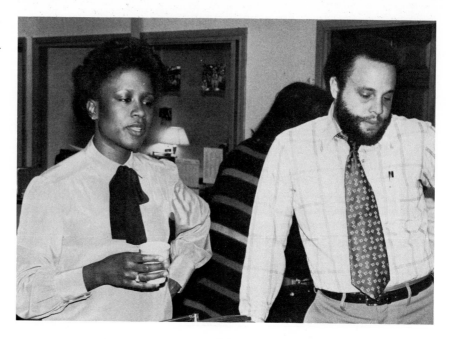

News Check. Monica Kaufman and assignment editor Morris Pyle of WSB-TV in Atlanta go over the wire news before preparing the 6 p.m. news program.

Figure 12.1 The news promo tells the viewer the stories that will be featured on a news program later in the day.

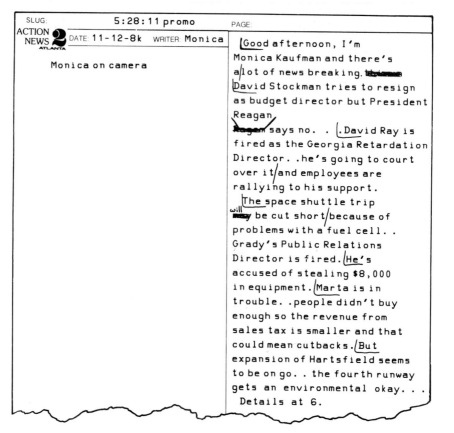

SLUG: 5:28:11 promo   PAGE:

ACTION NEWS 2 ATLANTA DATE: 11-12-8k WRITER: Monica

Monica on camera

Good afternoon, I'm Monica Kaufman and there's a lot of news breaking. ~~his news~~ David Stockman tries to resign as budget director but President Reagan ~~Reagan~~ says no. . .David Ray is fired as the Georgia Retardation Director. .he's going to court over it/and employees are rallying to his support. The space shuttle trip ~~may~~ will be cut short/because of problems with a fuel cell. . Grady's Public Relations Director is fired. He's accused of stealing $8,000 in equipment. Marta is in trouble. .people didn't buy enough so the revenue from sales tax is smaller and that could mean cutbacks. But expansion of Hartsfield seems to be on go. . the fourth runway gets an environmental okay. . . Details at 6.

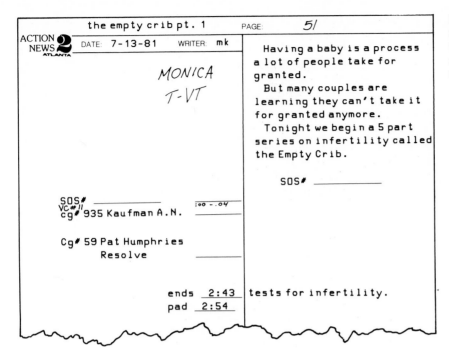

Figure 12.2 Series, which usually focus on matters that interest viewers, give reporters the opportunity to dig deeper into the news.

The script shown contains the following text:

the empty crib pt. 1   PAGE: 51

ACTION NEWS 2 ATLANTA   DATE: 7-13-81   WRITER: mk

MONICA

T-VT

SOS# VC#11 cg# 935 Kaufman A.N.   :00 - .04

Cg# 59 Pat Humphries
Resolve

ends   2:43
pad   2:54

Having a baby is a process a lot of people take for granted.

But many couples are learning they can't take it for granted anymore.

Tonight we begin a 5 part series on infertility called the Empty Crib.

SOS# _____

tests for infertility.

"When I come back up to the studio, it's time to look at the scripts that the reporters have written. They have been torn apart. White goes to the tele-synch operator. Blue to the show director. Green to the anchor who reads the piece. Goldenrod goes to the anchor who is listening. Pink to the show producer. Yellow to the editor."

Kaufman is on the set at 5:50 when she does a final read-through of the script.

After the show, she has hardly time to relax before preparing for the 11 p.m. news program. Usually, she goes out on a story for the late evening show.

"I try to make the 11 o'clock program different with new material. We update the 6 o'clock news whenever we can."

At 11:30 p.m., she takes a breather, and by midnight she is on her way home.

"At home, I try to read some magazines to keep up with what is going on in the world."

"I tuck myself in about 2 a.m."

Life for Kaufman is not always rush and more rush. Now and then she slows down to take on a major project that requires in-depth reporting and thoughtful writing. Often, these stories turn out to be series, one segment being presented each day.

Figure 12.2 shows the first page of the script for a series Kaufman handled, "The Empty Crib," an examination of the problems some couples have with infertility.

Clarity the Goal　　　Much of what we have been discussing in this textbook applies to newspaper copy, which is writing for the eye alone. Now we are discussing writing for the ear and the eye.

The first rule of broadcast news is that the story must be clear at once. Unlike the newspaper reader, the listener has no second chance to go over the material. Radio and television news is as fleeting as the wind—here for the instant, then gone.

There are several ways the broadcast news writer makes his or her copy clear.

Language　Broadcast news writers **use everyday words,** the language of conversation. Colloquialisms and contractions are acceptable. The style is informal. Look at some brief news items broadcast on the CBS television news program "Newsbreak":

> Mail carriers are still making their rounds, while postal unions and management are still going round and round. There was tentative agreement on a new contract early today, but later the deal fell through. Now negotiations have resumed, and the unions say they have no plans for a strike.

> Nato foreign ministers, meeting in Rome, today said nyet to Moscow—rejecting the Soviet demand for a moratorium on deployment of nuclear arms in Europe.

> A Singapore Airlines jumbo jet left Southeast Asia today with a new way to help passengers pass the time. The plane, bound for San Francisco, is fitted out with six slot machines—for high fliers.

Ideas　Broadcast news writers **simplify the complicated.** The story written for a newspaper plunges right into the heart of the event. The broadcast story often has a brief introduction before the theme is stated. Each of the three "Newsbreak" stories above has an introductory clause or sentence.

When the mayor and the city council disagreed over a proposal to increase the city sales tax from 3 to 4 percent—a week after another disagreement over taxes—the radio copy of a local station began this way:

> The mayor and the city council are feuding again. This time, the issue is the city's sales tax.

The writer used this as a brief introduction to the heart of the story. The writer then went into the details:

> The city council last night turned down a proposal to increase the city sales tax from 3 to 4 percent. Mayor George Grogan said the city faces trouble unless it takes in more revenue.

> And the only way the mayor can see to add to revenue is to raise the sales tax.
>
> But the council voted six to one against the increase.

Count the number of sentences in the story. Then count the number of words in each sentence. There are six sentences, and they contain the following number of words: 9, 9, 20, 14, 18, 10. Clearly, most of the sentences are short, much shorter than the sentences would be in the same story written for a newspaper. The average number of words per sentence in this radio news copy is between 13 and 14.

This leads us to the next point.

Brevity **Sentences are short** for broadcast stories. Long sentences cannot be read easily by the announcer, and the listener has a hard time following them. Here, side-by-side, are UPI news wire and broadcast accounts of a major story from Atlanta:

News Wire

ATLANTA (UPI)--Wayne B. Williams, flanked by his defense team and surrounded by sheriff's deputies in a packed courtroom, pleaded innocent today to charges that he murdered two of 28 young blacks whose slayings kept Atlanta on edge for almost two years.

Williams, wearing a dark suit and a shirt open at the collar, appeared before Fulton County Superior Court Judge Clarence Cooper under extremely tight security.

Movements into and out of the courtroom were tightly controlled, with deputies using electronic metal detectors to search each of the about 300 reporters and spectators who jammed the small room.

During the 10-minute session, the charges were read to Williams. . . .

Broadcast Wire

The man charged in two of the Atlanta slayings has pleaded innocent. Wayne Williams appeared in a packed courtroom today to answer to the charges that he killed two of 28 young blacks. The courtroom was under extremely tight security that included a search of everyone who entered. The judge tentatively scheduled the trial to begin October 5th. The 23-year-old Williams remains the only person charged in any of the 28 slayings that terrorized Atlanta for almost two years.

The news story continues for 20 more paragraphs. The first four sentences of the news wire story contain 106 words. The average sentence length is around 26 words. The five sentences of the broadcast story total 81 words. That averages to a bit more than 16 words per sentence.

We know the way to write short sentences. Follow the S-V-O style. Look at the broadcast version. Every sentence begins with a subject, and the verb usually follows the subject immediately.

All the news on a half-hour newscast would not fill the front page of a newspaper. The news on an hour program would run slightly more than one page.

Broadcast news has been described as a headline service. It is intended to give the listener or viewer only an outline of the event. A half-hour newscast may have as many as 20 news items crammed into the 22 to 23 minutes allotted to news. The 68 seconds that the CBS Newsbreak program has for news will have four to six items. One day there were seven. That's a bit less than 10 seconds for each story, one or two sentences a story. Altogether, the news script for a Newsbreak program contains about 170 words, which is the equivalent of a three-to-four-inch story in a newspaper.

In other words, there are more words in a routine traffic accident story in a newspaper than there are in the entire Newsbreak program, and on the longer television news programs most stories have fewer words than a newspaper story about a noncontroversial appointment by the governor.

Brevity—writing tightly—is the result of clear thinking. In order to write broadcast copy, the writer must be able to reduce news stories to their essence. The broadcast writer always asks himself or herself: **What happened here? Who said or did this?**

The answer, in simple S-V-O form, is the basis of the story.

The thinking process is the same, whether the news is gathered by a local reporter or is rewritten from the press association wires.

When stories are rewritten from the AP and UPI wires for television newscasts, these stories are described as **tell** stories or **readers.** That is, the anchor person tells the listener about them, instead of showing film or tape. Tell stories do not excite viewers, broadcast people believe. So the tell story must be brief as possible. Few tell stories run more than 20 or 30 seconds, which limits them to 50 to 75 words, the equivalent of one or two newspaper paragraphs.

In the CBS Evening News program we examined in chapter 1 there were eight tell stories. Not one ran more than 30 seconds. Even the stories with videotape were short. The lead story—the signing of an historic tax bill—ran two-and-a-half minutes, 365 words. The same story in *The New York Times* had 1,000 words. *The Washington Post* story of the event contained 1,200 words.

No one ever learned to write by memorizing rules, but there is one more suggestion before we look at how some professionals handle radio and television news.

Tense Use the **present tense** whenever possible. Broadcast writers frequently use the present tense in their leads. Newspaper stories almost always contain the past tense throughout. The broadcast version of the Atlanta slayings story used the verb *has pleaded,* which is the present perfect tense. The news wire story said that Williams *pleaded* innocent. This is the past tense.

The reason for using the present tense is simple. Broadcast news is supposed to give the listener or viewer the sense of immediacy, of events being covered as they happen. Sometimes, the present tense would sound silly, so the writer uses the past tense. Evening news programs use the past tense in looking back on events that occurred during the day.

If the mayor announced at a noon news conference that he will not seek reelection, the radio news account begins this way:

> Mayor George Grogan **says** he will not seek reelection. The mayor **made** his intention clear at noon today in a news conference. He **said** he wants to go back to running the family business.

Notice the present tense in the first sentence. The tense then switches to the past in the next two sentences when it describes the actual news conference statement. The logic behind using the present tense in the lead sentence is that his statement still holds true now. The present tense does not violate the truth.

In its seventh "World in Brief" newscast of the day, UPI's broadcast news staff wrote these leads on some of the news items:

Present tense	Portuguese air traffic controllers **are** engaged in a two-day boycott of U.S. flights in sympathy with the walkout by American controllers.
Present tense	A survey done by the University of Michigan **says** American consumers feel much better about the economy than they did a year ago.
Present tense	Country music star Willie Nelson reportedly **is** ill.
Present perfect tense	Elvis Presley's manager, Colonel Tom Parker, **has** vehemently **denied** allegations he defrauded Presley.

The Big Four

Broadcast news should be written:

Simply
moothly
uccinctly
traightforwardly

Several items did begin with the past tense. The writer had no alternative for these:

Five hundred people **attended** a memorial service honoring Elvis Presley at Memphis State University yesterday.

A youth evangelist and one hundred members of the First Assembly of God Church in Guthrie, Oklahoma, **made** a bonfire of rock music albums yesterday.

Incidentally, notice how short these leads are. They contain 23, 23, 8, 13, 15 and 25 words. Most newspaper leads run 30 to 35 words.

Not only are the leads and most sentences in the broadcast news story short, the stories themselves are short. Brevity is the key that unlocks the door to broadcast news writing proficiency.

Rewriting the Wires

Although radio and television stations have staff members who write and broadcast the news they gather, most broadcast news originates from outside the station. Except for the networks, which have correspondents scattered over the world and in major U.S. cities, most stations rely on the AP and UPI for their national and foreign news and for much state and regional news.

This news is rewritten by broadcast news writers and put into broadcast form. Smaller stations subscribe to only one broadcast wire and use the material just as it comes in. The stations that have a staff of news writers usually subscribe to both the AP and UPI news wires and rewrite these stories for broadcast.

One reason bigger stations rewrite the news wires is that news directors prefer that their writers see the original story, before it has been filtered by a broadcast rewrite person at the wire service. The wire service rewrite may neglect an aspect of special interest to local listeners, or it may be routinely written.

Shortly after 9 o'clock one morning in August, the press association news wires began to move a story they marked "urgent." Two Navy jets had shot down two Libyan jet planes in a dogfight over the Mediterranean Sea. The U.S. Defense Department stated that the Soviet-made Libyan planes had attacked the F-14 fighter planes, which had fired back.

Clash over the Mediterranean

In the CBS newsroom in New York, Mervin Block was preparing the Newsbreak television newscast, which goes on at 11:57 a.m. As he watched the wires move the story, he knew that it could not be told in the 10 or 15 seconds each item on Newsbreak is usually allotted. By 10 a.m., AP had moved three leads on the big story, and by 10:30, UPI was transmitting its fourth lead.

This was a big story. Did it mean Libya was planning to attack a neighboring country and wanted no U.S. surveillance? Was Libya's president anxious to demonstrate his nation's defiance of the United States, which he had described as the most dangerous country on earth?

Block had to monitor the wires for developments. Because the story was going to take more than a couple of sentences to tell, he could not wait long before sitting down with the thousands of words of AP and UPI copy to draft his broadcast story.

The people involved with the program—producer, editor, anchorperson and writer—agreed that the story would be given 40 or 45 seconds, which is long for a tell story. This meant Block had to boil down the wire stories to about 135 words.

After taking one last look at the wire and ripping off the latest leads, he went to the typewriter and began to write. He had half an hour, but he had been thinking about the story ever since he saw the first "urgent." He knew that he had to tell CBS television viewers the essential facts—that U.S. planes had downed two Libyan jets.

"There are some things I would change now," Block says. "Maybe I would use plane instead of craft on the first page of copy.

"But in broadcasting there are no second chances. I was reading a book the other day with the title *Done in a Day,* about newspapers. It describes the work that has to be done, all in a day, to produce a newspaper. But in broadcasting, it's done in minutes, sometimes seconds."

Block says that he always looks for the short word and that he tries to write short sentences that conform to the S-V-O sentence structure. For example, at one point in the script he used *taking part* instead of *participating.*

His script is shown in figure 12.3.

The broadcast news writer has to keep in mind that the story is to be read aloud by someone. This means that the copy should be prepared in a certain way. Stations differ in their rules for copy preparation but here are some suggestions.

Figure 12.3 Mervin Block explains how he chose the few words allowed him to convey the pertinent facts of the news story within the 45-second time limit.

BLOCK COMMENTS

This headline--admittedly a fragmentary sentence--gives the viewer a quick preview. The wire services said "off the coast of North Africa," but I jettisoned "the coast of" as needless. Near the top, I cite the source of the story. In broadcasting, attribution precedes assertion. Again, I took pains to name the source for the second assertion. My producer, however, might have thought the second sourcing was redundant, and he deleted it. Or he thought I was running long. Apparently, no reporter saw the dogfight, so we must make clear who told us. The wires quoted the Department of Defense, but I condensed it to "Pentagon," which has more punch. The wires also quoted the State Department; I reduced that to "Washington." We're constantly struggling for tighter scripts, even on two-hour newscasts. Although a viewer can't see quotation marks, I use them so the anchor can change his delivery. I use direct quotations seldom, and I say "quote" or "unquote" rarely.

After I gave the gist of the accusation, I reported the other side's response. And I tacked on a bit of background about the territorial claim. I couldn't take time to elaborate on the claim or to report on U.S.-Libyan relations. Nor did I waste time with name-dropping or name-calling. Until now, I hadn't identified the type of U-S jet. At 11:57 a.m., most of our viewers are probably housewives, and, chances are, few, if any, know an F-14 from an F-4 or even a 4-F. The wires said the Nimitz is nuclear-powered, but I saw no need to waste words about its propulsion. The AP said the encounter was "60 nautical miles" off Libya. I know that a nautical mile is about a mile and a seventh, which would make it nearly 70 miles. I wrote "almost"; years ago, my editor on the CBS Evening News told me an anchor can get a better grasp

A jet battle off
North Africa:
The Pentagon says
two Libyan jets
fighters attacked two
U-S Navy ᴲ⁻¹⁴ jets over
the Mediterranean
today. and the
~~Pentagon says the~~
Navy jets shot down
both Libyan craft.
Washington says the
attack against the
U-S jets was
``unprovoked'' and that
it took place in
``international air
space over
international waters.''
Libya says the U-S
jets violated air
space over its
waters, but Washington
does not recognize
Libya's territorial
claim. The U-S jets,
Ef-fourteen Tomcats
from the carrier
Nimitz, were taking
part in Sixth fleet
exercises. The Navy
says its jets were
almost seventy miles
off Libya when the
Soviet-made Libyan
jets fired at them.

(MORE)

```
on "almost." That editor also told me,        The Navy says neither
repeatedly, that viewers are only half-        of its planes was
listening. So I strive for simplicity.         hit. The State
My maxim: Make it minimal. That's one          Department has
reason that in the first sentence I            protested, and it
didn't mention "F-14." But the                 warned Libya against
director dug up a photo of an F-14, so          any new attack.
he prevailed upon the producer to
insert "F-14" high up. He obliged, and
I was shot down.
```

Copy Preparation

Name or initials of writer in lower right-hand corner.
Slug of story in upper right-hand corner.
Time the story takes to run is placed above slug.
Date goes in lower left-hand corner.

Use wide margins in preparing radio copy. The margins are normally set for 45 to 50 units and the length of lines is kept as uniform as possible. Depending on the speed of the announcer, each line will take about three seconds to read. Knowing this, the announcer can estimate how long it will take to read the story.

Television copy is prepared on two-thirds of the right-hand side of the page. The left-hand side is used for instructions, such as the name of the anchor or correspondent and whether the copy will be read over a film or tape (*VO* for voice over).

Each page is numbered and slugged at the top. At the bottom, an end mark is used when the story is completed—#, 30, END. The word *more* is written and circled at the bottom of pages of stories that are continued.

Each page should end with a complete sentence. If the page ends in the middle of a sentence, the announcer will be forced to pause as he or she reaches for the next sheet of copy.

So much for the basics of preparing copy. Next, some rules about writing style.

Style Rules

These rules have been used by broadcast news writers for many years to avoid confusion for the announcer reading the copy and to help the listener grasp quickly what he or she hears:

Numbers are spelled out.
Abbreviations are not used.
Titles are placed before names.
Initials of agencies and organizations are not used unless they are well known.
Quotes must be clearly introduced as direct quotes. "As the senator put it. . . . In the words of the president. . . . And here we quote the prime minister. . . ."

On Location. Monica Kaufman describes the action on the scene of a local news story.

Putting It Together. Television newscasts require the efforts of teams of writers, correspondents, technicians and on-camera journalists. Here, ABC news correspondent Frank Reynolds goes over a news item with a writer before air time.

Ten Seconds. Reynolds waits for the cue to start the "World News Tonight" on ABC.

Behind the Set. In the control room, technicians watch the monitors.

Writing Guidelines

We have already seen that broadcast news is written in simple, conversational language. The sentences are short, and they are usually in the S-V-O form.

Every word is selected to do something; every word has a purpose. Broadcast news is timed to the word. Omitting unnecessary words is the key to success.

Avoid using lengthy phrases and clauses to begin sentences. Get right to the point. When a source is being used, put it at the beginning of the sentence. Use action verbs. Stay away from adjectives and adverbs unless they are essential.

Introductory phrase

Avoid: Stressing the increased number of cars on campus, the Student Council has asked for more parking spaces near dormitories.

Improved: The Student Council wants more parking spaces near student dormitories.

Attribution

Avoid: There are two cars for every parking space, says Student Council President Tom Jarrett.

Improved: Student Council President Tom Jarrett says there are two cars for every parking space.

Action verb

Avoid: The Council was unanimous in its vote.

Improved: The Council voted unanimously.

Adjective

Avoid: Dean Albert Levine reacted with strong criticism of the vote.

Improved: Dean Albert Levine criticized the vote. Dean Albert Levine condemned the vote.

Leads A listener should not be overwhelmed with a long lead to a story. Complicated stories can be introduced with a general statement, such as:

The parking-space issue has heated up. Dean Albert Levine said this afternoon. . . .

The Russians want no part in the U.S. plan for feeding the hungry of the world. Soviet leaders said. . . .

Do not begin a story with the name of an unknown person. If you must, precede the name with the person's title or some identifying label. You can begin with a name if the person has what Mervin Block of CBS News calls "star quality." That means the President, the Pope, the governor of your state, a senator or congressman, your mayor.

For a story about the death of Robert Moses, who built many of the major highways in and out of New York City and a number of its major buildings, Block realized only New Yorkers would be familiar with the name, and then not all of them as Moses had been out of public life for many years. He was writing for a network news program. Here is how he began the obituary:

> The man credited with building even more than the Pharaohs of Egypt—Robert Moses—died in a New York City suburb today at the age of 92.

Here the identifying label is an arresting description. People will listen.

Do not start a story with a quotation. The listener cannot see or hear quotation marks and may think the words are those of the broadcaster. Some writers start with a quote and their next sentence is "Those were the words of. . . ." or "This advice, warning, challenge came from. . . ." Block says the technique does not work because it confuses listeners.

Story Telling Names make news in newspaper stories, but the fewer names in a broadcast story the better. Listeners are confused by lists of names and by a cast of characters in a story. One or two people in a story make for clarity.

If Roger Grimstead, a spokesman for the governor, says something, simply write: The governor's office says. . . .

If the secretary of defense, Allen Weinstein, issues a comment in a story about the President's defense bill and there are already too many names, just write: The Pentagon commented that. . . .

A newspaper story may have a major theme and two, three, even four secondary themes. The broadcast story should have a major theme and perhaps one other theme.

What It Takes

For those considering a career in broadcast journalism, the ability to write well under pressure seems to be what most broadcast news editors look for. A study by Professor Stephen Lamoreux of Colorado State University found that editors want writers who can write simple sentences in a conversational style. Many editors also expect the news writer to know grammar and to be able to spell.

Editors hire people who write lively, colorful copy and who have imagination, Lamoreux found.

Mastery of the writing craft is not enough, says Block. "The writer has to have a wide knowledge. He or she should know what is going on in the world. Also," says Block, "the writer should understand how things work—government, the criminal justice process, zoning boards, state government.

"The data bank in the writer's mind has to have a jillion bits of information because the writer must be able to retrieve a lot of data, and do it almost subconsciously.

"One of the problems with many broadcast writers at the local and network level is that they have insufficient experience and exposure to the world," Block says.

One of the ways to develop this experience and exposure is through reading. This is the easiest path for the young and inexperienced writer.

Summary

Broadcast writers try to follow these guidelines:

- **Use everyday language.** Instead of *impact on,* the writer uses *affect.* Instead of *interface,* the writer uses *match.*

- **Simplify complicated stories.** One way to do this is to begin a story with some background material: "Last month, the city council decided to revise the city's zoning regulations. Last night, it adopted a new master plan that will affect all new commercial and residential development in the city." Another technique is the headline to introduce a story: "Schools are open again." This could begin a story about the settlement of a long teachers' strike.

- **Use short sentences.** The listener cannot follow a long sentence. Any sentence over 25 words should be broken into two sentences. One way to cut down on the number of words in a sentence is to eliminate unnecessary words: "At this point in time" becomes *now,* "revenue enhancement" is changed to *taxes,* and such redundancies as "totally destroyed," "cold, hard facts" and "first annual" are eliminated. Introductory phrases and clauses are dropped. Stick to the S-V-O sentence construction.

- **Favor the present tense.** Give the reader the sense of immediacy by using the present tense for leads when possible.

- **Keep items brief.** Find the major theme of the event and concentrate on it.

Part Four
Story Types

Story Essentials

The beginning reporter is supposed to be able to do it all. Well, maybe not everything, but a lot. Even though the city editor may assign the beginner a beat, the editor also expects the new hand to be able to write personal items, turn out a feature about the volunteer program at a local hospital, make readers smile with clever brights and help out with weekend traffic accidents and obituaries.

On the small- or medium-sized newspaper—where most beginners start their careers—there are few specialists. Everyone has to be able to handle the basic types of stories.

The following three chapters will show you how to handle some of these basic stories. Chapters 13–15 look at the essential ingredients of a dozen different kinds of stories.

Every story that a reporter writes can be fitted into a type or category. There are game stories that sports writers do, fire and arrest stories police reporters write, meeting stories that a variety of beat and general assignment reporters cover and write. There are also: interviews, news conferences, obituaries, accidents, robberies, weather and personals. Each of these has distinct ingredients or elements that must be included in these stories.

Here is what we mean by the essential elements of the news story:

An obituary obviously must include the name of the person who died. Since the reader wants to know something about the person, every obituary must also include the person's address or home town and his or her occupation and accomplishments. There are other absolute necessities for the obituary, one of which was left out of the following wire service story. See if you can find out which essential is missing.

```
AM-HOBGOOD DIES, 180<
OLDEST WAR VETERAN DIES<
    ARKADELPHIA, ARK. (AP)-FUNERAL SERVICES
WILL BE HELD MONDAY FOR NORMAN HOBGOOD, THE MAN
THE GOVERNMENT CALLS THE NATION'S OLDEST WAR
VETERAN.
    HOBGOOD, WHO DIED FRIDAY, ENLISTED IN THE
ARMY IN 1898, SERVING IN THE THIRD KENTUCKY
VOLUNTEER INFANTRY DURING THE SPANISH-AMERICAN
WAR. THE VETERAN'S ADMINISTRATION SAID HE WAS
THE OLDEST OF 30 MILLION VETERANS LISTED IN ITS
RECORDS.
    ONLY ABOUT 250 VETERANS OF THE SPANISH-
AMERICAN WAR ARE LIVING, ACCORDING TO THE VA.
    THE KENTUCKY NATIVE ALSO WAS ARKANSAS'
OLDEST STATE LEGISLATOR. HE WAS ELECTED TO THE
STATE HOUSE OF REPRESENTATIVES FOR TWO TERMS IN
1925 AND 1927.
```

HOBGOOD, WHO LIVED IN AN ARKADELPHIA
NURSING HOME, FREQUENTLY WAS INTERVIEWED ABOUT
HIS STATUS AS THE OLDEST VETERAN. HE ALSO WAS
IN THE LIMELIGHT IN THE ANNUAL VETERANS DAY
CELEBRATIONS IN ARKADELPHIA.
     LAST YEAR, HOBGOOD WAS AWARDED THE ARKANSAS
DISTINGUISHED SERVICE MEDAL IN A VETERANS DAY
CEREMONY AT HENDERSON STATE UNIVERSITY.
     HOBGOOD WAS A LAWYER, TEACHER AND FARMER.
HE FARMED UNTIL HE WAS 99 AND PREACHED THE
SUNDAY WORSHIP SERVICE AT HIS CHURCH ON HIS
100TH BIRTHDAY.
     AP-NR-03-02 1413EST<

A few minutes after this story moved on the wires, an alert editor caught
the lapse and ordered a new story written with the essential information included. The new story was identical to the first except for this second paragraph:

HOBGOOD, WHO DIED FRIDAY AT THE AGE OF 108,
ENLISTED IN THE ARMY IN 1898, SERVING IN THE
THIRD KENTUCKY VOLUNTEER INFANTRY DURING THE
SPANISH-AMERICAN WAR. THE VETERAN'S
ADMINISTRATION SAID HE WAS THE OLDEST OF 30
MILLION VETERANS LISTED IN ITS RECORDS.

(In case you did not catch the blooper, the news writer had forgotten to
include the man's age, an essential ingredient of all obituaries.)

Journalists like to say that there are no rules for journalism. Since no event
is quite like another event, there can be no rigid rules for writing stories, they
say. It is true that no two basketball games are exactly alike. One may be an
easy victory, another may be won in the last three seconds. Even the games
won at the final buzzer differ. One may be won on a foul shot, another on a
desperation-heave from midcourt. A third might be won by a guard playing
his first game. Another game was not so much won by one team as lost by
another when the defense made a few blunders. And so on.

Every event—game, speech, interview, obituary, arrest, accident—is different from others like it, and the good news writer handles each differently,
no matter how many games he has covered, how many speeches she has had
to sit through, how many interviews he has conducted.

Yes, all events are different. Each should be handled with an individual
touch, with full attention to its unique characteristics. However, every basketball game story must include the score, the names of the teams, the key
plays and the names of the players scoring the most points. Every speech story
must include the main point of the talk, the speaker's name and his or her

Nonnegotiable
Essentials

title or occupation, the location of the talk, the response of the audience. All accident stories tell the reader or listener the names of those injured, where the accident occurred, the names of the drivers involved and the cause.

To sum up, there are rules for every type of story and they cannot be broken. They are nonnegotiable essentials. You can complain about being forced into a rigid style by these rules all you want. But break one of them and you will face the embarrassment of the wire service writer who neglected to put in the obituary the age of the Spanish-American War veteran.

These essentials can be placed anywhere in the story—in the lead, the middle, at the end. Placement is up to the news writer and his or her feel for the structure of the story. Regardless of placement, they must be included.

The most important element in one fire story in chapter 15 was that a man died because of his smoking habit, and that went into the lead—cause. Another fire story began with the damage done to a grain elevator—property damage. Cause and damages are essentials of the fire story. The writer has to determine—on the basis of what he or she has learned—which of the essential elements to put into the lead and which to place further down in the body of the story.

No list can predict the full dimensions of any story. The writer must be aware of the unique aspects of the story being written. Often, it is the unusual, the strange fact that makes the story that is being written different from other fire, sports or speech stories. If the fact is unique and significant, the writer begins the story with it—the tears in the firefighter's eyes as he carries the body of the child from the smoking ruins, the mistake of the base runner in the ninth inning, the sparse attendance at a meeting of school board candidates.

Journalism is not mechanical. It cannot be carried out by the number, like a drill team automatically stepping out its patterns. Journalism is an art that requires its practitioners to look with a fresh eye at each event so that the unique aspects of the event can be captured in the story. The eye must have a focus, a direction in which to begin looking.

The essentials in the next three chapters point the news writer in the proper directions for several types of stories.

To begin our examination of story types, we will look first at the interview. Editors say that the ability to conduct an interview and to write the story is one of the most important competences they look for in a new staff member. We will then go to other types of stories involving the spoken word—meetings, news conferences and speeches. In chapter 15, we will look at how accident and fire stories, obituaries, sports stories and personals are handled.

13

Spot News Interviews and Profiles

Looking Ahead

There are two types of interviews. Spot news interviews are used to develop information that supplements the news story. Profiles and personality interviews focus on the individual being interviewed.

To conduct a successful interview, the reporter should know something about the subject of the interview, ask simple and direct questions, listen and watch carefully. In writing the interview story, the reporter should use plenty of quotes, but only those that are directly related to the theme of the news story or feature.

The news story is the written version of what the reporter sees and hears. In this chapter and the next, we will be discussing what the reporter hears, though we won't ignore what he or she sees. Our main attention will be on what is said by sources in speeches and interviews and at meetings and news conferences.

What the reporter hears is the spoken word. Since the key to writing the news story is the realization that the story should reflect the nature of the event, we have a starting point for these kinds of stories: **Use quotes,** but not just any quotes. Use the quotes that capture the meaning of the event.

Of course, we want background material and description in these stories, too. But our stories will revolve about what we hear.

The interview is at the heart of just about every news story. Bank robbery or fire. Municipal budget or college basketball game. Campus rock group or sociology instructor with a new theory about student relationships. In every one of these stories, a reporter has asked someone for information.

In some of these stories, the focus is on the event. The interviews for these stories are called **spot news interviews** (fig. 13.1). In others, the emphasis is on the person. These stories are called **profiles.**

Figure 13.1 Interviews Make News. Information for the two major stories on page 1 of *The Hays Daily News* came from spot news interviews. The city's fire chief, an employee of the grain elevator and the elevator owner were interviewed for the fire story. For the story about the wheat crop, an economics professor, a banker, a chamber of commerce official and others were interviewed. The three stories described across the top of the page refer to profiles on inside pages for which depth interviews were conducted.

The spot news interview is used to supplement the theme of the news story. The interview itself is not the major element. The person being interviewed provides background material about the event.

Spot News Interview

Reporters interview police officers for information about crimes, fire marshals for possible causes of fires. Sports reporters talk to coaches and players for background material for their game stories. In each of these spot news interviews, the reporter is looking for supplementary material—the facts and background that will illustrate or highlight the event being described.

This usually leads the news writer to play down the person being interviewed because the focus is on the meaning of the event rather than on a personality. This does not mean that we ignore the source's direct quotes. We may find in them the quote that adds drama and interest as well as meaning to the event.

In the following story, a state highway patrol officer was the source of information about a fatal traffic accident. Look where the writer put the officer's quote:

Three people were killed in a grinding collision between a truck and an automobile on Highway 10, 15 miles north of Morgantown, the state highway patrol reported.

Those fatally injured were in the automobile. They were Albert Foster, 22, of 237 Western Ave.; his brother, Michael, 18, of the same address, and the driver, Bert Pierce, 21, of Tampa, Fla. The truck driver, George Allen, 48, of New Orleans, suffered minor bruises.

A state highway patrol spokesman, Robert Jackson, said the automobile apparently tried to make a U-turn off the westbound lane and moved into the path of the truck as it sped eastward.

"The car was demolished," Jackson said. "There were parts all over the road for 100 yards." Traffic was delayed on the eastbound section for 90 minutes, he said. . . .

Notice that the lead contains the major news theme—the deaths—and attribution. The next paragraph gives the names and identifications of the victims. The third paragraph describes the accident, and the fourth contains a good quote.

This is the standard approach to the spot news story. Since we have a dramatic quote, it is possible to use it high in the story:

```
Three people were killed in a grinding collision
between a truck and an automobile on Highway 10, 15 miles
north of Morgantown.
    "The car was demolished," said Robert Jackson of the
State Highway Patrol. "There were parts all over the road
for 100 yards."
    Those fatally injured were....
```

This version is an improvement because the direct quote captures the essence of the event—a horrible traffic accident.

Most information from sources for spot news stories is usually summarized or paraphrased. The careful reporter who listens attentively can sometimes find the quote that breathes life into the news story. A good direct quote is better than any paraphrase.

In a story about a refresher course offered by the School of Nursing at the University of North Carolina at Chapel Hill, a woman who had taken the course was interviewed. She had been a nurse, then married and had spent 20 years at home raising a family. She decided to return to nursing and took the nursing-update course. Here is a direct quote from the story in *The Coastline Times* of Manteo, N.C. It captures the story's theme:

"I would not have dared walk on a hospital floor without having gone back to school," she said. "There have been so many advances and so many changes."

Nothing earthshaking about the quote, but it does the job.

Generally, when an editor asks a reporter to interview someone the editor has a personality sketch or profile in mind. Here, the individual is the center of the story. Before we turn to the profile, some points have to be made about the business of interviewing.

Interviewing Techniques

Whether the interview is for a spot news story or a profile, the key to a successful interview is knowing what you want to find out. The spot interview often is conducted by telephone with busy sources. The reporter has to get to the point quickly. Because the people interviewed for profiles set aside time for the interview, the reporter cannot waste the subject's time fishing for information. Also, the reporter must appear to be knowledgeable. A firm grasp of the subject will usually make the person being interviewed more willing to open up.

Here are some guidelines for interviews:

- **Have a good idea of what you want to learn from the source or subject.**

- **Get to the point quickly.**

- **Ask if there is anything important you have not asked about.**

- **Ask the source if he or she can be called back should you need further information.** (Some sources will not take calls at home after they leave the office. Ask for the name of another person who can be called.)

The Profile

We are all curious, maybe even nosey. We want to know why the brightest young woman in the class suddenly quit school, how the elderly couple around the corner can afford a new Cadillac every year, why a happily married couple down the street suddenly separated. We wonder what kind of person Mick Jagger really is, how the new outfielder for the New York Yankees can spend all of his $1.5 million salary.

Most of our questions will never be answered, but some will—by a reporter writing a profile or personality feature. The fact that people have always been curious about the lives of others has made the profile the most frequently written feature story. Sooner or later, every reporter writes a profile.

Sometimes, the profile can be a small snapshot in a larger picture. In a series on Rhode Island's jewelry manufacturing business—the state's largest industry—Bruce Butterfield of *The Providence Journal-Bulletin* tells us something about Mary, a high school student who does part-time work in a factory. Butterfield lets Mary talk:

> . . . . Like, what I'm doing now. I stand up the entire time. I go in there for three hours and 45 minutes a day.
>
> It's in a room and you have metal that's melted down. I think it's twelve hundred degrees.
>
> There's people who've been working in there 25 years and they're still making less than $4 an hour.
>
> And they deserve more 'cause they're such nice people that work in there. And they just can't do anything else. They either don't have a high school diploma or they just have a high school diploma and there aren't many jobs in our society today for these people. And they're over 40.
>
> They deserve more.

These quotes tell us something about the factory and a lot about Mary. She works hard at an arduous job and is concerned about the people she works with. She is a decent young woman, and a bit naive: They deserve more, she says, because they are such nice people. But she is realistic about her co-workers' lack of education. She knows there aren't many jobs for people without an education.

"They deserve more." Mary's words make the reader put down the newspaper to reflect a minute about Mary. Although all we actually know about her is her name, we feel we really know her.

Our first requirement for the profile: It must capture the real person.

That may seem to be emphasizing the obvious. It isn't. Many profiles are written about people in public life—politicians, entertainers, athletes, television personalities, business leaders. These people cultivate a public personality. It is not easy to strip away the public-relations image.

Good profiles—good stories of any kind, for that matter—begin with good reporting. Here are four guidelines for successful interviews for the profile:

1. **Prepare carefully.** Know the subject matter and the person who is to be interviewed.
2. From these preparations, **devise a theme** or two as the basis of questions.

3. **Establish a relationship** with the subject that induces him or her to talk.
4. **Listen carefully and watch attentively.** Be alert to what is said and how it is said. Look around at the room or office for clues to the subject's interests, tastes, personal life.

Preparing for the Interview

Careful preparations begin with the newspaper or broadcast station library clippings about the subject matter and the person to be interviewed. The clippings provide background and suggest questions to ask at the interview. The next step is a quick look at references. The new college president may be listed in *Who's Who in America*. Although *Who's Who* is brought up-to-date frequently, biographical material should always be checked with the subject. The enrollment of the college she comes from can be found in the *World Almanac*.

If the new president is a specialist in a field, she may have written articles that are indexed in the *Reader's Guide to Periodical Literature*. Her comments about a subject in one of her articles could be the basis of the first question. Sources are flattered by a reporter's interest in them and their work.

When Mal Vincent of the *Virginian-Pilot* in Norfolk, Va., was preparing for an interview with actress Jacqueline Bisset, he went back to an interview he had with Bisset 10 years before.

Vincent had tried to interview Bisset on the set of a thriller in which she was co-starring with Alan Alda. In those days, Bisset had been cast in her movies as a sex object. She had done a nude scene in a surfing movie, "The Sweet Ride," and she had played a bedhopping jetsetter in "The Grasshopper."

At that time, Vincent had a definite personality in mind, the kind of young actress that moviegoers glance at in minor films and forget. But Bisset had surprised him then.

She had taken over the interview. "The name is Bisset," she had said at the outset. "It rhymes with *kiss it*."

When Vincent had tried to ask her about her relationship with actor Michael Sarrazin, Bisset had bristled. Although she had been widely publicized as living with Sarrazin, she refused to discuss the matter.

Vincent then tried women's liberation, a new phenomenon at that time.

"I have no intention of discussing women's rights with you," she had flared at him. "You wouldn't agree with me." She beckoned to her chauffeur and departed.

Bisset was a prickly subject for an interview, Vincent knew. In his preparations for his current interview he found that she was financing a movie in an attempt to convince critics she could act. As the coproducer, she had a stake in good publicity for the new film. She had to be patient with interviewers, Vincent knew. He also knew she had a mind of her own—as she proved in the new interview.

"I don't want to be a pinup," she told Vincent curtly. "I want to be something more than just an attractive woman. The public makes a mistake in labeling people that way."

Still bristling Bisset—but she stayed through the interview this time. Vincent knew how to approach her because of his preparations.

Vincent's preparations for his interview with Bisset point out the importance of figuring out some lines of questioning by having a tentative theme or idea for the story before the interview.

Devising a Theme

The depth interview is a confrontation between reporter-with-theme and subject-with-idea. By this, we mean that both interviewer and interviewee have points of their own they want to make. In Vincent's second interview with Bisset, she was trying to tell readers and moviegoers, through Vincent, that she is a serious actress, that they should forget her roles as a sex object, which had been stamped on the minds of the public by her scene in the movie "The Deep" in which she appeared in a wet, clinging, transparent T-shirt.

Vincent's new theme was the change from young starlet in grade B films to mature woman of 37 making serious movies. The interview went well because both themes, Bisset's and Vincent's, were parallel and not on a collision course.

Sometimes collisions are unavoidable. The reporter sent to interview a gubernatorial candidate for a profile knows that the candidate is a political novice, a person who has never sought public office. The reporter's theme is: What makes this man think he can handle the complexities of state government with no political experience whatsoever?

The candidate's campaign theme is: A new broom sweeps clean.

The reporter is too experienced in politics to buy that cliché without lots of proof. So the reporter will be pressing and probing the candidate to prove that he has some ability. Confrontation looms, unless the reporter can make the candidate relax and talk freely.

As we can see, the reporter devises a theme from checking the background of the subject and from the reporter's knowledge of the situation in which the subject is involved.

The theme or themes are launching pads for the reporter's questions. If nothing comes of the questions, the reporter works up new themes.

A profile or personality sketch cannot be a shapeless biography. There is no room in a newspaper, or time on a news program, for an endless recounting of a life or a situation. Every story must focus on a theme that limits the story to a specific situation involving the subject.

The profile of the new college president may have as its theme the fact that the appointee has been hired to make massive changes in the curriculum. The profile will be written with that in mind. Or the new president may be temporary, while the board of trustees tries to figure out a new educational policy and then seek out a person to match the policy.

A transitional appointee may not want to discuss this theme. It is up to the reporter to steer the source in the proper direction when the reporter is sure of the validity of the theme. This takes us to our third guideline for successful interviews.

Inducing the Subject to Talk

Reporters use many tactics to induce their subjects to talk freely and act naturally. Gene Miller of *The Miami Herald* says he tries to make himself as agreeable as possible during interviews.

"I nod a lot," he says, to appear to be agreeing with what the subject is saying and to encourage him or her to keep talking. "No tape recorder and no note taking if I suspect I'll turn off my man. The unpleasant questions always come last, often apologetically."

Miller's technique is the opposite of the confrontation tactics used by some television interviewers. After a while, a reporter learns the technique best suited to him or her. Of course, the nature of the interview will often determine the technique used. An interview with a manufacturer whose factory has been polluting the city's air and a nearby river cannot be much else but a confrontation.

The story is told of how Truman Capote, on an assignment from *The New Yorker* magazine, induced Marlon Brando to talk about his mother's alcoholism.

Capote flew to Japan where Brando was on the set of "Sayonara." They got together in the evening.

In his story for the magazine, Capote quoted Brando as saying: "I didn't care any more. She was there. In a room. Holding on to me. And I let her fall. Because I couldn't take it any more . . . breaking apart, like a piece of porcelain. I stepped right over her. I walked right out. I was indifferent. Since then, I've been indifferent."

Later, Brando was asked why he had been so open with Capote about such a personal matter.

"Well," said Brando, "the little bastard spent half the night telling me about all his problems. I figured the least I could do was to tell him a few of mine."

Ralph Ellison, the author of the classic about the lives of black Americans, *Invisible Man,* interviewed many people during the 1930's for the Federal Writers Project. Those were the days of the Depression, and few had jobs. Writers had a particularly hard time, and the government hired some of them to obtain first-person accounts of Americans of all kinds.

Ellison's technique for making people talk was similar to Capote's.

"I would tell stories to get people going, and then I'd sit back and get it down as accurately as I could."

For some people, a gentle nudge is all they need. For most, the reporter has to ask questions, a lot of questions.

Asking Questions

The first questions asked in an interview may be throw-away questions designed to put the subject at ease if the source is not accustomed to being interviewed. The first meaningful questions will reflect the theme that the reporter has in mind for the story.

"What I ask gives me my story," says Jane Brazes, a reporter for the *Cincinnati Post*. "What I don't ask I won't find out."

Answers to questions suggest additional themes. "When you think you have found an answer, you'll have found another question," Brazes says. The key to interviewing, she says, is to "find questions and never stop asking them."

When the author Gertrude Stein was dying, it is said that she looked up and asked—not "What is the answer?"—but "What is the question?"

Questions should be simple and direct. Larry King, whose radio talk program, "The Larry King Show," is carried by more than 200 stations around the country, is a skilled interviewer. He says that "if it takes you more than three sentences to ask a question, it's a bad question."

Complicated questions should be avoided. King recalls an interview Sandy Koufax did with the winning pitcher of a baseball game. Koufax, one of the greatest pitchers in the history of the game, was an inexperienced interviewer. He asked:

"In the game tonight, I noticed that in the fourth inning you took a little off your fast ball—you still had it in reserve because you had a 4–0 lead. Then, in the seventh inning, you used your curve ball. And in the ninth inning you went back to your fast ball and you still had it left."

King recalled, "All that the pitcher could answer was, 'Right.' "

King says the best question for the interviewer is "Why?" The object of the interview is to make the subject talk, and questions like, "Why," "How," "Give me an example of what you mean" induce people to talk.

Sometimes, silence can lead a person to talk. David M. McCullough, who interviews authors for the *Book-of-the-Month Club News,* says, "I found that a little silence often gets a better response than a pointed question."

Some experienced interviewers remain silent after a source or subject has made a particularly outrageous assertion. Except for a raised eyebrow, the reporter will not move. The interviewee has the feeling that the assertion isn't going down well, and usually he or she will feel obligated to fill the silence with an explanation, maybe a change of mind that moves closer to the truth.

Generally, the tactics used and the questions asked in an interview vary with the source and the kind of information sought. Many sources prefer to say little or remain silent. But a public official cannot be silent about public business, and reminding the source of that fact may be necessary to pry information from him or her.

By listening carefully, the reporter usually can find the one quote that best sums up the person or the event. When Wayne King was sent by *The New York Times* to cover a coal mine disaster in Colorado, King interviewed the brother of one of the 15 miners who had died. The man looked toward the western slope of the Colorado Rockies where the Dutch Creek mine is located and said, "That big mountain ate my brother."

King put the quote high in his story. It symbolized the life and death of the miner.

Listening and watching may reveal more than the words alone disclose. There is a language of gesture that says a great deal. The narrowing of a person's eyes as he or she speaks can underline a statement as emphatically

Listening and Watching

as boldface type in a written sentence. And if the source turns away as he or she says something, this may signal that the person is uncomfortable about his or her statement.

When the interview is conducted in the subject's home or office, notes are made of the furnishings, pictures on the wall, magazines on the coffee table or desk. These sometimes reveal a person's interests, tastes and concerns.

A well-known journalism professor covered his office walls with pictures of himself with famous people. Noticing this during an interview, a reporter concluded that the man's ego was monumental, that he needed to parade his fame to visitors. More than this, the reporter concluded that the professor—as famous as he was—had a sense of inferiority. The reporter filed away his observations for later use. Reporters often do this. Some save anecdotes and stories they hear for a year or more, until the right moment.

Howell Raines of *The New York Times* saved an anecdote a source gave him about a rising young politician. "I saved that quote because I knew that some day I would need it," Raines said. A year later he used it as the concluding anecdote in a perceptive profile of the young politician.

Taking Notes

Some reporters use tape recorders to take notes. Most use note pads. A few rely on their memory.

"I take notes a lot," Raines told Roy Peter Clark, who interviewed him about interview techniques. "If I'm working with a notebook, I bring it out early, and I take a pen out early. I do a lot of business with them. People then lose interest in your taking notes.

"If someone really gets cooking on something and I feel taking notes will be obtrusive, I won't take notes. Then, when the person is finished on that point—I've got a good memory—I'll take out my pad and write down what he said.

"But I try to be open about taking notes for two reasons. One, it establishes your authority. No one is going to come back to you and question a quote that he's seen you write down as it came out of his mouth. And two, these are people that are used to seeing reporters."

On- and Off-the-Record

The reporter's job is to write stories. Off-the-record interviews may help the reporter obtain background, but they do not lead directly to stories. Most experienced reporters are reluctant to go off the record, and they almost never bring it up.

"I never suggest putting anything off the record," Raines says. Most of those he interviews are experienced sources. They know that what they say is going to be used.

"I never put anything off-the-record retroactively," Raines says. "If they say to me, 'What I just told you is off the record,' they can say that all they want to, but I'm not bound by it. I'll usually tell them that, but I don't feel compelled to tell them that."

Raines does accept off-the-record information. When he does, he scrupulously follows certain ground rules: Off-the-record material may be used only on the grounds the source stipulates. Here are some ground rules sources may set:

Quotes are not to be attributed to the source but to "an official," or some such vague source.
The statement is to be paraphrased and used without attribution.
Material is to be used only if it is obtained from someone else and then not attributed to the original source.
For background use only—not for publication in any circumstance.

We are now ready to look over the essential elements of the profile or personality sketch.

Writing the Profile

Profile Essentials

Name and identification of the subject of the profile
Reason for profile (This is called the **news peg.**)
Background of person
Incidents and anecdotes from the subject and from friends and associates of the subject
Physical description
Direct quotes from subject and sources
Observations of the subject at work, home or play: mannerisms, gestures.
Strong ending

Most profiles are feature stories, and as such they must move quickly. Story movement is accomplished through the use of quotes, description, anecdotes and incidents.

The news peg for Vincent's story about actress Bisset was her new film, "Rich and Famous":

Delayed lead for first two paragraphs

> Hollywood—Don't call Jacqueline Bisset beautiful. Not if you want to get along with her.
> "I don't want to be a pinup," she says curtly, the famous gray-green eyes flashing. "I want to be something more than just an attractive woman. The public makes a mistake in labeling people that way."

News peg at the beginning of the third paragraph

> Currently, Bisset is chairman of the board—even if she is the only person on the board—of Jacquet Productions. As such, she is coproducer of "Rich and Famous," the plush, expensively mounted new soap opera movie that stars her as a respected novelist who has affairs, sometimes casually, with younger men. The film, currently showing at the Lynnhaven and Circle 6 Theaters, gives Bisset what she calls "a chance to prove,

Theme at the end of the paragraph

> once and for all, that I am capable of being a serious actress."

The last sentence of the third paragraph also serves as a transition or swing sentence. It takes the reader to a fuller explanation of the major theme of Vincent's piece—Bisset's attempts to prove she is more than a sexy pinup.

Notice that the news peg may not be the theme of the profile. Often, it is not. In a profile of the new college president, the news peg was the appointment. The theme was the appointee's ideas for revamping the curriculum.

The news peg tells the reader: Here is a newsworthy person. The theme says: Here's something interesting you ought to know about this person.

In his fourth paragraph, Vincent picks up the theme mentioned at the end of the third paragraph, Bisset's desire to be a serious actress:

> Although she thinks she has proved herself previously, she is aware that some critics haven't observed as much. "For some reason, critics like to take pot shots at me," she said. "In that way, my career has been similar to that of Candy Bergen, my co-star. We've both had our knocks from the critics."

(The complete story is in Appendix C.)

For a profile or personality sketch, the news peg need not be momentous. It may be as simple as the one used in the following profile by Timothy Weiner—Sonny Greer, a famous jazz drummer, is playing in New York City.

The story begins with a brief incident in Greer's life and shifts in the second paragraph to background. The third paragraph states the major theme—that Sonny Greer at 83 is still playing the drums and enjoying life. It continues with quotes from Greer and the pianist who plays with Greer.

Greer is described at the drums. We can see his "cannonball serve," the drumsticks doing a "tapdance on the high-hat cymbal."

The ending reinforces the theme with a good quote from Duke Ellington, with whom Greer played for 32 years.

All the elements of the profile are here. Notice that Weiner does not try to tell Greer's life story. No profile can be any more than a brief glimpse into a person's life. Here is Weiner's profile:

NEW YORK—When jazz great Sonny Greer was a kid, back in 1910, he had a single driving ambition: to be the world's greatest pool hustler.

Had Sonny not traded in his pool stick for drumsticks, he might never have teamed up with a young piano player named Duke Ellington in 1919. He couldn't have brought the Duke Ellington Orchestra to New York in the 1920s, where it gained fame as a worldwide paragon of jazz. And he might have spent most of his 83 years behind the eight-ball instead of behind his battery of drums and cymbals.

At an age when the rhythms of most people's lives have slowed to a crawl, Sonny Greer hasn't missed a beat.

Every Monday night at 8 o'clock, an impeccably dressed Greer sets up his drums onstage at the West End Cafe in New York City. Young admirers sit at the old gentleman's feet as he spins out stories of Harlem speakeasies and the halcyon days of jazz.

"My favorite place to play," Sonny said with a smile and a faraway gaze in his eyes, "was the old Kentucky Club. Fats Waller and me used to play duets there and sing risque songs. We'd play all night and come walking out of the club in the morning, the sun shining and all of us walking down Broadway laughing, feeling no pain. Those were good days, baby, oh yeah."

For 32 years' worth of good days, Sonny Greer's percussion was the beating heart of the Duke Ellington Orchestra. For thousands of nights he sat like a king on his throne, elevated above the rest of the band at center stage, surrounded by chimes, gourds, tympani, vibraphone and kettle drums, a great brass gong shining behind him like a halo.

In the 1930s and '40s, the Duke Ellington Orchestra was the closest thing to royalty the jazz world has ever known. But the band's fame didn't dampen the members' creative fires.

"While we were onstage," Sonny said, "as the evening progressed, we would experiment. If Duke liked it, he would keep it in. If he didn't, well, it cost nothing—throw it out, forget it.

"The guys in the band were amazing. They always had ideas, a million ideas. They were very creative. They created."

Sonny Greer is now the sole survivor of the original orchestra. He is probably the oldest jazzman active today. What keeps him going?

"Look, the drums are my life," he said, lighting a cigarette and cradling an Old-Fashioned glass of whisky. "I get a great pleasure out of playing and making the people happy."

Brooks Kerr, the 27-year-old blind pianist and Ellington scholar who plays with Sonny, said, "One thing that Sonny has that so few people of any age have is that desire to play. I think he lives to work and works to live."

At showtime, Sonny leads Brooks to the piano and seats himself at his drums. The drums, encrusted with tiny mirrors, sparkle in the spotlights. Brooks hits the first chords of "Take the 'A' Train" and shouts, "Sonny Greer, ladies and gentlemen!"

Sonny swats his snare drum with a flick of his wrist, the sound of a cannonball serve. His drumsticks tapdance on the high-hat cymbal. His bass drum pulses. Everyone in the audience is keeping time, their fingertips and feet following the drummer's beat, their bodies swaying slowly in unison.

Sonny's drums are talking. His drumming is musical syntax, giving structure to flowing musical language. And something more: echoes of Harlem, a conjuring of the past.

He's telling his life's story on the drums, distilling all those years of remembered rhythms into fluid syncopation. Listening to Sonny Greer is a trip back in time to the golden age of jazz. To hear him solo on the drums is to briefly recapture a classic style.

Sonny Greer's drum solo won't go on forever. But, as Duke Ellington once wrote, "Sonny Greer is an endless story."

Ending the Profile

A good idea in writing the profile is to use an incident or anecdote at the end of the piece that reinforces the major theme.

In his profile of Bruce A. Smathers, the son of a powerful political figure in Florida, Raines makes the point early in the story that Smathers' political future is dubious because he is not made of the steely determination of his father, "who," Raines writes, "never hestitated to backstab a friend for political advantage."

Raines writes of young Smathers high in his piece:

Bambi in the Jungle. Bruce Smathers, the subject of a searching profile by Howell Raines, and his wife at the time Smathers was a candidate for secretary of state. Raines showed that Smathers lacked the toughness and ruthlessness necessary to succeed in Florida politics.

. . . .With his fawn eyes and unlined face, he has more in common with Bambi than with the rapacious roebucks normally encountered in the political forests of Tallahassee.

Yes, Bruce Smathers says, smiling, he knows about those jokes that he is indecisive, that he would starve to death in a cafeteria line trying to choose between the Salisbury steak and the Spanish mackerel.

That rap, as Smathers tells it, is the price he must pay for having a trained mind and introspective nature.

"I have almost a repulsion of the easy answer," he says, and one hears in the scholarly tone echoes of Yale, where he won honors in economics. . . .

The picture Raines draws is clear. Young Smathers is an intelligent, decent person, perhaps unfit for the raw political infighting of southern politics. For his ending, Raines drives home his theme. The last two paragraphs read:

Perhaps Smathers' political gifts are that great, but many who know politics as it is played at the top question whether this young man loves it enough or is hard enough. Most people who make it as high as governor or U.S. senator have something—a hunger, a fire in the gut, a toughness—that one can sense. It is not necessarily a good thing to have, but it is essential to winning and surviving in office.

This is not the picture of Bruce Smathers that emerges from a story once leaked from his office—an intimate of Smathers was quoted as saying, "Somebody offered him some money for a vote and Smathers got up and went out of the room and threw up."

This is the anecdote Raines says that he had heard a year before and had saved for the time when he would need it. (The complete story is in Appendix C.)

If we could diagram the profile, it would look something like the illustration in figure 13.2.

Figure 13.2 Because most profiles are feature stories, they follow the same basic organization as the feature. All profiles should contain the elements diagrammed here.

14

Capturing the Spoken Word

Stories about meetings, panel discussions, news conferences and speeches must contain quotes that back up and buttress the theme the writer has selected for the lead of the story.

Meeting stories are of two types. They either focus on the decision reached or on the discussion. The decision or vote is the lead for the first type of meeting story. The consensus reached or the most significant issue raised in the discussion is the lead for the second type.

For **panel discussions,** the writer first looks for an area of agreement among the panelists to use as the lead. If there is no common ground, the writer may choose to single out the points made by one speaker.

News conferences can range over many subjects. The news writer selects the theme with the greatest impact on readers or listeners. Most news conferences are called for a specific purpose, and this is usually the lead.

Speeches have an even wider range of subject matter than the news conference. The speech story can concentrate on the speaker's main point, audience reaction or questions asked by reporters after the speech.

Much of the public's business is conducted in meetings. Important as they may be, few people attend them. It is the journalist's job to cover official meetings and to write clear, complete stories so that the people know what their appointed and elected officials are doing. Reporters are entitled to attend these meetings.

There are, of course, all kinds of meetings in addition to those of official bodies. The Parent-Teacher Association holds monthly meetings. College political clubs meet every so often. Church, civic and professional organizations meet regularly. Reporters are invited to attend these meetings.

The meetings of groups that are not financed with tax funds can be closed to the public and the press. A political club can call a closed meeting if it wishes. The board of the Kiwanis Club is not obligated to allow reporters to enter.

Once admitted to a meeting, a reporter can report anything that is said, unless the reporter is allowed to attend a meeting of a private organization that sets limits on coverage. When meetings are closed, the reporter can use anything else he or she obtains by interviewing those who attended the meeting.

Two Types of Meetings

Meetings usually have a purpose, and often the matter at hand is resolved by agreement or vote. Sometimes, there is only general discussion. Each type of meeting is handled slightly differently.

The story of a meeting that results in an action emphasizes the action taken:

> A bill to change West Virginia's 10.5-cents-per-gallon tax to a percentage of the wholesale price was soundly rejected by a joint House-Senate finance subcommittee yesterday by a vote of 9–2.

The meeting that does not result in any decisive action usually stresses the most significant part of the discussion:

> A student petition for more parking spaces on campus received sympathy but not much more from the trustees at yesterday's monthly meeting of the Board of Trustees.
> "We know it's a problem," said Alfred Breit, Board chairman. "But it is so complicated. . . ."

Meeting (Action Taken) Essentials

Vote, decision, agreement
Summary of the issue
Reason(s) for action taken
Arguments for and against issue
Names of those for and against, if important issue
Consequences of decision
Discussion leading to vote or action
Background of the issue
Significant additional issues discussed
Purpose, time and location of meeting
Additional agenda items
Makeup of audience and number attending
Statements, comments from audience
Significant departures from agenda
Agenda for next meeting

As we have often said, any one of these essentials can be the basis of the lead, and the story need not follow the order outlined in the list of essentials.

Here are some leads that are based on meetings in which a decision was reached. The leads stress the vote, agreement or decision.

Vote lead
The city commission voted unanimously last night to increase the property tax rate by $5.

Agreement lead
The County Bar Association agreed yesterday to allow Grant County lawyers to advertise certain legal services.

Decision lead
A group of parents today warned the city school board they will fight the proposed closing of the Donald Vogt Elementary School "by every possible means."

Another type of lead can be used when an action is taken. Readers usually want to know the consequences of an action, or what it means. The reporter who wrote the agreement lead above asked lawyers what the action would mean and was told the advertised legal services, such as divorce actions and drawing up wills, would probably cost less. With this information in mind, the writer decided to rewrite the agreement lead:

Consequence lead
It may be cheaper to draw up a will or file for a divorce in Grant County soon.

When the Alabama Public Service Commission granted permission to a bus company to run bus lines from a suburb into Birmingham, the reporter had two choices, a decision lead or a consequence lead. Judge for yourself which is better:

Decision lead
The Public Service Commission yesterday granted B&B Transport and Limousine Co. permission to run bus service from Alabaster to Birmingham.

Consequence lead
People who don't want to fight commuter traffic between Shelby County and Birmingham may soon have a new way to get to work.

Let's examine a meeting story in which an action was taken:

Decision lead

The Oldham County Planning and Zoning Commission yesterday recommended a denial of new zoning for a 68-unit townhouse and apartment complex in La Grange.

Next step

The recommendation goes to the La Grange City Council, which will make the final decision.

Summary of the issue

Terry and Donna Powell want a change from low-density residential to high-density residential zoning on 7.28 acres near Russell Avenue and Madison Street in a section of La Grange known as The Courts.

Audience, time of meeting; transition to discussion

About 50 people attended a planning commission hearing on the request yesterday. Charles Brown, county zoning administrator, said the commission cited these factors in voting against the rezoning:

Reasons for vote

✔The area contains suitable land already zoned for apartments.

✔Two other apartment complexes have been approved in the past year in or near La Grange.

✔The property is not close to such services as shopping areas.

✔The proposal conflicts with La Grange's comprehensive land-use and zoning plan.

Argument against proposal

Opponents from the neighborhood argued that the development would compound traffic problems. They also expressed concern that dynamite to be used during construction might damage their homes.

Argument for proposal

James Williamson, attorney for the applicants, contended that the apartments are needed. Some of them would have been reserved for the elderly and handicapped. The developers proposed building five townhouses and six apartment buildings.

—Louisville Courier-Journal

Meeting (Discussion) Essentials

Most important aspect of discussion: consensus (stated or implied);
  significant statement; strong disagreement
Arguments for and against issue(s)
Names and identifications of those for and against
Background of major issue(s)
Purpose, time and location of meeting
Additional matters discussed
Makeup of audience, number attending, comments
Statements, comments from audience
Significant departures from agenda
Agenda for next meeting

When the meeting does not lead to a decision, vote or action, the writer's task is more difficult. In this case, the writer may want to focus on what seems to be the consensus of the participants or on some significant statement made during the meeting:

Consensus
City council members last night displayed impatience with local residents who protested a proposed increase in the property tax rate.

Significant statement
City Councilman Garth Maguire told a delegation protesting a proposed property tax rate hike their opposition was "too strident, too narrow and too late."

Sometimes, what emerges is a strong disagreement:

Strong disagreement
City council members last night failed to reach any decision on the property tax rate increase City Manager Kelly Simmons proposed last week.

Panel Discussions

A panel or symposium is actually a meeting, but usually there is no intention to reach a decision. However, a consensus may emerge. If so, that should be the basis of the lead.

Most of the time panelists insist on going their own way, each person giving his or her opinions or findings. This puts the writer in a bind. Three, four or five people each merrily piping his or her own tune does not make for a smoothly written story.

Sometimes, the presentation of one speaker is clearly more newsworthy than that of the other speakers, and this becomes the lead, as in this story by Ray Cohn from *The Lexington Herald:*

Justice Secretary Says System Losing War Against White Collar Criminals

By Ray Cohn
Of The Herald Staff

White collar crime costs the country about $200 billion a year and the criminal justice system is losing the war against it, state Justice Secretary Neil J. Welch told a University of Kentucky symposium on crime and punishment last night.

Welch, a top FBI official before he came to Kentucky last year, said there has been an overwhelming increase in this type of crime.

"Profit is the motive," he said.

To illustrate the magnitude of the problem, Welch said that tax officials estimate $16 billion a year in taxes should be collected on interest income, but that only $2 billion is actually collected.

"We have won some battles," Welch said, "but we are losing the war."

He said that a conference was held about two years ago at University of California — Los Angeles on how to fight organized crime.

"You would think in 1980 we would have a strategy against organized crime, but we don't," he said.

Welch is credited as one of the masterminds of the FBI's Abscam investigation. In that probe, FBI agents posed as representatives of Arab sheiks and accepted bribes from congressmen and other public officials. The scandal resulted in the conviction of several congressman and Sen. Harrison Williams of New Jersey.

Neil J. Welch

Since becoming head of the state Justice Department in 1980, Welch has placed a heavy emphasis on combating white collar crime — and has come under fire for it.

At last night's forum he said "new leadership" is need to combat crime effectively.

He said in the past the emphasis in the United States has been "too oriented toward the legal system." The criminal justice system must now draw "on the finest business brains" to help fight white collar crime, he said, and greater use must be made of modern technology.

But Welch's approach was

oppposed by another member of the symposium panel, Dr. Ernest Yanarella, UK associate professor of political science. He said law enforcement officials must avoid the "nice lure" of technology as instruments of social control.

There was sharp **disagreement** among some panelists on a proposal made by a task force for U.S. Attorney General William French Smith to modify the exclusionary rule. Under that rule, evidence that police obtain illegally may not be admitted in court.

The national panel wants to permit the intoduction of such evidence if the police officer can show he made good faith effort to obtain it legally.

Yanarella said the position of civil libertarians is "that one has to make a difficult choice." But he insisted it is better to permit some guilty people to go free than "to permit great excesses."

Welch, on the other hand, said it doesn't make sense to exclude evidence because the police "may make a slight error."

Dr. Robert Granacher, a Lexington forensic psychiatrist, illustrated how difficult the issue can be.

He said "the killings in Atlanta stopped when that man was incarcerated." Yet, Granacher said, the suspect, Wayne Williams, will probably have to be released if a court rules that the fiber evidence the police seized from his home was obtained illegally

No other speaker is quoted but Welch until two-thirds down the story. The third speaker isn't even mentioned until the end of the story. The writer may have decided to give Welch top billing because of his experience as an FBI agent and his authoritative position as the state's top official in the justice system.

When it is possible, an area of agreement should be used as the basis of the lead. It may be that the speakers' only agreement is to disagree, and the subject of their disagreement can be the basis of the lead.

It may not be easy to find a common theme, but the reporter should try. Editors know that singling out a single speaker for the lead is the easiest lead to write. They value the reporter who has the ability to put the statements and ideas of different speakers together, to pattern his or her observations. The ability to extract a meaningful theme from what appear to be separate ideas is an art that every writer tries to cultivate.

Here is the beginning of a story for which the writer found a common theme:

High schools are not attracting the best teachers, panelists agreed last night in a discussion on the future of the public schools.

The panelists were not of one mind about most of the issues facing public education. But they did agree that a series of factors has made high school teaching unattractive.

The panel, which met in the Community College Auditorium, was sponsored by the college's department of education.

High school teaching has suffered from the following, the panelists said:

• Women are no longer forced to go into teaching because of limited opportunities in other fields. "Whole areas of professional life and business have opened to women," said Prof. Esther Josephs, associate professor of education at the College.

• The public has "little or no confidence in high schools, and morale is at the lowest point in years," said Raymond Peterson, principal of Lima High School. "No one wants to go into a field in which the public lacks confidence."

• Salaries are lower for high school teachers on the average than for any other field but social work, said Harry Metzger, an official of the state office of the National Education Association. . . .

Sometimes what is said is secondary to an incident in the audience, or even what is not said, as when speakers tiptoe around a controversial issue.

In the following story by Karen Ellsworth of *The Providence Journal-Bulletin,* who did and did not show up for a political meeting became the basis of the lead. Had any of the candidates said anything of significance, that would have been the lead. But Ellsworth concluded that most of what was said was not new. Instead, she decided on what her eyes, and not her ears, told her.

Her theme was apathy. Notice how her lead *shows* the reader there was public apathy.

PROVIDENCE—About half of the candidates for state general office and Congress attended a "Meet the Candidates" night at Rhode Island College last night, and they almost outnumbered the audience.

Every Republican candidate attended except James G. Reynolds, the Senate candidate. According to Doris McGarry, president of the Rhode Island League of Women Voters, his press secretary said he was ill. The league sponsored the event.

The only Democrats who attended were Robert Burns, the incumbent secretary of state, Dennis Roberts, candidate for attorney general, and Sen. Claiborne Pell. Neither independent candidate showed up.

About 30 persons, many of them students, attended the 2½–hour session in the lounge of Browne Hall. Mrs. McGarry said she didn't know whether to blame the low turnout on "illness or general apathy."

The format consisted of two-minute statements and questions from the audience, with the candidates each giving an answer and sometimes rebutting another's answer.

Only two candidates got to meet their incumbent opponents face-to-face. The livelier of those exchanges occurred between Burns and his opponent, Michael Murray, a Warwick city councilman. The Republican and Democratic candidates for attorney general, William A. Dimitri and Roberts, had just come from a live television debate on Channel 36 and they appeared a bit talked-out.

Reynolds' absence was particularly noted because of his charge last week that Pell had refused to face him head-on. At that time, Pell said he planned only two such confrontations, and one of them was last night's.

Burns said the first thing he will do when he is reelected is to work to reform recently-passed election laws.

The absentee and shut-in ballot law, which allows voters to have their ballots sent to the headquarters of a candidate who delivers it to their homes, is "wrong, wrong, wrong," Burns said.

News Conferences

The news conference has two scenes. Scene 1, the curtain raiser, consists of the statement by the person calling the press conference. The press politely hears out the message. Then Scene 2 begins, the questioning of the subject. Occasionally, but not often, a source will have an important announcement to make and not allow any questions. News can be made during both scenes.

The potential candidate for his party's nomination for governor announces he is pulling out of the race:

State Sen. Jack Felton said today he is withdrawing from the race for the Republican nomination for governor.

He pulled himself out of the contest at a press conference at the Simcoe Hotel.

"My plans now are to seek re-election to the legislature," he said. Felton's withdrawal clears the way for Ben Appleman, the only remaining announced candidate for the GOP nomination. . . .

Most often, the news comes out of the question-and-answer period when reporters try to dig out comments about pressing issues. At a presidential press conference, Ronald Reagan discussed general issues in an opening statement. The big news was made in answer to a reporter who asked how the United States could be sure a super-secret airplane Reagan wanted to sell to Saudi Arabia might not fall into the hands of unfriendly countries if the Saudi government were toppled.

Reagan replied there was "no way" the United States would stand by and let that government be overthrown.

The president's remark seemed casual, almost an aside, and the reporters went on to other issues. As the importance of his remark struck one reporter, he asked another question, and the president's reply was, again, brief.

All told, Reagan's comments on this issue occupied about a twentieth of the time of the news conference. Yet because of its importance—the United States implicitly warning all nations not to step into Saudi Arabia—it became the lead of the story. Because the reporters had only seven sentences from the president to back up their lead, they called a White House spokesman for comments and checked with a variety of sources. They also included considerable background.

The Boston Globe led its account this way:

President Ronald Reagan said yesterday that the United States would defend Saudi Arabia against any threat to take over the kingdom and cut off the flow of oil to the West.

Reagan's remark, which his aides acknowledged afterward constituted a major foreign policy pronouncement, was delivered as an aside to a question. . . .

News Conference Essentials

Major point of speaker
Name and identification of speaker
Purpose, time and location of conference
Background of major point
Major point in statement; major points in question-and-answer period
Consequences of announcement
Length of conference

The speech story is almost always based on the answer to the question: Who said what?

Speeches

Who: The speaker
What: The major theme of the speech

The key to writing speech stories is to isolate the major point the speaker is trying to make and then to select direct quotes that amplify this point. The major point goes into the lead, in the writer's own words. The quotes go into the body of the story.

Since speeches are often long and may include several themes, the reporter has to be choosy. A speech story should not include more than three or four of the speaker's points. There are exceptions—a major policy speech will be covered in detail—but the usual, everyday talk can be covered in a few hundred words.

Here is a speech story by Nicole Szulc of the *Los Angeles Herald Examiner*. Szulc selected the death penalty as the major point of the speech and placed it in the lead.

The second paragraph gives the name of the organization sponsoring the meeting. The third paragraph has a direct quote that amplifies the speaker's point, and the fourth paragraph contains background.

Notice that the other points made by the police chief are placed near the end of the story.

Gates urges homeowners association to support death penalty, '8,500 plan'

By Nicole Szulc
Herald Examiner staff writer

Los Angeles Police Chief Daryl Gates told some 300 Los Feliz residents last night they could contribute to stemming crime by supporting the death penalty.

At a monthly meeting of the Loz Feliz Improvement Association, which claims to be the largest and oldest home improvement association in Los Angeles County, Gates reminded the audience that two seats on the California Supreme Court recently had been vacated by two justices who favored capital punishment.

"You can help put a stop to crime by letting Governor Brown know how you want those Supreme Court vacancies filled," Gates said.

The police chief had been invited to speak to residents concerned about skyrocketing crime in their neighborhoods who are anxious to organize neighborhood watches or private security patrols. He outlined for them a three-fold plan to put a stop to violence.

Gates said the first point was to change the criminal sentencing structure, so "we can return to a system where if you commit a crime, you get punished."

Secondly, Gates pointed to the so-called "8,500 tax plan," which would provide funds to increase the city's police force to that number.

Next, Gates said, citizens have to learn to "become their brother's keepers," so neighbors know each other and can be "each other's eyes and ears" in trying to cut down neighborhood crime.

Neighborhood watches and security patrols are positive steps in the direction of crime prevention, Gates said, and he pledged the full support of the LAPD in bringing such organizations about.

Finally, Gates told the audience they must look into themselves in order to be able to defend themselves.

"If we hadn't won World War II, we probably wouldn't be here tonight discussing this," he said. "But now the greatest danger we face is from within."

Sometimes, something interesting that **happened** provides the main element for the story. During a political campaign in Wisconsin, the Republican candidate for senator was reciting the failings of his opponent and closed with, "I challenge him to deny these charges."

Suddenly, from the back, his opponent rose and shouted, "I deny every one of those charges," and he made his way to the stage. The **happening** obviously became the lead, and the confrontation between the two made up most of the story.

Speeches and speakers come in as many varieties as the offerings of a boardwalk ice cream parlor. There is the Kiwanis Club luncheon talk given by a member of the local chapter of the Audubon Society who discusses the need to save saltwater marshlands, and the recollections of a dentist before the county dental society about the early days of dentistry when Painless Parker cruised city streets in a horse-drawn wagon and extracted molars for 50 cents each.

Whatever the topic, whoever the speaker, the story must include certain essentials.

Speech Essentials

Name, identification of speaker
Major point of speech
Quotes to support main point
Purpose, time and place of speech
Nature of audience; prominent people in audience
Audience reaction
Background of major point
Speaker's dress, mannerisms, if important
Speaker's comments before and after speech, if any
Additional points made in speech
Material from question-and-answer period, if any

Writing the Lead

As we've said, the lead of the speech story generally answers the question: Who said what? It does so in S-V-O fashion, the speaker's name or identifying label first and what he or she said next.

Some editors prefer the lead reversed: What was said by whom.

> Rural Americans are not going to let high-voltage lines crisscross their homes, farms and ranches, two Carleton College faculty members said today.

The theory behind this structure is that often what was said is more important than who said it. For broadcast news writing, and increasingly for newspaper usage, the S-V-O structure is preferred.

The identification of the speaker is essential. This gives him or her the credentials to merit our attention. The identifying label usually establishes the speaker's credentials at once in the lead. We use a label when the name of the speaker will mean little to readers or listeners. With well-known people, the name alone usually establishes the person's authority to speak:

Identifying label	The owner of a chain of fast-food restaurants in the Midwest told a convention of food handlers here today that in 10 years a home-cooked meal will be unusual.
Identifying label	A University of Wisconsin historian said today that mass culture is a means through which men and women are manipulated.
Well-known name	Gov. William Blair said today his administration plans to increase aid to the state's colleges and universities that have suffered from federal cutbacks.

In addition to identifying the speaker and stressing the speaker's major point, two other essentials usually are placed in the lead:

Where the talk is given—location
To whom the speech is given—audience

It is not always possible to jam location and audience into the lead and still have a crisp lead:

> The head of a local architectural firm told members of the Engineers and Architects Club at their monthly meeting in the Miller Hotel last night that the proposed city hall may prove too costly to build.

To shorten such leads, drop the location and audience to the second or third paragraph:

> The head of a local architectural firm said last night that the proposed city hall may prove too costly to build.
> Preston Wilcox told the Engineers and Architects Club that the cost is estimated at $22 million. He spoke at the Miller Hotel.

The Audience

In our list of essentials, the word *audience* refers to those directly addressed. In Wilcox's talk, the audience is a local club. Audience can also mean the people the speaker hopes to reach through the press. Many speakers have the general public in mind when they speak. Wilcox obviously was intent on warning the public about the costs of constructing a new city hall.

The writer handled this aspect of Wilcox's talk by including background:

```
     Wilcox's talk comes in the midst of a controversy over
whether to go ahead with construction. Inflation--the
increased cost of labor and supplies--has sent costs
soaring.
     Taxpayer organizations oppose the construction that
was authorized by the city council in 1978. But local
unions and the administration of Mayor Fred Partell favor
going ahead.
```

Sometimes, as we have seen, the audience may provide the lead element. An unusually small audience for a presidential candidate's major speech can merit the lead, unless the candidate says something extraordinary. An unexpectedly large audience can be the basis of the lead as well.

Heckling or boredom at political speeches may be lead material. Significant questions from members of the audience may reveal more newsworthy information than the speech itself.

Constructing the Story

As in all the types of stories in this chapter, the speech story is built on direct quotes, the words of the speaker. Careful: the sign of the beginner is using a direct quote in the lead. A great orator is able to reach out and grab the audience and shake it with ringing sentences worthy of a lead. Such a speaker comes along once in a decade. Name one.

Most of the time, the writer begins with a paraphrase of the speaker's major point. This is followed closely by a direct quote that best makes the point.

The speech story is a blend of direct and indirect quotes, of the speaker's exact language and the writer's paraphrasings.

The basic elements included in the structure of the speech story are diagrammed in figure 14.1.

Caution Sometimes a writer is tempted to take a clever or flashy quote and put it high in the story to attract the readers' interest. This can create problems. Often, the quote is only the speaker's way of getting attention and may not relate to the news point. Placed high in the story, the quote may mislead the reader. The same caution should be taken with the anecdotes speakers sometimes use to spice their talks. Unless they lead directly to the news point, they should not be used high in the story.

Finding the proper material for the lead can be difficult. Some speakers dart from one subject to another, like a trout moving upstream, now here, now there.

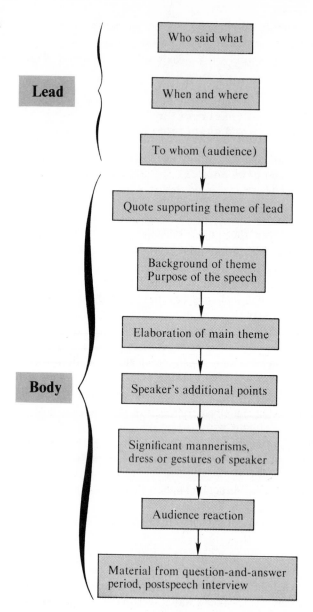

Figure 14.1 These elements are pertinent to nearly every speech story. The reporter must keep this structure and each of its elements in mind while listening to the speech.

A tipoff to the theme can be the title of the talk, if there is one. Watching the speaker's demeanor can indicate the emphasis of the speech. When the words come slowly and deliberately, the speaker is trying to stress his or her point. When the arms wave or a finger points, listen closely or follow the prepared text, pencil ready to underline.

When in doubt about the speaker's theme, ask the speaker. Post-speech interviews can sometimes turn up better leads than the speech itself.

Other times, the writer will find the lead in a point the speaker did *not* emphasize. Remember that the speaker is usually talking to a special audience, whereas you are writing for a general audience.

The manager of a local television station may be speaking to a women's club about the merits of programming for the mass audience. In passing, he may say that his station is cutting back on public affairs programming because "nobody watches those shows anyway."

The writer knows that the change in local programming is of greater interest than a generalized defense of situation comedies and quiz shows. To gather more details, the reporter may stop the speaker on his way out or call him at the station.

When a speaker does not explain a point adequately and the reporter cannot clear it up through an interview or telephone call, the story may have to include a sentence or two saying that the point was not clarified. The writer should not hesitate to do this. Otherwise, the reader will presume the writer neglected to explain something important.

An AP reporter covering a speech at an Asian population conference quoted a member of the Islamic Consultative Assembly as saying that the new regime in Iran had eliminated 114,000 prostitutes "who were the products of the disgraceful, satanic domination of America and lived at the highest level of wretchedness." To this, the AP reporter added his own comment, "She did not say how this was done."

Clarifying Ambiguous Statements

The texts of important speeches are often distributed to the press ahead of their delivery. Examination of the prepared text gives reporters time to study the material and to write without pressure. It also allows newspapers and broadcast stations to use the material—unless it is embargoed (restricted for use) until after delivery—ahead of the actual talk.

When prepared texts are used prior to delivery, the writer places in the lead or high in the story the phrase "In a speech prepared for delivery. . . ."

Reporters always cover important speeches with eyes on the text and ears on the speaker. News can be made by last-minute insertions to or deletions from the prepared speech.

Prepared Texts

The basics of writing the types of stories we have examined in this chapter are:

1. Catch the meaning or the drift of the event and put it in the lead.
2. Place the meaningful quotes that amplify and buttress the lead high in the story.
3. Give the setting of the event—location, nature of audience and time.
4. Include the possible consequences of what was said.

Summary

15

From the Office and On the Beat

Looking Ahead

Accident stories center on the names of the dead and injured.

Fire stories have two important themes: human casualties and physical damage.

Crimes, detection and **arrest** stories are usually written from police reports. Additional reporting gives these stories human interest. Stories from the police beat focus on the victim, nature of the crime and suspects or arrests.

Obituaries give the name, age, address and major accomplishment of the deceased.

Sports stories are most effective when the writer knows the sport and the players and coaches and when the writer makes the action, rather than supercharged language, propel the story. Game stories require the names of the teams, score, decisive play(s), strategy of players and coaches and the effect on standings.

Briefs or **shorts** include **precedes,** or **advances, personals** and other short items that run no more than five or six sentences. **Folos** are stories that follow up on a theme taken from another story. **Sidebars** emphasize an aspect of the main story printed nearby. **Roundups** combine two or more stories into one by finding a theme common to the stories and using that theme in the lead.

Weather forecasts and stories about unusual or extreme weather are given good play by newspapers and broadcast stations. When possible, use human interest.

Many editors assign their new reporters to the police beat as a way of introducing them to the community. Although at first glance this seems to be the way to see the town from the underside, the beat does give the reporter a quick overview of the city since accidents, fire and crime strike widely and at all levels of society.

Let's look at the traffic accident story first. The accident story is a staple of journalism. More than a million people are killed or injured every year in traffic accidents, and all but the largest newspapers carry stories of these accidents. Only the most minor—the so-called fender benders—are ignored or written in summary form in a column of briefs.

Accidents

In all accident stories, the names of the dead and injured must be reported. The victims are identified by age, address and occupation. The extent of the injuries and the condition of the injured are also given.

Accident Essentials

Names and identification of dead and injured
Time and location of accident
Types of vehicles involved
Cause (Quote official sources.)
Source of information
Names and identification of drivers and of others in vehicles if
relevant
Where dead and injured were taken
Extent of injuries
Condition of injured
Funeral arrangements, if available
Arrests or citations by officers

If the accident merits a long story because of its severity, add the following:

Damage to vehicles
Speed, origin and destination of vehicles
Unusual weather or highway conditions
Accounts by eyewitnesses and investigating officers

Caution Do not attempt to give the cause of an accident or information about excessive speed or drinking by a driver unless the information comes from an official source.

For minor accidents, only the first six essentials are included, as in this story about a car striking a pedestrian:

Auto Hits Man, Breaks His Legs

James Oates, 46, of 447 Dartmouth Ave. suffered two broken legs Thursday evening when struck by a car while crossing Bailey Avenue near LaSalle Avenue, police said.

He is reported in serious condition in the Erie County Medical Center.

Police reported that John Rinzel, 24, of 211 Doat St., driver, said the man stepped into the path of his vehicle from a parked car. He was not charged.

—Buffalo Evening News

For fatal accidents, material is also included about the victim, survivors and funeral arrangements:

Bullitt Man Dies in KY 61 Crash

A 34-year-old Bullitt County man, Jackie L. Boone, was killed Monday in a car-motorcycle accident near Lebanon Junction.

According to state police at the Elizabethtown post, Boone, of Route 1A, Lebanon Junction, was killed when the motorcycle he was riding was struck from the rear by an auto about three miles north of Lebanon Junction on KY 61.

Deputy Coroner J. B. Close said Boone died at the scene of a broken neck.

The driver of the auto, Marla Seay of New Albany, was not injured. No charges were filed.

Boone, formerly of Louisville, was a maintenance machinist for Naval Ordnance Station and a Navy veteran.

Survivors include his wife, the former Janice Goeing; a son, Jackie L. Boone; his parents, Mr. and Mrs. Witt Boone; four sisters, Miss Juanita Boone, Mrs. Norbert Carey, Mrs. Colleen Gipson and Mrs. Beth Lehner; and a brother, Robert Boone.

The funeral will be at 10 a.m. Friday at O.D. White & Sons Funeral Home, 2727 S. Third St., with burial in Resthaven Memorial Park.

Visitation will be at the funeral home after noon tomorrow.

—Louisville Times

Despite the frequency of vehicular accidents, the news writer can often find an interesting aspect to begin the story with instead of leading with the name and identification of the dead and injured and the location. Look at how a *Miami Herald* writer started a fatal accident story:

James D. Robinson of Opa-locka was driving in the proper lane when he died.

The car that killed him and seriously injured his wife and two small children was not.

In the next few paragraphs the writer gave full identification of those involved in the fatal collision, the location, where the injured were taken, and the extent of their injuries. The story ended with this paragraph.

Charges are pending, Broward Sheriff's Deputy Hal Samuels said. Altieri's blood was tested to determine if he had been drinking while driving, Samuels said.

Death or serious injury are not always necessary for an accident story to make the news. Massive traffic tie-ups, with the usual dented fenders and broken brake lights, also interest readers. So do the accident stories that have a humorous aspect, as this AP story does:

> MUSKOGEE, Okla. (AP)—A woman who stopped on a slick bridge here to scrape off her windshield drove off without a scratch, leaving 36 dented cars behind her.

Fires

Stories about fires usually are given good play. Fire stories interest readers, possibly because of our fear of fires. Whatever the reason, the beginner will likely find himself or herself handling a fire story within days, whether it is a farmhouse fire that causes $20,000 in damage or an apartment house fire that kills eight people:

HARRISBURG—A farmhouse six miles northeast of Harrisburg was badly damaged Sunday evening by a fire that began when the occupants of the dwelling were away.

Harrisburg Fire Chief Sonny Hanf said the two-story frame house, at 24661 Rowland Rd., sustained a loss of about $20,000. The building is owned by George Turney of Dallas and rented by Jim and Patsy Rosenberg, Hanf said.

According to Hanf, Jim Rosenberg returned to the house about 7 p.m. Sunday and found a bedroom in flames. Firefighters from Harrisburg and Halsey responded to the alarm.

Hanf said fire damage was confined to the bedroom area, although the rest of the house sustained smoke and water damage.

—Eugene (Ore.) Register-Guard

PATERSON, N.J. (AP)—Eight people died in a predawn tenement fire and 11 were missing yesterday after a man who had been spurned by a female resident allegedly set the building ablaze with a can of gasoline, authorities said.

Two dozen others were injured, "many of them jumping from windows," said police Sgt. Edward Hanna.

"The firemen were inside the building, crawling around on their hands and knees, feeling for people," he said. "Twenty minutes after I got there, they carried out three kids while the fire was really going. I never saw anything like it in my life."

Paterson Fire Chief Harold J. Kane said the bodies were found after firefighters gained control of the blaze that left more than 100 people homeless.

"We just hope it ends here. But we're waiting on a crane to help us go through what's left of the building,". . . .

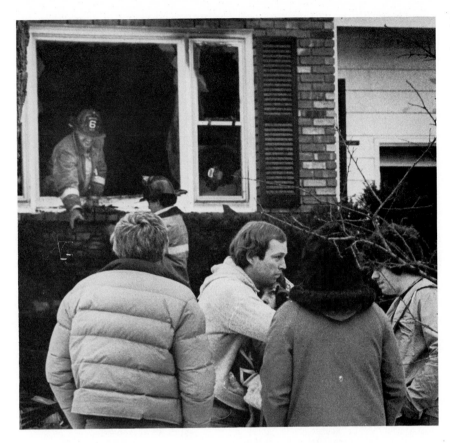

Burned Out. When someone is injured or killed, or the damages are large, the reporter selects from these for the lead. Home fire stories also center on the consequences to the residents—homeless, clothing gone, perhaps a valuable stamp collection or library gone up in smoke.

Fire Essentials

Deaths, injuries
Full identification of victims
Location
Type of structure
Official cause
Source of information
How victims were injured or killed
When and where fire started, and how and when it was brought under
    control
Rescue attempts
Where injured, dead taken
Extent of injuries
Investigation of cause
Damage to structure, cost, insurance coverage
Number of units and firefighters; amount of water used
Name(s) of fire company(ies) responding
Quotes of eyewitnesses, firefighters, residents of structure
Human interest details

Fires are frequent in large cities, especially in winter but they are not covered unless there is considerable damage, loss of life, traffic tie-ups, or a large amount of equipment is called out. In small and medium-sized cities, fires are usually covered even when there is no loss of life and damage is minor.

When a wooden grain elevator burst into flames one Saturday morning in downtown Hays, Kan., *The Daily News* sent reporters and photographers to cover the fire. Although the fire was brought under control in three hours and no one was hurt, the newspaper devoted almost all of the front page to the story and to a large picture. An inside page carried five photos and the continuation of the page one story.

In rural communities, fire is a great enemy, and coverage is thorough. The fire companies that answer the call are identified and the chief's quotes are usually used.

A farm fire that destroyed a feed barn, a tractor, a hay baler and 3,000 bales of hay received front page play in the *Georgetown News,* a weekly newspaper in Kentucky. The fire was caused by lightning. Ed Moore, chief of the Scott County Fire Department, was quoted in the story as saying:

"We just call this kind of thing an act of God. I've seen farms with lightning rods go up in smoke. Once the lightning flash causes a dust explosion in the hay, there's just nothing you can do to save the barn."

In the following story, a quote is used in the second paragraph and the names of the cities from which firefighters were dispatched is also included.

Brush fire threatens homes

WAVES—A brush fire driven by northeast winds scorched 12 acres near this Hatteras Island village Wednesday night, threatening several homes, before it was brought under control.

"Everyone on the island was involved," said Bert Austin, Dare County's chief deputy sheriff.

Firemen from Waves, Rodanthe, Salvo, Avon, and Buxton answered the alarm about 7 p.m. National Park Ser-

vice, Coast Guard, and N.C. Division of Forest Resources personnel assisted.

Austin said the flames reached within 50 feet of one home before the dry swamp grass was doused by firemen.

The fire started when an electric wire fell in the grass. The wire apparently had been damaged by the accumulation of salt, a common problem for utility companies in Dare County.

—*The Virginian-Pilot*
(Norfolk, Va.)

The Lead

When there are deaths or many injuries—as in the AP story from Paterson, N.J.—the lead must focus on this essential. When property is the only casualty—as in the Harrisburg farmhouse fire—then that is the basis of the lead.

Fires sometimes threaten homes in areas plagued by forest fires and brushfires, and this often provides the lead material, as in the story from Waves.

Now and then, a building of historical interest burns down. No one is hurt, and the structure has little financial value. But the fire has claimed a part of the past. Such stories are given good play, as was this story by Ed Kenyon from the *Eugene Register-Guard:*

Foley Hot Springs Burns

McKENZIE BRIDGE—Foley Hot Springs, once the queenly resort of the affluent seeking the healing powers of mineral waters, suffered a final indignity this week.

The once-stately lodge at the spa about five miles southeast of here, where many of the Willamette Valley's well-to-do spent their summers, was destroyed by fire Wednesday night.

Long faded from its glory years, the building had just one resident when fire, which apparently started in a wall behind a wood-burning furnace, spread rapidly.

Peter Runey, 22, son of the owners, was awakened by the fire and barely had time to throw his sleeping bag out a window and escape himself after making a futile attempt to douse the blaze with a fire extinguisher.

Runey's father, William, 60, latest in a family line which has owned the resort for 101 years, reflected sadly on the loss Thursday.

"It's not just the building," Runey explained. "There was an accumulation of three generations stored there."

The accumulation included a library of 3,000 to 4,000 books, a collection of old guns and tools and other equipment Runey used in his small logging business.

But the most prized possession was a desk which Runey's grandfather used when he served as mayor of Astoria in the 1870s. It was the grandfather, Peter Runey, who brought Foley Hot Springs into the family. . . .

Dennis Love of *The Anniston* (Ala.) *Star* describes how he heard about an unusual fire and then how he gathered the information for his story.

Death of a Smoker

"While on weekend duty one Saturday night, I got a tip while calling funeral homes throughout our seven-county circulation area. An employee said he was handling funeral arrangements for a 76-year-old man who died in a school bus fire the night before.

"An accidental death alone merits a brief story, but this man's age and obvious questions about why he was in the bus required further checking. I called the coroner, the sheriff's department and the fire department—all of which were represented on the scene—and pieced together the basic information.

"The old man, who lived with his brother in a rural part of the county, often slept in an old school bus he had converted into a camping vehicle. On this night he had apparently fallen asleep while smoking and was unable to escape the flames that rapidly engulfed the old vehicle. The coroner said there was no evidence of foul play."

Then Love began to try to reach relatives of the dead man to piece together the details. The coroner supplied the name of one relative who gave Love the telephone number of the family home, which he had not been able to find in the directory. He reached the victim's brother. This was a vital call.

"He gave me a first-hand account of what had happened, and he testified to his brother's love of cigarettes, which they were convinced caused the fire. He also said his brother recently had moved in with him from a nursing home and was not in the best of health and often needed assistance in moving around. I wrote down his comments and was ready to write the story."

Here is Love's story, and alongside it his comments about how he wrote it:

I had some colorful quotes from the brother about his brother's smoking habits, and since that had emerged as the consensus as to the cause of death, I decided to emphasize that angle in my lead paragraph. His age was also significant, as was the school bus setting, so I incorporated all of it in what I consider a somewhat clumsy lead. But it seemed to work.

FRUITHURST—Seventy-six-year-old Tom Jenkins' penchant for chainsmoking has been blamed for the fire which engulfed the old school bus in which he slept early Saturday and in which he died.

Next, the sequence of events were in order so I used the clearest and most official source I had—that of the coroner. I let him give the basic facts in the next three paragraphs, throwing in an aside about the victim's health in the third graf.

Cleburne County Coroner Hollis Estes said he and the Heflin Fire Department were summoned to the Coldwater community near Fruithurst shortly after 4 a.m. Saturday to find the old bus—converted into a camping vehicle—ravaged by flames.

The bus was parked in the front yard of the home of the victim's brother, Hubert Jenkins. Tom Jenkins was living with his brother while he recovered from a stroke he suffered earlier this year, according to family members.

Estes said the bedding in the rear of the bus apparently caught fire from a burning cigarette and spread rapidly throughout the vehicle. The coroner said there was no evidence of foul play and no autopsy would be performed.

Then I came back to the smoking angle, using my best quote from the victim's brother. I let him describe the chainsmoking habits, tell about the camper and the events leading up to his discovering the fire in progress.

"Lord, he (the victim) was always careless with his cigarettes," said Hubert Jenkins Saturday night. "He would just smoke one right after the other. Only thing we can figure is he got out there in the camper and fell asleep or something with one lit."

Jenkins said his brother, who left Golden Springs Nursing Home in April, spent a great deal of time sitting in the bus, which was equipped with a stove, refrigerator and other appliances.

"Friday afternoon, he said he was going out for some fresh air, and I watched him make a beeline for the bus," Jenkins said. "I checked on him later on and he was just sitting on the side of the bunk bed, said he wanted to stay out there a while longer."

Jenkins said his brother later told his daughter "he wanted to spend the night out there."

Around 4 a.m., Jenkins said he awoke to the sound of "something popping. It sounded like his old walking cane he used—I thought he was tapping on the side of the bus to get my attention. Before I could get to the door I could see the trailer" on fire. Jenkins said he believes the popping sound that woke him was .22-caliber cartridges exploding in the bus.

Jenkins said his brother needed some help in "getting around" after the stroke, but was at a loss to explain why the victim was unable to escape the flames.

He said the bus had a front and rear entrance, but the back door was blocked by the bed on which Jenkins slept. Estes said, however, that the body was found on the floor of the bus.

I closed the story with his brother's explanation.

"It just looks like when he woke up he tried to get out, but just didn't make it," said Hubert Jenkins.

Love said his story lets "the people who were involved answer the obvious questions: How and why did Jenkins die where he did, and why couldn't he avoid his death? My last phone call to the family of the deceased brought all that together, and helped to take the story a bit beyond the level of a routine police item."

Crime Stories

The main job of the police reporter is handling crime—reports of violent and property crimes, investigations and detection, and arrests. The police reporter may also cover the police and municipal or criminal courts to follow up the arrests he or she reports.

It is no surprise to anyone that crime is increasing. Few families are untouched by crime. A third of all households in the United States were affected by burglary or a violent crime in the 1980s. In towns where people never locked their doors, there is now a thriving business in burglar alarm systems. Automobile owners search for the switch, wiring or siren that will keep a thief from taking off with their Toyotas and Fords. In some cities, women are advised not to wear necklaces or earrings. Around college and university campuses, the number of rapes has doubled and tripled in recent years.

During the 1970s, the number of crimes reported to law enforcement officials increased by 50 percent. The FBI reports a property crime is committed every three seconds and a violent crime every 24 seconds. A rape occurs every six minutes and a murder every 23 minutes.

Almost every community in the country has contributed to these figures. This means that police reporters have had to be more discriminating in their reporting. If they did not, they would not have enough time to report the most important crimes in their cities and towns.

To help clear the way through this flood of police information, the police reporter usually concentrates on violent crimes and spends less time on property crimes.

Violent Crimes	**Property Crimes**
Murder	Burglary
Rape	Larceny
Robbery	Motor vehicle theft
Aggravated assault	

Crime Reports

Few police reporters have ever seen a crime committed. Yet they write about crimes every day, often with the intensity and drama of an eyewitness. Most of their information comes from crime reports. These are the forms filled out by officers who have investigated the crime. These reports may be augmented by interviews with the officers or their superiors and with those who witnessed the crime or were its victims.

Reporters determine the nature of the crime from the code number at the top of the crime report. The code number tells the reporter whether the crime is serious or minor.

Crime Essentials

Victim, full identification
Nature of crime
Date, time, location of crime
Violent crime: official cause of death or injury; weapon used; motivation; background of victim, if relevant
Property crime: value of loss; method of theft or entry
Suspects (no names unless charges filed), clues
Unusual circumstances
Quotes of witnesses, victim(s), police
Source of information

The following story about a violent crime was taken from a crime report. It begins with the nature of the crime and the victims. In the second paragraph, the victims are identified and their injuries described. The third paragraph describes the possible weapon and the questioning of two suspects.

Man, Woman Shot During Fracas in Field

A man and woman were shot about 10:40 p.m. Monday when gunfire erupted during what police called a "neighborhood-type" argument in a field at 34th and Forest.

The victims were identified as Tony Simmons, 20, of 5117 Woodland, who was listed in critical condition with a gunshot wound to the forehead, and Ms. Debra Williams, 21, of 3327 Tracy, in fair condition with a gunshot wound to the left hand. Both were admitted to the Truman Medical Center.

Police, who said they heard different accounts of the shooting at the scene, said they were questioning two persons in connection with the incident. A pump shotgun believed to have been used in the shooting was recovered on the porch of a home at 3329 Tracy, police said.

—Kansas City Times

Robbery

Beginning reporters sometimes confuse robbery, a violent crime, and burglary, a property crime. The difference is this: Robbery is a crime against a person. Burglary is a crime against property.

Robbery involves taking or attempting to take something of value from a person by force or threat of force or violence. The writer approaches robbery stories from two avenues—the value of goods stolen and the prominence of the person involved. Usually, the value of goods taken is the element chosen for the lead, but when a well-known person is robbed, that is the lead, regardless of the amount taken from the person.

Here is a typical robbery story:

A lone gunman held up the Thrifty Liquor Store at 42 First St. this morning and got away with $1,780 in cash, police said.

The owner, Martin Nolan, said that he was closing the store when a man in his thirties bought a bottle of wine. As Nolan opened the register, the man took a revolver from his jacket pocket and told Nolan to hand over the day's receipts.

On leaving, he warned Nolan against following him. But Nolan told police he managed to see the tall, thin man drive off in a 1979 blue compact car with Arkansas plates.

Burglary

Burglary is the unlawful entry of a structure to commit a felony or a theft. (A felony is a crime that is punishable by a year or more in a state or federal penitentiary.) In the case of burglaries, state law usually defines the dollar amount of stolen goods at which the theft passes from a misdemeanor to a felony. In some states, it is $250, in others $500, and so on. (A misdemeanor is a crime punishable by a fine or a term of less than one year in a city or county prison.)

When the loss in a burglary is considerable, the lead focuses on the value of the stolen goods:

Jewelry and personal items worth $50,000 were reported missing from the home of Victor Sewell, 560 Eastern Lake Ave., last night.

Police said Sewell told them he and Mrs. Sewell returned from a visit to friends about 11 p.m. and discovered the window to a bedroom at the rear of the house had been forced open.

Sewell, an attorney, told police he had purchased a matching diamond bracelet and necklace last week in London where he attended a law seminar. He said he had told no one of the purchase.

Police said the bedroom was the only room in the house that had been entered.

Detection

Police are understandably close-mouthed during the investigation of a serious crime, which makes it hard for the reporter to obtain material for a story during the detection-investigation stage.

Sometimes, the police will seek help from the press in locating a suspect and will provide information. Now and then a reporter will learn something the police want to keep confidential. Most police reporters will keep the material under wraps. They risk antagonizing sources if they use it. In the larger cities, the unwritten code is that a reporter may use anything he or she can learn. If the department cannot keep its people quiet, so be it.

Early information about suspects may compromise not only the investigation but the court case. A reporter must weigh all this before running any but officially sanctioned material.

Detection Essentials

Progress of investigation
Suspects
Additional clues
Personnel assigned to case
Summary of crime

Caution Only the most serious crimes are investigated by most big-city police departments. Generally, the greater the public interest, the more likely the police are to press an inquiry. The murder of a prominent person or a police officer will be investigated. But in large cities, the murder of a drug dealer or a drifter will be closed quickly. Burglaries, robberies and car thefts have, for all practical purposes, been decriminalized in large cities, unless the criminal is caught in the act. There is almost no follow-up investigation of these crimes.

Arrests

Some of the best crime stories are of arrests. Again, the information usually comes from a report, in this case an arrest report, which the reporter examines on his or her rounds of the police department. For arrests in serious crimes, the police or district attorney may call a news conference to make the announcement for all the media.

Usually, charges are filed on arrest, but sometimes a suspect is held for investigation. A suspect may be detained for a limited period until formal charges are filed. In the arrest story, the writer must be certain that the charges mentioned have actually been filed.

Arrest Essentials

Name, identification of person arrested
Crime person is charged with
Details of crime, including name and identification of victim
Circumstances of arrest
Officers involved in arrest
Source of information

For serious crimes, add these:

Investigation
Background of suspect
Motive
Circumstances of arrest announcement
Booking, arraignment, any other procedures

The Arrest Lead Generally, the lead to the arrest story is based on the name and identification of the person arrested and the crime that the person is accused of committing.

If the arrest is the result of extraordinary police detection or unusual circumstances, a delayed lead may be put on the story, with the arrest coming as a climax.

Here are some leads that emphasize different essentials:

Name, identification of person arrested

Two teenagers are in the Dade County jail, charged with first degree murder in the robbery and execution of a meat truck driver whose truck they hijacked. Robert Borton, 18 of 1981 NW 37th Ct., and his longtime friend, Carlton Derly, 19, of 2149 NW 24th Ct., were arrested Wednesday night.

The police arrested three brothers and accused them of breaking into a church yesterday in the suburb of Brookline.

The police identified the men as. . . .

Circumstances of arrest

HOUSTON—A one-armed busboy captured a fleeing gunman, tripping him twice and holding him in a headlock for police, after the gunman held up a restaurant and shot a cook, authorities said today.

Detail of crime

BALTIMORE—A suspect has been arrested in the weekend slaying of a department store manager who was found shot to death with his 3-year-old son standing over him, police said.

Investigation

Eleven South Americans were in custody today after a four-month investigation by the Sheriff's Department, Narcotics Bureau and U.S. Customs resulted in the seizure of $750,000 worth of cocaine, $139,500 in cash, a rifle, three handguns and a sizeable amount of gold jewelry, Undersheriff Sherman Block said yesterday.

What's Newsworthy? The size of the community and the amount of crime in it determine what kinds of arrests become news. In Detroit, Chicago, Los Angeles and cities of similar size, the arrest of a murder suspect may merit a few lines, if that, unless the victim is prominent or the crime had been given attention.

But in smaller cities and towns even the theft of some jeans and the arrest of a suspect is worth a story:

A Dress Barn employee was arrested Wednesday on a warrant charging him with stealing 49 pairs of blue jeans.

Joseph Scapella, 40, of 95 Trudy Lane was charged with second degree larceny in connection with the theft of the jeans valued at $1,302 and taken from a Dress Barn warehouse March 26, police said.

This story appeared in *The Advocate* in Stamford, Conn. The story is as long as a piece about an arrest for attempted murder in Chicago, which was carried by the newspaper only because of the grisly nature of the crime:

A resident of a West Side halfway house was charged Monday with shoving his roommate out of a third-floor window, then rushing downstairs and stabbing him 11 times as he lay in the alley where he landed.

The police charged Allen Taber with attempted murder. The victim, Fred Krumpe, was in critical condition with multiple fractures.

Analyzing the Arrest Story   Here is an arrest story with the list of arrest essentials alongside it:

Circumstances of arrest, crime committed	A special burglary detail yesterday chased and caught a suspect the officers believe responsible for a rash of house burglaries in the Tacoma Avenue area.
Charges	Karl Vogt, 31, of 967 Eastern St., was charged with burglary and possession of burglary tools.
Circumstances of arrest elaborated	Police said that Vogt was spotted by a detective in the special unit going from house to house along Tacoma Avenue. When he saw the man enter 98 Tacoma Ave. he radioed for the rest of the detail. Vogt awoke a tenant, John Strong, and then tried to flee but was arrested a block from the building.
	The detail was set up for round-the-clock surveillance of the neighborhood after several house burglaries were reported.
Officers involved in arrest	Detectives who made the arrest included Ray Miller, John Hazar and Bill Smith.

Obituaries

The Washington-based political reporter had finished his talk to the journalism class and asked for questions. He had just completed a five-state tour of the Midwest to sound out political feelings about the president.

"What was the strongest impression you got from your trip?" a student asked.

The reporter paused a moment before answering. "This isn't really a political matter," he said. "But when I was interviewing a woman in her kitchen in Iowa, I glanced over to the wall where she had some things clipped to a wallboard. At the top was a newspaper clipping behind a piece of clear plastic.

"It was the story of President Kennedy's funeral. The paper was yellow and frayed. It told me something about the woman's politics. But it also told me something about journalism. Here was the most basic journalistic story of all, an obituary, and it had been saved for all these years."

Obituaries are important to newspaper readers. They are among the most frequently read items in newspapers. A third to a half of the readers regularly read obituaries.

The Kentucky Post in Covington for years carried an obituary for everyone who died within the newspaper's circulation area. The *Post* would take special pains to obtain material. Every morning, reporters would call hospitals in the area for death reports, and funeral directors were expected to call the newspaper with material.

After a while, the obituaries began to take too much space. The newspaper decided to reduce the type size of its obituaries from eight points to seven.

"We got all kinds of complaints," says David Brown, the managing editor. "Since then we haven't fooled with them much."

For the *Post,* obituaries must include all the basic information and be tightly written.

Unlike the *Post,* the *Knoxville News-Sentinel* runs obituaries only of people prominent in the community or of those whose achievements merit attention. "To get a good death story, we stress trying to make the person live. We want it to be a personality piece of sorts about a person who had a family and friends and achievements," says Wade Saye, assistant managing editor of the *News-Sentinel.*

"Our goal is to really catch the personality of the person in the story."

For *The Cincinnati Post,* a person need not be prominent to be a good subject for an obituary. "We did an obit once on a bus driver whose name meant nothing to most people," says Leon Hirtl, managing editor of the *Post.* "But we discovered that many people knew him as the bus driver who sang."

For those newspapers that run most or all deaths in their obituary columns, most obituaries are written tightly as follows:

BOOS, EMIL A., 85, of 550 Ninth Ave. S., died Sunday (May 17, 1981). He came here 26 years ago from his native New Jersey, where he was a mail clerk for the U.S. Postal Service. Survivors include a sister-in-law, Mrs. Julian Anderson, St. Petersburg. Thomas A. Cooksey Funeral Home, Pinellas Park.

BORKMAN, FREDERICK J., 65, of 2732 58th St. S, Gulfport, died Friday (May 15, 1981). Born in Warren, Ohio, he was a veteran of World War II. He was a member of VFW Post 10110, Gulfport, and Sunshine City Post 6827 VFW, St. Petersburg. Survivors include a sister Marie Halsey, Cleveland. Robert D. Easter Funeral Home, Gulfport.

—St. Petersburg Times

These newspapers also run longer obituaries for those people considered newsworthy. But newsworthiness is sometimes an elusive guideline for an obituary. If the president of a local highway equipment firm is worth seven or eight paragraphs, why not the bookkeeper in his firm who emigrated from

Hungary as a youth 50 years ago? What made him leave home and family, and how did he fare on arrival? What were his struggles to educate himself? Did he struggle alone, or did he have help? Friends and relatives would know.

"There are a lot of missed opportunities for good stories with obituaries," says Jim Adams, city editor of *The Cincinnati Post.* "It's my philosophy that you treat the obituary the same as any other news story—get quotes and talk to people and try to give a face to the person you're writing about."

Obituary Essentials

Name, age, address and occupation of the deceased
Time and place of death
Cause of death
Date and place of birth
Survivors
Funeral and burial arrangements

These are the bare essentials. For the longer obituary, add:

Accomplishments and achievements
Memberships in organizations
Armed forces service
Anecdotes of friends and relatives

Usually, the basic material is made available by the mortuary handling the death. Material is also available from the advertising department, which receives a paid death notice from the funeral home. Occasionally, an obituary is called in by a person identifying himself or herself as a friend or relative. Be careful. Unless you know the person well, always verify the information by telephoning a relative or a mortuary. Some people call in phony death reports for the kick they get in seeing an obituary of someone who is very much alive.

Personal Details

Obviously, the obituaries of John Kennedy and John Lennon attracted readers. Readers are also interested in stories about the deaths of local people. Here, in capsule form, is the biography of someone we know or have heard about. We can read that the local Chevrolet dealer grew orchids as a hobby and had won prizes at local shows, or that the retired music teacher had set a national collegiate record for the 100-yard dash 50 years ago.

Obituaries balance these personal details with the obvious necessities—name, age, address, occupation, survivors, funeral arrangements.

The following obituary from the *Lexington* (Ky.) *Herald-Leader* includes the kind of detail that reveals, in just a few paragraphs, the story not only of a local businessman but of a whole class of people who pulled themselves up from humble beginnings:

Store Founder
'Al' Wenneker
Dies at Age 76

Alex "Al" Wenneker, a prominent Lexington businessman, died here yesterday. He was 76.

With a rented storefront on Main Street measuring only 12 feet by 30 feet, eight kitchen chairs, empty boxes used as shelves and a relatively small stock of shoes, Wenneker and his wife Mary opened for business back in 1935. The business, located at 155 East Main Street until 1979, was called Wenneker's Sample Shoe Store.

Although no longer at the Main Street location, Wenneker's Shoe Stores have become a very successful business chain here with locations at three of Lexington's shopping malls.

Wenneker was a member of Temple Adath Israel.

A native of St. Louis, Mo., he was the son of William Wenneker, a Russian immigrant, and Libby McDowell Wenneker.

Besides his wife, survivors include two sons, James E. Wenneker and William R. Wenneker, both of Lexington; four sisters; and three grandchildren.

The funeral will be at 3 p.m. Tuesday at W.R. Milward Mortuary — Broadway. Burial will be in Lexington Cemetery. Visitation is from 3 to 5 and 7 to 9 p.m. today.

Light Touch

The obituary does not have to be written in somber tones of black. If the deceased was known to be genial and easygoing, why not write an obituary to match his or her life? When possible, the obituary should offer a glimpse into the deceased person's life, a snapshot.

Here is the beginning of such an obituary from *The Milwaukee Journal:*

Services for Paul W. LaPointe, widely known Milwaukee restauranteur who was better known as "Frenchy," will be at 11 a.m. Tuesday at the Wittkopp Funeral Home in Plymouth. Burial will follow in St. John's Cemetery in Elkhart Lake.

LaPointe, 72, died Saturday, apparently of a heart attack, at his summer home on Elkhart Lake. He lived in Milwaukee at 2629 N.

Summit Ave.

A self-described workaholic, LaPointe owned and operated Frenchy's Restaurant at 1827 E. North Ave. from 1945 until he retired in 1975. In February 1979 he decided retirement was not for him and opened Paul's Small Cafe at 1854 E. Kenilworth Pla., just around the corner from his old restaurant.

In an interview in 1980, LaPointe spoke of his futile attempt at retirement.

"Just wait until you get to be 65 or 70 and you're just looking at four walls," he told a reporter. . . .

Joseph D. Robins was a popular man in his home town in Dalton, Mass. Everyone knew Joe. When he died in an airplane accident, the local weekly, the *Dalton News-Record,* carried his obituary as its number one news story following his burial. The obituary was written by Avice Meehan, the managing editor of the newspaper.

"I called Joe's two closest friends to find out what Joe was like," Meehan said. The nearby daily newspaper had carried a news story about the airplane crash, but by making several calls Meehan was able to reconstruct the accident in detail. She knew that her readers—Robins' friends and neighbors—would want to know just how Robins, a veteran pilot, had been killed.

She also knew that obituaries in the *Dalton News-Record* are read closely and carefully. "I wish we could do more with them than we do." Here is how she began the Robins obituary:

Death of a Pilot

Lead based on his accomplishment

Burial and funeral service

Age, cause of death

Anecdote about Robins' popularity

DALTON—Joseph D. Robins, a well-known flier and the most senior member of the Dalton Police Department, was buried Saturday in Ashuelot Street Cemetery following a Liturgy of Christian Burial at St. Agnes' Church.

His death at the age of 59 in a plane crash last week at the North Adams Airport has left this community shaken.

"This is a small department," said Police Chief Anthony Calabrese. "We are like a family here."

Since his death, officers have worn black bands on their badges. The flags at Town Hall and at Crane & Co. have flown at half mast. . . .

(The complete story is found in Appendix C.)

Meehan began her story with the latest material, the burial. She went on to describe in detail the funeral, the members of the honor guard and the burial service before she turned to the event that took Robins' life.

As we have said, the basic techniques explained in the writing chapters are used in all these story types. Here, Meehan uses her best quote up high, in the third paragraph, to show the loss felt by Robins' colleagues, and she uses a good observation, the black bands on the badges, in the next paragraph.

The Obituary Lead

Generally, a person's occupation, accomplishment or distinctive contribution to the community is placed in the lead to identify him or her:

Occupation

> Raymond T. Baron, former president of Paxton and Baron Co., book publishers, died yesterday in his home at 75 Arden Lane. He was 78 years old.

Accomplishment

> Mortimer Heineman, an advertising executive who helped create the slogan "Promise her anything, but give her Arpège," died yesterday following a heart attack. He was 74 years old.

Contribution

> Florence Gable Cerrin, long active in the local chapter of the American Red Cross, died yesterday at her home at 65 Eastern Parkway at the age of 94.

Funeral and **burial arrangements** can also be the basis of the lead. Some newspapers will try to vary their leads so that instead of every lead beginning with the report of someone's death, an occasional obituary will begin with the date, time and place of the funeral and burial.

> Services for Albert D. Scott, 79, of 156 W. Central Ave., will be held tomorrow at 11 a.m. in the Boulder Funeral Home.
> Burial for the retired pharmacist will follow in the Piedmont Cemetery in Oberlin.
> Scott died yesterday at his home after suffering a heart attack. . . .

When the death has ocurred a few days before, the lead will usually be based on the funeral and burial arrangements.

Delayed leads are rarely used for obituaries. If the delayed lead is in good taste, it is acceptable:

> Margaret Wilson did get her last wish.
> When she was told she had terminal cancer, the 73-year-old former high school teacher asked that she be buried in her ancestral family plot in Ireland.
> Next Tuesday, her ashes will be. . . .

An obituary should capture an important aspect of the person's life. If the deceased was an actor, the obituary emphasizes that from the beginning:

HOLLYWOOD, Calif.—Stage and film actor Arthur O'Connell, nominated twice for the best supporting Oscar, died here Monday. He was 73.

O'Connell made his American film debut with a small part in Orson Welles' "Citizen Kane." He went on to work with many of Hollywood's top stars, including Jimmy Stewart, Bette Davis, Marilyn Monroe, Elvis Presley and William Holden. . . .

A man who made his fame as an expert on reptiles was described this way in his obituary:

LAKE CITY, Fla.—Widely known snake handler Ross Allen, who planned to enliven this sleepy North Florida town with a tourist attraction called Alligator Town U.S.A., has died of cancer.

Mr. Allen, 73, had been ill for several weeks. . . .

When the author William Saroyan died, *The St. Petersburg Times* carried this lead on his obituary:

FRESNO, Calif.—William Saroyan, the boisterous, brilliant and reclusive American bard of Central California whose prize-winning books and plays underscored the dreariness of life—and who readily admitted he was as great a writer as his admirers said he was—died Monday of cancer in Fresno. He was 72.

Cause of Death

The cause of death is included in the obituary. Sometimes, a family will request that a terminal illness not be mentioned in the obituary. Some families feel that cancer-related deaths should remain private, and obliging newspapers use the euphemism a "long illness" to refer to such diseases. A "brief illness" is often used to describe a heart attack. The best guideline is to include the cause of death and let the editor decide whether to use it.

The St. Petersburg Times began one of its obituaries this way:

CLEARWATER—Anita Bilgore, a 35–year resident of Clearwater and the founder of Girls Clubs of Pinellas County, died Monday at Medical Center Hospital after a brief illness.

Nowhere was the cause of death given, but immediately beneath this obituary was another that began:

NEW PORT RICHEY—
Twelve-year-old Kathy Kruzlic, who battled terminal cancer for more than a year, died Monday at All Children's Hospital in St. Petersburg with her parents at her bedside.

Almost all newspapers and stations will give the cause of death when the deceased is a young child or the death was the result of an accident.

Some newspapers go behind the immediate cause of death. When Thomas Schippers, a well-known orchestra conductor, died of cancer, *The New York Times* received several letters asking whether Schippers had been a smoker. The information should have been included in the obituary, the *Times* admitted. The newspaper had included this information in the obituaries of heavy smokers who died of lung cancer, an editor stated.

Sudden Death When death strikes a young or middle-aged person suddenly, the story can be as much news story as obituary, as we saw with fatal accident stories. With sudden death stories, the cause of death is essential and must go into the lead. Here is how Rick Hampson of the AP began his story about the shooting of John Lennon:

NEW YORK--(AP)--JOHN LENNON, THE SINGER-
SONG WRITER WHO HELPED MAKE THE BEATLES MUSICAL
SUPERSTARS AND POP-CULTURE LEGENDS IN THE
1960S, WAS KILLED IN A LATE-NIGHT SPRAY OF
GUNFIRE OUTSIDE HIS LUXURY APARTMENT BUILDING.
    HE WAS THE CO-AUTHOR WITH PAUL MCCARTNEY OF
SUCH FAMOUS SONGS AS ``I WANT TO HOLD YOUR
HAND,'' ``YESTERDAY'' AND ``LET IT BE.''
    MINUTES AFTER THE SHOTS RANG OUT, POLICE
TOOK A SUSPECT INTO CUSTODY. EARLY TODAY, THEY
CHARGED MARK DAVID CHAPMAN, 25, OF HAWAII, WITH
MURDER. NO MOTIVE WAS KNOWN IMMEDIATELY.

Written under pressure shortly after Lennon was shot, the reporter had to balance the facts about the slaying and Lennon's background, which was obtained from the newspaper library.

Sometimes the exact cause of death is not known immediately, as was the case with the first stories about the death of Elvis Presley. In that case, the lead must give whatever information is available. Here is the lead written by Les Seago of AP:

```
    MEMPHIS, TENN.--(AP)--ELVIS PRESLEY, THE
MISSISSIPPI BOY WHOSE ROCK 'N' ROLL GUITAR AND
GYRATING HIPS CHANGED AMERICAN MUSIC STYLES,
DIED TUESDAY AFTERNOON OF HEART FAILURE. HE WAS
42.
    DR. JERRY FRANCISCO, MEDICAL EXAMINER FOR
SHELBY COUNTY, SAID THE CAUSE OF DEATH WAS
''CARDIAC ARRYTHMIA,'' AN IRREGULAR HEARTBEAT.
HE SAID ''THAT'S JUST ANOTHER NAME FOR A FORM
OF HEART ATTACK.''
    FRANCISCO SAID THE THREE-HOUR AUTOPSY
UNCOVERED NO SIGN OF ANY OTHER DISEASES, AND
THERE WAS NO SIGN OF ANY DRUG ABUSE.
    PRESLEY WAS DECLARED DEAD AT 3:30 P.M. 4:30
P.M. EDT AT BAPTIST HOSPITAL, WHERE HE HAD BEEN
TAKEN BY A FIRE DEPARTMENT AMBULANCE AFTER
BEING FOUND UNCONSCIOUS AT HIS GRACELAND
MANSION.
```

Localizing the Obituary

When a well-known person dies, a local follow-up is sometimes possible. The person may have been born or gone to school in town:

Robert Cowan, who served as governor from 1956–60, died today in a retirement home in St. Augustine, Fla. Cowan was born in Springfield and attended school here before moving to Gulfport in 1915. . . .

Sometimes, the local connection is less specific, as when the nation mourned the death of President John F. Kennedy. Then, local observances were the subject of many stories.

When John Lennon was murdered in New York City, newspapers all over the country localized the story with reactions of the fans of the Beatles and with the comments of musicians and music authorities about the impact of the Beatles on popular music. Here is how Mark Miller began the local follow for *The Berkshire Eagle:*

Mourning fans rush to buy Lennon, Beatles records

By Mark Miller

In the Berkshires as elsewhere yesterday, ways of dealing with John Lennon's death included talking out the sadness and irony of it, listening to Lennon and Beatles music, and buying Lennon and Beatles records and tapes.

However commercial, New Wave Music at 47 North St. was as fitting a shrine to Lennon as any. In the window, a black and white blowup of Lennon and Yoko Ono, taken from the cover of their new album, was draped with a black cloth. A large vase of red carnations, white chrysanthemums and green eucalyptus leaves stood in front of it.

For a nostalgic Beatles nut, inside would have been close to paradise on any other day. Six brown, ceiling-mounted speakers bathed customers all day in tunes and lyrics from early 1960s Beatles tunes to this year's Lennon-Ono double album.

The only thing wrong was the reason the Beatles had a monopoly on the music. People were not talking about it much, but rather thinking of their personal and collective loss. The lyrics of one song

counseled "whispered words of wisdom" and predicted, "There will be an answer. Let it be."

A customer idly fingered the records in a bin labeled "MISC. ROCK Q - T" and asked clerk Andy Hateman, "Did you have many people coming in for Lennon?"

Yes, Hateman answered, "and the Beatles are selling well, too."

Around mid-afternoon, some high school students who weren't yet born when the quartet of mopheads from Liverpool hit the Ed Sullivan Show started to show up in the store. Their attitude was respectful but tinged with indifference. They had missed part of the Beatles experience.

"Don't be afraid to go to hell and back," Yoko Ono sang from a cut on her and her husband's new album. "Don't be afraid to be afraid." Something like gunfire and ricocheting bullets are part of the song's sound effects.

Co-proprietor Brian Price said he began getting calls at home at 6:30 a.m. from friends asking him to save him a copy of Lennon and Ono's new two-record

album, "Double Fantasy."

His partner, John McLean, started down to Hartford, Conn., at about 7 a.m. to ensure that New Wave could replenish its supply of Lennon and Beatles albums.

"We've gone through about a hundred pieces at least," Price said of "Double Fantasy" at about 2:45 p.m.

By 6:30 p.m., New Wave had sold 200 "Double Fantasy" albums, including about 50 tapes. McLean had phoned to say he was on his way back with more. The store was down to 10 of the albums.

At other record stores in the county, response to Lennon's death was lighter, perhaps because their stocks were less voluminous. At The Record Hut at the corner of North and Eagle streets, a supply of 30 "Double Fantasy" albums was reduced to seven by 3 p.m. Eight tapes of the album were also sold, said Denise Pannozzo, a clerk. The store's sound system was not giving nonstop Beatles music but rather was tuned to a local radio station. Most of these, AM and FM, were

Lennon fans buy records
Continued on Page 17

Window Display Tribute. A music store in Pittsfield, Mass., decorated its window in memory of John Lennon after he was shot and killed in 1980. The photograph of Lennon and Yoko Ono is draped in black behind a vase of red and white flowers. A Christmas bulb and a Beach Boys' album remind the passerby that life goes on.

Story Types

Sports

A sportswriter once asked Carl Furillo, the great outfielder for the old Brooklyn Dodgers, how he learned to play the tough right-field wall in Ebbetts Field.

"I worked, that's how," Furillo replied.

And that, says the writer, Roger Kahn, is how a reporter learns to write sports stories. The first efforts may be as fumbling as the lead that a high school correspondent called in to a newspaper after his high school team had won a no-hit game:

> In the best-pitched game these
> old eyes have ever seen. . . .

Or the sport being covered may be as confusing as it was to Becky Teagarden, a sportswriter for the *Columbus* (Ohio) *Citizen-Journal* when she covered her first basketball game.

"I didn't know what was going on," she recalls. But she had the good sense to corner the coach after the game. She asked him, "Tell me, what happened out there?"

The high school reporter learned, too. His first task was to learn to keep himself out of the story. The reader is interested in the athletes and the game, not in the writer.

For most beginning sportswriters, the important lesson is that good sports writing is good writing. This means getting to the point quickly, stressing human interest, avoiding sports jargon and clichés, and giving the reader some insight into the game or the personality being described.

In other words, sports writers follow the principles of good writing that have been described in previous chapters.

School Sports

Sports writers who aspire to cover the Cleveland Indians, Dallas Cowboys or Golden State Warriors break in on school or nonprofessional sports. Although many people follow professional sports, many more are fans of the local high school or regional college teams. These fans expect the same quality of reporting and writing the fans of professional teams are given.

Look at the beginning of a story about a game between two Colorado high school baseball teams:

> Longmont pitcher Tim Fobes was in trouble in the seventh inning of the Trojans' 5–4 home-field win over Thompson Valley Friday afternoon. But coach Joe Brooks was not about to pull him out.
>
> "I walked out and told him we were going to win or lose with Tim Fobes," Brooks said after the game. Fobes survived the ordeal, but a game that Longmont appeared to have in its pocket suddenly became interesting.

John Gunn of the *Times-Call* in Longmont, Colo., is informative and entertaining in this lead. He gives the final score, and he provides the reader with a human interest detail. In just two sentences in his lead, Gunn has included several of the essential elements of the game story. (The complete story is in Appendix C.)

Game Story Essentials

The score
Names of teams, type of sport
When and where the game took place
Key incident or play
Outstanding player(s)
League
Scoring
Effect of game on league standings
Strategy
Crowd size; behavior, if a factor
Statistics
Injuries
Winning or losing streaks
Duration of game
Record(s) set
Postgame quotes

The Sports Lead

As we said, any of the essentials can be the major element that is placed in the lead of the story. Let's look at a Monday newspaper that carried the results of Sunday's schedule of professional football games. We'll see how some of the stories were handled.

None of the stories began with the score alone. All used an incident, a play, an outstanding player, or an injury along with the score. In one, the score was not even in the lead:

Outstanding player

GREEN BAY, Wis.—(UPI)— David Whitehurst, playing for the injured Lynn Dickey, ran for one touchdown and threw for three Sunday to lead the Green Bay Packers to a 34–24 victory over the Seattle Seahawks.

Dickey suffered a back injury last week. Whitehurst completed 19 of 31 pass attempts for 205 yards. Two of his scoring passes went to James Lofton and one to tight end Paul Coffman. . . .

Injury

ANAHEIM, Calif.—(UPI)— Jeff Rutledge came off the bench Sunday to rally Los Angeles to a 20–13 victory over the Detroit Lions in a performance that would appear to have earned him an opportunity to start, but the Rams' backup quarterback was in too much pain and too despondent to do much celebrating after the game.

His right thumb, thought to be dislocated and possibly broken, was in a splint, but what hurt even more was the possibility that the injury would cost him a chance to be the Rams' No. 1 quarterback.

Rutledge, who relieved Pat Haden midway through the third period, completed nine of 12 passes, including a 64–yarder to Preston Dennard early in the fourth quarter that set up a one-yard burst by Wendell Tyler for the winning touchdown.

But a few minutes later, Rutledge injured his thumb when he hit his hand against the helmet of Detroit's William Gay while following. . . .

Key plays

CINCINNATI—The Cincinnati Bengals cashed in on an unsuccessful gamble and an ill-timed Houston pass attempt just before the end of the first half Sunday to defeat the Oilers, 34–21, and take sole possession of first place in the AFC Central Division.

Clinging to a 14–7 lead with 1:44 left in the half, the Bengals held Houston on a fourth-down pass play at the Cincinnati 33 and scored in eight plays, the TD coming on an 18-yard pass from Ken Anderson to Cris Collinsworth with 40 seconds to go.

An interception by linebacker Reggie Williams 28 seconds later set up a 51-yard field goal by Jim Breech as time expired to give the Bengals a 24–7 lead on a 24–point second period.

"We were able to get 10 points just before the half. That was a big plus," said Bengals' Coach Forrest Gregg. "That probably was the turning point for us.". . . .

Outstanding player and key play

SAN DIEGO—Rolf Benirschke, named "Hero of the Year" by the NFL Players Association for his winning battle against an intestinal disease that nearly cost him his life, made another comeback Sunday—this one on the playing field.

He had missed an extra point after a touchdown early in the game, and it appeared to be a crucial mistake when the Kansas City Chiefs took a 20–19 lead over Benirschke's San Diego Chargers with little more than six minutes left on a 32-yard field goal by Nick Lowery.

Notice that the score does not come until the third paragraph because of the writer's decision to play up the human interest angle.

But Benirschke wound up the hero as he hit a 22-yard field goal with just 13 seconds left to give the Chargers a 22–20 victory.

"Any kicker, I think, likes it to come down to him," Benirschke said. "I just didn't want it to come down to us losing because of the missed extra point."

"I watched the situation developing, and I was hoping to get a chance for the field goal. We've lost two close games because of field goals in the last few seconds [to Chicago and Minnesota], so this time, it was our turn."

The story includes in the fourth and fifth paragraphs good quotes from a postgame interview. The sixth paragraph gives the effect on league standings.

The victory left the Chargers and Chiefs tied for first place with 6–3 records in the AFC West, with Denver, a half-game back, playing host to Minnesota tonight. . . .

Story Types

Record

This is a combination lead that includes mention of the record pass, the score and a human-interest angle. Notice how the writer goes into the rivalry between pass receiver and defender to give the story added interest.

TAMPA—(AP)—Tampa Bay tight end Jimmie Giles was glad to be on the receiving end of a club-record 81-yard touchdown play Sunday in a 20–10 victory over Chicago, but he was even happier that it came against Bears' safety Doug Plank.

Giles took a 21-yard pass from Doug Williams and beat Plank and the Chicago secondary in a 60-yard race to the end zone. It was Plank who last year knocked Giles silly during a 23–0 Chicago victory on national television.

Giles caught a long pass down the middle in that game, but Plank came up from behind and speared Giles with his helmet. No penalty throwing—begged was called, but Plank was later fined by the NFL.

"The biggest pleasure about it is being a big part of winning the football game," said Giles. "It made it even better because it was against him."

Strategy

The lead and the beginning of the story concentrate on a touchdown play. The reporter obtained the information in a locker-room interview.

NEW ORLEANS—(AP)—Alfred Jenkins had to do a little arm-twisting in the huddle Sunday to get Steve Bartkowski to throw his third touchdown bomb as the Atlanta Falcons drubbed the New Orleans Saints, 41–10.

"The first two were just plain old 'go' patterns," said Jenkins, the first Falcon to catch three scoring passes in a game. "The third one, I talked Steve into throwing—begged him in the huddle."

On the first touchdown reception, a 48-yarder, Jenkins ran past stumbling free safety Tommy Meyers. Jenkins later beat cornerback Mike Spivey on 60- and 47-yard scoring plays and added two more catches for a 179-yard total.

Atlanta (5–4) opened a 10–0 first-quarter lead on a 25-yard field goal by Mick Luckhurst and an eight-yard reverse by Wallace Francis. New Orleans (2–7) tied the score in the second quarter on a 28-yard field goal by Benny Ricardo and a 46-yard pass from Archie Manning to Guido Merkins.

From then on, it was all Atlanta as Jenkins caught his three TD passes.

| Be Imaginative | Imagination is vital to the sports story. There are so many sports, such a multitude of games that after a while the sports pages seem to swim in team names and numbers. Sports is the story of men and women straining mind and body to reach beyond their limits, of unusual people and strange events. The stories should reflect this. |

Imagination is vital to the sports story. There are so many sports, such a multitude of games that after a while the sports pages seem to swim in team names and numbers. Sports is the story of men and women straining mind and body to reach beyond their limits, of unusual people and strange events. The stories should reflect this.

When Nolan Ryan pitched his record fifth no-hit baseball game, the story was as much his nonchalance as the accomplishment. When a team, the Montreal Expos, cannot win a game against the Los Angeles Dodgers in their home park, the story of still another loss is the story of jinxes and superstitions.

"People forget about game scores in one hour," says T. J. Simers of *The Commercial Appeal* in Memphis. "But a story about emotion may stick with them for two hours." Simers is being sarcastic about the durability of a news story, but he does have a point.

The writer who captures the human dimension of the event creates a story the reader will remember, and this is what we all strive for in journalism—the story that makes the reader sit up and take notice.

Leads can focus on the small details unseen by fans in the stadium or watching on television:

> Paul Williams leaned a foot too
> far to his right last night, and that
> was the ball game.

This was the beginning of a story about a baseball team trailing 1–0 in the bottom of the ninth with two out. Williams had walked, the next batter had two balls and no strikes. And suddenly the game was over because Williams was picked off first base by the pitcher.

Structuring the Sports Story

When possible, the sportswriter tries to match the drama of the game with his or her account of it. The difference between the fans' observations and the sports story is the knowledge that the sportswriter takes to the game. This insight must be shown in the story. For this reason, sportswriters often like to begin their stories with the little things that are the turning points of the game, such as the base runner's too-long lead that abruptly ended a possible ninth-inning rally.

Increasingly, delayed leads are put on sports stories. The first paragraph or two may contain an incident, anecdote, a key play or a strategic move. Then, in the second or third paragraph, the writer gives the score. Next, a few paragraphs are devoted to the important points of the game—the scoring, significant substitutions, injuries, or changes in the standings.

If most fans already know the result of a game, it is a good idea to focus on a key play or turning point in the game:

Some clutch free-throw shooting by Paul Threet and a lucky bounce helped Park School clinch the co-championship of the Independent Athletic Conference basketball league.

Threet made both attempts in a one-and-one situation Thursday with seven seconds left in overtime as Park defeated visiting St. Mary's for the Deaf 62–61 in a game here. . . .

—*Buffalo Evening News*

Another technique is to use the comments and observations of the players or coaches involved in key plays or strategy. Most quotes are obtained in locker-room interviews after the game, a necessity for game coverage.

Sportswriters are enthusiasts. Sometimes they write as though they are covering the end of the world, not a game. This kind of enthusiasm leads to these excesses:

Restraint Essential

Shrillness This is a common ailment, especially of some television announcers. In football, every other play is accompanied by a rise in the voice. A writer can be shrill, too. A story written with high-pitch intensity from lead to end irritates the reader. Every game has pauses, contemplative moments, even dull periods. The story should not be dull, but it should not scream at the reader.

Overstatement Games sometimes are made into battles of titans, and the language of the story is exaggerated and pumped up. Writing of this sort often flows shamelessly during the games of traditional rivals—Green Bay Packers-Chicago Bears, Stanford-University of California at Berkeley, New York Knicks-Boston Celtics, Kansas-Missouri, New York Yankees-Boston Red Sox.

Mindless Emotionalism Fans do become excited by games. They have even been known to hurl beer cans at players and officials. Some fans become so involved with the action that it becomes a life-and-death conflict for them. Sportswriters have to reflect the intensity and the seriousness of sports, but they must also keep their distance. These are, after all, only games.

Extra Dimension

Most of those who turn to their newspapers to read of yesterday's games already know the results. They may have seen one game on television and heard the scores of others on television or radio. The reporter's task is to add an extra ingredient.

Emery Filmer, a sports reporter for *The Advocate* in Stamford, Conn., was covering a local team in the state baseball playoffs. On Tuesday, the team, the Stamford Catholic High School Crusaders, had upset the defending state champions, 2–1. Then, on Wednesday, Stamford lost 7–2 in the semifinal.

Advice for the Novice Sports Writer

Here are some do's and don'ts suggested by experienced sportswriters:

> Avoid commenting in straight game stories. Often, comments reflect lazy reporting.
>
> Use good quotes that reveal important aspects of the game. Avoid inane quotes.
>
> Be in touch with the reader. Too often, sportswriters write for each other.
>
> Don't sacrifice information for style. First, give the information. The style will come naturally.
>
> Don't use war references, such as "battling," or "troops being sent in." You're covering a game, not a war.
>
> Overstatement is the sign of the beginner. If anything, understate.
>
> Don't use sports jargon—*netminder, pigskin, hoop, horsehide.*
>
> Athletes are human, not gods. Avoid making them into heroes.

Filmer was writing for the Thursday newspaper. *The Advocate* is an afternoon newspaper, which meant that most fans following the local team already knew it had lost.

How would you handle this situation? A story that begins this way would be barely adequate:

> ```
> Andrew Warde High School defeated the Stamford
> Catholic High School Crusaders yesterday in the
> semifinal state baseball playoffs, 7-2.
> ```

There is nothing wrong with this lead, except that it repeats what many readers already know. How about this one:

> ```
> The Crusaders from Stamford Catholic High School hung
> up their gloves yesterday and will have to wait another
> year before trying for the state high school baseball
> championship. The Crusaders lost to Andrew Warde 7-2 in a
> semifinal playoff game yesterday.
> ```

Although this lead is also adequate, it says little more than the previous lead. All it does is add a picturesque, if not trite, phrase, "hung up their gloves."

Filmer was able to write an effective lead because he understood the key to the Crusaders' loss, the absence of their leading pitcher. He added a dimension to his story because of his knowledge of the team and the game. Here is how Filmer's story begins:

THE ADVOCATE

Sports

Tech girls take Fairchester League crown. Page 32.

Copyright 1981, Connecticut Newspapers Inc

STAMFORD, CONN., THURSDAY, MAY 21, 1981   31

Warde eliminates Catholic, 7-2

by Emery Filmer
The Advocate

Here are the two sides of the Stamford Catholic High School Crusaders:

On Tuesday night, they played a near-perfect game in upsetting the defending state champion Westhill Vikings, 2-1, in an FCIAC first-round playoff game. But on Wednesday, they fell behind 5-0 in the first inning and ended up on the short end of a 7-2 score against Andrew Warde, a club they had beaten 8-3 last month

So, what's the difference?

Roger Haggerty perhaps. After all, he wasn't pitching Wednesday.

"Knowing that we did not have to face Haggerty tonight was a definite factor in our favor," admitted Warde coach Ed Bengermino after his team had qualified for its first appearance in the FCIAC championship game.

Haggerty pitched a brilliant two-hitter against the heavy-hitting Vikings on Tuesday to vault the Crusaders into Wednesday's semifinal against the Eastern Division champions, Warde. It was Haggerty's sixth victory of the year and lowered his ERA to 1.82.

But, unfortunately, he can not pitch every day. And therein lies the difference in the Stamford Catholic Crusaders.

Wednesday, Catholic manager Mickey Lione tabbed lanky righthander Matt Reed to start against Warde. Now Reed has had a better-than-average season (3.95 ERA), but his three wins were the second most on the team.

The difference was apparent immediatly. The first five Crimson Eagle batters to face Reed all reached base, and all scored.

"Reed just didn't throw strikes," said Lione. "He was constantly falling behind

2 and 0 and 3 and 0 on everybody. So he had to come in with a lot of fat pitches."

Although he only walked one batter, Reed was never ahead of a hitter through the first five batters.

John Martin led off with a double and Mark Carlson followed with run-scoring single. So after two batters, Reed had allowed one run and two hits, which were the seven-inning totals for Haggerty a night earlier.

After a walk and a Greg Cantwell single, Joe Braun singled in the second run. After Reed retired the next man on a ground out which made it 3-0, Dan Schettino closed out the first-inning onslaught with a two-run single.

Before half of the crowd had arrived, Warde led, 5-0.

"We got beat by Haggerty last year and this year and both times he just blew us away," Bengermino admitted.

(Please turn to Page 32)

In the Newsroom

When the reporter arrived at his desk early one morning he could tell he would not be out on his beat for at least two hours. On his desk were a batch of papers, a couple of notes from the city editor and a telephone message. Without taking time for his usual chat with the reporter at the next desk, he set to work.

First, he looked through the papers. Several were announcements and press releases. One was about a regional history conference that would be held on the campus of the local college. Another concerned a skating party that would be held Sunday for a charity. The third was about a speech to be given by the governor next week. He put these in one pile, took a slip of paper and wrote *advances* on it and clipped the works together.

Another sheet contained a release from an army base about the promotion of a local soldier. He scribbled the word *personal* across the top of the press release.

He knew that he could handle these releases quickly. The others would take a little more time. One was an obituary, another required some calls to localize a wire story, and the third necessitated a call to the weather bureau for a weather story the city editor wanted for the newspaper's early edition.

Better get the easy ones out of the way first, he decided. He turned to the advances and the personal item. These would require short pieces. In fact, these tightly written pieces are called **briefs** or **shorts.**

Briefs

The trick to writing briefs, he had been told his first day on the job, is to give the reader the basics. "No frills, no ornamentation. The Five Ws and an H and get out of there fast," an experienced reporter had told him. No more than two or three paragraphs, unless the advance is about a big meeting of the city council that is coming up, or the personal is about the appointment of a new minister to the largest church in town, or the marriage in town next month of the 72-year-old senior U.S. senator.

Precedes

The reporter then looked over the seven-paragraph press release from the local college that detailed the history conference to be held next week. He wrote a precede:

The eighth annual Midwestern Conference of History Teachers will be held on the Hampden College campus next Thursday and Friday.

Registration will take place in McGuire Auditorium Wednesday afternoon and Thursday. The fee is $5. Sessions will be held in the Liberal Arts building.

The main speaker will be Prof. Felix S. Woodward of Oxford University. He will speak Thursday evening on "Breaking the Plains."

The smaller the newspaper, the longer the precede. Here is how the skating benefit story was written:

A fund-raising skating party to assist the Norwalk Community Hospital will be held Sunday at the Wheels Roller Skating Center at 61 Converse St.

There will be two sessions, from 7 to 9 p.m. and from 9:30 to 11:30 p.m. Music will be provided by "Soul Sounds." Admission is $3.

The income will be used to furnish a children's playroom in the hospital.

Here is an advance from *The Berkshire Eagle,* a daily newspaper with a circulation of 31,000 that stresses local news. The *Eagle* has room for stories like this:

A talk on bobcats in Massachusetts, part of the Berkshire Sanctuaries predator series, will be given tonight at 7:30 in the members room at Pleasant Valley Wildlife Sanctuary in Lenox.

Chet McCord, who is in charge of research for the state Division of Fisheries and Wildlife, will be the speaker.

While a graduate student at the University of Massachusetts, McCord studied bobcats on the Prescott Peninsula near Quabbin Reservoir in central Massachusetts. Using collars with radio transmitters, he studied the bobcats' movements and habitat preferences.

Fee for the talk is $1 for Massachusetts Audubon Society members and $2 for non-members.

The precede, or advance, tells people about events they may want to attend or at least want to know about. Knowing that the local school board will be considering a change in the busing policy, parents may call or write board members to express their opinions if they cannot attend the meeting. A family may not want to go roller skating but might send a donation to the community hospital after reading the short item about the benefit.

Precede Essentials

Event or activity planned
Date, time, place of activity
Purpose
Sponsor
Fee, admission charge, if any
Background, if a significant event

Personals

Names make news. In big cities, the names that make news are those of public figures—television personalities, the wealthy, politicians, athletes, the social set. In smaller towns, the names are those of neighbors, and their comings and goings are recorded in detail. These news items are called **personals.**

Here is the beginning of a personal item from "Notes on People" in *The New York Times,* circulation 850,000:

There were people who looked like George Burns, Goldie Hawn, Woody Allen and Katharine Hepburn. And there were quite a few who looked like Prince Charles and Lady Diana Spencer.

The party Tuesday night at Ted Hook's Backstage restaurant. . . .

Here are two personal items from the Hinsdale correspondent on the weekly *Dalton News-Record:*

Airman First Class Edward G. Barrett and Mrs. Barrett have returned to their home in Hampton, Va., after spending a week with their grandparents, Mr. and Mrs. Richard Boker.

The Ladies Aid Society will have a food sale suring the annual town meeting this Saturday. Ethel Perth and Julia Anderson are in charge of the event. Nancy Jenkins is in charge of the snack bar where homemade doughnuts and coffee will be available. Hours are 1 p.m. to 5 p.m.

Births, engagements and weddings, awards, retirements, promotions, confirmations, bar and bat mitzvahs, appointments—all are duly recognized.

"Small is beautiful," says Avice Meehan, managing editor of *The News-Record.* "Mainly we concentrate on the little things—items about the Boy Scouts, the high school junior that the Lions Club has selected to represent the club in the All-State Band at the district convention, the names of officers of the local Historical Commission."

The personal cements communities. It tells people about the successes, and sometimes the tribulations, of the family down the street, around the block and at the edge of town.

Some newspapers use personals imaginatively. When Waconah Regional High School held its graduation, *The News-Record* ran a paragraph about the plans of each of the graduates for colleges and careers.

Frank Availe, son of Frank and Karen Availe, County Road, Becket. Undecided.

Debra Wuinee, daughter of Mr. and Mrs. Robert Wuinee of 32 East Deming St., Dalton. BCC to study accounting.

Personal Essentials

Name, identification
Newsworthy activity
Connection of individual(s) to activity
Special or unusual activities in connection with the event

Personals are usually handled in a straightforward manner. If there is a special or unusual activity connected to the event, that can become the lead. A wedding held on the lawn of a summer home, a birthday party celebrated atop a mountain separate these events from the dozens of others the newspaper covers.

For weddings, the names of the bride and groom and the location of the wedding are carried in the lead. Also essential to the story are the background of the couple and the names of the parents:

Ann Margarita Poray and Marvin Abercrombie were married yesterday in St. John's Church.

The bride is a teacher in the Fairfield Junior High School. She was graduated from Weston College. Abercrombie is with the First National Bank in Fairfield. He is a graduate of Brown University.

The bride is the daughter of Mr. and Mrs. Phillip Poray of 62 Antonio St. The bridegroom is the son of Dr. and Mrs. Albert Abercrombie of Boston.

For engagements, the parents of the bride-to-be usually make the announcement and this is placed in the lead:

Mr. and Mrs. Burton V. Carroway announced the engagement of their daughter, Faye Elizabeth, to Robert Becker, son of Mr. and Mrs. Stanley Becker.

The wedding is planned for Sept. 21.

Ms. Carroway, 435 Eastern St., is a librarian with the state legislative service. Becker is a salesman for Reed Chevrolet and lives at 67 Marion Ave.

Small town newspapers carry stories about the celebration of wedding anniversaries (usually 25th, 35th, 40th and 50th).

Mr. and Mrs. W. J. Stagg were honored by their children in celebration of their golden wedding anniversary Saturday in the Reorganized Church of Jesus Christ of the Latter Day Saints. At the celebration, they renewed their wedding vows.

Mildred Forrest and William J. Stagg were married on July 25, 1933, in Lawrence, Kan. They have three married children and five grandchildren.

Most briefs can be handled quickly because few require additional information. The material that has been included in the announcement or press release is sufficient. Two points to remember:

1. If there is any indication of an unusual situation or circumstance in the material, check it out. There might be a good story hidden there.
2. Try to avoid running the press releases in the form given to you. They should be rewritten.

There are other stories that can be written from the office but require reporting and checking. Let's begin with a story that needs to be **localized.**

Localizing the News

The logic of localizing news stories is simple. As we learned in chapter 3, readers prefer to read about people and events close to them. Proximity, we learned, is a basic news determinant.

A local reporter is handed a wire service story that lists the names of 11 people who were killed in Ohio when the bus they were riding in collided with a truck. Two of those who died were local residents.

The reporter calls the local bureau of the AP to find out the names of the two local people killed in the crash and to ask if anyone from the local area was injured. He also makes a few calls to gather background information on the two people who were killed and the funeral arrangements.

An essential task is to make sure that the names are spelled correctly. They are often garbled in wire stories in such situations. Another is to verify that the people involved are actually from the local community. Mistakes do happen.

Here is the wire story:

```
    YOUNGSTOWN, OHIO--ELEVEN PEOPLE WERE
KILLED WHEN THE CHARTERED BUS IN WHICH THEY
WERE RIDING COLLIDED WITH A TRUCK ON U.S. 80
LAST NIGHT.
    THE DRIVER OF THE TRUCK AND 15 PASSENGERS
WERE INJURED. THE BUS HAD BEEN RENTED BY A
CHURCH GROUP, THE PRESBYTERIAN FELLOWSHIP
LEAGUE, THAT WAS HOLDING A CONFERENCE IN AKRON.
    WITNESSES TOLD INVESTIGATING OFFICERS THE
TRUCK SEEMED TO VEER INTO THE BUS AS THE BUS
TRIED TO PASS IT.
    NAMES OF THE DEAD ARE:
    ALVIN BAILEY, 59. . . .
```

The localized version began this way:

Two local residents were killed last night when the bus in which they were passengers collided with a truck on U.S. 80 near Youngstown, Ohio.

The dead are: Alvin Baily, 59, of 12 Belford Place and Charlene Dearborn, 21, of 68 Topper St.

The Associated Press reports they were attending. . . .

Localizing Essentials

Name of local person or situation that justifies localizing
General situation or background
Source of information–name of wire service or orgnization.

A **folo** is a story that follows up on a theme in another story. If a national educational organization reports that a growing percentage of high school graduates is putting off college, the enterprising reporter who sees the wire story hits the telephone to call area high schools, junior colleges and four-year schools. Folos usually run the day after the original story appears.

When President Reagan sent Congress a budget that would have cut back on services to the needy, reporters sought to determine the local consequences. Here is how one newswriter began her follow-up story:

Needy local residents would be severely hurt by Reagan administration proposals in Congress that would cut and restrict many federal programs.

This was the opinion of officials of several public and private organizations concerned with social, economic and health services for the poor here. Margaret Murtagh, executive secretary of the Family and Children's Services agency, a private organization, said:

"Half of the proposed reductions affect the poor. The budget seems to single these people out."

Another local agency, the Hospital and Home. . . .

Some people sit at home and paste stamps into albums, while others fly model airplanes. Most hobbies are perfectly safe. But some people climb mountains. Why?

This question occurred to several editors after an icefall entombed 11 mountain climbers under 70 feet of ice on Mount Rainer one Sunday in June, and just a few hours later five others died after a climbing party plummeted 2,000 feet down Mount Hood.

Reporters were sent out to find some local mountain climbers. Their answers made an interesting folo to the wire stories of the tragedies. Here is one local folo:

Contrary to the view of one well-known mountain climber, climbers do not attempt to scale mountains just because they are there.

"First, you have the beauty," said John Simac, 78 Harper Ave., who has climbed Mount Rainer in the state of Washington a dozen times, as well as other mountains.

"Then you have the challenge. Sometimes, it is almost too great," Simac said.

Then the challenge defeats the climber with frostbite and frustration. But sometimes the loss is greater. Last Sunday, 11 men climbing Mount Rainer were entombed when. . . .

Notice the insertion in the fourth paragraph of the **news peg,** the reason for the folo.

Reaction stories are folos. When the mayor of Boston described the city as "a racist city," the *Boston Herald American* followed up his accusation with reactions from various people. Here is how the folo by Greg O'Brien begins:

News peg—Reaction

Mayor Kevin H. White yesterday called Boston "a racist city," touching off a wave of reaction from politicians, church leaders, union officials and businessmen.

News peg elaborated

White, who has consistently rejected charges that racism is widespread in Boston, spoke extemporaneously yesterday to a group of 75 persons attending a Greater Boston Civil Rights Coalition conference. He concluded last winter, he said, that blacks and other minorities in Boston did not have equal access to "institutions around town."

Reaction elaborated

Reaction to the mayor's remarks differed widely. Lieutenant Governor Thomas P. O'Neill III said that racism wasn't confined to Boston, but was a statewide problem.

"It's not just the city," he said. "We've had a racial problem statewide. Keven White takes it on the chin when everything is thrust on one city. We have real serious problems statewide. Government is supposed to provide a brand of leadership that provides access, and that means everybody."

Folo Essentials

Reaction, response, local aspect of an event
Event that gives the folo its news peg
Summary

These are the absolute minimum essentials of the folo. The rest of the story should include the elaboration and buttressing of these essential elements.

The *Herald American* jumped on another story involving the city administration. This time the story was about a dress code that city hall employees were supposed to adhere to. The dress code contained the following provision for female city employees:

> Wearing apparel must be clean, neat and of a "business look" nature. Pants suits, dungarees, slacks or shorts will not be permitted at any time.

As soon as the code was issued, the *Herald American* assigned reporters to do a story on the new code. The newspaper also assigned a reporter to ask fashion designers for their reactions.

If the reaction story had appeared the next day, it would have been a folo. But since the reporter was able to report and write the story so quickly, the reaction appeared alongside the story about the code. In this case, the accompanying story about the comments of fashion designers became a **sidebar.**

Sidebar

A sidebar is a story that emphasizes an aspect of another story that is printed nearby. When Bonnie Britt did a series of articles for *The Houston Chronicle* on the dangers of insulation used in the construction of mobile homes, she wanted to get the reaction of the mobile home industry, which was being sued by a number of Texas mobile home owners.

Britt sought out the attorney for the industry. Although he was unwilling to comment, Britt dug into his background for the following sidebar that appeared alongside one of her articles in the series:

One of the ironies in the formaldehyde story is the involvement of former Atty. Gen. John Hill, who while in office obtained 440 injunctions and $5 million in civil penalties against polluters.

Hill is the lead attorney hired to defend the Texas mobile home industry in the 70 or so lawsuits filed by mobile home buyers irritated by indoor pollutants.

The second irony underlying Hill's defense of the industry is that formaldehyde irritation struck close to home. In this case, his grandchildren's home. Hill's grandchildren (ages 1 and 4) became sick after exposure to urea formaldehyde foam insulation in their parents' brick home, according to plaintiff attorneys Robert Bennett and Andy Vickery.

When asked why he would take so prominent a role in the cases if this were true, Hill would only say "No comment." . . .

Back to the hot dispute in Boston over pants and slacks for city workers. Here is how the *Herald American* played the main story and the sidebar, right next to each other:

Pants for women taboo in City Hall dress code

Employees angry

By ALAN P. HENRY
Staff Writer

There's a new dress code coming to Boston City Hall, one which many female city employees are already calling an insult to women.

Beginning next Tuesday, women who work in the building department will be banned from wearing pants or pants suits. They will be allowed to wear skirts or dresses only.

The new code, written by the Administrative Services department, reportedly will be phased in throughout the building and will apply to both sexes.

For women, the order reads: "Wearing apparel must be clean, neat and of a 'business look' nature. Pants suits, dungarees, slacks or shorts will not be permitted at any time."

For men, the order reads: "To regular personnel assigned to office, jacket, shirt and tie are required during working hours. Jackets may be removed while working or seated at a desk in the office, but

Continued on Page A8

Designers scoff

By ELEANOR ROBERTS
Staff Writer

Top New York and Boston fashion designers delivered a verbal kick in the pants to Mayor Kevin H. White yesterday.

The city issued a dress code banning women employees from wearing pants to work at City Hall.

"He's just another Boston fashion retard," said designer Alfred Fiandaca, who dresses Mrs. Johnny Carson, Joan Kennedy, Raquel Welch and Natalie Wood.

"Is he afraid his men aren't going to get their work done if women at City Hall wear pants?" he asked indignantly. "No one should dictate what a woman should wear.

"It's a personal intrusion on her liberty. It's sexual discrimination. Now, jeans and dungarees — I agree with him there.

"I'm no lover of pants although I design them for my clients. But there's nothing wrong in wearing a smartly tailored pair of pants with a jacket or blazer and a neat shirt or blouse to work."

Continued on Page A8

The essentials for the sidebar are the same as those for the folo. The news peg of the original story and the reaction or response are placed high up and close together.

In the dress code sidebar, the writer put a clever lead on the story that described the response. The second paragraph contains the news peg. The rest of the story is much like any other good feature: good quotes up high in the story, quickly paced sentences.

The **roundup** is frequently used to combine several stories into one. The roundup is based on finding an element common to two or more events and then writing a lead that reflects the common element. **Roundup Stories**

When a heavy fog covered the East Coast there were two boat collisions, one in New York, the other off Virginia. The AP put the two stories together. The common element in the lead was the fog:

The Staten Island ferry collided with a freighter in New York harbor and two freighters collided off Virginia Wednesday morning, as dense fog cloaked the East Coast. More than 80 persons were injured in the accidents, none seriously, and all four ships were damaged.

In New York, the ferryboat American Legion, carrying 2,500 rush-hour commuters, was near the Statue of Liberty when it collided with the freighter Heogh Orchid at about 7:20 a.m. injuring 83 persons, officials said.

"It looked like a large gray shadow coming out of the fog," said ferry passenger Matthew Bendix, 17.

Four of the 83 injured were hospitalized in satisfactory condition, and the others were treated and released, hospital officials said.

A Greek cargo vessel, the Hellenic Carrier, was taking on water and leaving a trail of diesel fuel as it limped toward Norfolk, Va., after it collided with another ship at about 7:20 a.m., said spokesmen for the 5th Coast Guard District headquarters at Portsmouth, Va.

The Greek ship's crewmen huddled in lifeboats for more than two hours before being rescued, Coast Guard officials said. Two were slightly injured, one suffering a sprained ankle and another treated aboard a Navy destroyer with a tetanus shot for cuts.

Mahfooz Hussain, who was at the wheel of the Hellenic Carrier when the two ships crashed, said there was a heavy blanket of fog over the area.

Notice that the lead includes both incidents. The body of the story amplifies each accident separately, one after the other.

Roundups are frequently used for traffic accident stories. You can spot them after a weekend or a holiday, or when bad weather has caused a number of accidents.

Roundup Essentials

Lead focuses on a common element
Body takes each incident or event and elaborates it in turn
Causes, consequences, quotes may be inserted high in story if they
    explain the situation

Weather Stories

The spectators in the large auditorium were filing out after having watched the second round of competition for Miss Iowa. The lines moved slowly, and people were chatting. But they weren't talking about Miss Muscatine's chances of making it to the finals, or the fact that Miss Dubuque seemed embarrassed about parading in front of a few thousand people in a skimpy bathing suit.

They were looking out the windows of the auditorium watching a hailstorm gather force, and the talk was about the weather.

"It'll tear up the crops pretty bad," one man said. "Wind like that is worse than hail when you come down to it."

Everybody talks about the weather, and every reporter takes a turn at doing the weather story. The television weather people have made the nation even more conscious of weather. The mobility of the population has made people interested in weather outside their immediate vicinity. The traveler en route to California wonders what the weather is like in San Francisco, and the Florida-bound family checks to see whether their Christmas holiday will be spent under blue skies in 80-degree weather.

All of us have friends or relatives in other cities and states. When a windstorm hits Washington, a flood strikes the midwestern states or a drought wilts crops and people in the Southwest, we sympathize and might even write or call our relatives or friends.

In short, weather is news.

Locally, people want to know what the forecast is, every day, and when there is anything out of the usual, they want a full story. If it is turning warmer, business people will put on lightweight suits. If rain is forecast, umbrellas and overshoes come out of the closet. If the weekend looks grim, the sports fans stock up on beer and snacks for a weekend of television sports.

Weather stories are often routinely written, but they need not be. When a heavy snowfall hit New York City, Meyer Berger, a gifted writer who covered local news for *The New York Times,* wrote that the storm "left tremendous drifts in the countryside, and in main urban avenues it veiled skylines, tufting skyscrapers and steeples with enormous white caps."

The daily weather forecast was taken out of the routine by H. Allen Smith of the old *New York World-Telegram* who wrote what may be the best one-liner in all of journalism:

Snow, followed by small boys on sleds.

Cooling Off. Human interest is an essential part of all news stories, even those about the weather. When the temperature flirted with the 100 degree mark, children in Baltimore took to the fire hydrants, and youngsters on a Kentucky farm cooled off in their mother's washtub.

As you can see, there are two types of weather stories, the daily forecast and the longer piece for unusual or extreme weather. Here are the essentials for both types:

Weather Essentials

> Forecast for next 24 hours
> Long-range forecast
> Most recent temperatures, humidity and precipitation
> Record highs and lows, if any

When weather is severe, the writer must consider the consequences. The effects are included along with the basics:

> Deaths, injuries, property damage
> Amount of precipitation (or drought)
> Strength of wind
> Any record(s) set
> Predicted duration of severe weather
> Consequences:
>> Traffic—roads blocked, accidents
>> Travel—air, bus, rail, local travel curtailed or stopped
>> Public services—power, water and telephone outages
>> Business—crops, tourism affected; business shut down temporarily
>> Schools—closings or changed hours

Writers try to show the consequences of unusual weather by introducing human interest, the effect of the weather on people. When unusually warm weather settled over western Massachusetts, *The Berkshire Eagle* reporter wrote that "large numbers of baby carriages blossomed forth on North Street and mopeds were seen put-putting about."

When the temperature reached 99 degrees in Baltimore on June 16—a record for that day—a reporter for *The Baltimore Sun,* had a novel idea for his story. He talked to youngsters at the zoo, and this became his lead. The desk then put the weather roundup in the body, and the story ended with a local reference.

It was a hot time in the old town, but it's not expected to last long

By Theodore W. Hendricks

Hot yesterday, were you?

Well, 7-year-old Christopher Frye, visiting the Baltimore Zoo on an end-of-school outing, summed it up for many people as city temperatures neared— but never reached—the 99-degree record.

"I feel ready to pass out," he said, laughing.

His friend, 6-year-old John Rau, also on the picnic with pupils from George Washington Elementary, showed how it was done. "You fall down like this," he said, as he stretched out full length on the asphalt.

As explained by National Weather Service experts, the heat was the result of warm, moist air from the South flowing over the Eastern United States and wrapping Baltimore in a sticky coat of searing temperatures.

The temperature peaked in the city at 98 degrees, hovering there for about two hours in late afternoon and missing the record of 99 set in 1957.

At the airport, where the Weather Service began keeping records in 1950, the highest temperature yesterday was 95 degrees—two degrees less than the record of 97, also set in 1957.

This region was not alone in having near-record heat.

Temperatures soared toward triple digits in the Southwest, and in Southern California the temperature hit 106 degrees in Palm Springs—the hottest spot in the nation and four degrees hotter than Monday's 102.

Fire fighters continued early yesterday to battle two dozen heat-spawned fires that began Monday night, burning 64 homes and 17,000 acres in six California counties.

There was little relief in the central states, where communities were attempting to recover from violent storms that have killed at least 22 people since the weekend.

More rain created new floods in Kansas, Texas and Indiana, where a South Bend construction worker drowned yesterday and two others were missing after they fell into a rain-swollen river when part of a bridge they were working on crumbled beneath them.

In Minneapolis and St. Paul, where a twister Sunday left 2 dead, 99 injured and $45 million in wreckage along a 15-mile path, about 16,000 homes and businesses still had no electricity.

While Baltimore's weather was uncomfortable for those outside or without air-conditioning, it did not appear to cause major problems.

The Baltimore Gas and Electric Company reported that it generated electricity at near record levels.

The state health department said the air quality Monday was "unhealthful,"

See WEATHER, A12, Col. 3

Part Five
Laws and Codes

16

Libel, Ethics and Taste

The laws of libel and privacy, codes of ethics and guidelines on matters of taste place limits on the journalist. **Looking Ahead**

Libel is the publication of material that causes a person to lose money, damages a person's reputation or exposes the person to shame and humiliation. A person who can prove he or she has been injured by a story or photograph can collect damages in a libel suit. Stories that are based on facts and are thorough, fair and impartial do not cause libel suits.

Privacy is the right of individuals to be left alone. A reporter cannot invade a person's home or use listening or recording devices to intrude on a person's privacy.

Ethics are not enforced by laws. They are understandings among journalists as to what is proper behavior for the practice of journalism. Some of these agreements are contained in codes. Others are the personal beliefs and commitments of journalists.

Taste—what society considers proper in the use of language and subject matter—changes with time, the nature of the audience and the nature of those involved in the event. Generally, material that may be vulgar, obscene, profane, or offensive is permissible if it is absolutely essential to the news story.

• The news story was like a dozen others that the newspaper had printed—a local resident had been arrested for drunk driving. But this one led to a libel suit.

• For several months, the reporter was underground. He had used a false identity to work his way into membership of the Ku Klux Klan for a series of articles on the organization that preaches hatred of blacks, Jews and Catholics. Some journalists questioned the methods he used to gather information for his articles.

• On their 6 p.m. news broadcasts, two Cleveland television stations reported that a coroner's examination of a 69-year-old woman murdered in a parking lot determined that the body was actually that of a man. The victim was Stella Walsh, a former woman's Olympic track champion and a well-known member of Cleveland's Polish-American community, which assailed the news reports of the two stations.

What was wrong, if anything, with these news stories? In this chapter, we will be looking at (1) libel laws, (2) journalistic ethics and (3) guidelines for matters of taste to find the answers to this question. First, to libel.

Libel

The news story reported that L. D. Sylvester of 536 Western Ave. had been arrested for drunk driving the night before and had posted bond. Several weeks later, Sylvester's lawyer sued the newspaper for libel. Sylvester said he had never been arrested. In fact, he had been out of town the evening that the newspaper had him careening down the center of town.

An error had been made, the editor learned on a quick check. There was nothing to do but settle out of court for several thousand dollars. The newspaper had no defense.

What had happened was simple, but devastating. In his haste at the police station, the police reporter had scribbled the man's name and address on his note pad. Drunk driving stories are not major events, and the reporter had been hurrying to get on to more important arrests.

Back in the office, the reporter could not read the address and looked in the telephone book for the address of L. D. Sylvester. He found the address as 536 Western Ave., which went into the story.

Actually, the arrested person was T. D. Sylvester of 561 Eastern Ave.

The incident reveals the cause of most libel suits: sloppy reporting and careless writing, the failure to check or verify potentially dangerous material.

Definition of Libel

Libel is the publication of material that injures a person by causing:

1. Financial loss
2. Damage to reputation
3. Humiliation, mental anguish or suffering

Newspapers do publish stories that cause people to lose their jobs and that damage their reputations. The Ohio congressman who put his mistress on his Washington payroll in a do-nothing job was exposed by reporters and defeated for reelection. No job and a tarnished reputation. Even so, the congressman did not sue for libel because the story was true. He knew a suit would be hopeless. The reporters had the sworn statement of the woman.

The true story can be printed or broadcast without fear. When the story is untrue, however, there is trouble. In the Sylvester incident, the story of his arrest was the only one of a dozen arrest stories that weekend that was erroneous. The other persons undoubtedly were humiliated by the news of their arrests. Unlike Sylvester, they had no grounds for a libel suit. The printed reports were accurate.

Sylvester, however, could prove that he was the victim of an error. Errors can be costly. Here is one that cost a magazine publisher almost a million dollars.

On March 2, 1976, the *National Enquirer* carried this item in one of its gossip columns:

The *Enquirer* and Carol Burnett

At a Washington restaurant, a boisterous Carol Burnett had a loud argument with another diner, Henry Kissinger. She traipsed around the place offering everyone a bite of her dessert. But Carol really raised eyebrows when she accidentally knocked a glass of wine over one diner—and started giggling instead of apologizing. The guy wasn't amused and "accidentally" spilled a glass of water over Carol's dress.

A month later, the magazine published a retraction admitting its report was wrong. But Burnett sued for libel. The television star testified that despite the retraction, the item had caused her great anguish and diminished reputation.

Burnett's lawyer claimed she had been the victim of defamation. One definition of libel is that it is published defamation, that is, written material that exposes a person to public hatred, contempt or ridicule, or injures the person in his or her business occupation.

The jury hearing the Burnett case felt that she had been so seriously defamed and had suffered such humiliation that it awarded her $300,000 in compensatory damages (for injuries actually suffered) and $1.3 million in punitive damages (to punish the *Enquirer*). A judge later lowered the total award.

Libel Defenses

There are three basic defenses against libel suits:

1. **Truth**   If the reporter can show that the defamatory material is true, the offended person may sue but the case usually cannot be won. It is not enough for the reporter to say he or she thought the material was truthful or that someone else said it was true. There must be proof of its truth. Truth is almost always an absolute defense in a libel suit.
2. **Privilege**   Anything said in a **public and official** legislative or judicial situation—whether it is true or false—can be reported. Legislative bodies include the city council, county commissions, state legislature and congress. In the courts, statements by attorneys, the judge and witnesses and any documents filed with the court are privileged.
3. **Fair Comment and Criticism**   Critics who assess the work of artists, authors, performers, sports figures and others who offer their services to the public may comment on the work or performance. The criticism must be based on facts and must not attack the personal life of the individual whose work is being assessed. The comment must not be malicious.

Anita and Elvis—The Reunion that Never Happened

The story in *The Commercial Appeal* in Memphis, Tenn., was a sensation to his fans: Elvis Presley had held a reunion in Las Vegas with Anita Wood Brewer, who had been Presley's "No. 1 girl" early in her singing career. Brewer had divorced her husband, the newspaper said, and joined Presley.

The story was dead wrong, and the newspaper printed a retraction. But the Brewers sued. In its defense, the newspaper claimed that both husband and wife were public figures—she was a well-known singer and he was a famous football star. (Brewer had been a college football star at the University of Mississippi and then played with the Cleveland Browns and the New Orleans Saints.)

A federal district jury court disagreed with the newspaper's defense and awarded each of the Brewers $400,000 in damages. The newspaper appealed to the circuit court of appeals.

This time, the newspaper won. The circuit court agreed that the Brewers were public figures despite the passage of time. If they wanted to sue, the court said, they had to prove actual malice, not negligence or carelessness. The U.S. Supreme Court refused to review the case.

In all of these defenses, the reporter is on safe ground if the report is a full, fair, impartial and accurate account of the event. If the story is so one-sided that it could be proved that the reporter intentionally singled out the critical or defamatory material, the reporter could be in trouble if someone sued.

The Sullivan Ruling

In 1964, the U.S. Supreme Court granted reporters some leeway for their mistakes. In a famous case, *The New York Times* v. *Sullivan,* the Court ruled that if a **public official** is the victim of a libelous story, the official must prove that the account was published with "actual malice." To prove actual malice, the official must prove in court that the material was published with:

1. The knowledge that it was false, or
2. The reckless disregard of whether the material was true or not.

Before this decision, the defendant had to prove that the defamatory material was the result of negligence or carelessness. Actual malice is much more difficult to prove.

The Sullivan decision took away from the individual state courts their control over libel actions. In its ruling, the Court said that a constitutional issue was involved—freedom of the press. This is why so many libel decisions are appealed to federal courts.

For a while, the Court's ruling about "actual malice" was extended to public figures and to private individuals involved in public or official matters.

Public Officials

Elected officials—mayor, governor, members of congress, legislators, city council members, etc.

High-level appointed officials—supervisors, inspectors, medical examiners, cabinet members, etc.

Police officers

Judges

Careful: Not all public employees are public officials.

Public Figures

People with power and influence—newspaper columnists, authors, radio and television personalities, popular performers, union officials

People involved in important public controversies who seek to influence the outcome—a person who vigorously and publicly opposes or supports a referendum, bond issue, candidacy

However, recent court decisions have restricted the definition of a public figure, so that now some public figures and most private individuals need only prove that the defamatory material was published or broadcast because of carelessness or negligence.

Any story that contains material that might injure someone's reputation should be treated carefully. Hasty, careless reporting and writing are dangerous. Some suggestions:

Avoiding Libel

Confirm and verify all defamatory material. A reporter should double-check anything that:

1. Questions a person's fitness to handle his or her job.
2. Alleges a person has committed a crime or has performed some act that constitutes a crime.
3. Implies or directly states that a person has a mental illness or a loathsome disease.

Make sure that questionable material can be proved true.

Be especially careful of arrest reports, damage suits and criminal court hearings. These stories cause more libel suits than all others, and almost all are the result of careless reporting or writing. Check names, addresses; make sure the defendant and plaintiff are properly identified.

Watch out for charges, assertions, claims. Just because someone says something and you quote the person accurately, this does not mean you have avoided libel. If a district attorney tells you he is investigating a business with a long string of lawsuits and you quote the official, you may lose a libel suit if the owner proves he has never been sued. If the district attorney makes the same statement in a court proceeding, or if he files charges and makes any allegations in them, the material may be used because it is protected by the defense of privilege.

Don't try to sneak in defamatory material by suggestion with such words as allegedly, *or* reported. These are not protections against libel.

When charges and accusations are made in a privileged situation, it is a good idea to check with the person being defamed. This demonstrates your fairness.

Watch out for words that a court may hold to be libelous. Some of these words and their context:

Subject	Dangerous Words
Commission of a crime	Swindler, thief, loan shark, shoplifter, bigamist, gangster, ex-convict
Performance in job or profession	Incompetent, failure, quack, shyster, hack, bribery, slick operator
Diseases that could cause a person to be ostracized	Wino, leper, sickie
Damage to a person's credit	Unreliable, bankrupt, gambler, cheat, failure
Lack of chastity	Loose, B-girl, hooker, seducer, immoral, streetwalker, adultery, prostitute
Lack of mental capacity	Screwy, nutty, strange, incompetent, out-of-it
Incite ridicule or contempt	Phony, coward, hypocrite, communist, fascist

Don't color the article with opinions. Watch out for personal enthusiasms that cause you to lose control of the writing.

Be careful of statements by police or court officials outside court.

Truth is a defense, but good intentions are not. You may not have meant to defame someone, but when your well-intended writing proves to be untrue, your intention is no defense.

A retraction of an error is not a defense. It may lessen damages and could eliminate punitive damages.

Careful journalists have no trouble with libel. The careless writer and the writer who stretches facts do get into trouble. The reporter who wants to impress an editor or readers sooner or later tumbles. Some lose their jobs. Others cause their publishers to lose money. A reporter for a Cleveland newspaper who invented quotes from a bereaved widow in an interview had a fascinating story. But it proved costly when she sued and won.

Another danger area for reporters is the private lives of individuals. Reporters cannot indiscriminately pry, peek and probe into the personal affairs of anyone they choose to single out.

Privacy

While truth is an almost complete defense against libel suits, truth is also the basis of suits that claim invasion of privacy. A newspaper publishes a picture of a scantily clad woman being led from an apartment house where she had been held captive. She sues, claiming the picture embarrassed and humiliated her. Her lawyer says that there is no argument about the truth of the incident but that the picture invaded her privacy.

The jury agrees and awards her $10,000 in damages.

A newspaper reporter is a guest at a party and includes details about the event in a feature story. The host and hostess sue, claiming their privacy was invaded—even though the reporter made it clear he would use material from the event. It takes three years of legal maneuvering and a three-week jury trial for the newspaper to avoid paying damages for invasion of privacy.

In their search for news, reporters gather material about the personal lives of people that can be embarrassing or unpleasant to those involved. Newspapers routinely carry hospital admissions, divorce actions, arrests and traffic violations. Reporters search out and interview the parents of children killed in automobile accidents and fires. Sunday supplements and magazines detail the sex lives of the stars and the drug habits and alcoholism of athletes. Television carries the shame and the grief of those involved in tragedy and crime into millions of living rooms.

These stories can be published and broadcast because the people are involved in legitimate news events. The drunk driver has no claim to privacy when he or she is arrested. The details of a divorce case may be published. The horrors of a nursing home fire and the sorrow of relatives may be shown on television.

However, when the press digs into private acts that are of no public interest or that are of no legitimate concern to the public, there can be trouble. The law of libel protects a person's reputation and character. The right of privacy gives the person the right to be left alone, unless the person is involved in a legitimate news event.

The right to privacy protects people from several kinds of activities that journalists engage in:

1. **Publicizing private matters**   Public disclosure of private facts and acts of an individual that are considered offensive can lead to legal trouble. Sensational material about a person's love life, health, business affairs or social activities can constitute invasion of privacy. If the acts are private and of no legitimate concern to the public, the material is dangerous.

   If a rock star talks about his drug habit, or an athlete reveals he is struggling with alcoholism, the information can be used. The courts have also ruled that personal material can be used if it concerns a **newsworthy person,** is of public concern and is not "highly offensive to a reasonable person, one of ordinary sensibilities."

   If the activity takes place in public or the information is in a public document—no matter how sensational or offensive—it can be used.

2. **Intrusion**   If the reporter forces himself or herself into a private area to gather news, this is intrusion. The intrusion need not be physical. The use of tape recorders, hidden microphones, cameras and any other kind of electronic equipment without the person's permission is intrusion, even if the material is not used.

   When a reporter misrepresents his or her identity to gain entrance, eavesdrops on personal affairs or trespasses, this is intrusion.

3. **Publicizing false material**   When a reporter tries to dramatize an event by inventing material, or when a television station produces a docudrama—a fictionalized account of an actual person or event—and defamatory material is used, the person may be placed before the public in what the law calls a "false light."

4. **Appropriation**   Use of someone's name or picture for advertising or for commercial purposes or for one's own use constitutes appropriation, unless consent is given. Legitimate news events can be covered, and no permission is needed. However, a feature story that uses the name and activities of a well-known person can be the cause of problems if the purpose of the story is to promote the newspaper's sales. In this situation, a court may rule that the story was designed to exploit the commercial value of the person.

An excellent guide to the laws of libel and privacy is *Synopsis of the Law of Libel and the Right of Privacy* by Bruce W. Sanford, published by Scripps-Howard Newspapers. The paperback edition is distributed by World Almanac Publications, 200 Park Ave., New York, N.Y. 10166. Sanford is with the law firm that represents Scripps-Howard and has lectured and written extensively on libel and privacy.

Journalistic Ethics

- A reporter for the Oceanside, Calif., *Blade-Tribune* wrote a column for the newspaper that was almost a word-for-word copy of a column by Art Buchwald. He was asked to resign.
- A columnist for the *Daily News* in New York invented characters and quotes in a story about a street clash between British soldiers and a gang of youths in Belfast, Northern Ireland. He was forced to resign.
- A sportswriter for *The Evening Tribune* in San Diego wrote a piece that contained material that had been published in *Inside Sports*. For using "certain phraseologies" from the magazine he was suspended from his job.
- A *Washington Post* reporter who won a Pulitzer Prize in 1981 for her moving story about an 8-year-old heroin addict was fired when it was discovered that her story was fiction. The *Post* returned the prize.
- Walter Cronkite accepted an appointment to the board of directors of Pan American World Airways after he stepped down from his long tenure as the anchor man of the CBS Evening News. Cronkite became a special correspondent for the network, and some of his work was to involve coverage of space programs with which Pan American had contracts. Cronkite was criticized for accepting the post on the ground it was a conflict of interest for him to accept money from an enterprise he would be reporting on. Six months after joining the Pan American board, Cronkite resigned from it.

These situations involve matters of journalistic ethics. Each is an example of a violation of one of the underlying rules of conduct for the journalist.

The journalist is expected to be truthful, to do his or her own work, to avoid pursuing any activity that would raise questions about his or her integrity. These and other ethical principles are outlined in various codes that newspapers, broadcast stations and national journalism organizations have adopted.

The codes prescribe responsibility to the reader or listener, accuracy, fairness and compassion. The code of the Society of Professional Journalists, for example, states that "the duty of journalists is to seek the truth." The code also states that "gifts, favors, free travel, special treatment or privileges can compromise the integrity of journalists and their employers. Nothing of value should be accepted."

In its code, the American Society of Newspaper Editors sets out six major categories:

1. **Responsibility**   The task of the journalist is to serve the general welfare by informing people so they can make judgments about the issues confronting them. Journalists should not abuse their power for selfish motives or unworthy purposes.
2. **Freedom of the press**   Freedom belongs to the people, and journalists must make sure public business is conducted in public. They must be vigilant against those who exploit the press for their purposes.

Newspaper Code of Ethics

The following guidelines are excerpted from the code of ethics of *The Register* and *Tribune* of Des Moines, Iowa:

An individual's own good judgment and integrity are the keystones of this code because it would be impossible to spell out every single question that might arise. . . .

Our management and employees must remain free of obligation to any special interest . . . avoiding all possible conflicts of interest or even the appearance thereof. . . .

MEALS—This code will continue the present company policy of having staff members pay for their own meals. . . . When it [is] impossible to pay for a meal beforehand or at the time . . . appropriate payment [shall be] sent later.

TRAVEL— . . . There are times when staffers ride with sports teams on chartered aircraft or with public officials on military aircraft or in chartered private aircraft with a political figure. On such occasions the company will send a check covering our staffer's share of the transportation.

TICKETS—It shall be our policy that no staffer accept any free ticket to any event. . . .

OUTSIDE EMPLOYMENT AND ACTIVITIES— . . . No employee will hold membership on boards of directors of corporations, or assume leadership or activist roles on boards or organizations about which this employee might be called upon to write stories, take pictures, edit copy or make editorial judgments.

. . . Working for a political candidate or party would be a clear conflict of interests for almost any staff member. . . . There is a flat rule against any employee producing publicity material for any public official, politician, government agency or sports team. . . . [No staff member shall] make public statements of opinion that will compromise that staff member's credibility on the job.

3. **Independence** Journalists must avoid conflicts of interest. They should accept nothing from sources nor engage in any activity that compromises or might seem to compromise their integrity.
4. **Truth and accuracy** The journalist must seek to keep the good faith of readers by assuring them that the news is accurate, free from bias, and that all sides are presented fairly.
5. **Impartiality** News reports and opinion should be clearly distinct. Opinion articles should be clearly identified as such.
6. **Fair play** Journalists should respect the rights of people in the news and be accountable to the public for the fairness and accuracy of their reports. Persons accused in the news should be allowed to respond.

(The Code of Ethics of the Society of Professional Journalists is included in Appendix D.)

We all have a sense of what is right and wrong. This sensitivity may have been influenced by our parents, schools or religious training. Some of our guidelines come from reading. For some young men and women, friends exert a powerful influence in establishing ideas of what is right and wrong.

For two days, a 16-year-old student at Milpitas High School in California bragged to his classmates he had raped and strangled his 14-year-old girl friend. He then led several friends to a remote spot in the foothills near San Jose and showed them her body.

Eight youngsters saw the body of the girl. Some covered it with leaves to hide it. One dropped a rock on her head to make sure the corpse was really that of a human being.

Not one of the youngsters informed the police.

An assembly-line worker, who had heard from friends that "a corpse was up in the hills," was shown the body by a student who had been taken to the scene by the 16-year-old. The worker called the police.

When word got out that the body had been recovered, some of the high school students criticized the worker for notifying the police. One described him as a "snitch . . . a fucking narc." The worker said that he had been hassled for his action. "I don't know if I'd do it again," he said.

Sheriff's Sgt. Gary Meeker wondered, "What the hell has happened to these kids?"

Sgt. Ron Icely of the Milpitas Police Department thinks he knows. "Usually when people are witnesses to a homicide, they come forward right away," he said. "But you have this code of honor (that says) forget about the girl on the side of the ravine and let's protect our buddy."

Although loyalty to friends is an honorable quality, at times we must respond to a greater demand on our loyalty, and this is to society. Journalists can use this commitment to society as a basis for establishing a personal code of behavior.

Responsibility and Independence

Journalism is a public service. Its purpose is to serve all the people by providing information gathered by men and women who are independent of commitments or obligations to any special group. The journalist places responsibility to the public above and beyond loyalty to an employer, a political party or friends.

The journalist is committed to the free and open flow of information. Passing on information is the journalist's duty. Thus, if a source or a friend asks that something be withheld from print or broadcast, the journalist must weigh the request against his or her commitment to inform the public.

If an editor, publisher or news director kills a story or removes information from a story on the ground that it will hurt business, advertising or friends of the newspaper or station, the journalist again must confront the situation from a moral perspective.

In both cases, the action the journalist must take is clear: See that the information reaches readers and listeners. As a result, some journalists have lost sources and some have quit their jobs rather than be a party to a cover-up.

Sometimes, this independence can be strained almost to the breaking point, as it is when reporters learn about something that the government wants kept secret because of "national security." In such cases, the reporter is confronted by a dilemma. In a democracy, the public is entitled to know what its government is doing. At the same time, revealing this information endangers security, according to the government.

Watching Power

This brings us to a second basic point in the formulation of a personal code of ethical behavior. The point is that journalists serve their readers and listeners by checking on power. They are in an adversary relationship to power. The power may be held by a dean, a corporation president, the mayor, or the president.

The founding fathers of this country made sure that journalists would be free of government interference or supervision so that the press could be a check on power.

If we go back to the first part of this chapter where we discussed libel, you can see the willingness of the federal courts to grant journalists wide freedom, even the freedom to make mistakes that libel officials. In the Sullivan ruling, the Supreme Court said that the press needed to be free of restrictions so that it can provide "the opportunity for free political discussion to the end that government may be responsive to the will of the people. . . ."

Reporters and their newspapers have confronted power at the highest levels, even at the risk of compromising what officials have said is "national security."

Given such power, the press can be an unchecked power itself. If government has no control over the press, what then is to protect the public from a free-wheeling, irresponsible press? Very little. And this is precisely why codes and guidelines—whether they are written and handed to reporters along with a style book, or are the reporter's personal beliefs—are so important.

Search for Truth

We have discussed two essentials for a personal code of ethics—responsibility to the public and independence from power. There are others for the young journalist to consider. A third is the mission to seek truth.

Most reporters understand that they should be truthful. But what is truth? At one level, it is the accurate reporting of what a source says in an interview. But the truth seeker must do more. On important stories, the reporter is obligated to dig into the background, the causes, the underlying layers of the event.

A tenement burns down. Three people are killed. The reporter quotes the investigators about the cause—faulty wiring. The reporter makes still another check, an independent check. Has the city any record of violations of fire laws against the building? Was the building really a death trap for its occupants?

A reporter who notices a pattern of fires in the area may even dig further and discover an arson ring, as a young woman working for a New Jersey newspaper did.

Not content with the official version, she checked records, looked at property transfers, examined insurance claims. She found that most of the fires were listed as being of suspicious origin, that they had been heavily insured, and that they were owned by local police officers. Several people had been hurt in the fires, and one person had been killed.

Reporters have little tolerance for any individual or any action that hurts people. This is the fouth point in our personal code. Journalists are concerned with the victims of unfair, illegal, discriminatory actions. They identify with the underdog.

Poses and Disguises

At the beginning of this chapter, mention was made of the reporter who adopted an identity in order to expose the Ku Klux Klan in his state. The use of poses and disguises is an old and frequently used device by investigative reporters. A *Wall Street Journal* reporter obtained a job in a factory in Texas and then revealed the company's harsh personnel practices and anti-union bias. A reporter for *The Washington Post* feigned mental illness and was admitted to a large mental hospital. She described the inadequate care given patients.

Lately, newspapers are questioning the use of this technique. They do not feel free to criticize others for illegal and underhanded actions in business and public life if they are themselves using questionable tactics to gather news.

Spies, snoops and informers are not respected in our society. Yet the newspaper whose reporters use poses and disguises do spy and snoop and then tell the story. It seems unethical, and it is. But it can be justified, under certain circumstances.

The reporter who is trying to formulate a personal ethical code might want to consider this point: When a critical condition exists in which people are endangered by a person or an organization, the journalist may use a tactic or a technique that otherwise would be considered unethical.

If the tactic will remove or publicize the danger, then the reporter may find justification for purposely misleading people from whom he or she intends to elicit information.

The journalist has a responsibility to the general society to serve as its watchdog, and sometimes this requires the warning bark of a brief story. At other times, it may be necessary to bite deeply into the situation. We punish the dog who bites unnecessarily, but we reward the watchdog that grabs the gunman by the arm, or threatens the thief's throat.

In the case of the Klan, its members have advocated violence against minority groups, and some Klansmen have been sentenced to prison for murder and conspiracy. The reporter who joined the Klan by using a pose may be thought of as providing a public service.

When such techniques are used, they should be described to the reader or listener. A tactic or technique used by a reporter that he or she is ashamed to admit in print or on the air should not be used in reporting.

Guidelines for a Personal Code of Ethics

Here are some additional points for the beginning journalist to consider for a personal code of ethics:

The willingness to admit errors

The determination to follow the facts, even if they lead in a direction you pesonally dislike or disagree with

A commitment to make yourself improve as a journalist so that you can better serve those who rely on you as their eyes and ears

Resistance to praise, the attractions of money, popularity and power—if any of these should stand in the way of writing the truth

An identification with those who suffer

The desire to make your town a better place to live in for all its people—youngsters in school, the sick in hospitals, the poor without jobs, the elderly without hope

A helpful booklet about journalistic ethics is published by the American Society of Newspaper Editors: *Playing It Straight: A Practical Discussion of the Ethical Principles of the American Society of Newspaper Editors.* The author is John L. Hulteng.

Self-examination

One last word on developing a personal code. Each of us knows when he or she is giving the best possible effort. Sometimes we cannot do our best because we have not pushed ourselves.

Only the journalist knows when he or she is not doing the best he or she can. To accept anything of ourselves but the best is unethical because the journalist's duty is to inform, and only the best effort informs fully.

In other words, the student and the professional journalist must always be checking themselves: Is this story telling people what they need to know about the event? Should I make one more telephone call, check another document before I let it go? Is this the precise word in this sentence, or should I try harder to find a word that describes the situation more accurately? Am I being honest with the reader in the way I've structured this story, or have I emphasized a secondary element because it is more dramatic?

The Obscene, the Indecent and the Profane

Go back a few pages to the section on journalistic ethics. Reread the part that is titled "A Personal Code." Was there something in this material that offended you, some word or reference that bothered you, that you would have preferred not to have read?

Flip the pages back still further. Look at the photographs in chapter 2. Were you uncomfortable when you looked at any of them?

In both places there is material that some people may consider offensive, a word and some photographs that are in questionable taste. The word is used in a quotation from a youth who condemned the worker who called the police to report the body in the foothills. He describes the worker as a "snitch . . . a fucking narc." The photographs are the grim, if not horrifying, pictures of the execution of members of Liberia's old guard.

Unquestionably, most people are bothered by obscene language and by explicit representations of death. Why, then, was the material used? Why did some newspapers that ran the story of the youngsters in Milpitas make the quote read: "f------ narc," whereas others used the actual language of the youth? And why did the Pulitzer Prize jurors think so much of the execution pictures they awarded the photographer a prize, while others turned away from the photographs in horror and condemned their use as another example of journalistic bad taste and sensationalism?

Because such questions are easier to raise than they are to answer, many people, and even some editors, have declared: Nothing obscene, profane or indecent should be published or broadcast. One example of how different newspapers chose to treat questionable material is shown in figure 16.1.

If the news is supposed to give the public a picture of reality, then a head-in-the-sand attitude deprives the public of essential information. Not only that, it is hypocritical. At the same time that some readers and listeners (and some editors as well) condemn the gossip columnist and are appalled by the picture of the dead motorcyclist lying in the street, they applaud the movies and soap operas that routinely parade incest, adultery, murder and nudity.

Here is a summary of a week's activities on a few of the TV soaps:

ANOTHER WORLD: Jerry, who was Clarice's caller, raped Clarice while in a schizophrenic fit. James accepted Steve after Steve revealed his identity to all at a posh whing-ding.

AS THE WORLD TURNS: Eric and Sofia got spaced out on joints laced with PCP. Lydia, Miranda's sister, arrived. Len was arrested in a gambling raid. James and Nick became restaurant partners, but Steve was quietly aware that James planned to use the eatery as a dope front.

THE DOCTORS: Billy sacked with Nola after seeing Greta and Theo doing the town. Maggie suffered pregnancy complications.

THE YOUNG AND THE RESTLESS: Karen lied to Jill saying that Andy sleeps around. Barbara, under the name Bobbie Smith, rented April's old room from Dorothy and Wayne.

Many viewers do their housework with one eye on these daily dramas. College students schedule their classes around their favorite soaps. And vacationers insist that their cottages come equipped with color TV sets so they can follow "All My Children," "Guiding Light" and "Search for Tommorrow."

Figure 16.1 Cover-Up.
Newspapers are sensitive to the possibility of offending their readers, as this display page from *Editor & Publisher* illustrates. After the advertisement for the movie ran untouched in *The Patriot Ledger* in Quincy, Mass., a group calling itself Morality in Media in Massachusetts complained the ad was vulgar and added to the "decivilization of society."

A cover up?

Different newspapers with different interpretations of what's offensive and what's not have used a variety of methods to cover up the model's buttocks in the ad for the latest James Bond movie. The Philadelphia Inquirer (top left) ran the ad as submitted; the Harrisburg Patriot (bottom left) cropped her buttocks out of the ad; the Philadelphia Bulletin, after running the ad as submitted, decided to add what appears to be a bikini bottom (top right); and the Pittsburgh Post Gazette (bottom right) added a pair of 'hot pants' to the original artwork.

EDITOR & PUBLISHER for July 11, 1981

Clearly, there are words, subject matter and pictures that should be off-limits. But how do we determine what they are? Do we refrain from using any material that would offend someone? Benjamin Franklin had no use for such a resolution to the problem:

> If all printers were determined not to print anything until they were sure it would offend nobody, there would be very little printed.

These days, when so much of what is newsworthy does involve unsavory matters, a great deal of news would be eliminated if we sought to offend no one. Crime is a major problem in our society, and many of the crimes are unspeakably violent and vicious. Do we refrain from running the brutal rape, the beheading of a five-year-old, the robbery gang that drove ballpoint pens through the ears of helpless patrons of a supermarket?

We need guidelines for the use of frank language, subject matter that is offensive and pictures that are gruesome.

Vulgar Language

Language that is obscene and profane is offensive to many people. They find words that refer to the sex act or to bodily functions to be unsavory. Many also have deep resentments against words that profane the deity.

Much of the hostility to such language stems from the desire to keep this kind of language from becoming acceptable speech. Taste is the sum of many value judgments about what is acceptable language or behavior. If such language is seen and heard frequently by young people, it becomes a part of their language and, possibly, will influence their behavior. Thus, adults—who are responsible for establishing values for their children—are anxious to hold the line against obscenity and profanity.

On the other hand, such language is part of everyday life. How do newspapers, radio and television stations tread the thin line between the extremes without falling on either side—offending well-intentioned people or cutting readers and listeners off from reality?

Let's start with the quote from the youngster angry at the man he described as a "snitch." *The Miami Herald,* which carried the quote as "f------ snitch," tried to walk the line. It did not run the obscenity, but by using the first letter and the exact number of dashes it was obvious to nearly all readers what the youngster actually said. I used the word *fucking* in this section. Why? Primarily to convey the intensity of the youth's feeling, but also because of the audience, the readers of this book. The *Herald's* readers range from grade school students to senior citizens, devout churchgoers and grandparents. The newspaper prefers not to risk offending them.

The readers of this book are men and women who know the language of youth. To have used dashes instead of the actual word would be, it seemed to me, insulting, condescending. If there is a young man or woman reading this book who has never heard the word, that is a rare person indeed these days. In addition, students are entitled to know the precise details of subjects they are studying. To sum it up, the word was used because it was **essential to the situation** and because the **nature of the audience** was such that the word would not be considered in poor taste. These two concepts are put in boldface because they are important guides in deciding whether to use certain kinds of language.

When Mark Patinkin and Christoper Scanlan of the *Journal-Bulletin* in Providence, R.I., interviewed the director of a job-training agency about unemployment among blacks, the official was frank, firm and forceful. This was reflected in his language. They quoted him as saying:

"It's a deep, deep problem," he said. "People don't realize it's an American problem. They say it's a black problem. It's a goddamn American problem and it requires the best energies of everybody to jump in and try and resolve it."

The profanity undoubtedly offended some readers of the newspaper. However, the writers chose to use it because of the intensity of feeling it revealed. The word was essential to the interview, they felt.

Some words are offensive in certain contexts, not in others. What do you think of this headline and lead from *The St. Petersburg Times?*:

Marie Osmond Says She Is a Virgin

Saying, "I have just as many passions as any other woman," Marie Osmond declares she is a virgin and a "square lady" in February's issue of *Ladies Home Journal.*

Celebrities raise the shades on their personal lives to allow journalists and the public to peek in. But that does not mean that every scene in every room need be described. Osmond has no objection to talking about her virginity, but what purpose does it serve in a newspaper? It adds nothing we need to know about the world.

So, what's the point? Marie Osmond's virginity is used to titillate readers, to give them the kind of excitement other media apparently dangle in front of their readers and viewers. In this sense, such stories do meet the competition—magazines, soap operas, movies.

If the editor desires to set a news policy in this direction, then editors and news writers must follow the policy. We now have a third guideline for determining what should be used—**the policy of the newspaper or station.**

Up to this point, we have been assuming that everyone agrees on what is offensive. The material we have used is clearly offensive to most people. But what is in poor taste to one person may be acceptable to another. The 16–year-old gang member and the Episcopal minister probably do not share the same definition of what is profane and what is obscene.

The truth is that there is no agreement on taste. There never will be. Just as some like licorice and others find it abominable, and just as some people will stand in the rain all night to buy tickets for a football game or an Elton John concert while others consider this a form of madness, so there can be no consensus on matters of taste.

However, we can say that opinions are changing, that overall there is a greater tolerance for what had been considered tasteless and offensive in what we read and see.

In 1905, the Brooklyn Public Library decided to ban from the children's room *The Adventures of Huckleberry Finn* and *Tom Sawyer* by Mark Twain. The librarians decided that the books were "bad examples" for children. The guardians of public morality often contend that their actions are intended to protect the young from contamination.

When Twain heard about the action of the librarians, he was contrite, and he made a public statement of his contrition.

"I wrote *Tom Sawyer* and *Huck Finn* for adults exclusively, and it always distresses me when I find that boys and girls have been allowed access to them," he wrote.

"The mind that becomes soiled in youth can never again be washed clean. I know this by my own experience, and to this day I cherish an unappeasable bitterness against the unfaithful guardians of my young life, who not only permitted but compelled me to read an unexpurgated Bible through before I was 15 years old.

"None can do that and ever draw a sweet breath again. . . ."

Mark Twain was poking fun at the zealous guardians of public morality. *Huckleberry Finn* and books by J. D. Salinger, Kurt Vonnegut and others are constantly under attack by these zealots. Those who seek to ban books are taken to the courts, which have held that book banning is unconstitutional.

If we look at the subject matter of the stories that newspapers and newscasts carry we can see similar changes in the attitudes toward journalistic subject matter.

Subject Matter

Subject matter as well as language that were once deemed unfit for readers' consumption are now their daily fare. Even the most conservative newspapers carry the unsavory details of trials and the sordid aspects of crime. The *New York Times,* which promised at its founding that it would not "soil the breakfast table," has carried stories about teenage prostitution (male as well as female) and some of the bizarre antics of celebrities.

The details of the rape of a 7-year-old child by two 6-year-olds and an 8-year-old were carried by the AP and were printed by many newspapers. Here is the beginning of this sordid story:

SYRACUSE, N.Y. (AP)—Two 6-year-old boys and an 8-year-old boy are accused of raping a 7-year-old girl in the back of a school bus and again in an apartment building, police say.

"If they're not the youngest, then they are certainly among the youngest" rape suspects in the state, Syracuse police investigator Rod Carr said.

The incident allegedly occurred Monday afternoon when the four children were riding home from school.

After allegedly raping the girl on the back floor of a moving city school bus, the three boys forced her into an apartment building where they attacked her a second time, according to a report issued by Carr.

Police were vague on the details of the alleged rape, and some medical experts said Wednesday a rape by boys so young would be physically "unusual." Dr. Gerald Nathanson, a pediatrician at Montefiore Hospital in New York City, said rape involving boys aged 6 to 8 would be "highly improbable."

But Carr said doctors at Crouse-Irving Memorial Hospital here confirmed the girl had been raped. The girl was taken to the hospital after her mother discovered her crying in bed, he said.

"We just received the medical reports, and, as unlikely as it may seem, it indicates that a rape took place."

The mother of the girl, whose name was withheld, said her daughter used to play alongside the three boys. . . .

This is a horrible story, clearly offensive to almost anyone. Why run it? Most of the newspapers that used it were not trying to peddle papers. They were, rather, trying to call attention to something terrible about the society we live in, to cry out that something must be very wrong if children can behave this way.

This leads to another guideline for our consideration: **Material that warns us or serves as a deterrent** may be used despite its tastelessness. Indeed, it is the shock value of the offensive material that drives home the point.

Billie Jean King

When a world-class tennis star was sued by a former close friend, the press had to make a major decision about subject matter. The tennis player, Billie Jean King, was accused in the suit of failing to carry out her promise to support her friend, who said she had been King's lesbian lover.

The suit, filed by a 33-year-old former hairdresser, stated that she had become intimate with King in 1972 and that the two had lived together in New York and Malibu, Calif. She asked for financial support and the Malibu home.

King was of sufficient prominence to make editors worry about the story. They could not ignore it because of King's prominence. On the other hand, people do make outlandish claims in suits. King denied the allegations.

Some editors buried the story on inside pages, others tossed it into the wastebasket, and some played it prominently. Many radio and television stations used it because of King's celebrity status as a sports announcer and tennis player.

Three days after King had issued a written statement denying the relationship and the promises alleged by the woman in the suit, King admitted she had once had a sexual affair with the woman suing her. Now, more newspapers carried the story, some of them playing it prominently on page one.

Many subject matters that were once taboo, like lesbianism, now are routinely written about—but not with the details that might offend people. When details about the last months of Elvis Presley's life were revealed, many newspapers were content to describe some of his personal antics as "kinky sex" without going into the details.

The Sex Industry

When Charles Bernsen of *The Commercial Appeal* was assigned to do a series of articles on the commercial sex industry in Memphis he had to see just what was being sold.

He says he went out to see his first peep show:

I remember coming out of the place, pausing to blink away the bright sunlight, and thinking: "How in the hell am I going to put what I just saw in the newspaper?"

The dilemma only got worse. I visited 12 more peep shows during the next eight weeks, including two that had "live show" booths in which patrons were urged to masturbate while they watched a naked woman writhe in feigned sexual ecstasy on the other side of a glass partition.

I went to 17 nightclubs that featured topless and/or bottomless dancers. In addition to watching the stage show, a partron could pay $5 for a four-minute "table dance" during which he often did more than just simulate the sex act with the naked waitress dancing between his outstretched legs.

I subscribed to a Memphis firm's obscene phone call service. (Pay them $20 and they send you a telephone number. Call the number and a woman will tell you what she'd like to do to you if only you were there with her.)

I subscribed to the same company's referral service for "swingers." (Pay them $20 and they send you the names and telephone numbers of folks in your area who are interested in getting together for a little mate swapping or group sex.)

I went to a public swingers club that said it offered "twosomes, threesomes, foursomes and moresomes" and did.

Bernsen and the newspaper were trapped in a dilemma. The commodity being peddled was bound to repel many readers, but the story had to be told because of the consequences of commercial sex. Much of it, Bernsen found, was controlled by organized crime, and its activities included "murders, beatings and attempted bombings." Also, it was big business in Memphis, grossing about $10 million a year.

"A business that big needs to be covered," Bernsen said. "That doesn't mean propriety should be tossed out the window.

"It doesn't do any good to write a story if your readers are going to gag on their orange juice and refuse to read it. But the business of selling sexual titillation can be reported fully and accurately without being titillating."

The policy that was adopted for the series was this: "If it was important to understanding how a part of the sex industry operated, we described or explained it in as much detail as possible. If it was superfluous, we avoided explicit detail that might be offensive."

This brings us to another guideline: **Explicit details of tasteless matters are avoided unless absolutely relevant to the story.**

Man or Woman?

Just what is relevant? This question came up with the story that we mentioned at the beginning of this chapter: the murder of Stella Walsh, the Olympic track champion and a mainstay of Cleveland's Polish-American community.

After the two television stations reported the coroner's finding that the examination revealed the body of 69-year-old Walsh was that of a man and not a woman, the community reaction was anger and hostility. Calls and letters protested the station's revelation.

The only local television station that did not mention the result of the autopsy was WJKW-TV, whose news director said that although the station knew of the sex angle it did not use it because: "We didn't think it was germane to the story. It was essentially a story of crime and violence."

Cleveland's two daily newspapers agreed with the news director's sentiments. An editor of the *Plain Dealer* said that the paper "felt there should be dignity in death."

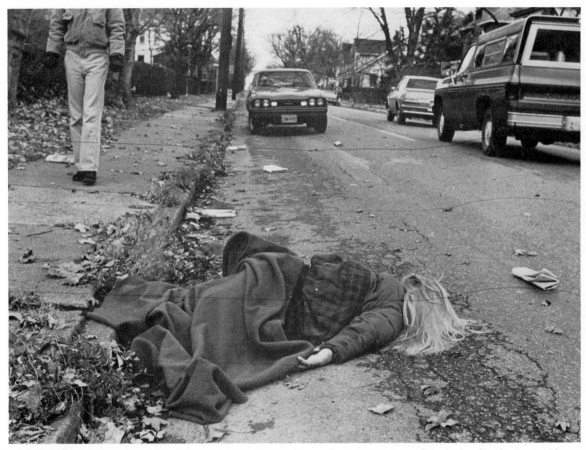

Legitimate or Irresponsible? When the *Columbus Citizen-Journal* ran this picture of the body of a nine-year-old girl who had been struck by a car, readers wrote and called to protest. They described it as tasteless, disgusting and irresponsible journalism. The newspaper defended its use of the photograph, saying it was a stark reminder to parents and to children of the dangers of city streets.

To these objections, the assistant news director of WEWS-TV said that the coroner's findings were the story.

The full story was run by the *Philadelphia Inquirer, Boston Globe* and *New York Times*. Only then did the Cleveland papers use the details.

Unquestionably, the coroner's findings were relevant. On the other hand, the local newspapers and WJKW were undoubtedly sensitive to their audience, the Polish-American community, many of whom wrote angry letters to the stations. WKYC-TV received 200 calls the night it used the story and 100 calls and letters over the next week, almost all critical of the reporting.

Photographs

The picture was stark and tragic: A little girl's body, half covered by a blanket, lay in the street where she had been struck and killed by a car.

As soon as the newspaper arrived in the homes of readers, the complaints began. Callers, then letter writers, complained that using the picture was irresponsible, that it was sensational journalism. Richard R. Campbell, editor of the *Columbus Citizen-Journal,* said that "the most common accusation was that the picture was tasteless.

"One reader called us coldhearted and tasteless and urged us not to forget discretion and compassion." Another reader said, "You have won first prize in the journalistic bad taste contest. Your prize for achieving this distinction is an all-expense paid trip to 'Sensational City' for the photographer and the editor who saw fit to print the picture."

Campbell said that the decision to run the photograph was his. His reasons, he said, were these:

> There could be no more dramatic way to point out to mothers and fathers and children, to drivers and pedestrians, the danger of carelessly stepping into the street. The proverb says one picture is worth more than 1,000 words. Here was such a picture.
>
> Secondly, it was part of our role of writing history.
>
> One father who appreciated our reason for using the photo said he showed it to his small sons, separately, and took the time to explain to each what happened to the little girl and why. That is what we expected the reaction to be.

If we look back at the guidelines for using material that may be in questionable taste, we can see that one of the reasons the picture was used was that it was hoped it would serve as a warning, a deterrent. The horror of the picture might register, as no written warnings can, the dangers to youngsters of playing in the street or darting out into the street.

Campbell also mentions the fact that this was part of local history. Of course, not every incident and accident is recorded by newspapers. The newspaper is, as historians are, selective. The editor chose to run this picture because it was a graphic demonstration of a part of every community's history—the appalling toll of traffic deaths.

"We gave our readers a slice of Tuesday's life in Columbus that they did not want to see," a reporter said about the protests. "Hank Reichard took the image of that broken little girl and hurled it in our faces so that we would have to look at her too.

"Hank made us care that a little girl had died when she should not have died, in a place that was terribly wrong for a child's death. He made us suffer."

Some of the same reasons can be given for the other photographs in this book that might have offended readers—the pictures by Larry C. Price of the execution on the beach in Liberia. These pictures did indeed show us history in the making.

Here are some guidelines for questionable language, subject matter and photographs: **Summary**

> *The material must be essential to the story being told.* Without the material, the point would not be made or would be diluted.
>
> *The audience must be taken into consideration.* If the great majority of readers or listeners would be offended, the material should not be used.
>
> *If the material serves as a warning then it may be used despite its offensive nature.*
>
> *Details of crimes, sex acts and other shocking actions should not be used unless absolutely relevant.*
>
> *If the event has historical significance, it should be used.*

Appendix A
Preparing Copy

1. Use copy paper, newsprint or some other nonglossy paper. Triple space. Use large margins left and right.

1. Use copy paper, newsprint or some other nonglossy paper. Triple space. Use large margins left and right.
2. Make a carbon of all your work. Retain the carbon.
3. In the upper left-hand-corner of the first sheet of all assignments, place your name, slug of story, news source and date. Thus:

Chamberlain
PHA-attended
10/7/83

4. On the first page, begin one-third down the page. Write on one side of the paper only.
5. If the story consists of more than one page, write *more* at the bottom of the page that is being continued, circle it. On the next page, put your name, "2" and slug at top left of page. Thus: Chamberlain-2-PHA. For the next page, make it 3, and so on.
6. End each page with a complete paragraph, not in the middle of a sentence.
7. Do not correct mistakes by backspacing and typing over. Cross out and retype. Never write over.
8. For simple errors, use copy editing symbols. (See fig. 10.2.) Do not confuse these with proofreading marks.
9. Never divide words at the end of the line. Hit the margin release and continue or cross out and begin word anew on the next line.
10. Keep copy clean. Retype hard-to-read sections and paste over, preferably with rubber cement.
11. Do not write more than one story on each sheet of paper.
12. End stories with an end mark: 30, #, or END.
13. Follow the stylebook. (See Appendix B.)
14. When finished, fold all pages together, in half, copy on the outside, reporter's name showing in the upper left.

Preparing Copy on a Typewriter

Writing on the VDT. Two students who are on the staff of the *Lumberjack,* the student newspaper at Humboldt State University in California, write their news stories on the video display terminal. The VDT is also used to edit stories and to store them on magnetic disks, which are then placed in a phototypesetter.

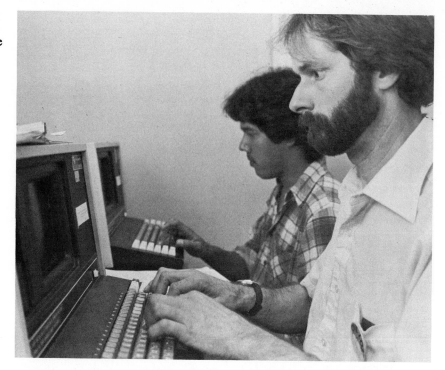

Preparing Copy on a Video Display Terminal

Most newspapers have traded in many of their typewriters for electronic equipment that has eliminated the costly and time-consuming process of typesetting a newspaper with hot metal. The electronic process is called phototypesetting.

Basic to the process are the video (or visual) display terminal, the phototypesetter and the processor.

The video display terminal (VDT) consists of keyboard and screen. The keyboard is used much like a typewriter, although it also has keys with special instructions for setting the type, moving copy around and editing.

The screen displays the copy as it is typed. Depending on the terminal model, 14 to 30 lines of copy can be seen on the screen.

The copy may be stored on a magnetic disk, a magnetic card or in some other storage device. It can then be called up for copy editing, which is also carried out on the screen of the terminal.

The edited version is sent to the phototypesetter, which sets the story according to the instructions of the news writer or editor. The story is produced on photosensitive paper that is placed in a processor.

In the processor, the paper is developed and a positive image or print is produced. The printed material is proofread and then placed on sheets for makeup.

For the news writer, keyboarding a story is faster and easier than using the typewriter. Since the system has a programmed set of instructions that justifies lines and hyphenates words, the writer does not have to return the

```
┌─────────────────────┐
│  Raw copy or notes  │
└─────────────────────┘
           │
           ▼
┌─────────────────────┐
│ Keyboarding the story │
└─────────────────────┘
           │
           ▼
┌─────────────────────┐
│ Editing on the screen │
└─────────────────────┘
```

┌──────────────┐   ┌──────────────┐   ┌──────────────┐   ┌──────────────┐
│ Typesetting │ → │ Processing │ → │ Proofreading │ → │   Makeup   │
└──────────────┘   └──────────────┘   └──────────────┘   └──────────────┘

carriage but types in an endless line. Corrections and other changes are made with the use of a cursor, a block of light that can be moved anywhere on the screen.

On newspapers whose terminals connect to a large storage computer, news writers can call up various reference materials, such as the newspaper's clippings on a subject. Reporters also can store their notes or partially completed stories, and with the use of their personal code numbers can call these up.

When the story is finished, it is read on the screen by a copy editor who also puts into the terminal a number of instructions about how the copy is to be set. These instructions are called *parameters*.

There are a number of different electronic typesetting systems, but the general procedure outlined here applies to all of them.

body type size The size of type used for the text of a news story. Size is measured in points, 72 points to an inch. The type size for newspaper stories ranges from 8 to 10 points.

cursor The location finder, a movable indicator used in editing copy on the VDT. The cursor can be moved up or down, left or right for insertions, corrections or deletions.

floppy disk A specifically coated platter made of plastic upon which copy is stored. The disc can then be used for editing and erased or saved.

format A specific set of commands for the phototypesetter that is stored in a memory unit and can be recalled. A format is used for sets of commands (called parameters) for frequently used material such as the one-column newspaper story, for example.

galley The processed material produced by a typesetting machine.

input Entering material for machine processing.

justification The addition of space between letters and words that allows a line of type to fill the line measure or column width.

Terminology for the
Electronic Newsroom

leading The amount of space between lines of type. Pronounced *ledding*.

line measure Width or length of a line of type, measured in picas. A pica is one-sixth of an inch; there are six picas to an inch.

OCR (Optical Character Recognition) An electronic method of "reading" typed pages or other printed material. Material that is placed in the OCR is scanned and recorded on magnetic discs. It can then be placed in a terminal for editing or into a phototypesetter.

parameters Specifications or instructions about the copy that is being put into the terminal. Common parameters include:
> type face
> point size of the body type
> line space (leading)
> line measure

phototypesetting Setting type by the controlled exposure of light on photosensitive paper or film.

pica A unit of measurement, one-sixth of an inch.

point A unit of measurement; a 1/12 of a pica. There are 12 points to a pica, 72 points to an inch.

scrolling Movement up or down of copy on a screen. The terminal screen carries a limited number of lines, usually a minimum of 14 lines. To see material that is not visible on the screen, the copy is scrolled up or down.

software The programming instructions that control the phototypesetter.

system The machinery (hardware) and programs (software) that together produce the final output for the press.

VDT (Video or Visual Display Terminal) A device used for input of material and to correct material before it is typeset.

Appendix B
Stylebook

The purpose of this stylebook is to set standards of consistency for abbreviations, capitalization, punctuation and other usage on which there may be differences of opinion. The stylebook makes the rules. This brief stylebook is based on common practices adopted by the AP and UPI for their stylebooks.

Abbreviations

Addresses, months, states and titles are often abbreviated.

Addresses Abbreviate Avenue, Boulevard, Street with specific address—1314 Kentucky St. Spell out without specific address—Kentucky Street, Fifth Avenue.

Months Abbreviate month with specific date—Jan. 25, 1927. Spell out when month stands alone or is followed by a year—January 1927.

States Abbreviate all states but the following when used with a city, in a dateline, or with party affiliation—Alaska, Hawaii, Idaho, Iowa, Maine, Ohio, Utah. Do not use Postal Service abbreviations. Spell out all states when standing alone.

Ala.	Fla.	Md.	Neb.	N.D.	Tenn.	Wyo.
Ariz.	Ga.	Mass.	Nev.	Okla.	Tex.	
Ark.	Ill.	Mich.	N.H.	Ore.	Vt.	
Calif.	Ind.	Minn.	N.J.	Pa.	Va.	
Colo.	Kan.	Miss.	N.M.	R.I.	Wash.	
Conn.	Ky.	Mo.	N.Y.	S.C.	W. Va.	
Del.	La.	Mont.	N.C.	S.D.	Wis.	

Titles Abbreviate titles before a name. When standing alone, spell out—The governor vetoed the bill.

Addresses

Use figures for the address number—3 Third Ave.; 45 Main St. Spell out numbers under 10 as street names—21 Fourth Ave.; 450 11th St.

Age

Infant Under one year of age.

Child The period between infancy and youth, ages one to 13.

Youth 13–18.

Man, Woman Over 18.

Adult Over 18, unless used in specific legal context for crimes such as drinking.

Middle-aged 35–55.

Elderly Over 65. Avoid when describing individuals.

Capitalization

Generally, follow a down style.

Proper nouns Use capitals for names of persons, places, trademarks, titles when used with names; nicknames of persons, states, teams; titles of books, plays, movies.

President Make it a capital when it precedes the name; lowercase in all other uses—President Hoover. The president.

False titles Generally avoid false titles—right fielder Tommy Jones; television star Babs Buchin. Put some titles after person's names with commas—Tommy Jones, right fielder, struck out. Lowercase the title if used to precede name.

Contractions

Avoid unless used in direct quotes or to set an informal tone to story.

Courtesy Titles

Miss, Mrs., Ms., Mr. are usually not used on first reference with the full name. Use Mrs. on first reference for clarity when a woman requests that her husband's first name be used or her own first name cannot be ascertained—Mrs. Bruce Berning. On first reference, use the woman's first name. Do not use Mr. in any reference.

Use the courtesy title for a woman on second reference, following the womans' preference: If married, use Mrs. unless she prefers Ms. If married and she prefers to be known by her maiden name, use Miss or Ms., if she prefers. If unmarried, use Miss on second reference unless the woman prefers Ms. For divorced women or women whose husbands have died, use Mrs. on second reference unless the woman prefers Ms.

Note: A number of newspapers drop Mrs., Miss and Ms. as well as Mr. on second reference—A Norfolk woman, Frances Savage, accused the judge of running a "three-ring circus." Savage made her charges in a letter to the editor.

Punctuation   July 6, 1957, was her birth date. (Use commas.) She was born in July 1957. (No comma between month and year.) **Dates**

Abbreviation   Abbreviate month with specific date—Feb. 19. Spell out all months when standing alone. With dates, use abbreviations: Jan., Feb., Aug., Sept., Oct., Nov., Dec.; spell out March, April, May, June, July.

Spell out one through nine; use figures for 10 and above. **Numerals**

Spell out a number when it begins a sentence—Fifteen members voted against the bill. Use figures when a year begins a sentence—1980 began auspiciously.

Use figures for percentages and percents.

For amounts of $1 million and more, use the $ sign and figures up to two decimal places with the million, billion, trillion spelled out—$1.65 million. Exact amounts are given in figures—$1,650,398.

When spelling out large numbers, separate figure ending in "y" from next number with a hyphen–Seventy-nine; one hundred seventy-nine.

A pronoun should agree with its antecedent in number, person and gender. **Pronouns**
The most common fault is a shift in (1) number or (2) person.

1. The organization added basketball and hockey to their winter program. (Wrong.)
   The organization added basketball and hockey to its winter program. (Right.)
2. When one wants to ski, you have to buy good equipment. (Wrong.)
   When one wants to ski, he or she has to buy good equipment. (Right.)

If the antecedent is singular, it is referred to with a singular pronoun. A singular pronoun is preferred with these antecedents: each, every, either, neither, someone, somebody, anyone, anything, anybody, everyone, no one, nobody.

A common error is to give teams, groups and organizations the plural pronoun:

The team played their best shortstop. (Wrong.)
The team played its best shortstop. (Right.)
The Police Department wants recruits. They need 1,500 applicants.
   (Wrong.)
The Police Department wants recruits. It needs 1,500 applicants.
   (Right.)

The nouns in the above examples are called collective nouns. If the noun is plural in idea, use the plural pronoun:

The family enjoyed their vacations.

Keep a good grammar book handy. No stylebook can adequately cover the complexities of the 13 punctuation marks: apostrophe, brackets, colon, comma, dash, ellipsis, exclamation point, hyphen, parentheses, period, question mark, quotation marks, semicolon. The following is a guide to frequent problems and usages:

Punctuation

Apostrophe Use for (1) possessives, (2) to indicate omitted figures or letters and (3) to form some plurals.

1. *Possessives:* Add apostrophe and "s" ('s) to the end of singular plural nouns or the indefinite pronoun unless it has an s or z sound:
   The woman's coat. The women's coats.
   The child's toy. The children's toys.
   Someone's pistol. One's hopes.
   If the word is plural and ends in an s or z sound, add apostrophe only:
   Boys' books. Joneses' farm.
   If the word is singular and ends in an s or z sound and has one syllable, add apostrophe and "s."
   James's hat. Jones's application.
   If the word is singular, has more than one syllable and ends in an s or z sound, add apostrophe only:
   Stevens' invention. Velazquez' paintings.
   Note: if the second s or z sound is necessary for broadcast purposes, then add the apostrophe and "s."
   The hostess's gown.
2. *Omitted figures or letters:* Use in contractions—Don't, can't. Put in place of omitted figure—Class of '84.
3. *To form some plurals:* When figures, letters, symbols and words are referred to as words, use the apostrophe and "s."
   Figures: She skated perfect 8's.
   Letters: He received all A's in his finals.
   Symbols: Journalists never use &'s to substitute for the ands in their copy.

Caution: The pronouns ours, yours, theirs, his, hers, whose do not take the apostrophe. Its is the possessive pronoun. It's is the contraction of it is.

Note: Compound words and nouns in joint possession use the possessive in the last word:

Everybody else's homes.
His sister-in-law's book.
Carter and Kennedy's party.

If there is separate possession, each noun takes the possessive form:

Mondale's and Kennedy's opinions differ.

Brackets Check whether the newspaper can set them. The wire services cannot transmit brackets. Use to enclose a word or words within a quote that the writer inserts—"Happiness [his note read] is a state of mind." Use for paragraph(s) within a story that refer to an event separate from the datelined material.

Colon The colon is usually used at the end of a sentence to call attention to what follows. It introduces lists, tabulations, texts and quotations of more than one sentence.

It can also be used to mark a full stop before a dramatic word or statement—She had only one goal in life: work. The colon is used in time of day, 7:45 p.m.; elapsed time of an event, 4:01.1, and in dialogue in question and answer, as from a trial.

Comma The best general guide for the use of the comma is the human voice as it pauses, stops and varies in tone. The comma marks the pause, the short stop:

1. He looked into the hospital room, but he was unable to find the patient.
2. Although he continued his search on the floor for another 20 minutes, he was unable to find anyone to help him.
3. He decided that he would go downstairs, ask at the desk and then telephone the police.
4. If that also failed, he thought to himself, he would have to give up the search.

Note that when reading these sentences aloud, the commas are natural resting points for pauses. The four sentences also illustrate the four principles governing the use of commas:

1. The comma is used to separate main clauses when they are joined by a coordinating conjunction. (The coordinating conjunctions are: for, nor, and, but, or.) The comma can be eliminated if the main clauses are short—He looked into the room and he froze.

2. Use the comma after an introductory element: a clause, long phrase, transitional expression or interjection.
3. Use the comma to separate words, phrases or clauses in a series. Also, use it in a series of coordinate adjectives—He was wearing a long, full cape.
4. Set off nonessential material in a sentence with comma(s). When the parenthetical or interrupting nonrestrictive clauses and phrases are in the middle of a sentence two commas are needed—The country, he was told, needed his assistance. Other uses of the comma:

Use a comma with full sentence quotes, not with partial quotes—He asked, "Where are you going?" The man replied that he was "blindly groping" his way home.

To separate city and county, city and state. In place of the word "of" between a name and city—Jimmy Carter, Plains, Ga.

To set off a person's age—Orville Sterb, 19, of Fullerton, Calif. In dates—March 19, 1940, was the date he entered the army.

In party affiliations—Bill Bradley, D-N.J., spoke.

Caution: The comma is frequently misused by placing it between two main clauses instead of using the period or semicolon. This is called the comma splice:

The typewriter was jammed, he could not type his theme. (Wrong.)
The typewriter was jammed. He could not type his theme. The typewriter was jammed; he could not type his theme. (Right.)

Dash Use a dash (1) to indicate a sudden or dramatic shift in thought within a sentence, (2) to set off a series of words that contains commas and (3) to introduce sections of a list or a summary.

The dash is a call for a short pause, just as the comma and the parenthesis. The comma is the most often used and is the least dramatic of the separators. The parenthesis sets off unimportant elements. The dash tends to emphasize material. It has this quality because it is used sparingly.

1. He stared at the picture—and he was startled to find himself thinking of her face. The man stood up—painfully and awkwardly—and extended his hand in greeting.
2. There were three persons watching them—an elderly woman, a youth with a crutch at his side and a young woman in jeans holding a paperback—and he pulled her aside out of their view.
3. He gave her his reasons for being there.
   —He wanted to apologize;
   —He needed to give her some material;
   —He was leaving on a long trip.

(*Note:* This third form should be used infrequently, usually when the listing will be followed by an elaboration.)
The dash is also used in datelines.

Ellipsis   Use the ellipsis to indicate material omitted from a quoted passage from a text, transcript, play, etc.—The minutes stated that Breen had asked, "How many gallons of paint . . . were used in the project?" Put one space before and one space after each of the three periods. If the omission ends with a period, use four periods, one to mark the end of the sentence (without space, as a regular period), three more for the ellipsis.

The ellipsis is also used by some columnists to separate short items in a paragraph.

Do not use to mark pauses, shifts in thought, or for emphasis.

Exclamation point   Much overused. There are reporters who have gone through a lifetime of writing and have never used the exclamation point, except when copying material in which it is used. The exclamation point is used to indicate powerful feelings, surprise, wonderment. Most good writers prefer to let the material move the reader to provide his or her own exclamation.

When using, do not use a comma or period after the exclamation point. Place inside quotation marks if it is part of the quoted material.

Hyphen   The hyphen is used (1) to join words to express a single idea or (2) to avoid confusion or ambiguity.

1.   Use the hyphen to join two or more words that serve as a single adjective before a noun—A well-known movie is on television tonight. He had a know-it-all expression.
     Caution: Do not use the hyphen when the first word of the compound ends in "ly" or when the words follow the noun—He is an easily recognized person. Her hair was blonde black.
2.   (a) Avoid ambiguity or (b) an awkward joining of letters or syllables by putting a hyphen between prefixes or suffixes and the root word.
     a. He recovered the chair. He re-covered the chair.
     b. Re-enter, macro-economics, shell-like.

Parentheses   Generally, avoid. They may be necessary for the insertion of background or to set off supplementary or illustrative material.

Use period inside closing parenthesis if the matter begins with a capital letter.

Period   Use the period at the end of declarative sentences, indirect questions, most imperative sentences and most abbreviations.

The period is placed inside quotation marks.

Question mark   The question mark is used for direct questions, not indirect questions.

Direct: Where are you going?
Indirect: He asked where she was going.

The question mark goes inside quotation marks if it applies to the quoted material—He asked, "Have you seen the movie?" Put it outside if it applies to the entire sentence—Have you seen "Guys and Dolls"?

Quotation marks Quotation marks set off (1) direct quotations, (2) some titles and nicknames and (3) words used in a special way.

1. Set off the exact words of the speaker—"He walked like a duck," she said. He replied that he walked "more like an alley cat on the prowl."
2. Use for book and movie titles, titles of short stories, poems, songs, articles from magazines and plays. Some nicknames take quotation marks—Sen. Henry "Scoop" Jackson. Do not use for nicknames of sports figures.
3. For words used in a special sense—An "Indian giver" is someone who gives something to another and then takes it back.

Punctuation with quotation marks:

The comma—Use it outside the quotation marks when setting off the speaker at the beginning of a sentence—He said, "You care too much for money." Use inside quotation marks when the speaker ends the sentence—"I just want to be safe," she replied.

The colon and semicolon—Always place outside the quotation marks—He mentioned her "incredible desire for work"; he meant her "insatiable desire for work."

The dash, question mark and exclamation point—inside when they apply to quoted matter only: outside when they refer to the whole sentence—She asked: "How do you know so much?" He asked himself, what's the meaning of "know so much"?

For quotes within quotes, use single quote mark (the apostrophe on typewriter) for the inner quotation— "Have you read 'War and Peace'?" he asked. Note, no comma is used after the question mark.

Semicolon Usually overused by beginning reporters. Unless there is a special reason to use the semicolon, use the period.

Use the semicolon to separate a series of equal elements when the individual segments contain material that is set off by commas. This makes for clarity in the series—He suggested that she spend her allowance on the new series at the opera, "Operas of the Present"; books of plays by Shaw, Ibsen and Aristophanes; and novels by Tolstoy, Dickens and F. Scott Fitzgerald.

Avoid stereotyping women or men. Be conscious of equality in treatment of **Sexism** both sexes.

In writing of careers and jobs, avoid presuming that the wage earner is a man and that the woman is a homemaker.

The average worker with a wife and three children. . . . . (Wrong.)
The average family of five. . . . (Right.)

Avoid physical descriptions of women or men when not absolutely relevant to the story.

Use parallel references to both sexes—the men and the women, not the men and the ladies; husband and wife, not man and wife.

Do not use nouns and pronouns to indicate sex unless the sex difference is basic to understanding or there is no suitable substitute. One way to avoid such subtle sexism is to change the noun to the plural, eliminating the masculine pronoun: Drivers should have their licenses.

Personal appearances and marital and family relationships should be used only when relevant to the story.

When in doubt about spelling, consult an accepted dictionary. Use the first **Spelling** spelling listed. If the word is not listed, do not use it unless it is a direct quote.

Exact times are often unnecessary. Last night and this morning are acceptable **Time** substitutes for yesterday and today, if appropriate. Use exact time when pertinent, but avoid redundancies—8 a.m. this morning should be 8 a.m. today or 8 o'clock this morning.

Use figures except for noon and midnight.
Separate hours from minutes with a colon—3:15 p.m.

Appendix C
Complete Stories

Without Heat: It's a Way of Life for Them

by Mary Ann Giordano

It is warm and bright in Marie Walker's kitchen. Four flames glow on the aging stove as a pot of water boils steadily. The door of the oven is open, and she sits in front of it, her sock-covered feet propped on the door as the gas heat warms her toes.

It is the only hot spot in the apartment, the only place in the entire building where warm breath does not send puffs of vapor into the air.

A thermometer in a front room, where the sun shines through a window, registers 52 degrees. That is warm, the Walker family says. Saturday it reached a high of 39 degrees inside.

It is so cold the pipes burst in the four-story apartment building at 58 Gates Ave. in Bedford-Stuyvesant and the six members of the Walker family must take turns drawing water from a hydrant on the street.

Water from hydrant

None of the Walkers like that chore. They say it "embarrasses" them to have to use the wrench on the hydrant in front of their apartment to draw enough water for their cooking and washing needs.

Sometimes they fight over "whose water" it is. They say they never appreciated water so much in their lives.

But that is not their only hardship. When the pipes burst, their toilet stopped working, and the bowl remains filled with water. Their friends have been startled in answering the door to find one of the Walkers out of breath in the rush to a workable toilet.

The Walkers—60-year-old Marie; her daughter Sarah and Sarah's three children; and another daughter Ethel and Ethel's son—had thanked God every morning this winter for the mild weather. They thanked God because they knew they faced cold weather without any heat. Last week, their prayers ran out.

Still hasn't lost her smile

"We got very religious this winter," says Ethel Walker, a 28-year-old marketing student who manages to keep a constant smile on her face as she tells of her struggle for decent housing.

"I mean very religious," she says. "Every morning we would wake up and say, thank God. It's warm again today."

It is not the only time the Walkers

have prayed for such things. For more than three years, they have been the only tenants in their eight-apartment building. They have prayed to keep the junkies out, prayed the rats will have enough to eat elsewhere and will stay away from them, and prayed that they will soon be able to move.

Marie Walker has lived at 587 Gates Ave. for 20 years. It was a nice building when she moved in, she says. Then the landlord abandoned it and the city took it over. It was sold then to another landlord who more than quadrupled the rents.

Rent control and more than 15 years in that building saved Marie from a substantial rent increase.

High rents drive tenants out

When the other tenants could not afford to pay the high rents and moved out, she was left alone. She's been alone with her family in the building ever since. Only the junkies who populate the lower floors at night and the rats who seem to own the place are there to keep them company.

Since then, the building—like the neighborhood around it—has continued to deteriorate. Last winter, after many nights without heat, the boiler broke for good.

The Walkers learned to live without hot water, heating small amounts on the stove and visiting friends for baths. They accepted things when their new landlord told them the building wasn't profitable enough for her and she was pulling out. It wasn't until the water stopped completely that things became unbearable.

"It's bad enough when you can't get no hot water, but when you can't get no water . . . " Marie Walker says, her voice trailing off as she shakes her head.

Chill affects her arthritis

She rubs her swollen right knee from time to time, trying to massage the arthritis out of her joints. The cold and the broken windows in her rear bedroom—covered only by sheets of heavy plastic—do not help her soreness during the night. The stove burning steadily and the heaps of blankets only take the stinging chill from the air.

Ethel and Sarah and Sarah's 2-year-old daughter, Crystal, share two twin beds pushed together in the front room. Harry, 11, and Tyrone, 9—Sarah's sons—and Jamel, 7—Ethel's son—sleep together in a nearby room.

The Walkers do not sleep soundly. Ethel and Sarah leave a light burning in their room through the night to let would-be arsonists know someone lives there.

"All someone has to do is set a match to this place," Sarah says sadly.

They sleep with a prayer that the meager lock on the front door will discourage the junkies from coming in, they say, and they address the rats as "Mr." and "Mrs."

"We have to ask them, can we sleep tonight, is it okay if we sleep?" Sarah jokes.

Hopes to get city housing

No lack of enterprise has contributed to the Walkers' situation. They have tried to get out. Ethel has been approved for Section 8 housing and is simply awaiting a vacancy that can offer her better conditions than she has. Sarah is trying to get into city housing with her mother, and has been on the phone constantly to get help.

It has not been easy for them. After almost four years, Ethel lost her job as secretary with an engineering firm in cutbacks. The job loss eliminated a substantial source of income for the family, and is also making it difficult for Ethel to move into a Section 8 apartment. It is also making it difficult for her to study, as she pursues a goal of becoming a broadcast journalist.

Sarah says she and her mother simply waited too long to get out. They kept waiting for better, but things kept getting worse.

"We're past scared," Ethel says. "We're at the bottom now and the only way to go is up."

"There ain't nothing left but for us to die," Marie Walker said. Then, shuffling off her slippers, she pulled her legs up over the oven door, pushed her feet back inside, and leaned back in the warmth.

—The *Daily News* (N.Y.)

A Family Still Asks for Home

Chapter 2

by Mary Ann Giordano

The plumbing is still broken, the heat is still out, the junkies and rats still roam freely through the lower floors, and the Walker family of Bedford-Stuyvesant is still looking for decent housing.

Three weeks after an article appeared in The Daily News detailing the plight of the seven members of the Walker family, they are still trekking through the maze of housing regulations—cruel realities that confront New Yorkers searching for livable housing.

A vacancy notice was posted on their building at 587 Gates Ave. last week after the housing code inspectors found the place uninhabitable. Now, 60-year-old Marie Walker, her daughters, Sarah and Ethel, and the daughters' four children, are on waiting lists for other apartments.

Meanwhile, they are still drawing all their water from the fire hydrant in front of their apartment and storing it in bottles kept over the unworkable sink.

They still must run to the apartments of friends and neighbors to find a workable toilet.

Warmed by sun

The boiler remains broken and they are still gathering in a frontroom of the house to be warmed by the sun when it streams in through the window.

The gas stove is lit often to provide heat to the rear of the house, and last month the Walkers paid $85 for gas and electricity. That price was estimated, however. The meter readers could not enter the basement to get the true readings because it has remained flooded with several feet of water from when the pipes burst.

20-year residents

There is housing available for the Walkers, housing authorities said. But the Walkers are looking for better than they have. They are looking for the security they thought they had for most of the 20 years they lived at 587 Gates Ave.

But a change in landlords and hefty rent increases drove all the tenants out of that building, and for the last two years, the Walkers have been the only tenants in the four-story building.

Protected by rent control, they continued to pay their $49.12 a month until early fall, when the landlord stopped purchasing oil and told them she was abandoning the building.

Their attempts to get out of the building have not been easy, they said. It took until earlier this month for housing inspectors to arrive, and they did not post the vacate notice until last Thursday.

Then, Sarah Walker was counseled by the Department of Relocation, who took her application for emergency housing. Sarah said the counselor told her he could place her, her two sons, her toddler daughter, and her mother, in temporary housing. She said he told her it would be three to five months before she could place them in permanent housing.

"I was very upset," Sarah said. "We really don't want to move into the hotels, either, because they're trouble, too. But we can't stay here for three to five months."

Sarah said she is hoping to get into public housing but, knowing there is a lengthy waiting list for such apartments, she is hoping to get any apartment with better conditions than those in which her family is living.

Meanwhile, Ethel Walker is looking for a Section 8-subsidized apartment for herself and her son. A broadcast major at New York City Community College in Downtown Brooklyn, she has been trying to look for apartments in between studying and attending classes. She is also looking for a job.

"You try to do better. You try to get out of it," Ethel said. "I'm just trying to make it out here."

—The *Daily News* (N.Y.)

Chapter 2

Hollywood Sun-Tattler

HOME Edition

Home Delivered 90¢ a Week Call 925-5511

Vol. 52 — No. 178   Hollywood, Florida Tuesday, July 28, 1981   38 Pages In 5 Sections

Massive search launched for boy, 6

By Charlie Brennan
Sun-Tattler staff

Adam Walsh disappeared from Sears Monday afternoon

Reve Walsh usually leaves her son in the toy department at Sears while doing her shopping at the Hollywood Mall. He's always there waiting for her.

But Monday was different. Adam Walsh, 6, wasn't there waiting. The Hollywood child hasn't been seen since 12:30 p.m. Monday.

"Everybody's working this one," says police spokesman Fred Barbetta. "Everybody wants this kid to show up."

Adam is the only child of John and Reve Walsh of 1801 McKinley St.

"He's very sheltered," Walsh says. "We never let him out of our sight. He even went on business trips with me."

Hollywood police, the Broward Sheriff's helicopter search team and 47 members of Citizens Crime Watch teamed up Monday night to search for the child throughout Hollywood. Their efforts so far have proven fruitless.

Undaunted, police and the Crime Watch volunteers fanned out again late this morning, hoping to find a trace of the vanished child.

"Even if we have to retrace from last night, we're going to look all over," Barbetta says.

Adam, a student at St. Mark's Lutheran School, was last seen wearing a red and white striped Izod shirt. He was dressed in green Adidas shorts, yellow sandals and a beige captain's cap. He is missing one front tooth and has straight,

Charlie Brennan at Work.

sandy colored hair and hazel eyes.

Barbetta says 22 patrol officers requested overtime duty early this morning at the end of their normal shifts so they could continue looking for Adam.

"We've got the whole detective bureau on this one, the whole patrol — everybody," Barbetta says.

Adam's parents appeared before television cameras at 10:10 this morning to make a plea for the child's return, saying: "Look for landmarks, Adam. Look for landmarks, and you'll be able to find your way home."

The Walshes have consulted a psychic, who has worked in the past with police in locating missing persons. The psychic, identified only as a Dr. Fisher, has given them information that their

please see **SEARCH, 8A**

Adam Walsh, 6, Vanished.

son may have left the mall heading south.

"We seem to think he left the Hollywood Mall in a panic, but we don't know for sure in what direction," Walsh says. "He's a very bright child and very shy — very introverted."

The psychic was able to tell the Walshes details about their child he would have had no way of knowing. For example, the psychic knew the name of a Texas girl scheduled to visit Adam next week. They were to have attended a performance of "Peter Pan" in Miami Beach.

There are many theories about what may have happened to Adam. His parents have reason to believe he may have been seen getting into a late-model white car with a CB antennae. "But that's just conjecture," Adam's father says.

Mrs. Walsh says she was just a few aisles away from her son when he was last seen.

"I told him I would be in the lamp department," she says. "He said 'I know where you'll be, Mommy,' he told me."

A second theory Mrs. Walsh proposed is that there was reportedly an altercation in Sears about the time of Adam's disappearance involving two white teen-agers and two blacks. Adam, his mother says, may have fled the store in fear.

The extensive search launched late last night by Crime Watch volunteers working with the police sent teams down back alleys looking in garbage cans, dumpsters and anywhere else a clue to the boy's disappearance might be found. They found nothing.

Hollywood police have distributed a flyer to Florida Power and Light workers, Southern Bell crews and letter carriers in hopes those people might see Adam during the course of their daily routine.

Referring to the response to Crime Watch and other citizens helping with the search, Barbetta says, "I've never seen a response like this. It's just fantastic."

Tony Sodl, 58, is one Crime Watch member who combed the area near Johnson Street and 28th Avenue from midnight until 2 a.m. He was on hand at the police station to resume the search. "I'll look all day, if we have to," he says.

Chapter 4

Old Hitler:
A Shark Hunter's Obsession

by Jeff Klinkenberg

Ron Swint moaned in the dark about the shark called Old Hitler, the largest shark in Tampa Bay, as traffic roared by on the Skyway Bridge. Somebody in a car shouted and Swint automatically winced. He has been hit by beer cans thrown from passing cars. A huge truck rumbled by so fast the bridge shook. Diesel fumes hung in the air.

The first shark to come along was not Old Hitler, but it was a big one, a shark Swint later estimated at 500 pounds, a shark that swallowed a three-pound live ladyfish bait and swam toward the lights of Tampa. The shark almost killed Swint.

Swint was pulling on the shark rod with all his strength when the line snapped. His own momentum carried him into the lane of traffic. The truck never slowed down, but Swint was quick enough to scramble back onto the sidewalk with his expensive rod and reel. Shaken, he said: "That's why I never drink when I'm out here. You need all your faculties to fish for sharks. If I'd had a few beers tonight, I may not have been quick enough to get out of the way. I've almost been pulled in the water by sharks, but this was the first one that almost got me killed by the traffic.

"And that wasn't even Old Hitler."

Four times Ron Swint has hooked the shark he calls Old Hitler and four times it has escaped. "Last year I wasn't even a challenge," Swint said. "Old Hitler ripped me off." Last time Swint was ready. "Old Hitler took 1,500 yards of line and I turned him. I thought I had him. Then my line broke."

Swint is obsessed by Old Hitler, the most intimidating shark in the bay. Old Hitler, Swint says, is a 22-foot hammerhead. Its head is 5½ feet wide. Old Hitler, Swint says, weighs 1,500 pounds, easy. If Old Hitler is indeed that large, it is twice the size of the biggest hammerhead ever taken on rod and reel. The world record, captured off Jacksonville in 1975, weighed 703 pounds and was 14 feet long. Swint intends to catch Old Hitler and break the record. "That SOB is mine," Swint said, voice, rising in the night. "I'm gonna get him."

It was 11 p.m. near the main span of the Skyway, the bridge from which Swint fishes nightly for sharks, and he was prepared for another titanic tussle with Old Hitler. His face now illuminated by the eerie glow of a gasoline lantern, Swint said with reverence: "Old Hitler has attacked boats. They've had to close beaches a couple of times. Old Hitler is . . ." His narration was interrupted by the clicking drag of his enormous fishing reel filled with 2,500 yards of 80-pound test line. Something large had picked the bait from the bottom and was swimming away.

Swint, who had recovered from his near miss with the truck, picked up his rod and harnessed it to his chest. With one hand he tied a rope to a hole in the sidewalk. A big shark could pull him from the bridge. Occasionally, Swint ties himself to the structure with the rope.

The shark swam slowly away from the bridge. "Old Hitler hits softly," said Swint, a 32-year-old St. Petersburg resident who says he retired from Ohio so he could fish for sharks in Florida. "Old Hitler," Swint said, "will take line out so my reel makes five or six clicks. Then he takes off against the full drag. It's the most amazing thing you'd ever want to see."

But this shark wasn't Old Hitler. It was probably a pup, a shark that weighed less than 200 pounds, because it didn't even swallow the bait. It mutilated it, then abandoned it on the bottom.

"Even when I don't catch a fish, having a run is the most exciting thing in the world," Swint said.

Three years ago, Swint got it in his mind to devote the rest of his life to catching sharks. He had a good job in Columbus, Ohio, he says, as the product manager for a pollution firm. He made a good salary, he traveled, he was unmarried, "and I read in some books that Tampa Bay was the second best place for sharks in the world, second only to Australia. And shark fishing was about the only thing I'd never done. And I'd seen people retire at 65 and drop dead eight days later, so I figured it was a good time to retire. At 29." And so he did.

He works part time now, for The Tackle Box, a fishing store on U.S. 19. He repairs rods and reels. He is good at the work. Sometimes he does a little bartending for a friend. He has a lot of time to fish, on the Skyway at night, for sharks. "I think there's a lot of sharks in the bay because they follow the ships in from the Gulf," said Swint, a tall, muscular man who wears a necklace made from shark cartilage. "Those ships throw their garbage overboard and the sharks must follow it in."

There's a fortune to be made from sharks, Swint says enthusiastically, and he is just now looking into that prospect. A world record shark, he says, will be worth $1.5 million from endorsements from tackle businesses. A nine-foot shark, he says, is worth $5,000 if correctly processed.

A 200-pound shark will yield 190 pounds of delicious meat, he says. "But the trouble is nobody does it right," he said. "Lot of guys shoot sharks before they land them. Even from the Skyway. You kill a shark and you ruin it. Their bladders explode and the flesh will be contaminated by urine."

Swint lands sharks alive and immediately removes internal organs. He says he sells the flesh to private parties for $1 a pound. He also tans the hides, he says, and sells them to people who use them to make women's apparel, belts and wallets. From the jaws of a large shark he can make 300 necklaces, which sell for $9 each, he says. He can make five canes, at $40 each, from the backbone cartilage.

But Swint has more than a mercenary interest in sharks. "I would rather fight a shark then any other fish," he said. "There's something special about them."

The shark expeditions begin before dark, when Swint drives his aging, odiferous station wagon—he transports dead sharks on the roof—to the Skyway. He stops the car near the main span—"This is dangerous and illegal. I've been fined $25 for doing it"—and unloads four fishing rods, a large tackle box, two buckets, rope, a bridge gaff, pads, a jug of Kool-Aid and two gasoline lanterns. He unloads his car in less than a minute. Then he drives to the end of the bridge, parks, and walks a mile back.

When it gets dark, Swint ties a lantern to the bridge and dangles it six inches above the water. The light attracts small fish, which Swint catches on a spinning rod. He uses the small fish for bait to catch ladyfish, which in turn are used to entice the sharks on his big outfit, a size 16/0 reel that sits on a rod as thick as a broomstick. The rod and reel, which Swint bought after eight months of studying sharks, weighs 25 pounds. He says he paid $1,200 for it.

To get his bait away from the bridge, he ties a balloon to the line with thread. The balloon drifts with the tide away from the bridge. When the bait is carried a sufficient distance, Swint pulls hard on his fishing rod and the balloon breaks loose. The bait sinks to the bottom.

"It's never boring out here," Swint said. "I can catch ladyfish all night while I wait for a shark run. Sometimes I catch tarpon. I've caught tarpon, boy. I've gotten exactly 72 this year. They swim right under my lantern sometimes. But I break off tarpon, or cobia, or grouper, or snook—whatever I might have on—if I hear my big rod going out. There's nothing like a shark."

The hardest part of catching a big shark from the bridge is landing it. The fight, Swint says, is often short. He lets sharks tire themselves out, then reels them in. But when he pulls them to the bridge, the work begins.

He first drops a rope around the tail of the shark—that often takes some nifty maneuvering; the shark won't cooperate—and hoists it from the water. When he can't lift it higher, he ties the rope to the bridge. Then he loops another rope around the head of the shark and lifts. When he can't pull that any higher, he lifts the tail rope. "It works like a winch," Swint said. "I've pulled 300 pounders in by myself."

Last September 24 he caught a shark he couldn't work himself. But he was lucky that night. He was fishing from the jetty of Pass-a-Grille. It took him 45 minutes to reel in the tiger shark, estimated to weigh 970 pounds. Swint tied it to the jetty, but he wasn't strong enough to bring it in.

Swint phoned a towing service for help, he says. The first three towing services did not believe him. "I told the fourth service that my car was broken down," Swint said. "When the guy arrived, I told him my car was okay but I needed some help down on the jetty. He pulled up my shark."

Last summer Swint says he lived four days on the Skyway. He slept during the day on the sidewalk. Old Hitler never touched his baits.

—*The St. Petersburg Times*

Disco Does Wonders For Radio Station

by Geoff Walden

New York—Last July 24th, at 5:59 p.m., WKTU-FM, "Mellow 92," was playing Neil Young's soft-rock song, "It's Over."

At 6:00 p.m., WKTU-FM, "The new, Disco 92," was playing Donna Summer's The Last Dance."

For Donna Summer, the song went on to win this year's Oscar for Best Original Song, for the movie, "Thank God It's Friday." For the radio station, the song was the start of the all-disco format that has made WKTU the most-listened to station in America, with an average of 275,000 people tuning in every quarter hour.

As Mellow 92, WKTU had about a 2 percent share of New York's radio audience according to Michael Ellis, who selects the station's music. That meant that 20 stations in New York alone had more listeners than WKTU, Ellis said.

As of February (the latest figure), Disco 92's New York audience share was 10.3 percent, higher than the country's perennial radio leader, New York's all-top-40 station, WABC-AM.

"It was the first double-digit share for a New York station in several years," Ellis said.

Six months after WKTU went all-disco, its ad rates had more than quadrupled, from $60 to $280 per minute.

Other stations around the country have caught "Saturday Night Fever," too, but "their results have been uneven," Ellis said. He believes that "New York is the disco capital of the world," and there are many reasons for the music's failure to beat as loudly in other cities. He thinks a city has to be fast-paced, heavily urbanized and ethnic for disco to command a large share of its radio market.

"The Sun Belt is less receptive to disco than the Snow Belt, with the exception of Miami, which is probably one of the two or three biggest disco markets," he said. Miami, he explained, has a large Cuban population, which like New York's Puerto Rican community, is keeping time to disco's pulse.

But Ellis cautioned against looking upon disco as an ethnic phenomenon. "Disco crosses race, class and age," he said, adding that older people like disco better than rock. He thinks WKTU is the number-one station among listeners as old as 50.

Ellis sees the origin of disco's popularity as a rebellion from rock's increasing sophistication.

"Rock was exciting when it was new in the '60's, and you had superstar groups," he said. "But when it matured, it got artistic and esoteric. It was higher-quality music, but it was losing its common touch.

"Punk and disco broke with rock. They were throwbacks to simpler beats, and they were more accessible. But punk didn't catch on, because it was too anti-social. Disco never threatened anybody."

Disco has become so popular in New York that two other major stations besides WKTU are thriving by pumping out disco refrains (one is WABC, which has changed its format to majority disco).

Ellis foresees more disco stations arising nationwide, and he advocates WKTU's setup for them.

The format is relaxed and informal. The disc jockeys avoid "radio" voices, and they trade banter with the newscasters. Newscasts are held to 92 seconds. DJ's occasionally announce, "You're listening to America's No. 1 station," but on the air WKTU generally understates its success. The setup is almost diametrically opposite to the frantic, jingle-filled style of WABC.

Also, WKTU plays no commercials from midnight to 5:30 a.m., and from 12:30 p.m. to 1:30 p.m., every day.

David Rapaport, the station's general manager, says that WKTU has the fewest ads of any successful commercial station in New York. "We believe too many commercials can lose your audience," he said. "We could be making considerably more money if we took more ads."

Marc Cichon, WKTU's operations director, says that the station's rise reflects the general ascendancy of FM.

"Originally, FM was heard only in homes and only by a limited audience," he said. "Now, more or less every new car has FM."

Cichon said that AM stations are as much concerned over the decline of their whole radio band, as they are over the fall of individual stations. He said that AM is going to test stereo transmission (it has always delivered monaural sound).

The question for WKTU, stereo FM, is, will disco keep in step with changing times?

Ellis answers, "I think disco will continue to be popular through the '80's. It's been growing since '73, and it has yet to peak."

—Columbia News Service

"I don't apologize for any of my work. I hate people putting down things they do. I hate the negativeness of apologizing. When I did each of the movies, I did them in good faith. If they didn't turn out so well, so what? I'll make more."

Beauty and Bisset: not just a pretty face

By MAL VINCENT
Virginian-Pilot Entertainment Editor

HOLLYWOOD—DON'T CALL Jacqueline Bisset beautiful. Not if you want to get along with her.

"I don't want to be a pinup," she says curtly, the famous gray-green eyes flashing. "I want to be something more than just an attractive woman. The public makes a mistake in labeling people that way."

Currently, Bisset is chairman of the board—even if she is the only person on the board—of Jacquet Productions. As such, she is co-producer of "Rich and Famous," the plush, expensively mounted new soap opera movie that stars her as a respected novelist who has affairs, sometimes casually, with younger men. The film, currently showing at the Lynnhaven and Circle 6 Theaters, gives Bisset what she calls "a chance to prove, once and for all, that I am capable of being a serious actress."

Although she thinks she has proved herself previously, she is aware that some critics haven't observed as much. "For some reason, critics like to take pot shots at me," she said. "In that way, my career has been similar to that of Candy Bergen, my costar. We've both had our knocks from the critics."

But Bisset isn't taking the situation without a fight. Since she has a plethora of offers to play gorgeous, glamorous beings, such as the ones she had in "The Greek Tycoon," "Who is Killing the Great Chefs of Europe?" "The Deep," "Airport," and "Murder on the Orient Express," she has decided to form her own company—primarily to produce films starring herself in serious roles.

"I'm the only asset the company has at the moment," she admitted. "There are no secretaries buzzing around. I do it all myself. I don't know enough yet."

She managed, quite adequately, though, to get the $10 million-plus remake of the old Bette Davis-Miriam Hopkins film "Old Acquaintance" (1943) produced at a time when many thought a film starring two women would be a risky box office gamble.

They simply don't make movie glamour girls the way they once did. When Rita Hayworth was the love goddess of the world, she simply took orders from Columbia's Harry Cohn and went from one exotic movie adventure to the next. Ava Gardner, often called one of the greatest screen beauties of all time, was forced to obey the orders of MGM, which shuffled her from one decorative part to the next——fulfilling the public demand that she do little other than look gorgeous.

Times have changed. Today, Jacqueline Bisset, age 37, knows what she wants and is taking matters into her own hands. "I don't want to do nudity, but it's not because of morals. It's more because I'm shy—physically. I mean, I don't think I have a great figure."

Her male fans, who are numerous, might disagree, especially those who remember a nude scene she did in a surfing movie called "The Sweet Ride" in 1968 or her steamy role as a bedhopping jetsetter in "The Grasshopper" in 1970. Those with shorter memories can drool over the highly publicized wet T-shirt scene in "The Deep" in 1977.

"Oh, yes. I knew you'd bring up 'The Deep,'" Bisset mused. "That was the very opposite of what we've been talking about. It didn't quite make for a ladylike image for me, did it? The whole thing was forced upon me. After all, that scene was shot under 60 feet of water. I was thinking more about surviving the whole thing than I was about how that T-shirt would look. Besides no one knew it would look that transparent underwater." (Does she really believe this? Yes, she appears to be serious.)

"'The Deep' did a lot of good for my career. It threw my career into a very public position, though, and that's not me."

☐ **Please see Bisset, Page B9**

Bisset not just a pretty face

☐ **Bisset, from Page B1**

Bisset is known to be paranoid about the press. TV host David Letterman says she is the most difficult interview he ever conducted. And our first encounter was not the rosiest.

It was on the set of "The Mephisto Waltz," a 1971 occult-thriller co-starring Alan Alda. "The name is Bisset. It rhymes with kiss it," was her opener. She was in a dither because the director of the film had just suggested that she do a semi-nude scene. Even though she had done such scenes before, she felt compromised because the requirement was not in her contract. At the time, she was widely publicized for her live-in relationship with actor Michael Sarrazin, who had a notable, if fleeting, career, particularly as Jane Fonda's costar in "They Shoot Horses, Don't They?" One question about him, and she bristled. Asking her about women's liberation did more harm.

"I have no intention of discussing women's rights with you," she announced. "You wouldn't agree with me." When advised that interviews are usually to get only her opinion, not that of the interviewer, she called her chauffeur and departed in a huff.

Ten years later, Jackie is more polite, perhaps because she has money invested in the new film. She does ban photographs during interviews, however. Like the glamour girls of old, she has approval of any pictures that are released to the press.

She prefers to talk about films she has made in Europe, such as Francois Truffaut's critically acclaimed "Day for Night," in which she played a screen glamour girl. "It's necessary to make big Hollywood films to keep your position and power within the industry," she said, "but I must occasionally run off to Italy or France and make a little picture. I have to do it. I have to emotionally play those parts."

She admittedly is irritated by having to talk to strangers who don't really know her. "I've made 35 movies and maybe they've seen me only in 'The Deep' or 'Bullitt.' It's hard to explain an entire person when all you know of them is maybe their toenail. When they try to be nice to me by saying I'm a star, it makes me crazy.

"I don't apologize for any of my work. I hate people putting down things they do. I hate the negativeness of apologizing. When I did each of the movies, I did them in good faith. If they didn't turn out so well, so what? I'll make more."

Jacqueline Fraser Bisset was born in Weybridge, England of Scottish-French-English parentage. "My mother wanted me to go to the university, but I wanted to be independent. Besides, they already had to pay my brother's school fees. My father sided with me and said that if I went to the university, I'd probably just end up getting married."

At 18, she became a photographer's model. By the mid-'60s, she was playing sexy bits in British films, then went to Hollywood where she was groomed as a starlet and became an international star as Frank Sinatra's leading lady in the 1968 movie "The Detective." She scored again that same year by costarring with Steve McQueen in "Bullitt."

One of her teachers at 20th Century-Fox studios in those early years was George Cukor, the famed "woman's director" who has directed everyone from Greta Garbo to Katharine Hepburn. "He was tough back then. He was very much in charge on 'Rich and Famous' too. He's a master at pacing and at handling pauses. He'd say to us 'move at a good pace girls. Faster, ladies.'"

Cukor, 82, has been the subject of recent controversy when published reports claimed that Bisset actually directed "Rich and Famous" to suit herself and that he merely was a decorative fixture on the set. She denies this. "Making a movie is a collaborative effort. Who can say where one job started and another stopped? I made my contribution, but not as a director. I do hope to be a director someday, but it wasn't on this film."

Candice Bergen was chosen, with Bisset's approval, for the costarring role of a Southern girl who is a lifelong friend and rival. "Candy is such a mixture of vulnerability and strength," Bisset said. "She's a very, very, funny woman. I'm surprised that she hasn't been playing comedy all these years. But then, she is so beautiful. People think beautiful women can't be funny. Anyway, this is a great comedy role for her. She speaks French too. When I was growing up, we always spoke French in my home. I immediately feel close to someone who speaks French."

Critics have pointed out that the characters played by Jackie and Candy seem directly opposite, and that audiences may well question how these two would remain friends. "I think they never would have been friends at all if they hadn't been roommates in college," Bisset said. "Candy plays a straightforward person and I play a sophisticate. We'd both like to be like each other. Friendship is inexplanable. One may well wonder why any of our friends put up with us."

As for analyzing herself, Bisset, in a rare, revealing mood, pondered and said: "I have this bourgeois, middle-class, streak in me. It's in conflict with the rest of me. On the one hand, I'm free. On the other hand, these bourgeois attitudes envelope me. I'm constantly fluctuating between the two."

She seems cool, collected, haughty and very much in charge. The beauty who's going to beat the system.

But her double standards rear their heads again in a parting zinger that contradicts the pat personality we think we've perceived.

When asked what is most difficult about her job, she answers: "Putting on my makeup in the morning. It's a tremendous effort to reach the level of looks that people expect from me. There's a conscious effort not to disappoint people."

The curse of beauty lives on. Long may it live.

Smathers Learns to Live with a Background Deep in Politics

Chapter 13

by Howell Raines

TALLAHASSEE—Will the son also rise?

That question hangs like a storm cloud over Florida Secretary of State Bruce A. Smathers, whose role as a public official seems almost incidental to his larger role as son and political heir of George A. Smathers, former U.S. senator, intimate of presidents and a bigtime Miami-Washington lawyer.

As he sits in a state capitol where he is widely regarded as the bumbling puppet of his father's ambition, Bruce Smathers says he has, at 33, learned to live with the heavy burden of his sonship.

"I finally figured out that whatever I do or however far I go in public office that'll always be there," he reflected. "I think of John Kennedy and all the talk that whatever he did, his father was in the background pulling the strings. I don't think he ever got over that. It's just something you live with."

Living with the Smathers political legacy is not easy, if you listen to the talk around Tallahassee and within the secretary of state's own staff. As long as a year ago, the senior Smathers was pushing his son to jump into the 1978 governor's race, a former adviser confided. "He's very ambitious for his son."

Bruce Smathers indicates that he is unsure what office he will seek in 1978 or, for that matter, in 1980, when the U.S. Senate seat he yearns for will be up for grabs. His political conversation seems based on one certainty, however: he must run because he is who he is.

Yet the legacy George Smathers created for his son is not an unmixed blessing politically. In his four years in the U.S. House and 18 years in Congress, George Smathers established a reputa-

tion as a man who never hesitated to backstab a friend for political advantage.

As a result, many in Florida politics would delight in visiting the sins of the father upon the son, and political circles fairly buzz with cruel jokes.

The handsome young man sipping coffee in the rather grand office Florida taxpayers provide the secretary of state seems an unlikely target for all this random vilification. With his fawn eyes and unlined face, he has more in common with Bambi than with the rapacious roebucks normally encountered in the political forests of Tallahassee.

Yes, Bruce Smathers says, smiling, he knows about those jokes that he is indecisive, that he would starve to death in a cafeteria line trying to choose between the Salisbury steak and the Spanish mackerel.

That rap, as Smathers tells it, is the price he must pay for having a trained mind and an introspective nature.

"I have almost a repulsion of the easy answer," he says, and one hears in the scholarly tone echoes of Yale, where he won honors in economics. "The easy answer reads well. You get a lot of attention and a headline. But the easy answer may not be the best answer."

Smathers' critics put it less kindly. The world had decided that Panhandle blacks Freddie Pitts and Wilbert Lee had been wrongly convicted of murder but Smathers could not make up his mind to sign the pardon. He agonized for months over the Florida barge canal. Even Gov. Reubin Askew, notorious for his forebearance, has been known to joke about Smathers' leisurely decision-making.

"The complaint that has always been made of me," Smathers continued, "even within my own family, was that I always gave a complicated answer to any question. My father used to kid me that if you ever go into politics, you're going to be like Adlai Stevenson, who, when asked a question, explores every alternative."

There it is again—the family, father, the anchors of Bruce Smathers' existence, for better or worse. "I've often told him," said Assistant Secretary of State David McNamara, 'Bruce, if you were a foot shorter, had your brother's looks and another name, you'd be standing in the line looking for a job.' "

That judgment, which sounds harsh, is offered in affection. At 53, after a lifetime of "having worked for politicians in the servant role," he thinks that Bruce Smathers is the hottest political talent in Florida—a "well packaged" natural vote-getter.

McNamara gave up his job as city clerk of Jacksonville to serve as Smathers' chief of staff and political mentor. There is no escaping the feeling that McNamara fills another role, that he has been sent over by the senator and his powerful allies in the old Ed Ball machine to serve as coach and surrogate father to Bruce Smathers. "We've been friends for a long time," McNamara replies obliquely when asked about his relationship with George Smathers. "We were in the Marines (together) . . ."

Whatever the relationship, Dave McNamara can provide insight into Bruce Smathers' upbringing. He is different from the other pols in Tallahassee because he grew up differently. He belongs to a special category of American princes—the children of wealth and power whose foreign travels were chaperoned by the American embassies, who dreamed in their Ivy League dorm rooms of going back home and getting into politics in the manner of, say, the Kennedys.

In so many ways comfortable, Bruce Smathers' world could also, as McNamara tells it, be harsh and demanding.

"His father sent Bruce and (brother) John off to get a good education," said McNamara. "He told them to make 'A's and keep their names out of the papers. Bruce and John never had to hustle dishes at the fraternity house, but their old man is so conservative that he didn't give them a nickel they didn't need. . . . Bruce and John went dutifully off to college and got a good education like they'd been told to do. Their old man is the kind that wouldn't hesitate to belt the hell out of either one of them."

Bruce Smathers recalls those years of youthful adventure with enthusiasm. There were good times with New York Timesman's "Scotty" Reston's sons in Mexico and Sweden, and the sweetness of his one major rebellion against his father, which was his enlistment in the Navy's underwater demolition service. But those years apparently left him with that sense of separateness that so often afflicts the children of the privileged in this democratic age.

"Bruce feels a sensitivity about being born with a silver spoon in his mouth," McNamara said. "Once he said that on a podium when I was with him, and I told him after his speech, 'Bruce, don't ever say that again. You don't have to apologize for who your parents are.' "

A desire to see how the other half lives apparently played a part in the major blunder of Bruce Smathers' political career. One evening during the 1974 campaign, he found himself rolling down the road in a motor home with Ku Klux Klan Imperial Wizard Bobby Shelton of Tuscaloosa, Ala., and Florida KKK chief John Paul Rogers.

Not even George C. Wallace, who likes Shelton and owes him political debts from the old days, hangs around with Shelton anymore. But there was Bruce Smathers of Yale and the Florida Law Review, traveler in 41 counties, speaker of Spanish along with some French and Italian, friend of the Kennedys. There he was with Bobby Shelton.

"That was an example of naïveté," said Smathers, who claims that he stumbled into the meeting. "I had never met a Klansman. Initially, it was interesting. You know, 'What does he think about?' Then after it's over, you think, 'Jesus'—pardon my language—'what a disaster.' And you want to just wipe it out, forget it ever happened."

In fact, Smathers did try to forget that meeting ever happened, initially denying to reporters that he had talked with the Klansmen. When he did acknowledge it, he said he had not told the truth in the first place because "I was tired."

It is a tribute to the power of the Smathers name that he survived that incident, which would have wiped out most other candidates. He went on to become, at 31, the youngest secretary of state in Florida history.

The curious thing about the Klan experience—if one accepts Smathers' contention that he stumbled into it—is that it fits a pattern of political clumsiness that has afflicted him since his days as a Jacksonville state senator.

Once he gave a pro-Israel speech there before an audience of Arab-Americans who sympathized with the Palestine liberation movement. Halfway through his speech, Smathers recalls with wonder in his voice, he had to be escorted out through a baying crowd that wanted to tear him limb from handsome limb.

Smathers strolls into embarrassing situations, a former aide said, because although "brilliant," he is also "spacey" and "absent-minded." Those who have guided his career so far are constantly "worried about him losing his brief case and looking like a bungler."

Appearances aside, even those who joke about Smathers' indecision concede that he has done a pretty good job of running the secretary of state's office, and that raises the onerous question of what to do in 1978.

That question does burden Smathers. He tries to dodge interviews where he thinks that the subject of the governor's race will come up and his staff has orders to carefully screen calls from reporters to find out what they want to talk about.

Officially, Smathers says, he is running for re-election. Yet the governor's race being urged by his father and, according to some reports, Mrs. Bruce Smathers, is a tantalizing possibility. Imagine, governor of Florida at 35. (Right now Smathers seems less attracted to the option of running for lieutenant governor as Atty. Gen. Robert I. Shevin's running mate. He does not think much of the job and key aides to gubernatorial candidate Shevin have a lively contempt for Smathers.)

McNamara, whose office connects to Smathers' through a door that is seldom closed, thinks that there is still plenty of time to pick the best shot, so formidable are his young charge's gifts.

"Some guys have such natural political skills, and that's where I put him. It's not contrived. He was born and raised in it. . . It's ridiculous to try to advise a guy like that. When the time comes, he'll know what to do and it'll be right."

Perhaps Smathers' political gifts are that great, but many who know politics as it is played at the top question whether this young man loves it enough or is hard enough. Most people who make it as high as governor or U.S. senator have something—a hunger, a fire in the gut, a toughness—that one can sense. It is not necessarily a good thing to have, but it is essential to winning and surviving in office.

That is not the picture of Bruce Smathers that emerges from a story once leaked from his office—an intimate of Smathers was quoted as saying, "Somebody offered him some money for a vote, and Smathers got up and went out of the room and threw up."

—*The St. Petersburg Times*

Chapter 15

New York Fights Youth Crime With Tough New Offender Law

by Richard Higgins

New York—Rafael Torres and Hector Valdez sat at the brown wooden table, playing Superman coloring books, combing their hair, waving and occasionally shouting to friends in the room.

It could have been a scene out of the South Bronx junior high school where they are enrolled in the eighth grade. But it was the beginning of an arson and multiple murder trial in the Bronx Criminal Courthouse and the two skinny, squirming boys were not there to learn; they were the defendants.

At night, the boys are taken to a special, isolated section of the city's sprawling jail on Rikers Island, where three dozen others await court appearances on charges from robbery to murder. They are all 13-to-15-year-old juveniles, children of the city's ghettos who have become symbols of New York's new effort to crack down on juvenile crime.

Their presence at Rikers is just one dramatic result of a new state law that sends 13-to-15-year-old juveniles accused of certain serious crimes directly into the adult court system. Until Sept. 1, 1978, when the new juvenile offender law took effect, youths under 16 were handled exclusively in Family Court. More than 600 juveniles have been arrested under the new law, one of the strictest in the nation.

The new law allows 13-year-olds charged with murder and 14- and 15-year-olds charged with murder and several other serious felonies—such as rape, arson, aggravated assault and robbery—to be tried as adults. Thus youths who are too young legally to buy liquor, vote, drive or even quit school can be sentenced to life in prison if convicted of murder.

Under the old law, the most Rafael Torres and Hector Valdez could have received in Family Court was 18 months in a secure facility of the State Division for Youth and three and one half years of supervision.

New York's new law is in step with a trend toward toughness in juvenile justice systems across the country. As violent youth crime increasingly disturbs the public, the 1960s quest for rehabilitation is giving way to strident demands for punishment. Two dozen states in recent years have enacted measures to beef up the punitive power of their juvenile courts or to permit the waiver of youths from juvenile to adult courts. Connecticut is now considering a bill similar to the New York law.

The juvenile offender law has sharply divided the state's criminal justice system since it was hastily passed in the wake of two brutal murders committed by 15-year-olds. In the midst of his then-faltering re-election campaign, Gov. Hugh Carey reversed his stand and embraced the law.

The city's district attorneys and police say the law was needed because youths under 16 were becoming heavily engaged in serious crime—even in heroin traffic and murder contracts—on the assumption that they had virtual "immunity" against significant punishment in Family Court.

State Senator Ralph J. Marino, a Long Island Republican and staunch backer of the new law, believes it was needed to halt "rampant youth crime" because the therapeutic orientation of Family Court wasn't working. "If these hoods commit adult crimes, let's treat 'em that way," he said. "It'll probably be good for 'em."

But civil libertarians and children's advocates have denounced the law as "Draconian" and "brutalizing," and charged that it particularly victimizes poor and minority youths.

"It's a demoralizing regression," commented Carol Sherman, a lawyer for the juvenile rights division of the New York Legal Aid Society, the chief defender of youths in court. "The notion that the city is being run rampant by murderous youths is a myth being exploited by politicians."

She pointed out that police arrests of juveniles for murder decreased from 110 in 1974 to 44 in 1978.

Under the juvenile offender law, youths whose cases start out in Criminal Court may be transferred at any point to Family Court, if the judge and prosecutor agree it "serves the interest of justice."

One reason the law has stirred so much controversy is that more than three-fourths of the juveniles arrested under it have had their cases transferred to Family Court or had charges against them dropped. The reason for this, say Legal Aid lawyers and, privately, some judges, is that police are bringing inflated charges.

"Typically, we're defending kids involved in schoolyard brawls, such as a 14-year-old beating up and stealing a radio or skateboard from a 13-year-old classmate," said Charles Schinitsky, attorney-in-charge of Legal Aid's juvenile rights division. Because such cases involve weapons or the use of force, they may be prosecuted as first degree robbery.

Schinitsky said such "nonsense cases" comprise about 80 percent of the juvenile offender cases. He charged that

hundreds of youths were being unnecessarily exposed to the adult court system, where, he said, they are "stigmatized as criminals."

City prosecutors hotly deny the charge, John J. O'Donnell, chief juvenile prosecutor in the Manhattan District Attorney's office, said many "so-called schoolyard brawls" involve vicious attacks and serious injuries. "Is it less criminal if the victim is another youth?" he asked.

Several Family Court judges have said they support a proposed amendment to the junvenile offender law that would start all youth cases in the Family Court, but allow only the most serious to be waived up to the Criminal Court. "It makes more sense that way," said Judge Edith Miller of the Manhattan Family Court.

Since Family Court remains confidential, youths whose cases do not belong in Criminal Court would be protected, Miller said. Other judges said such a move would save the state time and money.

The response of anti-crime Republicans in Albany to such a move is likely to be cool. Senator Marino's reply to such a change was terse: "Over my dead body. If anything, we'll beef it up." To the anxiety of Legal Aid lawyers that youths are being brutalized in court, Marino answers, "It's brutalizing to be stabbed."

Although New York prosecutors, like Bronx District Attorney Mario Merola, think that the new law is having a deterrent effect because "word has gone out on the streets that the old, easy days are over," many judges are not so sure. One Brooklyn Family Court judge said, "Either youth crime will decrease, or we'll start seeing 12-year-old drug runners and hit men."

—Columbia News Service

Dalton Mourns
Joseph Robins

DALTON — Joseph D. Robins, a well known flier and the most senior member of the Dalton Police Department, was buried Saturday in Ashuelot Street Cemetery following a Liturgy of Christian Burial at St. Agnes' Church.

His death at the age of 59 in a plane crash last week at the North Adams Airport has left this community shaken.

"This is a small department," said Police Chief Anthony Calabrese. "We are like a family here."

Since his death, officers have worn black bands on their badges. The flags at Town Hall and at Crane & Co. have flown at half mast.

A delegation of police and fire officers, led by Chief Calabrese, formed an honor guard at the funeral. The state police, Pittsfield Police, Dalton Fire Department and American Legion were represented. The bearers, all members of the Dalton Police Department, were Daniel Casey, Edward Croughwell Jr., Lawrence Higgins, Daniel Filiault, John Bartels and Dennis Croughwell.

All three Selectmen, William Moody, Thomas Callahan and William Glendon, attended the funeral as did representatives of Crane & Co., where Mr. Robins had been employed for 34 years as supervisor of maintenance at the stationery factory.

The flag that draped the casket was presented to Mrs. Robins, the former Marion Garneau of Hinsdale, by Fred Little and Eugene Trostle of the American Legion. The Rev. John Koonz, pastor of St. Agnes' Church, celebrated the liturgy and said the prayers at the grave.

Mr. Robins died Wednesday, April 22, when his single-engine Citabria struck several trees on the eastern approach to the North Adams Airport, went out of control and landed upside down just short of the runway. The plane immediately burst into flames, hampering any rescue efforts.

Investigators have ruled out mechanical failure as a cause of the crash and have relased the plane to co-owner John Fisher of East Greenbush, N.Y.

Many of those who knew Mr. Robins and flew with him are still at a loss to explain the accident.

"He was an overly safe pilot," said Jeffrey Moody, a frequent flying partner. "He wouldn't take a chance. If he knew a risk was there, he didn't want a part of it."

Mr. Moody, who was taught to fly by Mr. Robins, went on to say, "He loved flying for the pure and simple love of flying. He liked the peacefullness, the sense of command."

Mr. Robins, a pilot for more than 30 years and a flight instructor for much of that time, was flying to North Adams to meet George Kendall, owner of the Windsor Airport and Berkshire Hills Aviation.

Mr. Kendall, one of the first on the scene, said the pilot was coming into the airport behind one of his planes and may have altered his flight plan because of that.

"Because of the traffic, he slowed up a little. The trees were there and he was looking forward and he just couldn't see the trees," Mr. Kendall said. "For the first time he did something out of the normal, did something he never did before."

Mr. Kendall, who is a former Delta Airline pilot, learned how to fly from Mr. Robins when the Dalton Airport was still operating in the Pease Avenue area.

Mr. Kendall said the sun on Wednesday night was "the brightest I've ever seen." He said a combination of different factors led to the crash. Observers have said Mr. Robbins tried to climb back up, but failed in the attempt.

"If anyone could have pulled out of it Joe could have. He could land between matchsticks," Mr. Kendall said. "This time I couldn't get to him in time. He was an outstanding guy who no one will ever forget."

Continued To Page 12

Joe Robins

Continued From Page 1

In 1974, Mr. Robins landed in the trees while taking off from the Windsor Airport after the engine in his Piper Cub stalled. On that occasion, Mr. Kendall arrived on the scene with a ladder to aid the treed flier.

Mr. Robins learned to fly at Berkshire Aviation Enterprises in Great Barrington, following World War II. He worked there as a flight instructor and charter pilot and later at Mohawk Valley Airport in North Adams.

He was manager of the old Dalton Airport owned by Norm Bellanger and at one time kept as many as 16 planes there. With his brother William, he ran a flying school there. The Dalton Airport closed in 1953 and since then, Mr. Robins flew out of the Pittsfield Airport and later out of the Windsor Airport, a facility he helped build.

Mr. Robins was born in Pittsfield, son of Joseph Robins and the late Agnes Carroll Robins, who died in 1980.

He was educated in Dalton schools and was an Army veteran of World War II.

Mr. Robins, of 29 Otis Ave., had been employed by Crane & Co. for 34 years and as a reserve officer in the Police Department for 29 years.

He was a member of the Dalton American Legion, Deputy Sheriff's Association, Massachusetts Police Association and the Aircraft Pilots and Owners Association.

Joseph D. Robins

Mr. Robins was a communicant of St. Agnes' Church.

In addition to his wife and father, Mr. Robins is survived by a son, Michael J. Robins of Dalton; two daughters, Nancy Giglotti of Dalton and Joanne Clevenger of East Hampton; a brother, William Robins of Hinsdale and four grandchildren.

"He was my right hand man," said Thomas Sedgwick, superintendent of the stationery factory. "I don't know what I'll do without him."

sports

LONGMONT DAILY TIMES-CALL   WEEKEND, MARCH 28-29, 1981   19

Longmont survives Eagles' surge

By JOHN GUNN
Times-Call Staff Writer

Longmont pitcher Tim Fobes was in trouble in the seventh inning of the Trojans' 5-4 home-field win over Thompson Valley Friday afternoon. But coach Joe Brooks was not about to pull him out.

"I walked out and told him we were going to win or lose with Tim Fobes," Brooks said after the game. Fobes survived the ordeal, but a game that Longmont appeared to have in its pocket suddenly became interesting.

Fobes entered the game in the final inning in relief of Trojan ace Tim Valencia. Valencia was razor sharp in his first effort of the season, hurling one-hit baseball through six innings and striking out 13 Eagles.

But Thompson Valley's six innings of frustration were vented as the Eagles began making contact and scored four runs.

Thompson Valley inaugurated its rally when junior pitcher Dan Spare, who relieved starter Mark King in the sixth, stroked a single to center field. Spare stole second base and raced home when first baseman Mike Amundson doubled.

Amundson's hit advanced Eagle left-fielder Roger Collister, who had drawn a walk, to third base. Third baseman Scott Tilson then belted a Fobes pitch to deep left field that got some help from a stiff west wind and cleared the fence for a three-run homer.

But Longmont's defense stiffened. The next two batters flied and grounded out, preserving the save for Fobes.

The wind did not play favorites, however. Right fielder Ken Kissner, leading off the third for the Trojans, also clubbed a home run over the fence in left.

Kissner's shot put Longmont ahead 2-0. The hosts had gone ahead by a run in the first inning when Valencia, who went three-for-four with two runs batted in, brought second baseman John Rhoads home with a sharp single up the middle.

Longmont struck for its final three runs in the fourth. Kevin Haakensen tallied one when he scored from first after a base hit to left by Trojan shortstop Tom Fobes was misplayed by Collister. Kissner, two-for-three on the afternoon, later singled Fobes home and scored when Valencia doubled.

Valencia's pitching made the difference in the contest and Brooks was quick to acknowledge the senior's work.

"Valencia was pretty sharp and very quick with his fastball," the Longmont coach said. "He gave us a chance to get the game in hand. I haven't seen him throw that hard all spring."

The non-conference win put the Trojans, snowed out of their scheduled opener last weekend, at 1-0. Thompson Valley fell to 0-2.

Longmont is at home again this morning as the Trojans play host to North Denver at 10:30.

Appendix D
Code of Ethics

The following is a code of ethics published by the Society of Professional Journalists (Sigma Delta Chi, 1973):

The Society of Professional Journalists, Sigma Delta Chi, believes the duty of journalists is to serve the truth.

We believe the agencies of mass communication are carriers of public discussion and information, acting on their Constitutional mandate and freedom to learn and report the facts.

We believe in public the truth as part of the public's right to know the truth.

We believe those responsibilities carry obligations that require journalists to perform with intelligence, objectivity, accuracy, and fairness.

To these ends, we declare acceptance of the standards of practice here set forth:

RESPONSIBILITY: The public's right to know of events of public importance and interest in the overriding mission of the mass media. The purpose of distributing news and enlightened opinion is to serve the general welfare. Journalists who use their professional status as representatives of the public for selfish or other unworthy motives violate a high trust.

FREEDOM OF THE PRESS: Freedom of the press is to be guarded as an inalienable right of people in a free society. It carries with it the freedom and the responsibility to discuss, question, and challenge actions and utterances of our government and of our public and private institutions. Journalists uphold the right to speak unpopular opinions and the privilege to agree with the majority.

ETHICS: Journalists must be free of obligation to any interest other than the public's right to know the truth.

1. Gifts, favors, free travel, special treatment or privileges can compromise the integrity of journalists and their employers. Nothing of value should be accepted.

2. Secondary employment, political involvement, holding public office, and service in community organizations should be avoided if it compromises the integrity of journalists and their employers. Journalists and their employers should conduct their personal lives in a manner which protects them from conflict of interest, real or

apparent. Their responsibilities to the public are paramount. That is the nature of their profession.

3. So-called news communications from private sources should not be published or broadcast without substantiation of their claims to news value.

4. Journalists will seek news that serves the public interest, despite the obstacles. They will make constant efforts to assure that the public's business is conducted in public and that public records are open to public inspection.

5. Journalists acknowledge the newsman's ethic of protecting confidential sources of information.

ACCURACY AND OBJECTIVTY: Good faith with the public is the foundation of all worthy journalism.

1. Truth is our ultimate goal.

2. Objectivity in reporting the news is another goal, which serves as the mark of an experienced professional. It is a standard of performance toward which we strive. We honor those who achieve it.

3. There is no excuse for inaccuracies or lack of thoroughness.

4. Newspaper headlines should be fully warranted by the contents of the articles they accompany. Photographs and telecasts should give an accurate picture of an event and not highlight a minor incident out of context.

5. Sound practice makes clear distinction between news reports and expressions of opinion. News repots should be free of opinion or bias and represent all sides of an issue.

6. Partisanship in editorial comment which knowingly departs from the truth violates the spirit of American journalism.

7. Journalists recognize their responsibility for offering informed analysis, comment, and editorial opinion on public events and issues. They accept the obligation to present such material by individuals whose competence, experience, and judgment qualify them for it.

8. Special articles or presentations devoted to advocacy or the writer's own conclusions and interpretations should be labeled as such.

FAIR PLAY: Journalists at all times will show respect for the dignity, privacy, rights, and well-being of people encountered in the course of gathering and presenting the news.

1. The news media should not communicate unofficial charges affecting reputation or moral character without giving the accused a chance to reply.

2. The news media must guard against invading a person's right to privacy.

3. The media should not pander to morbid curiosity about details of vice and crime.

4. It is the duty of news media to make prompt and complete correction of their errors.
5. Journalists should be accountable to the public for their reports and the public should be encouaged to voice its grievances against the media. Open dialogue with our readers, viewers, and listeners should be fostered.

PLEDGE: Journalists should actively censure and try to prevent violations of these standards, and they should encourage their observance by all newspeople. Adherence to this code of ethics is intended to preserve the bond of mutual trust and respect between American journalists and the American people.

The codes have come about because of the realization that the press has enormous power and that this power can be abused, misused and misdirected. The codes are helpful, but no code can force a reporter or news writer to do anything. The choice between right and wrong is up to the individual.

Glossary

These definitions were provided by the press associations and working reporters and editors. Most of the brief entries are from the *New England Daily Newspaper Study,* an examination of 105 daily newspapers, edited by Loren Ghiglione (Southbridge, Mass.: Southbridge Evening News Inc., 1973).

Print Terms

add An addition to a story already written or in the process of being written.

assignment Instruction to a reporter to cover an event. An editor keeps an assignment book that contains notations for reporters such as the following:

> Jacobs—10 a.m.: Health officials tour new sewage treatment plant.
> Klaren—11 a.m.: Interview Ben Wastersen, possible Democratic congressional candidate.
> Mannen—Noon: Rotary Club luncheon speaker, Horlan, the numerologist. A feature?

attribution Designation of the person being quoted. Also, the source of information in a story. Sometimes, information is given on a not-for-attribution basis.

background Material in a story that gives the circumstances surrounding or preceding the event.

banger An exclamation point. Avoid. Let the reader do the exclaiming.

banner Headline across or near the top of all or most of a newspaper page. Also called a line, ribbon, streamer, screamer.

B copy Bottom section of a story written ahead of an event that will occur too close to deadline for the entire story to be processed. The B copy usually consists of background material.

beat Area assigned to a reporter for regular coverage. For example, police or city hall. Also, an exclusive story.

body type Type in which most of a newspaper is set, usually 8 or 9 point type.

boldface Heavy, black typeface; type that is blacker than the text with which it is used. Abbreviated bf.

break When a news development becomes known and available. Also, the point of interruption in a story continued from one page to another.

bright Short, amusing story.

bulldog Early edition, usually the first of a newspaper.

byline Name of the reporter who wrote the story, placed atop the published article. An old-timer comments on the current use of bylines. "In the old days, a reporter was given a byline if he or she personally covered an important or unusual story, or the story was an exclusive. Sometimes if the writing was superior, a byline was given. Nowadays, everyone gets a byline, even if the story is a rewrite and the reporter never saw the event described in the story."

canned material See boiler plate.

caps Capital letters; same as uppercase.

caps and lower case Initial capital in a word followed by small letters. See lowercase.

clip News story clipped from a newspaper, usually for future reference.

closeup (broadcast) Shot of the face of the subject that dominates the frame so that little background is visible.

cold type In composition, type set photographically or by pasting up letters and pictures on acetate or paper.

column The vertical division of the news page. A standard-size newspaper is divided into five to eight columns. Also, a signed article of opinion or strong personal expression, frequently by an authority or expert—a sports column, a medical column, political or social commentary, and the like.

copy Written form in which a news story or other material is prepared.

copy desk The desk, often horseshoe in shape, around which copy editors sit to read copy. The slot man sits inside the horseshoe and is in charge of the desk. (For newspapers that use copy paper and edit with pencil.)

copy flow After a reporter finishes a story, it moves to the city desk where the city editor reads it for major errors or problems. If it does not need further work, the story is moved to the copy desk for final editing and a headline. It then moves to the mechanical department.

correction Errors that reach publication are retracted or corrected if they are serious or someone demands a correction. Libelous matter is always corrected immediately, often in a separate news story rather than in the standard box assigned to corrections.

correspondent Reporter who sends news from outside a newspaper office. On smaller papers often not a regular fulltime staff member.

crony journalism Reporting that ignores or treats lightly negative news about friends of a reporter. Beat reporters sometimes have a tendency to protect their informants in order to retain them as sources.

crop To cut or mask the unwanted portions, usually of a photograph.

cut Printed picture or illustration. Also, to eliminate material from a story. See trim.

cutline Any descriptive or explanatory material under a picture.

dateline Name of the city or town and sometimes the date at the start of a story that is not of local origin.

deadline Time at which the copy for an edition must be ready.

dirty copy Matter for publication that needs extensive correction, usually because the reporter has made indecipherable markings on copy.

edition One version of a newspaper. Some papers have one edition a day, some several. Not to be confused with issue, which usually refers to all editions under a single date.

editorial Article of comment or opinion usually on the editorial page.

editorial material All material in the newspaper that is not advertising.

enterprise copy Story, often initiated by a reporter, that digs deeper than the usual news story.

exclusive Story one reporter has obtained to the exclusion of the competition. A beat. Popularly known as a scoop, a term never used in the newsroom.

feature Story emphasizing the human or entertaining aspects of a situation. A news story or other material differentiated from straight news. As a verb, it means to give prominence to a story.

file To send a story to the office, usually by wire or telephone, or to put news service stories on the wire.

filler Material used to fill space. Small items used to fill out columns where needed. Also called column closers and shorts.

flag Printed title of a newspaper on page one. Also known as logotype or nameplate.

free advertising Use of the names of businesses and products not essential to the story. Instead of the brand name, use the broad term camera for Leica or Kodak.

futures calendar Date book in which story ideas, meetings and activities scheduled for a later occurrence are listed. Also known as a futures book. Kept by city and assignment editors and by careful reporters.

good night Before leaving for the day, beat reporters check in with the desk and are given a good night, which means there is nothing further for the reporter from the desk for the day. On some newspapers, the call is made for the lunch break, too. Desks need to know where their reporters are in case of breaking stories.

graf Abbreviation for paragraph.

Guild Newspaper Guild, an international union to which reporters and other newspaper workers belong. Newspapers that have contracts with the Guild are said to be "organized."

handout Term for written publicity or special-interest news sent to a newspaper for publication.

hard news Spot news; live and current news in contrast to features.

head or headline The display type over a printed news story.

head shot Picture featuring little more than the head and shoulders of the person shown.

HFR Abbreviation for "hold for release." Material that cannot be used until it is released by the source or at a designated time. Also known as embargoed material.

identification Personal data used to identify a person: name, title (if any), age, address, occupation, education, race, religion, ethnicity. The identifying characteristics used are those relevant to the story. Generally, we use name, age, occupation, address. To lend authority to the observations or statements of sources, we give their background.

Racial Identification

Figure G1

One editor's guidelines:
1. Use racial identification in a story that tells about the achievement of the race or some member of the race.
2. Use racial identification when the point of the news story hinges upon race.
3. Do not use racial identification in minor crime news.
4. Do not use racial identification in news stories that reflect discredit upon the whole race, or tend to discredit the whole race.

Race, religion, and ethnicity are used infrequently and are subject to continuing discussion. (See Figure G1.) In obituaries and crime stories, the readers want as much identification as possible. In general news stories, logic should indicate relevancy: Toledo readers are not interested in the home address of the North Carolina senator who collapses in a hotel and dies. But the newspaper in his home town of Raleigh will insert the address in the press association copy.

insert Material placed between copy in a story. Usually, a paragraph or more to be placed in material already sent to the desk.

investigative reporting Technique used to unearth information sources often want hidden. This type of reporting involves examination of documents and records, the cultivation of informants, painstaking and extended research. Investigative reporting usually seeks to expose wrongdoing and has concentrated on public officials and their activities. In recent years, industry and business have been scrutinized. Some journalists contend that the term is redundant, that all good reporting is investigative, that behind every surface fact is the real story that a resourceful, curious and persistent reporter can dig up.

italics Type in which letters and characters slant to the right.

jump Continuation of a story from one page to another. As a verb, to continue material. Also called runover.

kill To delete a section from copy or to discard the entire story; also, to spike a story.

lead (pronounced leed) First paragraph in news story. In a direct or straight news lead it summarizes the main facts. In a delayed lead, usually used on feature stories, it evokes a scene or sets a mood.
Also used to refer to the main idea of a story: An editor will ask a reporter, "What's the lead on the piece?" expecting a quick summary of the main facts.

Also: A tip on a story; an idea for a story. A source will tell a reporter, "I have a lead on a story for you." In turn, the reporter will tell the editor, "I have a lead on a story that may develop."

localize Emphasizing the names of persons from the local community who are involved in events outside the city or region: A local couple rescued in a Paris hotel fire; the city police chief who speaks at a national conference.

lowercase Small letters, as contrasted to capitals.

LTK Designation on copy for "lead to come." Usually placed after the slug. Indicates the written material will be given a lead later.

makeup Layout or design. The arrangement of body type, headlines and illustrations into pages.

masthead Formal statement of a newspaper's name, officers, place of publication and other descriptive information, usually on the editorial page. Sometimes confused wtih flag or nameplate.

morgue Newspaper library.

mug shot See head shot.

new lead See running story.

news hole Space in a newspaper allotted to news, illustrations and other nonadvertising material.

obituary Account of a person's death; also called obit.

offset Printing process in which an image is transferred from a printing plate to a rubber roller and then set off on paper.

off the record Material offered the reporter in confidence. If the reporter accepts the material with this understanding, it cannot be used except as general background in a later story. Some reporters never accept off-the-record material. Some reporters will accept the material with the provision that if they can obtain the information elsewhere they will use it. Reporters who learn of off-the-record material from other than the original source can use it.

No public, official meeting can be off the record, and almost all official documents (court records, police information) are public information. Private groups can ask that their meetings be kept off the record, but reporters frequently ignore such requests when the meeting is public or large numbers of persons are present.

op-ed page Abbreviation for the page opposite the editorial page. The page is frequently devoted to opinion columns and related illustrations.

overnight Story usually written late at night for the afternoon newspapers of the next day. Most often used by the press services. The overnight, or overnighter, usually has little new information in it but is cleverly written so that the reader thinks the story is new. Also known as second-day stories.

play Emphasis given to a news story or picture—size and place in the newspaper of the story; typeface and size of headline.

P.M. Afternoon or evening newspaper.

pool Arrangement whereby limited numbers of reporters and photographers are selected to represent all those assigned to the story. Pooling is adopted when a large number of persons would overwhelm the event or alter its nature. The news and film are shared with the rest of the press corps.

press release Publicity handout, or a story given to the news media for publication.

proof Reproduction of type on paper for the purpose of making corrections or alterations.

puff or puffery Publicity story or a story that contains unwarranted superlatives.

quotes Quotation marks; also a part of a story in which someone is directly quoted.

rewrite To write for a second time to strengthen a story or to condense it.

rewrite man Person who takes the facts of stories over the telephone and then puts them together into a story and who may rewrite reporters' stories.

rowback A story that attempts to correct a previous story without indicating that the prior story had been in error or without taking responsibility for the error.

running story Event that develops and is covered over a period of time. For an event covered in subsequent editions of a newspaper or on a single cycle of a wire service, additional material is handled as follows:

New lead—Important new information;
Add and insert—Less important information;
Sub—Material that replaces dated material, which is removed.

sell Presentation a reporter makes to impress the editor with the importance of his or her story; also, editors sell stories to their superiors at news conferences.

shirttail Short, related story adapted to the end of a longer one.

short Filler, generally of some current news value.

situationer Story that pulls together a continuing event for the reader who may not have kept track as it unfolded. The situationer is helpful with complex or technical developments or on stories with varied datelines and participants.

slant To write a story so as to influence the reader's thinking. To editorialize, to color or misrepresent.

slug Word or words placed on all copy to identify the story.

source Person, record, document or event that provides the information for the story.

source book Alphabetical listing, by name and by title, of the addresses and the office and home telephone numbers of persons on the reporter's beat and some general numbers—FBI agent in charge in town, police and fire department spokesmen, hospital information, weather bureau.

spike Six-inch long nail on which stories are placed for later use or because they are rejected. "Spike it," means to kill a story. Stories put "on the hook" are rejected.

split page Front page of an inside section; also known as the break page, second front page.

stringer Correspondent, not a regular staff member, who is paid by the story or by the number of words written.

style Rules for capitalization, punctuation and spelling that standardize usage so that the material presented is uniform. Most newspapers and stations have stylebooks. The most frequently used is the common stylebook of the United Press International and the Associated Press.

stylebook Specific listing of the conventions of spelling, abbreviation, punctuation, capitalization used by a particular newspaper, wire service. Broadcast stylebooks include pronunciations.

sub See running story.

subhead One-line and sometimes two-line head (usually in boldface body type) inserted in a long story at intervals for emphasis or to break up a long column of type.

take Page of copy, also known as a book.

text Verbatim report of a speech or public statement.

thumbnail Half column-wide cut or portrait.

tight Full, too full. Also refers to a paper so crowded with ads that the news space must be reduced. It is the opposite of the wide open paper.

tip Information passed to a reporter, often in confidence. The material usually requires further fact gathering. Occasionally, verification is impossible and the reporter must decide whether to go with the tip on the strength of the insider's knowledge. Sometimes the reporter will not want to seek confirmation for fear of alerting sources who will alter the situation or release the information to the competition. Tips often lead to exclusives.

titles Mr., Mrs., Miss, Ms., Secretary of State, Police Chief, Senator are formal designations and may be used before the person's name. Usage depends upon the station's or newspaper's policy. False titles—Vietnam war hero, actress, left fielder—are properly used after the name: For instance, Nate Thurmond, the center . . . instead of Center Nate Thurmond. . .

trim to reduce or condense copy carefully.

update Story that brings the reader up to date on a situation or personality previously in the news. If the state legislature appropriated additional funds for five new criminal court judges to meet the increased number of cases in the courts an update might be written some months later to see how many more cases were handled after the judges went to work. An update usually has no hard news angle.

VDT Video display terminal, a part of the electronic system used in news and advertising departments that eliminates typewriters. Copy is written on typewriterlike keyboards and words appear on attached television screens rather than on paper. The story is stored on a disc in a computer. Editing is done on the terminals.

verification Determination of the truth of the material the reporter gathers or is given. The assertions, sometimes even the actual observation, do not necessarily mean the information is accurate or true. Some of the basic tools of verification are: the telephone book, for names and addresses; the city directory, for occupations; *Who's Who,* for biographical information. For verification of more complex material, the procedure of Thucydides, the Greek historian and author of the *History of the Peloponnesian War,* is good advice for the journalist: "As to the deeds done in the war, I have not thought myself at liberty to record them on hearsay from the first informant or on arbitrary conjecture. My account rests either on personal knowledge or on the closest possible scrutiny of each statement made by others. The process of research was laborious, because the conflicting accounts were given by those who had witnessed the several events, as partiality swayed or memory served them."

wire services Synonym for press associations, the Associated Press and United Press International. There are foreign-owned press services to which some newspapers subscribe: Reuters, Tass, Agence France Presse.

Broadcast Terms

actuality An on-the-scene report.

audio Sound.

cover shot A long shot usually cut in at the beginning of a sequence to establish place or location.

cue A signal in script or by word or gesture to begin or to stop. Two types: incue and outcue.

cut Quick transition from one type of picture to another. Radio: a portion of an actuality on tape used on broadcast.

cutaway Transition shot—usually short—from one theme to another, used to avoid jump cut. Often a shot of the interviewer listening.

dissolve Smooth fading of one picture for another. As the second shot becomes distinct, the first slowly disappears.

dolly Camera platform. Dolly-in: move platform toward subject. Dolly-out: move platform away.

dub The transfer of one video tape to another.

FI or **fade in** A scene that begins without full brilliance and gradually assumes full brightness. **FO** or **fade out** is the opposite.

freeze frame A single frame that is frozen into position.

graphics All visual displays, such as art work, maps, charts and still photos.

jump cut Transition from one subject to a different subject in an abrupt manner. Avoided with cutaway shot between the scenes.

mix Combining two or more sound elements into one.

montage A series of brief shots of various subjects to give a single impression or communicate one idea.

O/C On camera. A reporter delivering copy directly to the camera without covering pictures.

outtakes Scenes that are discarded for the final story.

pan or **pan shot**   Moving the camera from left to right or right to left.

remote   A taped or live broadcast from a location outside the studio. Also, the unit that originates such a broadcast.

segúe   An uninterrupted transition from one sound to another; a sound dissolve. (Pronounced seg-way.)

SOF   Sound on film. Recorded simultaneously with the picture.

SOT   Sound on tape. Record simultaneously with picture on tape.

trim   To eliminate material.

V/O   Reporter's voice over pictures.

VTR   Video tape recording.

zoom   Use of a variable focus lens to take closeups and wide angle shots from a stationary position. By using a zoom lens an impression can be given of moving closer or farther away from the subect.

Credits

Photos

(left): Bernard Drew, *The Dalton News-Record;* (top right): © 1981 Worcester Telegram & Gazette, Inc.; (bottom right): *The Evening and Sunday Bulletin.*

p. 4: John Titchen of the *Star-Bulletin,* Honolulu; p. 8: Hong Kong Government Information Services, © 1981. Used with permission; p. 9 (top): Guy Liu/UPI; p. 9 (bottom): Arthur Tsang/UPI; p. 13: CBS News Photo; p. 15 (top): Melvin Mencher; p. 15 (bottom): Bernard Drew, *The Dalton News-Record;* p. 19: Susan Plageman, *The Berkshire Eagle;* pp. 21, 23: *The Providence Journal-Bulletin.* Photo by Bob Thayer.

pp. 32, 33: Wide World Photos, Inc.; p. 36: Melvin Mencher; p. 37: Ken Elkins, *The Anniston Star;* pp. 46, 47: © 1980 Larry C. Price/*Fort Worth Star-Telegram.*

p. 53: ABC NEWS; p. 54: Joel Librizzi, *The Berkshire Eagle;* pp. 57, 61: Jack Kirkland, The *Knoxville News-Sentinel;* p. 59 (top): Joseph Noble, *The Stuart News;* p. 59 (bottom): Pepperdine University; p. 65: Jack Kightlinger, The White House; p. 68 (top): Susan Plageman, *The Berkshire Eagle;* p. 68 (bottom): Jess Andresen, The *Daily News Tribune;* p. 69: Stewart Bowman, *The Courier Journal and Louisville Times Co.;* p. 71: Ken Elkins, *The Anniston Star;* pp. 76, 77: *The Free Press* (Mankato, MN); p. 78: *The Wall Street Journal;* p. 80: Ruben Ramirez, *El Paso Herald-Post.*

(left): Leslie Jean-Bart; (top right): Melvin Mencher; (bottom right): *New York Daily News* photo by Michael Lipak.

p. 89 (top): Perry Werner, *The Hays Daily News;* p. 89 (bottom left): *The Providence Journal-Bulletin.* Photo by Bob Thayer; p. 89 (bottom right): Melvin Mencher; p. 90: Jeff Widener, *The Evansville Press;* p. 91 (top left and right): Joe Luper, Pepperdine University; p. 91 (bottom): Bill Wright, Pepperdine University; pp. 95, 98, 101: Terry Keys, *The Kentuckian;* p. 105: Jean Pierre Rivest.

p. 111: Robert Dikerson of *The Cincinnati Post;* p. 118 (top and middle): Pepperdine University; p. 118 (bottom left): Terry Keys, *The Kentuckian;* p. 118 (bottom right): Joe Luper, Pepperdine University; p. 119: Stewart Bowman, *The Louisville Times.*

Part One

Chapter 1

Chapter 2

Chapter 3

Part Two

Chapter 4

Chapter 5

Part Three   (top right): R. Gene Gaillard, *Greenville News;* (bottom right): Ruben Ramirez, *El Paso Herald-Post.*

Chapter 6   p. 132 (top): Pepperdine University; p. 132: Warner Brother Records; p. 133 (top left): Alex Robertson, Pepperdine University; p. 133 (bottom): Joe Luper, Pepperdine University; p. 135: Jean Pierre Rivest, *The Gazette* of Montreal; p. 143: Al Cabral, *Albuquerque Tribune.*

Chapter 7   p. 151: Terry Keys, *The Kentuckian;* p. 153 (left): Joe Luper, Pepperdine University; p. 153 (right): Pepperdine University; p. 157: Rafael Trias, *The San Juan Star;* p. 159: Terry Keys, *The Kentuckian;* p. 164: Robert Burke, *The Sunday Courier and Press;* p. 166: Stewart Bowman, *The Courier-Journal.*

Chapter 8   p. 184 (top): Mona Oxford, Pepperdine University; p. 184 (bottom left): Leslie Jean-Bart; p. 184 (bottom right): *The St. Petersburg Times;* p. 185 (top): Kathy Strong, Pepperdine University; p. 185 (bottom): Terry Keys, *The Kentuckian.*

Chapter 9   p. 201: Susan Plageman, *The Berkshire Eagle;* p. 205: Stewart Bowman, *The Courier-Journal;* p. 209: Thomas L. Brossart, *The Daily News;* p. 228: Douglas Hand, *Country Journal.*

Chapter 10   p. 252 (top left), p. 253 (top): Joe Luper, Pepperdine University; p. 252 (bottom left): Bill Wright, Pepperdine University; p. 252 (right): Terry Keys, *The Kentuckian;* p. 253 (bottom left): Terry Keys, *The Kentuckian;* p. 253 (bottom right): Bill Wright, Pepperdine University.

Chapter 11   p. 272: *New York Daily News,* photo by Michael Lipak; p. 273: The Hartford Ballet; p. 274: Al Cabral, *Albuquerque Tribune.*

Chapter 12   pp. 284, 294 (top): Karen Clark; pp. 294 (bottom), 295: ABC NEWS.

Part Four   (left): James Madison University; (top right): *The Hays Daily News;* (bottom right): Karl Schumacher, The White House.

Chapter 13   p. 304: *The Hays Daily News;* p. 316: *The St. Petersburg Times.*

Chapter 15   pp. 339, 358: Susan Plageman, *The Berkshire Eagle;* p. 379 (top): Richard Childress, *The Baltimore Sun;* p. 379 (bottom): Stewart Bowman, *The Courier-Journal.*

Part Five   (left): Terry Keys, *The Kentuckian;* (top right): *Editor and Publisher;* (bottom right): Hank Reichard, *Columbus Citizen-Journal.*

Chapter 16   p. 400: *Editor and Publisher;* p. 401: William E. Vance, *The Orient,* Ball State University; p. 407: Hank Reichard, *Columbus Citizen-Journal.*

Appendix A   p. 412: Wayne Floyd, *The Lumberjack.*

Appendix C   p. 429: *Hollywood Sun-Tattler.*

Text and Line Art

Chapter 11	*The Philadelphia Bulletin:* Stories on pp. 264, 265–66. Used with permission. *Pantheon Books:* Story on p. 271 by Studs Terkel. *Working: People Talk About What They Do All Day and What They Think of While They Do It.* Copyright © 1972 by Pantheon Books, a Division of Random House, Inc. *Birmingham Post-Herald:* Story on pp. 275–79. Used with permission.
Chapter 12	*WSB-TV:* Figs. 12.1 and 12.2. Used with permission. *United Press International:* Story on p. 287. Reprinted by permission of United Press International. *CBS:* Fig. 12.3. Used with permission from CBS.
Part Four	*Associated Press:* Stories on pp. 300–301. Used with permission.
Chapter 13	*The Hays Daily News:* Fig. 13.1. Used with permission. *The Providence Journal-Bulletin:* Story on p. 307. Used with permission. *The Virginian-Pilot* (Norfolk, Va.): Story on pp. 313–14. Used with permission. *New York, New York:* Article on pp. 315–16. *New York, New York,* edited Donald H. Johnston, Arno Press, New York City, copyright © 1981. *The St. Petersburg Times:* Story on pp. 315–16. Used with permission.
Chapter 14	*The Courier-Journal:* Story on pp. 321–22. Copyright © 1981. Used with permission. *The Lexington Herald:* Story on p. 324. Used with permission. *Providence Journal-Bulletin:* Story on p. 326. Used with permission. *Los Angeles Herald Examiner:* Story on p. 328. Used with permission.
Chapter 15	*Buffalo Evening News:* Story on p. 336. Used with permission. *The Louisville Times:* Story on p. 337. Used with permission. *Eugene Register-Guard:* Stories on pp. 338, 341. Used with permission. *Associated Press:* Story on p. 338. Used with permission. *Virginian-Pilot* (Norfolk, Va.): Story on p. 340. Used with permission. *The Anniston Star:* Article on pp. 342–43. Used with permission. *Kansas City Times:* Story on p. 345. Used with permission. *Lexington Herald-Leader:* Excerpt on p. 352. Used with permission. *The Milwaukee Journal:* Story on p. 352. Used with permission. *The Dalton News Record:* Story on p. 353. Used with permission. *Associated Press:* Stories on pp. 356–57, 376–77. Used with permission. *The Berkshire Eagle:* Stories on pp. 358, 369. Used with permission. *The Advocate:* Story on p. 367. Used with permission. *Boston Herald American:* Stories on pp. 373–74, 375–76. Used with permission. *Houston Chronicle:* Story on p. 375. Used with permission. *The Baltimore Sun:* Story on p. 381. Used with permission.
Chapter 16	*The Des Moines Register and Tribune:* Material on p. 394. Used with permission. *Editor & Publisher:* Fig. 16.1. Copyright © 1981 by Editor & Publisher Co., Inc. Reprinted with permission. *Associated Press:* Story on p. 404. Used with permission. *The Commercial Appeal:* Story on pp. 405–6. Used with permission.
Appendix B	*Stylebook:* Reprinted from *News Reporting and Writing* by Melvin Mencher, 1981. Dubuque, Iowa. Used with permission of Wm. C. Brown Company Publishers.
Appendix C	*Daily News:* Stories on pp. 425–28. Copyright © 1980 New York News, Inc. Reprinted by permission. *Hollywood Sun-Tattler,* a Scripps-Howard newspaper: Story on pp. 428–30. Used with permission. *The St. Petersburg Times:* Stories on pp. 430–32, 437–39. Used with permission. *New York, New York:* Articles on pp. 433–34, 440–41. *New York, New York,* edited by Donald H. Johnston, director of Columbia News Service, Arno Press, New York City, copyright © 1981. *The Virginian-Pilot* (Norfolk, Va.): Story on pp. 435–36. Used with permission. *The Dalton News-Record:* Story on pp. 442–43. Used with permission. *Longmont Daily Times-Call:* Story on p. 444. Used with permission.

Index

Melvin Mencher is professor of the Graduate School of Journalism at Columbia University. He joined the Columbia faculty in 1962 after teaching at the University of Kansas. He worked for the United Press, was the statehouse correspondent for *The Albuquerque Journal,* handled investigative reporting for *The Fresno* (California) *Bee* and covered political and social developments in Central America for *The Christian Science Monitor.* He was a Nieman Fellow at Harvard University. He is the author of *News Reporting and Writing* (also published by Wm. C. Brown).

About the Author